Faith in Fiction

Faith in Fiction

The Emergence
of Religious Literature
in America

David S. Reynolds

Harvard University Press
Cambridge, Massachusetts
London, England
1981

Copyright © 1981 by the President and Fellows of Harvard College

This book has been aided by a grant from the Andrew W. Mellon Foundation

Library of Congress Cataloging in Publication Data

Reynolds, David S   1949–
    Faith in fiction.

    Bibliography: p.
    Includes index.
    1. American fiction—19th century—History and
criticism.   2. Religion in literature.   I. Title.
PS374.R47R49   813'.009'382   80-20885
ISBN 0-674-29172-7

To
Pamela Minkler

Acknowledgments

I would like to thank several scholars whose assistance was invaluable. I am deeply grateful to Richard Bridgman for his constant advice and encouragement. Henry F. May's enthusiasm and constructive criticism was extremely helpful. I also appreciate John Henry Raleigh's careful reading of my manuscript. I am indebted to Henry Nash Smith, who first aroused my interest in religious fiction, and to Leo Marx and Benjamin DeMott, who inspired me to pursue the study of American literature.

I was greatly aided by the staff of the University of California, Berkeley, library, especially those behind the desk of the Newspaper and Microprint Room who located scores of microfilms for me, and by the staffs of the Pacific School of Religion and the Graduate Theological Union libraries.

I appreciate Ruth McKeether's excellent typing and her patient cooperation.

My family and friends were most supportive during several years of research. Special thanks go to Pamela Minkler, to whom I dedicate this book.

Contents

Illustrations

Introduction

The rise of religious tolerance and diversity in nineteenth-century America was accompanied by an increasingly widespread tendency to embellish religion with diverting narrative. At the same time that the novel was being attacked by conventional clergymen, many writers believed, with Caroline W. Thayer, that "the light, unthinking mind, that would revolt at a moral lesson from the pulpit, will seize, with avidity, the instruction offered under the similitude 'of a story.' "[1] The Oriental and visionary tale, historical fiction about Biblical times, the domestic novel, and the Social Gospel novel were successive subgenres in the movement from cautiously allegorical to more confidently realistic religious fiction. By 1871 Mark Twain could assert that the gospel of Christ comes "filtered down" to nineteenth-century Americans through stage plays and *"through the despised novel and Christmas story* . . . and NOT from the drowsy pulpit!"[2]

This filtering process provided refuge for various writers tired of theological niceties and polemical debate. Catherine Sedgwick, weary of "the splitting of . . . theological hairs" and "utterly useless polemical preaching," found in the novel a means of rhetorically overcoming religious opponents while advancing a simple code of morality and pious feeling.[3] William Ware, E. P. Roe, and Charles Sheldon were nineteenth-century ministers who became popular novelists after discovering in fiction a pleasing package for their religious views. Harriet Beecher Stowe and Elizabeth Phelps Ward were two of several female novelists who questioned the orthodoxy of their clergyman fathers in fiction.

In 1796 the Calvinist Timothy Dwight had declared, "Between the Bible and novels there is a gulph fixed which few readers are willing to pass."[4] By 1896 a sufficient bridge over this gulf had been constructed to allow the Reverend Charles Sheldon to read chapters from his latest novel to his Topeka congregation. A firm scaffolding for this bridge was built between 1785 and 1850, a time of widespread liberalization and secularization of Christianity, when a growing number of American writers and clergymen, dissatisfied with traditional theology, adopted fictional modes and devices with the aim of refreshing doctrine.

Analyzing religious fiction written between 1785 and 1850 helps in understanding a transitional period of central importance in American history. Religious changes during this period left an indelible mark on the quality of both popular and elite culture in America. Intellectual doctrine gave way in many circles to a simpler affectionalism, Calvinist constraint to evangelical persuasion, passive expectancy of divine grace to active preparation for it. The dramatic growth of the Baptist and Methodist churches, with their mass-oriented approaches and theological simplifications, initiated an increase in American church membership that would continue its upward trend until the 1950s. Antebellum American religion was centered in a highly modified Calvinism and a fervent Methodist Arminianism. It was reformist, democratic, noncontemplative, millennial—a progressive, patriotic Christianity. Religious change between 1785 and 1850 affected elite American culture as well, as a series of heresies on the part of some sophisticated thinkers gave rise to the deist, Unitarian, and Transcendentalist controversies, which contributed to the flowering of New England.

Thus, pious fiction emerged during a century when, in Henry Steele Commager's phrase, religion prospered in America while theology went slowly bankrupt.[5] This antebellum fiction occupied a crucial position between Puritan religious literature, which had generally been confined to exposition or illustration of orthodox dogma, and post–Civil War religious best sellers, the most popular of which, like *The Gates Ajar* and *Ben-Hur,* were nonsectarian and quite secular.

Since early American religious fiction was in large part a rebellion against conventional religious literature, it is useful to review briefly the literary modes that had been used by American writers during the seventeenth and eighteenth centuries. Because of Puritanism's strongly doctrinal tradition, imaginative religious literature before 1780 had taken the conservative forms of poetry, allegory, history, and cautious sermonic anecdote. Anne Bradstreet, Edward Taylor, and Jonathan Edwards produced artistically varied but theologically analogous vivifications of the Puritan cosmos. While these and other writers sometimes departed from the Puritan plain style, none of them seriously contravened the underlying doctrinal standard for stylistic conservatism established in the preface to *The Bay Psalm Book* (1640), a standard epitomized in John Cotton's famous statement, "God's altar needs not our polishings."

Puritanism's caution about polishing God's altar signaled a mistrust of literary embellishments that might sully the divine with the human. Hatred of Rome engendered an antipathy toward excessively sensuous, material representations of a God who was considered inscrutable and totally other. Anything that delighted or amused the senses at the expense of concentration on theological truth was to be avoided in writing as well as in worship. The Puritan tended to limit his diction, his images, and other literary devices to those he could find in the Bible, which one writer called the "unpolished" Book of God written "with great simplicitie and wonderful plainnesse."[6] The Puritan saw the Bible as sacrosanct, beyond human alteration or improvement. Ramus had taught Puritans to think of rhetoric not as a system with rules of its own but as one dependent on logic, nurturing a style that was meant to reflect the reasonable order of the created universe.

Of course, as many scholars have pointed out, almost from the start these Puritan literary ideals were compromised by secularizing forces in culture and theology. Although Puritans generally eschewed earthly embellishment in the interest of preserving doctrinal purity, we do find in seventeenth-century journals and sermons records of the lives of ministers and important townspeople, stories of early piety, tales of captivity, allegories of warfare between Christ and Satan, and, of course, the grand narrative of the errand. However, fiction and undisciplined imagination remained anathema well into the eighteenth century. For example, in 1726 Cotton Mather advocated a more "poetic" religious style and at the same time declared that "the powers of darkness have a library among us," a "cursed library" filled with "romances and novels and fictions."[7] Similarly, the revivalist George Whitefield preached in 1739 that reading "trifling, sinful Compositions" like "Plays and Romances" precluded entrance to heaven.[8]

Between 1730 and 1790 Edwardsean Calvinism transcended former Calvinist literary attitudes by reemphasizing the radical difference between nature and grace, between imagined and true salvation. Jonathan Edwards and his followers constantly stressed the unreliability of human portrayals of godly things. Edwards said that a person might be emotionally moved by a beautiful physical description of heaven and angels or of human beings behaving ethically or of Jesus' ministry among the poor of Galilee and yet remain unsaved in the corrupt realm of "mere nature."[9] Such stories and descriptions Edwards called "external ideas in the imagination," alien to the sweet inward "sense of . . . spiritual beauty" that constitutes true faith. Satan, Edwards said, deludes the soul with "immediate suggestions of facts and events, pleasant voices, beautiful images, and other impressions on the imagination."[10]

Between 1785 and 1850 many Americans, reacting against such restrictive literary attitudes, began writing religious fiction designed to inspire the reading public with familiar descriptions of angels and heaven, portraits of moral behavior, examples of the operations of faith in society and history, and the story of the human Jesus. The adaptation of religion to human experience was impelled first by the Scottish Common Sense philosophic movement and later by English and Continental romanticism. The former encouraged earthly observation over abstract logic, ethical behavior over expectancy of grace; the latter emphasized imaginative intuition of God in nature and the worth of the common man.

While critics continued to be numerous and vocal, endorsements of religious fiction began to come from several respectable sources. In 1783 Hugh Blair, the Scottish clergyman and rhetorician who found literary applications for the Common Sense philosophy, praised "fictitious histories" as "one of the best channels for conveying instruction, for painting human life and manners, for showing the errors into which we are betrayed by our passions, for rendering virtue amiable and vice odious."[11] Not only was Blair's *Lectures on Rhetoric and Belles Lettres* widely read in America, but his praise of the moral possibilities of fiction was repeated by writers of various American denominations. In 1797 Royall Tyler reported that New England wanted something more diverting than "some dreary somebody's Day of Doom."[12] The next year Parson Weems, canvassing the South, found a demand for less theology and more novels. As the pious matron of William Hill Brown's *Power of Sympathy* noted: "Didactick essays are not always capable of engaging the attention . . . We fly from the labored precepts of the essayist to the sprightly narrative of the novelist."[13] Added validation for fiction was discovered in the Bible itself. In 1811 Isaac Mitchell became the first of several American novelists to cite Jesus' parables as prototypes for modern religious stories. In 1829 the novelist and critic Samuel L. Knapp wrote that such Common Sense philosophers as Dugald Stewart and Thomas Reid had "almost entirely superseded" Jonathan Edwards, whose theology now seemed "obscure and involved." Knapp explained, "When Edwards wrote, it was thought that abstruse subjects were not susceptible of embellishment; but Stewart has convinced the world that there is no subject so knotty and knarled which the skill of a master cannot adorn and polish with the charms of imagination." Efforts to adorn and polish religion, Knapp noted, were seen both in novels, which had "given truth some of her ornaments," and in sermons, which had taken on "the charms of literature and taste."[14]

The imaginative embellishment of religion in fiction was manifested by several kinds of stories and novels written by Americans in the six decades following the Revolution. First, roughly between 1785 and 1820, came Oriental tales that redirected European fictional models with the aim of indirectly subverting orthodoxy. Though some explicit satire on Calvinism appeared in Oriental guise, generally these Eastern stories took the more oblique, benign forms of visionary contemplation of angels and heaven, allegories of religious pilgrimage, and moral exempla. These tales, which often appeared in magazines of the day, were written by religious outsiders—rationalists, liberals in the main—with the design of counteracting determinism and gloom on behalf of the notions of perfectibility, divine benevolence, and universal salvation. One device of Eastern fiction, the vision of angels and heaven, also appeared in several non-Oriental stories. By 1830 the visionary mode had come to be used for overtly anti-Calvinist purposes by several American novelists.

As time passed, Oriental and visionary tales came to be absorbed into and then displaced by more realistic affirmative fiction written by liberals, Calvinists, and Roman Catholics. Novels and stories by New England liberals became the major corpus of American religious fiction before 1850, as evidenced by the works of Catherine Sedgwick, Lydia Maria Child, Sylvester Judd, and William Ware and his brother, Henry Ware, Jr. Hostile to both the content and style of received doctrine, these and other liberals used fiction early in their careers to gain rhetorical victory over religious opponents and then, in their less controversial later works, to endorse moral action.

Meanwhile, a thin but steady stream of Calvinist novels was produced throughout the period. Although the orthodox writers were at first more respectful of Puritan tradition than the liberals, after 1830 they too began to concentrate on earthly misbehavior and ethical redemption.[15] The convergence of orthodox and liberal fiction in a secular center was signaled in the 1850s by the similarities between Susan Warner's *The Wide, Wide World* and Maria Cummins' *The Lamplighter;* it made little difference that the first of these pious best sellers was written by a Presbyterian and the second by a Unitarian. The secularizing process was also manifested in Biblical fiction, which grew from early theoretical paraphrase and cautious Biblical dialogues to Christian martyr narratives and at last to novels about the Bible itself. Roman Catholic fiction, though always more intellectual than the Protestant stories, similarly passed from the doctrinal works of Charles Constantine Pise to the more sentimental novels of Charles Cannon, Anna Dorsey, and others. Even satirical and combative novels, in which the values of the affirmative fiction were mocked, reflected the pattern, as witty polemical satire gave way to vehement caricature and sensationalism. As religious fiction came to be written increasingly by moderate Calvinists of the religious mainstream, established ministers and religious publishing houses began to utilize fictional devices; in popular sermons and tracts, secular illustration and anecdote came to predominate over logical exposition.

The growth of religious fiction in America signaled a significant shift in normative religious discussion. This fiction moved progressively away from the Puritan ideals of anecdotal restraint, logic, strict Biblicism, and unsullied spirituality. Thematically, religious fiction replaced a wrathful Divine Judge condemning to hell depraved humanity with a responsive Divine Friend offering a comfortable heaven to all who behaved morally at home and in society. Stylistically it replaced rigorous exposition of dogma with diverting narratives in which outward secular crises and consummations supplanted inward self-analysis and contemplation as the center of faith. By the end of the nineteenth century several informed commentators declared that fiction had become the major vehicle of mass inspiration in America, a generalization confirmed by the immense popularity of religious fiction after the Civil War and the widespread use of narrative devices by American clergymen and tract writers.

The role of religious fiction in increasingly secular nineteenth-century culture is an unwritten chapter in the intellectual history of America. Literary critics have discussed the growth of a Transcendentalist aesthetic out of Boston Unitarianism. Historians have traced modifications of Calvinism that made conservative belief available to the masses. But the emergence of a popular religious aesthetic has yet to be studied. The subversion of dogma through fiction can be compared with religious change on more elite literary levels; early pious fiction helped prepare for the artistic use of Christian typology in major American works by detaching religion from its doctrinal moorings and placing it in a new secular context. At the same time, this fiction was a significant cultural phenomenon that eventually engendered such works as *The Gates Ajar, In His Steps,* and *The Robe.* Shortly after the Revolution, American writers of religious fiction began polishing God's altar, initiating a process that has continued to this day.

I

The Oriental Tale and the Visionary Mode

*I*N A JULY 1825 REVIEW of the Englishman James Ridley's *The Tales of the Genii,* the *New York Mirror* denied that writing Oriental tales was "beneath the dignity of a clergyman." Indeed, the reviewer asked: "Why should a clerical gentleman not employ his leisure time in innocent amusement, and moral instructions, (though it be in the shape of romance,) with the same charity and good opinion of mankind that others enjoy? We are of the opinion that moral lessons conveyed by example, and through the medium of an innocent tale, will, with many, have a more salutary effect than volumes of dry and undigested sermons. The scriptures abound in romance and sublime poems—our Saviour spoke in parables."

Ridley's volume had first appeared in 1764; the *Mirror*'s defense was a belated response to a school of religious fiction that had seen its greatest vogue in America between 1780 and 1820. During that period, various American rationalists and liberals used Oriental and visionary fiction to combat gloomy, determinist religion on behalf of a milder faith in human perfectibility and divine fairness.

The Oriental tale permitted writers to make their ideas palatable and to subvert opposing doctrines while avoiding rigorous debate. At first liberal only in the oblique sense of endorsing benevolence and toleration, Eastern tales became progressively more satirical of established denominations, especially the Calvinistic ones. After 1825, when less distanced kinds of religious fiction became fashionable, the Oriental tale became mainly adventurous and nonspeculative, although it did contribute to the rise of Biblical fiction.

The visionary mode, in which an angel gives moral or religious advice, appeared in some Oriental tales, in a group of non-Oriental stories, and in several novels of the period. A genius appears to the protagonist in a dream vision, usually in a moment of meditative solitude. The angel displays the rewards of virtue and the wages of sin either through visions of heaven and hell or through allegorical landscapes. The protagonist is enjoined to walk the path of moderation between passion and coldness, hilarity and gloom. The visionary mode answered an impulse to visualize a loving, accessible Deity; at the same time it gave heavenly sanction to the potentially unpopular view that man could earn salvation through good works.

After 1810 visionary episodes in American fiction became first more elaborate and detailed and then more directly applied to actual life. In a few novels written between 1810 and 1830, an angel flies with the hero to other parts of the universe to visit not only model societies but heaven itself. After 1820 several novelists commissioned human angels—visionary heroines described in angelic terms—to operate redemptively in the world. In several novels the visionary mode was used as a way of undermining opposing viewpoints without engaging in polemical discussion. For example, the heroine of Sylvester Judd's *Margaret* (1845), exasperated by a logical orthodox sermon, goes into the woods and has a vision of Jesus and John, who embrace her while ignoring the Calvinists who try to draw near. This use of visionary devices seems to have been purgative, as many authors, apparently considering the battle won, dispensed with angel imagery and with attacks on enemies in their later works, preferring to describe religious duty in real life. The visionary mode endured and came to be used by Presbyterians, Methodists, and Catholics, as well as by satirists such as George Lippard and Cornelius Mathews. After the Civil War the visionary protagonists of novels written by Elizabeth Phelps Ward, Annie T. Slosson, and others of the *Gates Ajar* school would visit comfortable heavens to see old friends, watch Beethoven conduct his own symphonies, and meet Biblical figures. Thus, in the course of a century, the allegorical celestial vistas of the early tales were slowly transformed into the earthly heavens of the religious best seller.

Oriental and visionary fiction occupied a pivotal position between colonial religious literature and the nineteenth-century religious novel. The landscape of these tales was regulated in such a way as to change a tyrannical and enigmatic Christianity into a positive, benign force. "Anti-Calvinism" is too strong a phrase to describe this strategy, at least in its early stages. The tales reflected a benign liberal reflex more than a conscious subversion of Puritan theology. Yet the appearance of loving angels and well-lighted paths to heaven, pitted against cruel tyrants wielding arbitrary power, does suggest metaphors used by American liberals from Charles Chauncy to William Ellery Channing, who regularly called liberalism reasonably benevolent and orthodoxy darkly despotic. Moreover, a sample list of Oriental tale writers reveals a group of Americans known for their aversion to Calvinism: Benjamin Franklin, Royall Tyler, Samuel L. Knapp, William Ware, Caroline Hentz. In a more general sense, the process of objectifying the divine and placing trust in human choice involved a repudiation of orthodoxy's firm stand on God's ineffability and man's incapability. The authors of Oriental and visionary tales brought kindly angels into the direct view of a humanity that was not as sinful as Calvinism had maintained. In doing so, they created America's first body of inspirational fiction.

1

The Oriental Connection

"All the fairy tales of Aladdin," wrote Emerson, "or the invisible Gyges or the talisman that opens kings' palaces or the enchanted halls underground or in the sea, are only fictions to indicate the one miracle of intellectual enlargement." In the Oriental tale "man passes out of the torpid into the perceiving state" and "sees things in their causes, all facts in their connection."[1]

By inference, the Oriental tale would seem a natural product of the Enlightenment; and it was. In the eighteenth century, Eastern fiction was a common literary outlet for various English and Continental advocates of such intellectual enlargement: Montesquieu, Steele, Addison, Defoe, Johnson, Goldsmith, Walpole, Voltaire. In religious belief, these writers ranged from moderate liberalism to skepticism, but they were linked in their use of the Oriental tale to question the orthodox establishment. Giovanni Marana's *Turkish Spy* (1684, tr. 1687), an Italian work widely read in America, portrayed a Mohammedan spy in Paris attacking Christian bigotry and defending deists as "Men of great Morality and Goodness, far exceeding the *Zealots* of the Age in true Virtue and pious Actions."[2] Similar sentiments were expressed by Montesquieu's spy in *Persian Letters* (1730). Later in the century, Marana and Montesquieu were praised by Voltaire as worthy philosophers to be grouped, on the basis of their Eastern fiction, with Toland, Bayle, and Montaigne. Voltaire himself directed the Oriental tale to even more skeptical ends in *Zadig* and in parts of *Candide* and the *Philosophical Dictionary*. In England the tendency of writers to clothe rationalist ideas in Oriental dress became so common that in 1746 one critic charged that Confucius had become "the Pope of Deism."[3] Four decades later the tales were being attacked with a suspicion approaching paranoia:

> A *free-thinker* can easily assume all shapes; which is not surprizing, if we reflect that a man who holds to nothing is best able to *act* everything; as stage-players who personate all characters are said to have none themselves. He is sometimes seen in the guise of a Chinese, talking notably of Confucius: Anon he is a Turk, and lavishing his praises on Mohammed: Next, perhaps he is a Magian, and then you hear wonderful things of Zoroaster: And thus by turns you may find him a Gymnosophist, a Talapoin, a layman or a priest, a Jew, or even a Christian: His business is to play the opinions of mankind upon one another with an eye to their common destruction, and to erect upon their ruins a monument to UNIVERSAL SCEPTICISM.[4]

Americans were more interested in the positive, inspirational possibilities of Oriental fiction than were the Europeans.[5] Charles Brockden Brown preferred the "simple and natural" Eastern tales of Goldsmith to "the pompous and gloomy fictions of Johnson," saying "Goldsmith is, in this particular, as benign, cheerful, and agreeable as Johnson is morose and melancholy."[6] The Unitarian William Bentley used Oriental fiction as a standard of hopeful religion: "Come, cheerfulness, and find a seat with us. The tales of Asia, and the borrowed romances of Europe, know thee not so well as we."[7] In the 1780s and 1790s American writers avoided the pure adventure and sensationalism that was beginning to characterize the English tales at the time. Thus "Osmyn of Bassora," an Eastern story submitted to the *Columbian Magazine,* was rejected because, as the editor wrote to the author, the tale was "prettily written, but to what end? Unless rendered subservient to the interests of virtue, compositions of this kind are unworthy of attention. However distinguished, they are but a splendid nothing."[8]

Yet American tale writers, though more didactic and less pointedly skeptical than the Europeans, frequently used the Oriental motif for advancing religious ideas that were aligned against the tenets of New England orthodoxy. These ideas included the unity and universal benevolence of God; the ultimate reward of virtue; perfectibility; the accessibility of the divine through nature; toleration; and the supremacy of behavior and experience over logic. Such beliefs were still unpopular in the predominantly Calvinist milieu of late-eighteenth-century America. Oriental fiction was congenial to a tendency among American liberals to avoid strict theological debate. A contributor to *Massachusetts Magazine* explained in 1789: "The style of eastern nations is . . . peculiarly adapted to inculcate truths, that in themselves are disagreeable and unpleasant. Such truths delivered in plain and direct language, would disgust, and the hearer would close his ears against instruction." The Oriental tale can "force conviction on the mind, before prejudice takes the alarm, or has time to make opposition." Exposition might alienate the reader, "But when the same truths are disguised in parables, or fables, a man may be surprised into attention ... Our Saviour himself adopted this mode of instruction."[9]

American authors between the Revolution and the Civil War used the Oriental tale for religious purposes in four general ways. First, the doctrines of some Eastern religions, particularly Islam, were found to be analogous to certain tenets of American liberalism; thus, for several writers, the Oriental tale provided a convenient camouflage for satirizing orthodoxy and promoting toleration. This type of subversion usually took place in captivity narratives, in which American sailors taken prisoner by Turks or Algerians report on Eastern manners or religion, and spy stories, in which Oriental visitors to America write home about doctrinal controversies and other aspects of American life. A second kind of Oriental tale describes visions of angels and the afterlife experienced by a distressed protagonist, who receives comfort from the prospect of salvation. A third group of tales uses allegorical landscapes or characters to dramatize correct and incorrect moral choices. A fourth group studies human efforts to achieve happiness on earth, usually pointing out that virtuous poverty and submission are more rewarding than wealth and intellectual endeavor. Between 1780 and 1800 the second and third types predominated, while the fourth type provided a fictional staple for magazines until about 1850. Because of its more controversial nature, the first type was never as prevalent as the others, though it did produce some of the longer, better-known tales written between 1785 and 1820. Also, it set an example of indirect satire which was observed in the other tales, as the use of Oriental personae for religious commentary had ironic import in a country that had traditionally consigned Orientals to hell. Because it exaggerates an anti-Calvinist tendency that is implicit in nearly all the tales, this group will be studied first.

West Meets East

Islam, the Eastern religion most commonly invoked by the tale writers, stood in a similar relation to Christianity as liberalism did to New England orthodoxy. Muslims saw Jesus as good but not divine, God as one and just, and man's will as free and efficacious despite God's omnipotence. Such precepts corresponded roughly to three major strands in American liberalism—Arianism, Unitarianism, and Arminianism. Although the Koran rode the line between determinism and human agency, early reform groups within Islam—particularly the Qadarites and Mu'tazilites—had permanently influenced Muslim thought by arguing persuasively for the latter. Other aspects of Islam that some liberals found appealing were its belief in intermediary angels and its allowance for imagination and fables in religious writing. These beliefs answered the liberal impulse to replace Puritanism's inscrutable God with more personable, accessible divine agents and polemical theology with a more figurative mode of religious discussion.

An Oriental tale that illustrates the connection between Islam and liberalism is Royall Tyler's _The Algerine Captive_ (1797). Having mocked Calvinist polemics in _The Bay Boy,_ Tyler turned to the Oriental captivity narrative to specify his religious preferences. In the novel, the New England Calvinist Updike Underhill, captured and made a slave by Algerians, learns from a Mullah the "gentle precepts" of Islam, including the unity of God, the perfectibility of man, and the final reward of good works. Underhill is told that Islam is more ethical and rational than Christianity, which has spawned persecution and sectarian strife. The Mullah, a learned convert from Greek Christianity, eulogizes Mohammed for "expressing the Arian opinion" of Jesus and replacing polytheism with a belief in "the Unity of the Deity."[10] Underhill expresses customary Western complaints about Islam: it is warlike; its paradise is too sensuous; its moral code is not strict. The Mullah replies that Christian history has been "a detail of bloody massacre" (II, 61), that "a sensual heaven is no more imputable to us than to you" (II, 63), and that the Koran forbids intemperance and gambling, which the Bible does not. In a direct slur on Trinitarian theology, Tyler has the Mullah say that in the Koran, "You will learn the unity of God, which, notwithstanding the cavil of your divines, your prophet, like ours, came into the world to establish, and every man of reason must believe" (II, 64). God is described as attentive and responsive, a pitying God whose tears "shall quench the glowing flames of the bottomless pit" (II, 175). Islam is also said to stress various social duties: charity, kindness to the aged, tenderness to idiots, and so forth. After visiting impressive mosques at Mecca and Medina, Underhill learns that his father has bought him out of slavery. He returns to America still denouncing Algerians as a ferocious race but advocating respect among nations.

The Algerine Captive created a stir in New England religious circles. _The Monthly Anthology and Boston Review_ attacked Tyler for making Christianity come off second best in the debate with Islam: "The author has so decidedly given the Mollah the best of the argument, that the adherence of Updike to Christianity seems the effect rather of obstinacy than of conviction. We enter our solemn protest against this cowardly mode of attacking revelation. It has not even the merit of novelty. Voltaire set the example—and a herd of petty novelists, who thought that to be impious, was to be a Voltaire, have gladly shown their wit at the expense of their religion."[11] Tyler replied that his novel supported "the sublime doctrines, morals, and language of the Gospel Dispensation" while exposing "the Mahometan imposture."[12] Indeed, the novel does pay lip service to orthodoxy by making periodic ejaculations against the

Mullah's paganism, but these, like the author's rejoinders to his critic, are transparent ploys to protect his somewhat dangerous views. In the "Spondee Essays," Tyler noted that fiction is especially adapted to readers "insensible to sound argument and incapable of logical deduction."[13] *The Algerine Captive* avoids logical argument by disguising anti-Calvinism behind the protective mask of Islam.

A similarly sympathetic use of Islam occurs in "Mahomet: A Dream" (1791), a tale in *New York Magazine*. The protagonist, granted the power to call forth any dead person of his choice, selects Mohammed, whose spirit rises majestically before him. The prophet holds a copy of the Koran that emits "a luminous ray, which convinced me that it was full of that Deity whose power and glory it so awfully announced."[14] The Christian hero, like Tyler's Underhill, instinctively calls Mohammed an impostor, but a heavenly voice defends the prophet as "a great man" who "first taught the idea of a Divinity who observes all our actions; and who, according to them, will dispense a just retribution" (507–508). Not only was Mohammed the first to preach salvation through works and a practical moral system, but he also initiated religious fiction, showing man how "to embellish his morality and religion with the charms of fable." Instead of distorting truth, fable improves it, for "a religion purely metaphysical, could not have been understood at that time, nor perhaps could it be understood even at this day." Theorizing logically about God can be "tedious and uncertain," and "even in these more enlightened days" the effective use of "a little innocent deceit" in fiction could help "bring about an useful revolution" (508).

This tale makes daring use of Islam to endorse divine benevolence, human morality, and religious fiction. The statement that Muslims initiated the idea of a God who dispenses just retribution on the basis of man's works implies a rejection of the doctrines of divine wrath and human depravity. The plea for imaginative religious literature has overtones of the common liberal attitude that Calvinism was a constricting system of logical metaphysics. The author has thus designed his Oriental tale to be a part of a revolution against both the content and style of received doctrine.

Humanity in Algiers (1801) couples the captivity narrative with the dream of Mohammed to make a plea for toleration. The preface announces, "Taught and accustomed from infancy to think our own religious creed the only mark of civilization, we can scarcely think it possible that a Mahometan could possess a feeling heart, or perform a virtuous deed."[15] The novel aims to show that there is indeed humanity and religion in Algiers. An American sailor captured by Algerians is promised his freedom under the legacy of the dead philanthropist Azem, whose autobiography forms the main narrative. Azem is a servant of the wealthy Selictor and Sequida. Lamenting his servitude, Azem asks "a God that loveth and rewardeth virtue" for freedom (23). His prayer is answered after his mistress dreams of Mohammed, who reveals a heavenly landscape that can be reached only by a deed of charity. Once free, Azem marries, succeeds in business, and dies leaving his fortune to buy the freedom of one slave per year.

Although not as doctrinally specific as Tyler's novel, this tale does dramatize the message of its preface by portraying the efficacy of a Muslim's prayers. The novel's target is not Calvinism in particular but religious exclusiveness and gloom of any sort. Azem prays to the "Universal Father of all men" (23), a God whose chief message is "Of one blood have I created all nations of men that dwell upon the face of the earth" (98–99). This echoes the standard rationalist outlook, which denied Christianity's uniqueness while extolling the One Spirit behind all creeds. The anonymous author occasionally seems to mix Islamic and Christian concepts, as when Azem wonders when each member of God's "great family . . . shall do by others as he would wish that they should do by him" (24). The landscape of Sequida's dream vision combines the symbology of Christian salvation with the lush beauty of the Mohammedan heaven. In sum, the novel emphasizes the interchangeability of Islamic and Christian concepts by combining them in an appealing whole.

This subversion of creedal narrowness is also evident in Peter Markoe's *The Algerine Spy in Pennsylvania* (1787). The novel consists of letters sent home by the Algerian spy Mehemet from various European ports and finally from Philadelphia. His second letter contains a "digression in favor of toleration" in which he argues that "the followers of Mahomet have been more indulgent to those who profess christianity, than the different sects of christians have frequently been to each other."[16] On his journey Mehemet encounters a rabbi who, sounding as much like a Calvinist as a Jew, discourses on Adam's fall, and "from this improbable fiction he inferred the supreme degeneracy of man" (57). The rabbi treacherously reports to the Algerian government that Mehemet is a Christian who has deserted his country. The exiled Mehemet settles in Philadelphia, where he is converted to Christianity. Trained by Islam to dislike a "religion involved in metaphysical subtilties" (79), he adopts a simple faith in "but one God" and moral duty (121). By having his hero embrace Christianity, Markoe protects himself from the charge of infidelity, having already used the Oriental guise to voice his disagreement with religious exclusiveness, the doctrine of original sin, and metaphysical theology.

A later novel of a Muslim spy in America, Samuel L. Knapp's *Ali Bey* (1818), replaces such indirect satire with a detailed critique of sectarian controversy and fashionable religion in New England. Ali Bey, a Muslim disguised as a Frenchman, comes to Boston to convert America to Islam. Boston is the place where a breach into Christendom can be made, since "this garrison in appearance so formidable, is weak, divided, and mutinous," with "a mighty schism" between Calvinists and liberals "opening a door to the healthful breeze of truth."[17] Bey finds Americans engaged in destructive theological warfare, which he hopes to replace with Islam's faith in good works and toleration. He notes that Unitarians denounce Calvinists for being dark, hopeless, and rigid, while Calvinists call Unitarians cold, imprecise, and nonreligious. Bey finds Calvinists to be spokesmen "of another age, when metaphysicks were in vogue," dreary reactionaries who preach "obsolete and abstruse subjects to audiences little able to comprehend them—while the rest of the world has grown *practical,* and is returning to common sense, both in religion and philosophy" (19). To effect Boston's conversion to Islam, Bey decides to woo the Unitarians, whose "good disposition and research are unclenching the hold of error and preparing their minds for the true faith" (113). After more discussion of America's religious battles, Bey concludes: "To those who are offended with the fanaticism of the one party or the levity and affectation of the other, we should offer simplicity, sincerity, solemnity, truth" (119).

Thus, a small but significant body of American fiction between 1785 and 1820 capitalized on similarities between Islam and liberalism to make disguised attacks on orthodoxy and to call for a benevolent religion of works. The Oriental tale permitted a freedom of doctrinal exploration and satire that was available in expository prose only at the risk of the writer's reputation. In the case of Tyler's *Algerine Captive,* the Oriental shield was perilously weak, leaving the author open to charges of heresy and cowardice; but in all the tales a self-protective indirection is apparent. Updike Underhill vows "to steer the middle course of impartiality" between positive and negative views of Islam,[18] and his periodically hostile reactions to the Mullah's teachings serve to disguise Tyler's liberal inclinations. "Mahomet: A Dream" teaches that fiction involves "a little innocent deceit," an idea that is reflected in the hero's initial objections to Muslim doctrines he is taught to admire. *Humanity in Algiers* and *The Algerine Spy* serve up palatable mixtures of Christianity and Islam in tales of adventure. Knapp's *Ali Bey* professes to be a translation of an Arabic manuscript, and in the preface "the translator deems it proper to observe that he has nothing to do with the statements or speculations of the author" (4).

In one magazine story this indirection through fiction is itself the major theme. "Zaman" (1784) portrays a young man being taught by a sage "how truth may be presented to its enemies." The neophyte is given a volume of Koranic fables which convince him of "the necessity of veiling truth, in order to render it acceptable to mankind." Taking this pious fiction as a stylistic guide for his future writing, Zaman declares to the reader: "I will continue to revere truth; but will render its image less shocking to your eyes."[19] As we have seen, several early American authors tried to render potentially shocking truths less offensive by packaging them in the Oriental tale.

Although Islam was the most appropriate shield for the American tale writers, Benjamin Silliman's *Letters of Shahcoolen* (1802) and George Fowler's *The Wandering Philanthropist* (1810) show that other Oriental religions could be used to similar ends. Silliman's work consists of letters written from Philadelphia by a Hindu philosopher to a friend in Delhi. Seemingly more conservative than most Oriental spokesmen, Shahcoolen begins by lambasting various forms of contemporary skepticism, ranging from freethought and Jeffersonian republicanism to Mary Wollstonecraft's feminism. However, the second half of the book is devoted to establishing quite daring connections between the Hindu and Christian scriptures. Shahcoolen notes that while Christians may "excel the Hindus in reason and taste, . . . the Hindus leave them far behind in flights of imagination, and beauty of expression."[20] He goes on to make an exegetical "comparison between the famous Gitagovinda and the Song of Solomon," in which he praises both for their "rich, brilliant and poetical" language (99). Thus, Silliman has carefully arranged his Hindu letters. By courting orthodox sympathy through his opening indictments of infidelity, he feels free to conclude his volume with rather unorthodox Biblical commentary.

In Fowler's *Wandering Philanthropist* Confucianism provides the framework for a less oblique analysis of American religion. Fowler's Chinese visitor finds religion in America to be narrow and contradictory. When asked by his American host to abandon his religion for Christianity, the visitor points up "the great difficulty of suddenly believing a religion of which I scarcely ever heard the name until I left my native country."[21] Faith, he claims, is not absolute but is rather the product of education and nationality. The visitor lauds America's abolition of state religion, but he is confused by the country's baffling variety of sects. In fact, he is "disposed to wonder how Christianity, if it was clear in its doctrine and consistent in its parts, could give rise to so many different, and even contradictory, creeds, and . . . ready to believe that if it is not actually false, must at least be very obscure and doubtful"(186–187). This confusion increases when he visits various American churches. The most sensible thinker he meets is a deist who points out the Bible's absurdities and says: "It is from this obscurity and contradiction of the bible, that there have arisen so many different sects, each drawing their creed from different texts, and while they have preached humanity to the rest of the world, have set the example of intolerance, and persecution among each other" (261). The Chinese visitor concludes that dogma should be replaced by a simple faith in "the dignity of human nature" endorsed by God (300).

Thus, some American authors between 1785 and 1820 found in Oriental religions, particularly Islam, a safe perspective from which to comment on American religion in a way that was often liberal and sometimes freethinking. Though varied in tone and emphasis, their tales were linked by a common use of correspondences between Oriental doctrine and progressive American ideas. The indirection that characterized most of these tales grew from the potentially heretical nature of the ideas they contained.

Angels, Allegories, and Exempla

Whereas the captivity and spy narratives established a dialogue between Americans and Orientals who were trying to seek doctrinal connections, the three remaining types of pious Eastern tales—the visionary, the allegorical, and the secular moral—seem to have presupposed such connections, eschewing creedal and sectarian debate on behalf of moral affirmation. These more characteristic tales were concerned less with controversy than with consolation. Their typical message was that man's longings and needs are answered by a protective God who rewards virtue with earthly contentment and heavenly bliss. This theme, which would inform much nineteenth-century religious fiction, represented a break from Calvinism's view of an angry God who threatens man with hell, ignoring human attempts at virtue and arbitrarily rewarding only a predetermined elect.

Oriental tales describing visions of angels and the afterlife stood at the abstract beginning of a fictional line that would extend through the nineteenth century to the *Gates Ajar* school after the Civil War. The impulse to pictorialize the divine—to make heaven and angels tangible, familiar—constituted a tacit rejection of the Puritan doctrine of God's ineffability and otherness. Jonathan Edwards had said that "all imaginary sights of God and Christ and heaven . . . and all impressions of future events, and immediate revelations of any secret facts whatsoever" are merely "external ideas" of the imagination. Especially reprehensible was "the pretended immediate converse, with God and Christ, and saints and angels of heaven."[22] For Edwards, the divine and supernatural light "is no imagination or idea of an outward light or glory, or any beauty of form or countenance, or a visible lustre or brightness of any object." Thus, a man "may be affected with a lively and eloquent description of many pleasant things that attend the state of the blessed in heaven, as well as his imagination be entertained by a romantic description of the pleasantness of fairy land," and still remain unregenerate.[23]

Harriet Beecher Stowe would write in 1859 that Jonathan Edwards had knocked out the rungs of the ladder connecting earth with heaven.[24] But Edwards was not the only Calvinist who distrusted visions of heavens and angels. In 1696 Increase Mather declared, "*Men ought to be very cautious of admitting or hearkening unto pretended Angelical Revelations.*"[25] Mather considered most angelic visions to be frauds. For instance, "*Mahomet's* Angel, from whom he pretended to receive his new Religion was a Devil: For in the *Alcoran* there are contradictions, and therefore falsehoods which cannot proceed from a good Spirit: No good Angel ever told a lye" (14). Mather pointed out that Luther prayed that God "would not reveal anything to him by Dreams or Visions, but by his Written Word" (7). In 1712 another Calvinist, Edward Tompson, declared: "We do now live so much in, and by Things sensible, that we have but little commerce with Angels, nor do we commonly care for more." Angels are so much purer than man that "when we have Exhibitions of them they terrify us."[26] Joseph Fish in 1755 stressed that angels are immaterial beings without "*Parts,* or *Shape,*" invisible to us "Worms of the Dust."[27] And Samuel Hopkins equated the belief in angelic intervention with a denial of Christ's divinity. Since Christ is "infinitely higher and greater than all the angels in heaven," an angel's proposal to God on behalf of a sinner "would not only be rejected, but would itself be an act of high rebellion, and carry in it the most abominable contempt of GOD and his law."[28]

Oriental tales initiated the fictional reconstruction of the visionary ladder. The visions that Calvinists had suspected became commonplace in tales that revealed not only alluring angels but heavenly landscapes as well. As an essayist for *Massachusetts Magazine* wrote in 1794, the "visionary fables of the heathen" are implicitly Christian legends that teach us, "It is not strange that a lively and pious imagination should gradually personify, and deify, the attributes, and favours, of so unsearchable, august, and beneficent a Being."[29] Not only did many Oriental tales seek to personify God, but they began to glimpse paradises filled with the colors, sounds, and other pleasant things that Puritans had consigned to the deluded imagination. They suggested that man was worthy to converse with angels and to receive the promise of salvation through works. In most tales, especially those written before 1810, heavenly visions were granted but then curtailed by celestial agents who concluded by reminding the protagonist of his earthly duties. Yet even abbreviated revelations offered the consolation of a happy futurity to the virtuous. The miracle of intellectual enlargement which Emerson associated with Oriental tales was reflected by fiction that illustrated man's ability to scan the divine.

In 1746, the year Edwards was denouncing imaginary pictures of angels and heaven, the Boston *American Magazine and Historical Chronicle* published "The Meditation of Cassim the Son of Ahmed, or, An Emblematical Description of the Resurrection," which appears to be the first Oriental tale written by an American. This story set the pattern for many later Eastern tales: a solitary protagonist holds a mountain-top conversation with an angel who discourses on heavenly bliss and earthly duty. At the beginning of the tale, the weary Cassim walks from town to the top of a mountain where he contemplates nature's beauties and feels "the flames of a holy transport." Sensing a kinship with "the departed spirits of good men," Cassim asks:

Don't the inhabitants of paradise thus admire the works of God? Does not the harmony of their praises rove thro' the bowers of bliss, and soften the murmurs of the streams of life? Are they not overflowed with a flood of joy, when they search the labyrinths of creation, and range through the dominions of the Supreme Being? Methinks I beheld them lift up their admiring eyes, from the fields green in an eternal flourish, and, with a strengthened and enlarged ken, penetrate into the remote space of aether. They view the systems that compose our universe, and their intellects are stretched and crowded with the ample vision.[30]

Cassim wonders how spirits, lacking human senses, can fully enjoy the countryside and wildlife of heaven. Suddenly there appears on a distant peak an angel, who says, "Don't perplex your mind but rest assured that the unembodied souls among us are perfectly holy and happy, far beyond thy glimmering conception" (547). But the angel goes on to answer Cassim's questions about the afterlife by comparing the resurrected body to the transformation of a silkworm into a butterfly. "Thus," concludes the angel, "shall the bodies of good men be raised, thus shall they shine, and thus fly away" (548). Cassim is enjoined to leave off his worries about heaven and apply himself to earthly tasks.

Couched in this tale are several ideas of religious liberals: the Book of Nature which leads to revelation; the benevolence and accessibility of God; the salvation of the virtuous. Cassim's fancy of spirits gamboling in "soft and indulgent" climates, verified by the angel's image of the butterfly, suggests that most men are moving not toward Calvin's hell but rather toward a comfortable land of plenty. Although the final message of the tale is that heaven is ultimately incomprehensible to man, most of the tale is devoted to amassing physical details of celestial life, including hills, birds, streams, spices, and gems. The author uses the Oriental mode to indulge his curiosity about heaven and then recants at the end, perhaps to help deflect orthodox criticism. At the same time, he quietly jettisons the Calvinist doctrines of depravity and grace by having his angel request man merely to "love your maker, converse with your own heart, and delight in doing good" (547).

Benjamin Franklin's "Arabian Tale" (1779), although less detailed than "Cassim," shows another anti-Calvinist using the visionary format to indulge curiosity and answer philosophical questions. The Oriental tale suited Franklin's distaste for polemics. After a few years of religious disputation in his youth, Franklin learned that "if you wish to instruct others, a positive, dogmatical manner in advancing your sentiments may provoke contradiction and prevent a candid attention."[31] Franklin's cheerful "Arabian Tale" safely dramatizes the deistic views he had baldly stated in two early essays, "Of Liberty and Necessity" and "Articles of Belief and Acts of Religion." These essays had asserted divine benevolence and human morality but had expressed misgivings about evil and about God's distance from man. The latter issue was partly resolved in the "Articles" by Franklin's statement that "the INFINITE has created many beings or Gods . . . exceeding wise and very good" who are links in the upward chain.[32]

"An Arabian Tale" allowed Franklin to visualize and to converse with one of these celestial beings on the problem of evil. In this story the "good magi-

cian" Albumazar climbs each night to the top of Mt. Calabut, where he talks
with "genii and spirits of the first rank, who loved him, and amused him with
their instructive conversation." To one genius Albumazar speaks "with rap-
turous piety" of God's goodness but expresses his puzzlement over the existence of evil. The genius asks him to contemplate the scale of being from an
elephant to an oyster and then reveals a reciprocal scale upward "from an elephant to the infinitely Great, Good, and Wise." Perceiving this universal
order, Albumazar is relieved of his anxieties about evil.[33]

Another tale that offers a view of the Great Chain is "Moclou, or the
Dreamer" (1788). Depressed by the world's vices, Moclou falls asleep and
dreams of a being who "walked, touched, spoke, and heard, although it had
neither feet, hands, mouth, or ears." The being announces itself as "the center
and first cause of all things: the Alpha and Omega, of all nature." Revealing
to Moclou a chain running through the universe, the angel points out that on
one side of the chain lies beautiful order and on the other horrid confusion,
symbolizing life as seen by God and by man. On the verge of receiving a final
revelation, Moclou awakes. The tale ends by explaining that "the august secrets which were about to be revealed to Moclou, are far above the weak understanding of the author; nor would he dare attempt to lift the impenetrable
veil, which hides them from human reason."[34]

Like "Cassim," this tale withdraws from the heavenly vision it begins to cre-
ate, saying that certain august secrets are beyond the anonymous writer's ken.
The recoil here is put in semi-Calvinist terms, as the revelation of the Great
Chain is checked by a reminder of man's insignificance and God's sovereignty.
But again, this appears to give an orthodox cast to a potentially unorthodox
vision. The first half of Moclou's dream comes close to reducing the Alpha
and Omega of the Bible to a walking, breathing human being. Not only is
God made anthropomorphic, but Moclou is momentarily given an expansive
view of celestial order which strict Calvinists would have called above man's
limited vision.

The angels who appear in Oriental tales are ordinarily not wrathful and
vindictive but rather benevolent and responsive to good works. "An Eastern
Apologue" (1789) enforces the moral that the "Supreme Arbiter of our lot,
who made man and virtue, never leaves without pleasure the heart of the
good, nor a benevolent action without reward."[35] Similarly, the hero of
"Orasmin and Almira" (1790) is comforted by a being who says, "Cease . . .
to doubt the mercy and justice of the Supreme Being, who though he acts by
unknown springs and seeming severities, is ever watchful for the happiness of
the virtuous, and perfectly consistent in all his laws."[36] The genius of "Salah:
or The Dangers of Habit" (1793) announces himself as "one of those beneficent beings that keep a watchful eye over the children of the dust, to guard
them from the calamities they have not merited."[37] And "The Enchanted
Rose" (1795) is designed to show "that there is no act of humanity, however

insignificant it may appear at the time to us, but the great Author of universal benevolence will, in his own proper time, amply repay us tenfold."[38] Oriental angels thus embodied the liberal view that man's good deeds are not ignored by a supervening, wrathful Deity but are carefully recorded and rewarded by a Divine Friend.

"The Visions of Aleph" (1789) portrays a dying man's visions of heaven and hell to provide an unusually detailed picture of the afterlife. While contemplating the beauties of the sunrise, Aleph sees "the angel of peace," who announces, "Now thou shalt taste the cup of heavenly happiness." Suddenly the earth seems to be lit by a hundred suns, and Aleph is carried upward into "a new existence." The earth recedes to a distant point, and Aleph sees "the Son of Heaven" sitting on "a throne of stars."[39] Feeling "the ravishment of unspeakable bliss" at being among "sanctified spirits," Aleph revels in heavenly joy:

> My soul was filled with the soft melodies of spiritual hymns: myriads of angels saluted me with the smiles of transport, and I was bathed in the tears of rapture: the soft dews of heaven moistened my heart, and diffused through it the sweets of delicious love. I beheld again the angel of peace, and under his wings my soul advanced in delight to the throne of the *Most High*. Millions of angels and archangels filled the heavens with one voice, saying, Holy, Holy, Holy! A cloud of incense arose before the throne of immaculate purity and love! (21).

Waking from this happy dream, Aleph is now granted a brief view of the "shadows of sin" and "the gulph of grief unutterable" (21). Aleph thanks Allah for these visions, assuring his family that "we shall meet again in the abodes of peace, and never separate ... Hearken only to the voice of virtue, and with Aleph be happy" (22).

This tale attempts a rather daring reproduction of celestial ecstasy. It strains to create the kind of "lively and eloquent description of ... the state of the blessed in heaven" which Jonathan Edwards had held suspect. Like other visionary Oriental tales, it objectifies the divine, rendering it palpable and physically alluring. The Oriental mode allows imaginative freedom for conjuring up the sensuous details of heaven. It provides a vehicle for envisaging "the Son of God" and "the *Most High*" under the pretext of seeing Mohammed and Allah, thereby deflecting the charge of sacrilege that might result from a direct account of Jesus and God. It draws from a fund of imagery presumably Oriental but potentially Christian: the angel of peace, sanctified spirits, incense, archangels, hymns. Also, hell is reduced to a black gulf of sin and guilt, and is made avoidable through proper conduct. Salvation is stripped of its uncertainty and complexity, as man is asked simply to "hearken ... to the voice of virtue" in order to join his relatives in heaven.

In some Eastern fiction of the period, heaven, although not as closely ana-
lyzed as in the above tales, controls the plot by providing hope and an incen-
tive to virtue. The disillusioned Selim of "The Happiness of a life regulated by
the Precepts of Virtue" (1784) is told that although "thy sight at present is
imperfect . . . thou shalt soon put off the veil of mortality, and thou shalt then
be capable of surveying thoughts that are now invisible."[40] The hero of "The
Contemplant" (1786), led by the untimely death of his son to view God as
wrathful and indifferent, is consoled by "Gabriel, the angel of peace," who reveals the soul of the son in heaven.[41] In "Almet, the Dervise" (1793) an angel
points to a distant celestial garden which is reached "by virtue; and virtue is
possible to all."[42] The bereaved widower of "Ibrahim and Almira" (1797) is
assured by a celestial agent that his wife and children are secure in the "eternal
mansions of felicity," awaiting his arrival.[43]

Hell is deemphasized in Oriental tales, whereas heaven is posed as attainable
by the virtuously inclined. This Arminian theme reverses the emphasis of earlier imaginative literature in America, which concentrates on depravity and
damnation. Eastern tales provide an oblique answer to the Calvinist scheme by
guaranteeing a blissful eternity to those willing to observe a simple code of
moral action. They begin to shift the balance away from Michael Wiggles-
worth's *The Day of Doom* (1662) and toward Elizabeth Phelps Ward's *The
Gates Ajar* (1869).

The next group of religious Oriental tales, allegories enforcing proper moral
decisions, are also transitional. In most of these stories the protagonist is offered a choice between ethical alternatives—honesty and falsehood, prosperity
and adversity, gaiety and gloom. These alternatives are objectified—that is,
embodied in landscapes, people, or objects. The main action illustrates the exemplary happiness or misery resulting from the protagonist's choice. Reason,
contentment, and sobriety are found preferable to imagination and sensual indulgence. Though vaguely indebted to such works as *The Divine Comedy* and
The Pilgrim's Progress, these Oriental tales redirect traditional allegory and
point toward nineteenth-century popular novels. Showing the influence of the
Scottish Common Sense philosophy, the tales reduce moral imperatives to easily distinguishable objects, simplifying a process that in Dante and Bunyan
was complex and agonizing. Whereas Bunyan's Christian must battle enemies
who are emblems of interior doubts and shortcomings, protagonists of Oriental tales either observe such battles from without or else combat behavioral
rather than spiritual infirmities.

This simplification of moral choice is seen in several Oriental allegories of
the period. "Prosperity and Adversity" (1792) embodies opposing philosophies in two women, the first attractive but shallow and the other plain but
strong. The tale contrasts the marriages of two Phoenician brothers, Uranio
and Felix, to these women. By selecting Prosperity, Uranio finds transient en-

joyment and untimely death. By choosing Adversity, Felix learns submission and gains "a virtuous mind, . . . an unblameable life, and a death full of good hopes."[44] Similarly, in "The Choice of Abdala" (1796), the hero, a prince, is told by an angel to select a wife from a group of three women—Tristina the grave, Hilarana the gay, and Serena the placid. By choosing the last, Abdala adopts the qualities of moderation and reason which make him a good ruler.[45] The protagonist of "Zaman" (1784) is led to a mountain top where "all nature in his eyes served as emblems of truth."[46] Honesty is symbolized by the sun, falsehood by reptiles and shifting winds. Zaman learns that if his soul "abhors falsehood, it will become resplendent in the sight of the Eternal Being as the centre of light" (48). "The Talisman of Truth" (1795) and "Hamet" (1812) allegorize the conflict between imagination and reason, lauding the victory of the latter.[47] In these tales "conversion" comes not when man recognizes his moral inability and God's supervening grace, as in the Calvinist scheme. Rather, it results from the confidence in an innate ability to choose between right and wrong.

"Timur" (1790) combines a lesson on the vanity of riches with an allegorical vision. The Persian farmer Timur, robbed in the woods and left for dead, has a dream vision of the River of Life which teaches him that "the enjoyments of sense are short and deceitful, while those of virtue are permanent and certain; . . . to the upright of heart are reserved those superior pleasures that flow from love of Deity and from charity towards man."[48] Timur's vision contains symbols that seem like holdovers from Puritan allegory—whirlpools, fog, bubbles, chastizing ministers. Yet these are painless and distanced compared to obstacles in Bunyan like the Slough of Despond and Hill Difficulty. On the River of Life, Timur's boat is prevented from sinking by a good genius, and religious duty is reduced to love of Deity and charity toward man. Also, Oriental reverie provides a way of combining allegory with a more realistic fictional mode, as Timur awakes from the dream and applies the teachings of the vision to daily life. This story shows how the Oriental tale could form a bridge between the self-contained Puritan allegory and the more secular religious fiction of the nineteenth century.

"Salah: or The Dangers of Habit" (1793) follows a similar pattern, as a discontented rich man is comforted by a dream of a landscape symbolizing the stages of life. As in "Timur," the allegorical vision is contained by a framework story of initial longing and final fruition. The hermit Salah, unhappy after forty-eight years of contemplation, one day dreams of an angel who reveals to him the huge Mountain of Life. The narrow, uncrowded road of reason and religion leads to the Temple of Felicity atop this mountain, while a more inviting downward thoroughfare leads to the precipices of Ambition, Despair, Intemperance, and Indolence. Learning that the high road can be attained by the correction of daily habits, Salah awakes, vowing to observe the dictates of rational religion.

Despite its Dantesque overtones, "Salah" is characteristic of American Oriental allegories in its modification of horrific or enigmatic aspects of the religious pilgrimage. The author stresses that his beneficent angel will ward off unmerited calamity. Also, sin is identified with correctable habit rather than with inescapable depravity. A premonition of Bushnellian nurture is contained in a passage extolling the lessons of education. And man's educability is implied in the angel's advice to observe and learn. Not only are traditional sins like despair and habit converted into objects avoidable through reason, but the tale as a whole keeps evil at a comfortable distance. In effect, the reader is twice removed from the precipices and pits of the mountain, as the allegory is a distant panorama revealed to a sleeping protagonist. Therefore, the painful immediacy of encounters with sin and hell in Dante and Bunyan, or in the damnation sermons of American Calvinists, is removed. When Salah awakes to a beautiful dawn with the resolve to behave better, the reader feels that the high road of religion is not so unattainable after all.

This softening of traditional allegory also occurs in "The Vision of Almet, the Dervise" (1793). The discontented Almet has a mountain-top dream of the benevolent angel, Azoran, who says: "The book of nature thou hast read without understanding; it is again open before thee; look up, consider it and be wise."[49] Azoran reveals two landscapes: an edenic garden beyond which lies a gloomy desert, and a bleak, mountainous terrain leading to a fertile country. Dazzled by the first scene, Almet wants to enter it, until he sees a dejected man walking along the garden path with his eyes fixed on the ground. In the second scene he notices a traveler who smiles and looks ahead despite the rocky path. Azoran explains, "That which makes every station happy, and without which every station must be wretched, is acquired by virtue; and virtue is possible to all."(277).

Like "Salah," this tale simplifies both the choices and the goals of the religious pilgrim. The reader and the protagonist are again distanced from peril by the use of a panoramic landscape contained in an Oriental dream vision. Despite the message that the religious path is forbidding, a universalist optimism is contained in Alzoran's declaration that "virtue is possible to all." As in "Timur" and "Salah," evil is made passive and unresisting by being objectified in nature. In Bunyan, Satan's emissaries appear not only in natural but in human form, with active power to attack and imperil Christian. In the American allegories, sin is usually converted into objects—rocks, caves, cliffs, gardens—which can be sidestepped by proper moral choice. In the poetic prelude to the second part of *Pilgrim's Progress,* Bunyan noted a widespread tendency "to counterfeit / My pilgrim" and singled out New England as the place where his work was "trimmed, new clothed, and decked with gems."[50] In the Oriental allegories written by Americans, the Christian pilgrimage is "new clothed" to be made less austere and forbidding.

*   *   *

The last group of religious Oriental tales depict the operation of religion in the world, usually pointing out the vanity of power, riches, or intellectual endeavor. Whereas Eastern fiction about the afterlife and religious pilgrimage appeared mainly between 1746 and 1800, these tales began to be written in the 1780s and continued to appear in American magazines until the Civil War. Like the spy and captivity narratives, these tales show a distrust of religious narrowness and gloom. With the visionary and allegorical fiction, they revise traditional literary versions of angelic intervention, human struggle, and moral choice. Like all the tales, these find in the Oriental mode an opportunity for indirection in the promulgation of progressive religious attitudes. Reflecting the increasingly secular imperatives of American culture, the religion in these tales becomes more dependent on narrative development than in the other kinds of Eastern fiction. Therefore, these tales provide a bridge between the early otherworldly or allegorical stories and the more secular, plot-oriented religious fiction of the nineteenth century.

In William Munford's *Almoran and Hamet* (1797) and Henry Sherburne's *The Oriental Philanthropist* (1802), religious commentary is wedded to fast-paced adventure. Munford's work, a dramatic adaptation of an Oriental tale by John Hawkesworth, announces its chief subject to be "Morality and Religion."[51] Munford's novel centers on the trials of Hamet, joint king of Persia with his brother Almoran, as the latter seeks to take by guile and by force both the kingdom and the love of the beautiful Almeida. Almoran relies heavily on supernatural aid to carry out his subversive schemes, as a genius appears to him constantly and gives him a magic talisman enabling him to change identity at will. But Almoran's wickedness becomes suicidal, and in the end the genius proves to be friendly to the reason and morality that Hamet has exercised throughout. A morbid preoccupation with predestination, human depravity, and damnation contributes to Almoran's downfall, while a reliance on divine benevolence and free will protects Hamet. In his quest for arbitrary power, Almoran is "depriv'd of reason's guidance"; Hamet, in contrast, heeds the liberal advice of the dervish Omar: "God has appointed man to run his course. / His will is free . . . / Your freedom is the noblest gift of God" (47, 49). Since man is a free agent, the genius moralizes at the end, we must learn to "regulate / Our minds by reason, and the laws of virtue" (107).

Sherburne's *The Oriental Philanthropist* also endorses liberal precepts in a tale of political intrigue. Sherburne's preface commends the "silvery channels" of fable and allegory for communicating "essential truths" to "those readers who are apt to be disgusted with dry treatises of morality."[52] The "essential truths" of this novel prove to be aligned against orthodox values. The tale shows the Chinese prince Nytan being imprisoned by an evil minister, Sanden, and then being rescued by various supernatural agents: magical pictures, talking birds, fairies, flying chariots. Escaping to an East Indies island, Nytan makes philanthropic journeys throughout mainland Asia, Africa, and Europe. He spreads principles of ethical living and democracy, and he marries a Persian princess who helps him establish a new kingdom free of gloom and tyranny.

Like Munford, Sherburne portrays the victory of a faith in perfectibility and benevolence over mysterious, determinist religion. In the preface, Sherburne says that the lack of confidence in God's "love and tender compassion" is "unbecoming and shameful to a rational being" and "is the source of every evil" (8). In the novel "the sects of enthusiasts, and the promoters of fanaticism" (22)—especially Sanden's fire worshippers—are at the bottom of Nytan's miseries, while angels "incessantly employed in works of benevolence" (23) insure his salvation. As the author explains, "A religion that contains in its bosom the seeds of vice and oppression, and which tends to enflame instead of destroying vicious inclinations, ought to be exposed by every friend of virtue and mankind" (23). Nytan lauds man as "Heaven's fairest image! . . . exquisitely divine" and decries those who believe in innate depravity. In Nytan's new kingdom, fanatical fire worshippers are banned, while principles of moral rectitude and human dignity are advocated. In sum, Sherburne has followed Munford's lead by supplanting a belief in divine wrath and human depravity with a more benevolent view of God and man.

Almoran and Hamet and *The Oriental Philanthropist* show how the Oriental tale could provide a secular enactment of the clash between opposing religious systems, with victory given to the liberal side. These tales subtly invoke the Revolutionary spirit of egalitarianism, since they attack both religious and political tyranny. Nytan's utopian nation free of dictators and fanatical fire worshippers is analogous to what some liberals of the newly formed American republic envisaged as an ideal America free of King George and Calvinist enthusiasts. Likewise, Munford's plan to expose the evils of arbitrary power can be linked with the liberal rejection of an arbitrary, capricious God and an authoritarian ruler. Such political metaphors would continue to be used by anti-Calvinists well into the nineteenth century. In 1830, for instance, the freethinker Robert Dale Owen called the orthodox God "some eastern tyrant," "a despot" opposed to truth, which is "a plain republican."[53] In a broader condemnation, Emerson declared in 1838 that "this eastern monarchy of a Christianity" is enslaving man, suppressing his divinity.[54]

Some of the Oriental tales I have already discussed make use of such political images in connection with liberal religion. In "The Choice of Abdala," the son of a cruel tyrant, after marrying Serena, becomes the rationally pious ruler that his father was not. Updike Underhill of Tyler's *The Algerine Captive* learns from his imprisonment that "when men are once reduced to slavery, they can never resolve, much more achieve, any thing, that is manly, virtuous, or great."[55] *Humanity in Algiers* describes the escape from slavery of both the Algerian Azem and the American narrator, enforcing the author's Arminian prayer, "Thou art a God that loveth and rewardeth virtue, although found in the meanest slave; and must certainly hate and punish vice, though covered by the title of master, or the pomp of gold."[56] Though not anti-Calvinist in any direct sense, such protests against Oriental tyranny have overtones of republican religion which are particularly significant in light of the liberal commentary appearing elsewhere in these works.

Other tales depict the lamentable transformation of the hero into a ruler possessing the power of salvation and damnation over his subjects. The restless Zohar of "The Discontented Man" (1784) asks the friendly angel Firnaz for the throne of Arabia, wishing to be "the master of mankind, resembling the God of the earth, the arbiter of destiny." Zohar's wish is granted, but his dictatorship is soon toppled by a popular revolt and replaced by democracy. By the end, the chastened Zohar has learned to leave off the search for arbitrary power and to respect "the immortal being which reigns within me."[57] A similar lesson is taught to a tyrant in "The Paradise of Schedad" (1797). Schedad, the ruler of Yemen, tries to exhibit godlike control by creating a garden paradise for his subjects. He issues an edict allowing admittance into the garden only to those who, "neglecting every superfluous virtue, shall believe sincerely in us, and shall submit themselves without reserve to our divine will." When his people become bored with the paradise, Schedad prepares a second edict that would "create a hell, where unbelievers and impious persons should no longer mock him" (136). The tyrant is finally dethroned and imprisoned in his own heaven, showing that "there is a supreme God, who confounds the projects of impiety; and who has only promised happiness to virtue."[58]

The accounts of Zohar and Schedad give an anti-Calvinist coloring to the traditional mirror for magistrates mode. In their efforts to emulate the divine, these rulers assume qualities that liberals often associated with the God of orthodoxy. Zohar would dispense blessings and destruction to become an implacable arbiter of destiny. Schedad creates a heaven and a hell and pronounces his subjects powerless to determine their own fates. In both tales, this determinist, tyrannical ethos falls before a belief in human dignity and divine fairness.

Examples of the fourth kind of Oriental tale that I have discussed dramatize the contest between two religious value systems—tyranny, predestination, enigma, and emotion versus democracy, self-determination, clarity, and reason. This contest appears in slightly altered guise in a group of tales which expose the illusory nature of wealth and knowledge on behalf of virtuous poverty and contentment. These stories usually depict an indigent protagonist desiring material or intellectual advancement, being given them by a genius, becoming disillusioned with them, and returning to his former life having learned that virtue is its own reward. Like Samuel Johnson's *Rasselas,* these tales underscore the vanity of human wishes. But Johnson's vision, which verges on a cynical denial of any sort of absolute verity, is contained in the

American stories by a concluding encomium to contentment and piety. Brockden Brown's distaste for Johnson's "morose and melancholy" Eastern fiction appears to have been shared by several of his contemporaries.

Susanna Rowson's "Uganda and Fatima," which appears at the end of *Mentoria* (1794), a novel on female education, exemplifies this kind of Oriental tale. Elsewhere in *Mentoria*, Rowson advises parents to teach religion not through "long prayers" or "books of dull theology" but through example, remembering that "the useful and ornamental branches of education [are] to be combined."[59] In her Oriental tale she displays how this combination can be achieved in fiction. Her heroine, Fatima, is a poor shepherdess who envies the princess Semira, the pampered mistress of a vizier. Fatima is transformed by the fairy Uganda into the vizier's new favorite. But "the Vizier was passionate, capricious, jealous, and extremely cruel," so that Fatima is merely in "splendid slavery" (97). Changing Fatima back into a cottager, Uganda enjoins her to "humbly take the blessings within thy reach, enjoy them and be happy" (101).

A similar pattern is followed in two magazine tales of the period, "Hassan" (1795) and "Amorvin" (1806). Because of its secular emphasis, this motif lasted into the nineteenth century while the other types of religious Eastern fiction were dying out or being displaced by a more realistic school of pious fiction. The continuing popularity of this idea can be explained in part by the attempt of many American authors to envisage a moral panacea for vicissitudes of actual life, as opposed to the more heavenly and allegorical concerns of the pre-1800 tale writers. By discounting reveries of happiness, these tales were part of a general rejection of the visionary mode during this period. As the hero of "Hamet" (1812) learns, "The visionary, who wastes his time in the indulgence of idle abstraction, and permits his fancy to transport him whither she pleases, will soon be brought to the sense of suffering reality, by some of those inevitable wants which are the common lot of humanity."[60]

The Later Oriental Tale

This sense of suffering reality crept increasingly into the American Oriental tale, tilting the balance from the divine to the secular. While most of the tales written before 1820 were religious, the large majority of the some two hundred tales written between 1820 and 1860 were adventurous or historical. As early as 1806, this shift was registered by an essayist in Brockden Brown's *Literary Magazine and American Register* who noted that Eastern tales tend "to accustom the mind rather to wonder than to inquire; and to seek a solution of difficulties in occult causes, instead of seriously resorting to facts." Oriental tales should thus "originate in true pictures of life" and present "resemblances of man as he really is."[61] By 1833 one American author could defend experiential moral fiction by aspersing bygone Orientalism: "Founded on fact, and sanctioned by experience, it is to be hoped that this history, will meet with a more favorable reception than exploded romances of giants and enchanters, than fairy tales or Persian fables; which, by being destitute of probability as well as truth, must prove insipid and disgusting to every reader of sentiment and taste."[62] And in 1837 the *New York Mirror,* which had in 1822 praised Ridley's religious Oriental tales, gave "A Caution to Novelists," which asserted: "Beautiful as are the tales of the Arabian nights, and perennial in the delight which they have afforded to successive generations, they yet lack many of the elements which are now deemed indispensable in fictitious composition; such, for instance, as the close discrimination of character, the ingenious complication of plot, and above all, the close adherence to the realities of life and achievement, without which the critical doom of narrative authorship, in these modern days of perfectibility, is certain and speedy, and without hope of appeal."[63]

Religion in the later Oriental tales, instead of controlling, began to be controlled by such fictional devices as plot, scenic description, and psychological portraiture. Indeed, all imaginative religious literature entails, to some degree, a delicate balancing of didacticism and entertainment, spiritual message and diverting story. Bunyan, for example, felt compelled to warn readers against "playing with the outside of my dream" and to direct attention to "the substance of my matter."[64] Likewise, Orestes Brownson wrote that religious fiction attempts a difficult combination of divine contemplation, which demands stasis and reason, and plot, which is based on action and emotional change.[65] Many of the pre-1800 tales discussed above, particularly the visionary and allegorical tales, tried to achieve a kind of spiritual stasis by removing the protagonist to a scene of solitary communion with God and nature. In this sense, these early tales harked back to the Puritan tradition of private meditation, as exemplified by Anne Bradstreet's "Contemplations," Edward Taylor's "Preparatory Meditations," and the nature passage in Jonathan Edwards' *Personal Narrative.* The later tales began to define religion in terms of a sequence of human events, in which the reader's apprehension of the religious message is governed by the author's manipulation of plot, description, and sentiment. This was true of the spy and captivity narratives that flourished between 1795 and 1820, as well as of the adventurous and romantic tales, which lasted until the Civil War period. Fiction became a way of trying on various religious alternatives without arguing seriously about any of them. It helped to detach doctrinal discussion from its intellectual moorings, placing it in a relative world of dialogue, forward plot movement, and pathos.

The secularization of the Oriental tale reflected an increased valuation of the religious significance of daily life. Yet it also signaled growing qualms about the intellectual viability of doctrine and about religious absolutes in general. There is a spiritual restlessness about such works as *The Algerine Captive, Letters of Shahcoolen, The Wandering Philanthropist,* and *Ali Bey.* Samuel

Knapp could adopt the Oriental mask to propose sardonically the conversion of America to Islam, but beneath the humor lies a serious realization that American religion was becoming divided, mutinous, and aristocratic. Similarly, George Fowler's Chinese visitor can wittily point out the deficiencies of American sects and yet remain unconsolable, learning that those "who have discarded all systems of religion . . . passing from one gloomy chimera to another, have at last ended with denying the existence of a universe, the existence of a God, and the existence of themselves."[66] The pious endings of the American *Rasselas* imitations often seem like stoic pleas for the exercise of virtue in the face of uncertainty and illusion. In a more general sense, the absence of religion in many of the later Oriental tales signifies an abandonment of religion for experience, as meditation and conversion come to be seen as less important than episodic adventures about Arabian warriors, Barbary pirates, and caliphs in love.

Accordingly, several religious Oriental tales written after 1810 are exempla on the superiority of moral behavior to metaphysical, logical polemics. "The History of Aden" (1815) describes the failure of human reason to achieve certainty.[67] Aden seeks fulfillment in science, political power, and religious speculation, only to end in anxious skepticism. At last Aden meets a sage who tells him to act piously without trying to probe divine mysteries. This use of experience as solace for intellectual exhaustion shows the influence of Scottish Common Sense. As Sydney E. Ahlstrom has noted, the Scottish philosophy was in nineteenth-century America "a vast subterranean influence, a sort of water-table nourishing dogmatics in an age of increasing doubt."[68] Tales like "Aden" grasped the behavioral essentials of faith after metaphysical speculation came up short.

James Kirke Paulding's "Musa; or, the Pilgrim of Truth" (1847) is a later example of this more chastened kind of religious Oriental tale. In "Selim" (1833), "Musa, or the Reformation" (1833), and "Murad the Wise" (1844), Paulding had adopted the Oriental persona to denigrate sectarian intolerance and religious reformism. His later tale describes the effort of a wandering Muslim to discover the true religion. Musa travels throughout Asia and Europe only to become confused by the contradictory doctrines of jarring churches. Thus, "Every step . . . that he proceeded in his search after truth, only seemed to render its existence more doubtful."[69] Returning to Baghdad, Musa dejectedly tells a hermit that God and virtue do not exist. But the hermit argues that Musa's travels have proved just the opposite: since all men worship God, there must be a God; and we must be tolerant of all religions. Musa returns home to become a benefactor, having learned that truth consists merely of "reverence for the Creator of the world, and charity toward all his creatures" (32). As in "Aden," redemption for the religious seeker lies in simplistic religious duty after the failure of the intellect to discover truth.

This sense of suffering reality began to be manifested even in visionary tales, which before 1800 had been the most consoling kind of Oriental fiction. In Laughton Osborn's *The Dream of Alla-ad-Deen* (1838), a vision of heaven and hell leads to a disturbing realization of universal transience. Unlike such earlier visionary heroes as Cassim and Salah, Alla-ad-Deen is forced to contemplate a wide range of human suffering and to confront the reality of man's insignificance. The visionary landscape is closer to worldly experience than it had been in the pre-1800 tales.

Two stories of love and soldiership, *The Templar* (1822) and Samuel Spring's *Giafar al Barmeki* (1836), typify the later Oriental tales by making religion subservient to adventure. *The Templar* traces the captivity and rescue of the Turkish princess Orina during a war between Christians and Muslims. Orina is converted to Christianity as a result of her love for the heroic St. Armand, who saves her from torture. From Armand she "found that all Christians were not bigots and cruel-hearted: having always been taught to venerate the Redeemer as a great prophet, she soon learned to adore him as a beneficent Saviour."[70] *Giafar al Barmeki* subsumes religious commentary to a complex sequence of events involving Turkish-Roman battles, political intrigue, and romance. Some of the hallmarks of the early religious stories remain. For instance, the Muslim is said to be "a firm believer in the unity of God," detesting Christians who "were thought to worship a plurality of gods." And a dervish teaches the heroine that the end of religion is "to make man tolerant and happy."[71] Such passages, which appear occasionally in the book, use Islam as a prototype of liberalism and toleration in a familiar way. However, Spring is far more concerned with the development of plot than with religious reflection.

William Ware's *Zenobia* (1838) epitomizes the problems of purveying affirmative Christianity in an Oriental mode that had come to be dominated by secular adventure and by a weighing of philosophical alternatives. *Zenobia,* customarily cited as one of America's earliest religious novels, has been interpreted in various ways that emphasize its inspirational, Christian characteristics. However, Ware's novel is more complex than most commentators have recognized. In light of my argument that Eastern fiction in America began as a vehicle for liberal views, it is no accident that the first best-selling novel by a prominent American Unitarian minister was Oriental. And given the history of the American Oriental tale, especially its history after 1800, it is no accident that *Zenobia* is indirect, circuitous, and predominantly secular.

Instead of consistently endorsing Christianity, Ware weaves it into a plot of military confrontation and places it in a dialogue with various pagan systems. At one point in the book, when the Greek philosopher Longinus is asked if his thought is influenced by Christianity, he replies that he has not read the Bible: "Yet even as a piece of polished metal takes a thousand hues from surrounding objects, so does the mind; and mine may have been unconsciously colored and swayed by the truths of christianity, which I have heard so often stated and defended."[72] This statement is an apt description of Ware's literary technique, since the entire novel may be viewed as a prismatic "piece of polished metal" in which religion "takes a thousand hues from surrounding objects"—from Greeks, Romans, Persians, from atheists, stoics, Platonists, from warriors and lovers, from despots, democrats, laymen. Christianity is filtered down, refracted through various systems, applications, personalities. The only dedicated Christians in the novel—Probus and the hermit St. Thomas—remain background figures, while vocal pagans or "half-Christians"—Julia, Zenobia, Longinus, Gracchus, Aurelian—assume center stage. Lucius M. Piso is the first of Ware's three epistolary spokesmen, who would come to include Nichomachus of *Probus* (1838) and Julian of *Julian* (1841), who are religiously neutral. As in *The Algerine Captive, Ali Bey,* and "Aden," the Oriental tale becomes a vehicle not of ecstatic affirmation but rather of tentative, sometimes anguished exploration.

Throughout the novel Ware creates an unsystematic dialogue between Christianity and epicurean materialism, Platonism, atheism, and polytheism. Queen Zenobia says that philosophy's greatest service would be to prove "the certainty of a future existence, in the same satisfactory manner that Euclid demonstrates the truths of geometry" (II, 145). Later, Longinus declares that he believes in a future state "as implicitly as I believe the fifth proposition of Euclid's first book" (II, 233). Yet far from providing Euclidian proof of an afterlife, the novel leaves heaven as an unsupported conjecture and forges from several philosophies a creed of action and goodness in the face of uncertainty. Even St. Thomas, who has seen Christ, says: "We can theorize and conjecture without end, but cannot relieve ourselves of doubts. They will assail every work of man. We wish to repose in a divine assurance. This we have in christianity" (I, 184). But the assurance in which Ware reposes is less divine than it is secular, less Christian than it is eclectic. Probus's praise of Christianity's "practical aim and character," his belief that it is "no fanciful speculation nor airy dream" (I, 262), is similar to the atheist Gracchus' faith in "the lines of duty: . . . not in any fancies or dreams; but in the substantial reality of virtuous actions" (II, 224). Likewise, the activist creed of Longinus, Zenobia, and Julia is not distant from that of Thomas, who says, "Christianity teaches, that in goodness, and faithfulness to the sense of duty, lies the chief good" (I, 180).

An outlook that can gather the atheist and the Christian, the materialist and the Platonist into a formless center of virtuous action verges on denying the spiritual and intellectual validity of any religion. Like Knapp, Fowler, and Paulding, Ware tests a variety of philosophical possibilities only to perceive the futility of speculation and the necessity of reducing faith to its behavioral essentials. As in *The Templar* and *Giafar al Barmeki,* martial action provides a way of deflecting unresolved otherworldly discussion into secular channels. Explicit discussion of Christianity is limited to two chapters, and the author is primarily concerned with portraying Zenobia's heroic resistance of Aurelian's invading army. In general, *Zenobia* bears out Orestes Brownson's point about the incompatibility of the novel and religious reflection. Ware's characters discuss religion only during brief moments of stasis or solitude—in the hermit's cave, in a prison cell, in Zenobia's boudoir. Once Ware turns to the main plot, religion is left behind. Action is sought as a release from the difficult juggling of philosophies and creeds attempted in the meditative chapters. In fact, Ware's espousal of the novel form itself reflects a failed minister's abandonment of systematic religious investigation on behalf of experiential fiction. Not only could Ware turn to the Oriental mode to advocate an uncomplicated creed of loving duty, but he could repose in the security of narrative development when exposition of this creed became bothersome.

By the late 1830s, therefore, the now sophisticated Oriental tale could offer a kind of secular redemption to a prominent American religious figure who later confessed to having made a "mistake for life" in joining the ministry in the first place.[73] The case of William Ware brings up another issue concerning religious Eastern fiction. Mukhtar Ali Isani places Ware's last novel, *Julian,* in a group of Oriental novels and short stories based on the Bible.[74] I choose to defer comment on these works until my discussion of Biblical fiction. However, Isani's classification is significant because it points to the fact that in the 1830s and 1840s several American writers came to view the Bible as a potentially exciting Oriental tale readily transformable into fiction. In this sense, such post-Civil War novels as *Ben-Hur, The Robe,* and *The Big Fisherman*—all of which accent Biblical drama with accounts of Eastern customs and manners—have roots in the early Oriental tale.

As a whole, the group of Oriental tales I have discussed make up the first body of religious fiction in America. Often obvious and simplistic, these tales nevertheless exhibit both the possibilities and problems of inspirational fiction in general. The various kinds of Oriental tales can be viewed as precedents for later types of American religious fiction. The visionary tale presaged a preoccupation with angels and heaven that would surface continually in American fiction from *The Power of Sympathy* through *Oldtown Folks* to the novels of the *Gates Ajar* school. The Oriental allegory began a simplification of Dante and Bunyan that would be emulated by the likes of Edmund Botsford, D. J. Mandell, and George Cheever and be satirized in Nathaniel Hawthorne's *The Celestial Railroad.* The spy and captivity narratives began a doctrinal dialogue that would be seen in several kinds of popular fiction after 1820; they also fed into a stream of religious satire that ran from Philip Freneau through George Lippard to Mark Twain. The moral stories reflected an overall tendency to secularization. And the historical and romantic tales that became popular after 1830 helped pave the way for the Biblical novel. In sum, the Oriental tale was a crude incubator for nearly every variety of American religious fiction.

2

Earth Above, Heaven Below

The non-Oriental visionary mode was manifested in three general ways in American fiction written between 1785 and 1850. It appeared in novels and stories whose main emphasis was the vision of angels or the afterlife. It occurred more frequently in the form of visionary episodes in novels with a more secular emphasis. In time it came to be embodied in protagonists characterized as human angels acting redemptively in the world.

The pattern of secularization noted in the Oriental tale was also apparent in the American visionary mode. Not only did visionary episodes become less distanced and allegorical during the period as a whole, but within the careers of individual novelists an early reliance on visionary techniques was often displaced by an increasing concern with religion in human experience. The visionary mode, like the Oriental tale, began primarily as a means of combating religious gloom and determinism. After 1820 such authors as Catherine M. Sedgwick, Sarah J. Hale, and Sylvester Judd exploited it for explicitly anti-Calvinist purposes. But as time passed it came to be used by some writers who were not religious liberals—by Presbyterians, Methodists, Roman Catholics, and secular satirists. Like the Oriental tale, it came to be a variegated literary phenomenon directed at diverse religious ends. In most cases it provided a means of circumventing logical debate about problematic religious or philosophical issues.

The visionary mode appears to have sprung from various religious impulses. It provided a rebuttal to eighteenth-century critics of miracles and divine revelation. Such spokesmen of the skeptical Enlightenment as Hume, Gibbon, and Paine had threatened to strip religion of its divine sanction by dismissing accounts of God's intervention as unsupported hearsay. The early visionary tales, several of which began with a recognition of the tenuous state of religion, posited the reality of angelic intervention in contemporary life. Fiction was thus a way of asserting God's miraculous presence without proving it. In addition, the visionary mode applied Lockean sensationalism and Scottish Common Sense to didactic ends. The fictional angels and the lessons they uttered divested faith of its enigmatic, metaphysical aspects, making it palpable and experiential. Lastly, visionary tales initiated a fictional search for kinds of mediation between man and God that Puritanism had held suspect.

Whereas Calvinists admitted the validity of only certain kinds of celestial revelation, the visionary mode opened the door to divine visitants who were usually religious but rarely Biblical or even identifiably Christian. In time, angelic imagery in Protestant fiction was drawn from Greek and Roman polytheism, American Indian faiths, and Roman Catholicism. For example, Catherine Sedgwick's Hope Leslie and Harriet Beecher Stowe's Mary Scudder are angelic heroines referred to as Catholic saints who intervene on behalf of sinful characters. In this connection the protagonists of several religious novels after 1820 came to be identified with redemptive angels. While characters in the pre-1820 visionary tales ordinarily received religious instruction and heavenly information from visiting angels, in some important later novels the protagonists themselves became angels with the power to give such instruction to others.

The Visionary Mode Before 1820

Two of the earliest fictional works written in America, *The Golden Age* (1785) by "Celadon" and Francis Hopkinson's "An Extraordinary Dream" (1792), exemplify the early use of the visionary mode. Written at the time when American religion was at a nadir, these tales show how fictional angels could be summoned to help man build on the ruins of faith. Both authors betray a painful awareness of the disarray of contemporary religion, and both invoke fictional angels for divine solace.

In *The Golden Age,* the pious Revolutionary War veteran Celadon, troubled about the future of his nation, dreams of "a wondrous form" with "an ineffable sweetness in his looks, and nothing vindictive in his aspect."[1] When the startled Celadon asks how the angel could "condescend to visit this wretched, fallen, and offending world," the angel explains that he belongs to "a bright squadron of Seraphic warriors" who protected America during the Revolution and who will insure the stability of the new nation (6). When Celadon complains that American religion has been reduced to "a plant in the drought of summer" which lacks its "original verdure and fragrancy" (13), the angel declares that the millennium will be ushered in by the conversion to Christianity of Indians, Negroes, and Jews. Christianized Indians and liberated slaves will be given their own states in the West, Savagenia and Nigrania, where they will grow pious and sedulous. Similar states will be given to Jews and to Dutch and Spanish immigrants. Celadon is eager to learn more about the millennium, noting that the Bible and theologians give us "probable conjecture at most," while "the document of an angelic teacher, might be relied on with the firmest belief, and trusted in with indubitable dependence" (15). The angel says he is "not allowed to proceed," but he comforts Celadon with simple moral advice before disappearing.

Despite the familiar recoil from final revelation here, the author has used the visionary mode to outline a relatively concrete millennial plan. The tale offers angelic resolution of combined problems: the potentially destructive factions of a multinational society and divergent interpretations of the millennium. The visionary mode has enabled the author not only to imagine the conversion of religious opponents but to detach angelic revelation from its traditional moorings. The assurance that the angel has nothing vindictive in his aspect opposes the doctrine of divine wrath. Celadon begins in amazement at God's concern for a wretched, fallen, and offending world but ends with the knowledge that social concern and moral behavior can lead to salvation. An undercurrent of doubt is apparent in the acknowledgment of the nation's religious indifference and the obscurity of Biblical texts. Stating that answers can be found neither in the Bible nor in theology, the author places indubitable dependence on a fictional angel to create a kind of supra-Biblical religious authority. The angel's moral advice at the end is a culmination of the tendency of the tale to promote divine benevolence and human perfectibility in the face of cultural complexity and theological confusion.

Francis Hopkinson's "An Extraordinary Dream"gives different answers to similar religious problems. The sleeping protagonist meets an angel who reveals the garden of human knowledge with a tree in the center representing religion. This tree was "once the glory of the whole scene," but theologians' "several *systems* and *improvements*" have "reduce[d] it to a mutilated, useless, and deformed trunk."[2] Two other trees, Logic and Metaphysics, are in the "most useless and untoward spot" of the garden (8). Healthier are the trees symbolizing Law, Physic, Poetry, and Music. The angel declares that through man's own efforts "the several branches of NATURAL PHILOSOPHY" (9) will flourish in time, leading to the revivification of religion.

Just as Celadon called American religion a dying plant, so Hopkinson calls it a useless and deformed trunk. Having noted the debilitating effect of metaphysical theology on the tree of religion, Hopkinson turns to more secular areas of human experience to restore the tree. The visionary mode enables him to do this without a great expenditure of intellectual energy. By reducing large topics like metaphysics and logic to trees in a garden, Hopkinson can caricature religious polemicism without discussing it logically. Moreover, his allegorical sanctification of Enlightenment thought prepares for a passage in an essay appearing in the volume shortly after the visionary tale: "The happiness or misery [of afterlife] will not be determined by the unalterable decree of the omnipotent Creator, but will more probably depend upon the temper and capacity of the soul of each individual to become an angel of light, or a fiend of darkness. We cannot reasonably suppose that God will forcibly compel any man to be either happy or miserable. Good and evil are set before us, and our wills must determine the choice" (I, 53). Having used a fictional angel to jettison metaphysical theology, Hopkinson turns to the essay to argue that man can be an angel of light with an inborn capability for moral choice. Incorporated into the text of the essay, the angel of the dream becomes equivalent to man himself.

A similar movement from allegorical to overt optimism occurs in Enos Hitchcock's *Memoirs of the Bloomsgrove Family* (1790), a novel of domestic education which contains a visionary episode. Bloomsgrove is a storytelling father who uses the visionary mode to enforce his religious sentiments. Before telling his visionary story to his children, Bloomsgrove explains that he has no difficulty in believing that God can have "access to our minds in such a manner, as, by a vision or dream, to stamp upon it things necessary for our information or encouragement; and that too by such images, as cannot fail to express their meaning."[3]

In Bloomsgrove's tale a young man in search of his wife travels along dark and dangerous roads. One night the terrified youth falls asleep and dreams of a "visionary ladder" connecting earth and heaven on which "those benevolent agents who are supposed to be always attendant on good men, seemed to be constantly ascending and descending." (I, 74) Above the ladder stands God, who addresses the youth "in the language of paternal affection, assuring him of his favor and protection" (I, 75). The man goes on to find his wife and lead a piously sober life.

After telling this story Bloomsgrove gives his children cheerful religious instruction, avoiding "any of those frightful notions of the Deity, which were formerly thought to constitute religion" (II, 201). The Calvinist God is called a "severe and unforgiving" being, the worship of whom is "superstition" motivated by "fear and dread." In the Puritan system "weak minds" were "rendered abject and servile," while "the bold and inconsiderate became totally negligent of religion." Only the "more rational notions of the Deity" of recent times have dispelled this gloom (II, 201). Bloomsgrove tells his children "to look up to God as their heavenly father and friend," as a "kind and benevolent" being who is "always countenancing the virtuous, and rewarding them, if not in this life, yet most certainly in a life to come" (II, 198).

In Hopkinson and Hitchcock, therefore, we see the visionary story used as preparation for religious exposition. This maneuver is underscored elsewhere in the books by explicit references to a distaste for logical debate. Both writers place visionary tales at the beginning of their volumes to suggest that their antitheological, benevolent outlooks have the endorsement of heaven. Significantly, the visionary mode is detached from the more expository accounts of religion and morality elsewhere in these volumes. Hopkinson's angelic allegory and Hitchcock's description of the visionary ladder are instructive but self-contained fictional exempla. In more sophisticated religious fiction by later writers such as Catherine Sedgwick and Harriet Beecher Stowe, visionary imagery would be absorbed into the central action of the story, planting the celestial ladder more firmly in terrestrial experience.

Several magazine tales of the 1790s show that Americans could use the visionary mode to forge religious fiction with devices borrowed from late-Augustan graveyardism.[4] In England the philosophical use of graveyard devices had reached its peak with the publication of Edward Young's *Night Thoughts* (1743) and Thomas Grey's *Elegy Written in a Country Church Yard* (1751). By the 1790s the English Gothic mode had become primarily adventurous and sensational, as evidenced by the fiction of Horace Walpole, "Monk" Lewis, Clara Reeve, William Beckford, and Ann Radcliffe. In the American tales, graveyard trappings are utilized to create an atmosphere of meditative communion with nature and to inspire comforting visions of angels or heaven. Gothic fear in these stories is softened into religious melancholy, and supernatural visitation is designed to console rather than terrify.

The impulse to modify English literary models noted in visionary and allegorical Oriental tales is evident in these stories, which are hardly Gothic or graveyard fiction at all. Ruins and graves become another way of placing spiritual struggle outside the soul. The awareness of evil is no shattering sense of personal depravity, but rather an instructive gloom before a mildly frightening nocturnal scene. The cemetery and ruins are ready-made catalysts for metaphysical vision. And again, the dream vision itself places the panorama of sin safely in the distance while indulging the author's curiosity about angels and the afterlife. As in the tales by Celadon, Hopkinson, and Hitchcock, the vision is terminated by a return to daily experience and a recommendation of good works.

Between 1790 and 1815, changes in the American visionary mode occurred that parallel those described in connection to the Oriental tale. The careers of two novelists, William Hill Brown and Charles Brockden Brown, show early experimentation with visionary devices being replaced by a later concern with secular experience. In some novels of the period—Brockden Brown's *Wieland*

(1798) and *Edgar Huntly* (1799) and Isaac Mitchell's *The Asylum* (1811)—this experiential assessment of the visionary mode was evidenced by the explained supernatural, which attributed apparently miraculous phenomena to natural causes. Mitchell's work was joined by Caroline W. Thayer's *The Gamesters* (1805) in applying the visionary form to realistic religious ends, as protagonists have visions of dead friends or relatives. Susanna Rowson's *Charlotte Temple* (1791) and *The Inquisitor* (1793) embodied saving angels in religious characters who helped redeem others. Thus, during this period there was a movement away from the allegorical or abstract visionary story, as represented by the pre-1795 tales studied above, toward the more complex, secular visionary tales and episodes which began to appear after 1815.

William Hill Brown's two novels, *The Power of Sympathy* (1789) and *Ira and Isabella* (1807), evidenced a visionary-to-secular pattern that would be visible in the careers of several later American novelists. The protagonist of the first novel, Harrington, distressed by the discovery that his intended is in fact his long-lost sister, has a visionary dream of an angel who conducts him first to the gates of hell and then to heaven. Indirectly Brown advances the doctrine of works, showing heaven and hell to be the reward of earthly behavior. Also, he uses the visionary mode to lend supernatural retribution to his tale of seduction.

In *Ira and Isabella* Brown dispenses with visionary exempla. He laments in his preface "the loss of fairyism" and *"the extinction of the eastern manner."*[5] Brown says he feels freer than before *"to allure the untutored mind to the practice of virtue by an example which is rewarded, and to deter it from vice by the representation of its misery"* (xii). In the novel the replacement of supernaturalism by humanistic morality is enacted in such passages as: *"Reverence thyself* is a maxim said to be descended from heaven" (94); and "Religion is an ornament and a bulwark. Is it not the soul of stability? take it then, and find in your own soul the firm, unshaken character you wish to assume" (98). By relinquishing fairyism, Brown converts the Arminian sentiments of Harrington's dream into a plea for religious exertion in daily life, placing salvation fully in the hands of man himself.

A more famous example of changing views of the visionary mode is the literary career of Charles Brockden Brown, who similarly moved from the visionary to the secular, from an identification of religion with solitary communion to an interest in the workings of faith in human society.

Brockden Brown's prenovelistic stage was characterized in large part by visionary musing. In his 1789 "Rhapsodist" contributions to the *Columbian Magazine,* Brown begins by declaring that "the life of the rhapsodist is literally a dream."[6] Like other visionary tale writers of the period, he finds it "utterly impossible" that God should send angels "upon errands hurtful or pernicious to the sons of men" (8). Therefore, he is "void of terror" when "the film is removed from his eyes, and he beholds his attending genius, or guardian angel, arrayed in ambrosial weeds, and smiling with gracious benignity upon the bold attempts of the adventurous pupil" (8). Brown writes that both religion and poetry "seek a gayer prospect, and a visionary happiness in a world of their own creation" (9). The rhapsodist's main delight is "to mingle in the pastimes of angels" (11).

As Brown's letters between 1790 and 1793 reveal, his visionary inclinations during this prefictional period even tinged his attitude toward love and friendship. Several of his letters to Henrietta G———, who is often called a benevolent angel, read like religious visionary tales. Similarly, in an undated early letter to his friend William Wood Wilkins, Brown calls himself "a visionary" and states: "My pinions . . . *are dipped in heaven* . . . They are fitted only to accelerate the speed of angels and to enable the airy messenger, who at thy divine command wanders through eternity, to perform more quickly the behests of God."[7] When Wilkins died, Brown dreamed of him in heaven. Likewise, an early poem, "Devotion, An Epistle" (1794?), is full of heavenly and angelic references.

It is difficult to identify the reasons for Brown's rejection of the visionary mode, although frustrated love and the death of friends may have contributed to a general disillusionment. Actually, though, his opening address as president of the Belles Lettres Club betrays an early awareness of the precariousness of visionary ideals: "In the bosom of retirement and leisure we are apt to pour forth a visionary beauty and proportion upon the scenes around us, which vanish away when we come to examine them more nearly, and to try them by the unfailing test of experience."[8] By 1796 he began to mistrust angelic meditation, writing a friend: "I am sometimes almost in doubt whether he that was last year a visionary has not now become a lunatic, whether the objects around me are phantoms or realities." In the same year he confessed to his brother his "endeavor to *reason down* my perturbations, and dispeople by mere energy of argument the aerial work of 'calling shapes and beckoning shadows dire!' "[9]

By 1801, when his major fictional work was behind him, the man who had once loved solitary walks and "visionary transports"[10] wrote in his journal: "What a wretched possession is solitude. Intelligence and sympathy beaming from eye to eye, constitute all the happiness of man. Nature owes all her charms to her alliance with images flowing from socieity."[11] In the fictional history he completed in 1805, *Sketches of a History of the Carrils and Ormes,* Brockden Brown turned from the psychological introspection of his major novels to social historicism. Religion in this work is studied not in its effect on the solitary protagonist—as it had been in "The Rhapsodist" and in *Wieland, Edgar Huntly,* and *Ormond*—but rather in its connections with society and the world. Brown has a character in *Carrils and Ormes* say that all images of heaven "must necessarily correspond with the objects of terrestrial experience," since "Heaven . . . is but a splendid improvement of earthly plans." Al-

though during this period Brown married a minister's daughter and pro-
claimed himself "the ardent friend and the willing champion of the Christian
religion," his eyes became more closely fixed on the world than on heaven.[12]
In 1803 Brown ran an article in *The Literary Magazine and American Register*
on "The Impropriety of Looking into Futurity" which enjoined man to abandon impious attempts at visualizing angels and heaven and to confine himself
to "the narrow sphere around him" with the aim of learning only those things
that will "render him useful in life."[13] The last published writings of Brown's
life were purely historical pieces in his *American Register or General Repository of
History, Politics, and Science.* These are at the opposite end of the literary spectrum from his early "Rhapsodist" sketches. In her obituary notice, his wife
could laconically sum up his life as follows: "In early life he delighted to indulge in the visions of fancy, and the productions of his juvenile pen bear the
stamp of that character . . . For the last five years of his life he abandoned the
regions of fancy, and devoted himself exclusively to more solid and severe
pursuits."[14]

It violates the complexity of Brown's writings to say simply that he passed
from visionary rhapsodist to romancer to secular historian. On the other
hand, a rough pattern to this effect is suggested not only by the comparison
between his early and late work but by changes within his brief fictional
career. Paradoxically, his novels become more secular and social even as they
become more affirmatively Christian. The compelling quality of his first four
novels—*Wieland* (1798), *Ormond* (1799), *Edgar Huntly* (1799), and *Arthur
Mervyn* (1799–1800)—derives in part from a creative tension between the miraculous and the human, passion and reason, dream and reality. The visionary
mode, which Brown said nearly made him lunatic, provides a fund of imagery
for the depiction of dementia or nightmare, as when Wieland hears divine
voices commanding him to kill or when Arthur Mervyn and Edgar Huntly
have frightening dreams of resurrected corpses and dark pits.

In his last novels, *Clara Howard* (1801) and *Jane Talbot*(1801), Brown
abandoned psychological obsession on behalf of requited love and religious
conversion. Thus, the latter work commends a character whose "faith was
steadfast and rational, without producing those fervours and reveries and
rhapsodies, which unfit us for the mixed scenes of human life, and breed in us
absurd and phantastic notions of our duty or our happiness: . . . his religion
had produced all its practical effects, in honest, regular, sober and consistent
conduct."[15] Brown has exchanged his early celestial rhapsodies for an interest
in the operations of religion in "the mixed scenes of human life."

Brown is at his best when he detaches the visionary mode from didacticism
and places it in an extracreedal realm of terror. In this sense, he is the first
American novelist in a school that would come to include Poe, Hawthorne,
and Henry James, who connect reverie and supernatural visitation with psychology rather than with doctrinal commentary or religious comfort. The

being who commands Wieland to kill his wife is distant from the "guardian angel . . . smiling with gracious benignity" who had assured the young Rhapsodist of God's kindness. Edgar Huntly's nightmarish experience in the black cave is distant from the angelic reveries of the younger Brown. The same is true of Arthur Mervyn's dream of an ominous interview with Fielding, who stabs him. Unlike the more didactic writers I have discussed, Brown approaches artistry by recognizing the demonic underside of the visionary mode and by achieving an aesthetic equipoise between various attitudes to the divine. Like the other writers, he is least satisfactory when he endorses divine benevolence through the visionary mode ("The Rhapsodist") or when he interprets affirmative religion in terms of human experience (*Jane Talbot*).

Brown's contribution can be appreciated by an analysis of the use of the visionary mode by another American Gothic novelist, Isaac Mitchell. Throughout *The Asylum; or, Alonzo and Melissa* (1811) the religion emphasized in Mitchell's preface relieves the gloom, and the visionary mode is utilized to diminish rather than increase the terror of endangered characters. Alonzo often assures Melissa that their virtue will be rewarded in heaven, and at one point Alonzo has a comforting vision of Melissa's spirit in "the celestial regions of glory."[16] Mitchell's characters' views of the divine are closer to those of Brown's Rhapsodist than to those of Wieland, Clara, or Edgar Huntly. Like the American graveyardists, Mitchell utilized visionary devices not to probe the psychology of terror but rather to advance a religion of hope.

Alonzo's momentary view of Melissa's soul represents a phenomenon in American fiction that would be developed by such novelists as Harriet Beecher Stowe, Elizabeth Phelps Ward, and Annie T. Slosson. The vision of deceased friends or relatives—as opposed to abstract angels—seems to have begun in Caroline W. Thayer's *The Gamesters* (1805). Thayer briefly experiments with realistic visionary techniques through the kind of deathbed scenes that would become a staple of later religious fiction.

Another modification of the visionary mode that began during this period was the portrayal of human angels or earthly mediators who act redemptively in the world. This device signaled a humanization of the angels in the earlier visionary tales. In nineteenth-century religious fiction it would become common to portray angelic heroines who are redeemers of sinful characters. But before 1810 overt uses of this technique were rare in American fiction. To grant redemptive power to a human being, particularly a lay person, implied a rejection of the strict Calvinist view of man as helpless without God's grace.

Only *Charlotte Temple* (1791) and *The Inquisitor* (1793) by the Episcopalian Susanna Rowson make explicit use of the human angel. In the first novel, the redemptive function is assumed by the matronly Mrs. Beauchamp, who has "the benignant aspect of an angel of mercy." When she visits the dying Charlotte, the latter exclaims, "Angel of peace and mercy, art thou come to deliver me?" Beauchamp's attention to the doomed girl is called "an action in which even angels are said to rejoice," and she talks of religion "in the accent of a pitying angel."[17] Here we see the supernatural genius of the visionary tale being integrated into the fabric of the sentimental novel. A human being begins to function as a divine intermediary. After being consoled by her human angel, Charlotte makes a profession of faith and dies with her eyes raised to heaven.

In *The Inquisitor* Rowson makes a bolder attempt to instill divine qualities into a human character. The narrator of the story wishes he possessed the capability for "visiting unseen, the receptacles of the miserable, and the habitations of vice and luxury" with the aim of "rewarding and supporting merit; or withdrawing the veil, and discovering the aspect of hypocrisy."[18] A kind genius appears and gives him a magic ring which will make him invisible. In the course of the novel the invisible rambler, promoting a religion of good works and cheer, visits a gambler, a businessman, a drunkard, a libertine, an East Indian, a Calvinist preacher, and others. By converting her hero into a divine agent, Rowson has created a being who is at once a personal mediator for the virtuous and a celestial scourge of the wicked.

Like several other American novelists, Rowson turned from the visionary mode in her later works. After *The Inquisitor* she made no extensive use of the supernatural, even in its humanized form. In *The Fille de Chambre* (1793) and *Sarah* (1813), she scatters benign religious passages through stories that are mainly secular. *Biblical Dialogues* (1822), in which Rowson retells the Bible story in terms of what she describes as "profane history," deemphasizes angelic visitation. By the time she wrote *Charlotte's Daughter* (1828), Rowson had reduced religion to a simple code of Christian nurture and active benevolence. Unlike her ostracized mother, who had to be redeemed dramatically by an angelic intermediary, Lucy Temple is raised by a polished Episcopalian priest who teaches her "the principles of morality, and the plainest truths and precepts of religion."[19] Opening a school for young ladies and marrying well, Lucy undertakes "various and comprehensive schemes of benevolence" (184). Angelic intervention is unnecessary for a heroine who is the self-sufficient and socially integrated opposite of her erring mother.

Thus, between 1790 and 1815 we find tentative yet significant explorations of realistic versions of the visionary mode that would become extensively used by American authors after 1820. Enos Hitchcock and William Hill Brown transformed the allegorical visionary stories of such earlier writers as Hopkinson and Celadon into novelistic episodes. Susanna Rowson and Caroline Thayer introduced human angels and deathbed visions of friends. Charles Brockden Brown became the first American novelist to escape the didactic shackles of visionary contemplation and rise to a higher artistic level. Isaac Mitchell followed the lead of earlier American graveyardists by seeing pious possibilities in Gothic models. Some of these writers, especially the two Browns and Rowson, established a pattern of secularization—early experimentation with the visionary mode followed by an abandonment of it—that would characterize the careers of several later writers. In sum, early American fiction contained, in inchoate form, nearly every variation of the religious and nonreligious visionary mode.

George Fowler's *A Flight to the Moon* (1813) was a transitional work between the early visionary tales and the more elaborate later ones. Fowler, who in *The Wandering Philanthropist* had used the Oriental spy format to criticize American sectarianism, turned to the visionary mode to envisage not only extraterrestrial societies but heaven itself. The hero, Randalthus, is taken by an angel to the moon, which is inhabited by simple people who observe a nonmetaphysical religion of works. On the moon Randalthus dreams of flying to other ideal places, including heaven, where spirits live in bucolic bliss close to God. At one point, wondering if he is dead instead of dreaming, Randalthus feels "the emotions of a saint, who, having literally burst the chains of death and escaped the persecutions of a bigoted or blood-thirsty world, beholds the gate of heaven opening to receive him, sees the light of the countenance of the Great Eternal, hears the melting . . . sounds of golden harps, the joyful acclamations of innumerable hosts of angels; and meets all the joys of everlasting felicity."[20] The angel flies with him over yet more glittering celestial regions, and then they hover halfway between the moon and the earth so that Randalthus can observe all nations and their histories. He sees Confucius, Jesus, Mohammed, and various American religious figures, noting that "opinions on divine subjects are various and contradictory" (167). The lesson to be learned from theological wrangling is that "by refined disputation we may reason ourselves out of the plainest truths" (169). After visiting yet another heavenly utopia on the planet Mercury, Randalthus awakes and finds himself on earth.

Such a summary only hints at the lavish celestial imagery sustained by Fowler for nearly two hundred pages. In this novel the visionary imagination has burst from the confines of its pre-1800 circumspection and attempted to probe the heart of divine mysteries. No longer is heaven a distant allegorical panorama or a fleeting revelation followed by cautious recoil. Rather it is a society, or various societies, observing an ideal nontheological code of benevolence. Fowler uses the visionary mode in ways that are unparalleled in American fiction before 1820. Not only does he see the world and heaven from God's angle of vision, but at moments he seems to become God himself, as the tentative assurances of man's perfectibility that occurred in the pre-1800 tales give way to an exuberant proclamation of man's divinity. Moreover, the visionary mode permits Fowler to embrace God like a saint in heaven and to see all the major religious leaders of history, including "an amiable person named Jesus" (123).

Despite the almost pristine joy of the liberated visionary imagination in *A Flight to the Moon,* there is in the book an undercurrent of negativity which, as mentioned above, began to be seen in the Oriental tale during this period. Fowler's spiritual restlessness in *The Wandering Philanthropist* is evidenced here by a somewhat frantic flight to various parts of the universe in search of truth. A note of desperation sometimes creeps into the account of celestial delight, and the dream within a dream is an exponential multiplication of visionary devices, as though one dream and one angel will no longer suffice.

As in other American fiction, the visionary mode here is not a comforting enactment of received doctrine but rather a firm repudiation of it. Theologians such as Jonathan Edwards and Samuel Hopkins prized pointed doctrinal discussion. In contrast, such Oriental and visionary tale writers as Tyler, Knapp, and Fowler dramatized the failure of theological controversy to produce anything but destructive persecution. At the end of his tour of human history, Fowler's Randalthus witnesses a great explosion which reduces the world to ruins. On these ruins he sees man rebuilding from a savage to a civilized state and then being blown up again and again in a cycle of annihilation and reconstruction. This, explains Fowler, represents the end result of "the blood that different sects and different tribes have shed in support of their religious tenets" (167). Fowler's portrait of universal ruin and rebuilding can be seen as a metaphor for American religious fiction, which in large part was built on the ruins of strictly logical discussion of doctrine. Beneath the prevailing optimism of American religious fiction lay a chastened realization that the pious imaginative writer must depend on other things than reason for divine certainty. Early in his career, the religious fictionist was wont to envisage divine or human angels, as though creating imaginary gods would validate the existence of a real one. Later, he often turned to secular experience as a way of illustrating the operability of nondoctrinal piety in the world. In many cases, fiction was a device for infusing divine endorsement and human emotion into a faith which for many authors had lost its rational buttresses.

The Visionary-to-Secular Pattern in Sedgwick, Child, and Judd

Three authors who began writing fiction after 1820—Catherine Sedgwick, Lydia Maria Child, and Sylvester Judd—followed the visionary-to-secular pattern while they abandoned logical religion. Each of these writers, having rejected Calvinist polemics, turned to the novel after a nearly devastating crisis of faith. Fiction became a way of reconstructing faith on the ruins of metaphysical theology. Although associated with New England liberalism, none of these writers found a true spiritual home. They all considered Calvinism severe, Transcendentalism mystical, and Unitarianism flawed despite its gratifying creedlessness. Their novels reveal three liberal imaginations finding divine and earthly supports for faith, first through the visionary mode and later through secular morality. In each case we find an ongoing dialectic between what Judd called simply "the ideal and the real," a dialectic manifested by early experimentation with visionary devices followed by modification and final abandonment of them. The first novel of each of these writers wages war on Calvinism, using the visionary mode as a rhetorical weapon. The later novels seem to assume that orthodoxy has been defeated, abandoning disputation for the depiction of religion's connections to the real. A study of the careers of these three novelists provides important insights into shifting attitudes to the visionary mode in the post-1820 period.

Catherine Sedgwick was using visionary metaphors to attack Calvinism long before the publication of her first novel in 1822. In 1812 she wrote that her brother Charles's religious letters were "like angels' visits," which counteracted "all the sermons I hear in a month, and all the writers on human depravity, with Hopkins at their head."[21] "If an angel was to vouchsafe me the honor of a visit," Catherine wrote, "she would not come with words so sweetly soothing as those dictated by a brother's partial kindness" (90). In describing how her sisters Frances and Eliza escaped "the horrors of Calvinism" (68), Sedgwick established the two poles of the defiance of orthodoxy that would extend through her long fictional career. The imaginative Frances "would spread her wings and rise up into a purer atmosphere, bright with God's presence" (68). Eliza, in contrast, calmly kept her eyes fixed on practical moral duty. In her first three novels, Catherine's religious heroines embodied the visionary and angelic qualities of Frances. After *Clarence* (1830) Catherine increasingly questioned the visionary mode and opted for the experiential religion represented by Eliza.

Catherine started writing fiction during a period of religious indecision, even though *A New England Tale* (1822) was undertaken as a Unitarian tract. She joined New York's First Church in 1821; but in the same year she called herself a religious *"borderer"* (256), detesting Calvinism yet disappointed with Unitarianism, which she found rationalistic and cold. She respected her minister, William Ware, but she disliked his dry pulpit manner. She wrote in 1821 that Unitarianism lacked "seriousness and holy fervor" (145). Twenty-six years later she would still be saying that "there is some radical defect in it, or in its ministration, that prevents its general diffusion" (301). She refused to follow other liberals into Transcendentalism, for she thought Emerson's outlook lacked "a sound, rocky foundation, and clear atmosphere of good sense" (316). As a religious borderer, she never mentioned Unitarianism in her novels, though she showed its influence. Instead, she fabricated a kind of hybrid "fictional faith." In her early novels she sought to supplant Calvinism with visionary intermediaries deriving from various sources—from Methodism, Quakerism, romantic intuitionalism, Roman Catholicism, American Indian religions, and Oriental faiths. Later she turned to portrayals of domestic piety, social religion, and active benevolence.

Sedgwick's first two novels, *A New England Tale* (1822) and *Redwood* (1824), utilize visionary devices to combat, respectively, Calvinism and skepticism. These novels contain both angelic heroines and visionary episodes. Jane Elton, who in the course of *A New England Tale* exposes the follies of orthodoxy, is surrounded with celestial imagery. As a child she feels "as if an angel were really walking beside me."[22] As an adult she is referred to as "an angel on earth" (102), "an angel of goodness" (131), one of the "earthborn angels" (151). One character tells her, "You need not hide your wings—I know you—there is none but an angel would look upon me with pity" (138). The visionary theme takes on a more supernatural coloring in the characterization of Crazy Bet, an amalgam of Methodist enthusiast and Wordsworthian lunatic seer. A frequenter of camp meetings, Bet instinctively hates the logical Calvinism of Jane's protectress, Mrs. Wilson. Bet often refers to Jane as an angel, and one night she has a visionary episode witnessed by Jane. While leading Jane through the woods, Bet climbs a nearby mountain and has a "heavenly vision" of the "I AM" (129–130).

While using these visionary devices to suggest her anti-Calvinist characters' divine nature and closeness to God, Sedgwick represents orthodoxy as a tyrannical system which results in indolence and crime. Jane's childhood acquaintances, David and Elvira Wilson, embody the evil fruits of a Calvinist upbringing (he ends up a religionless criminal, and she runs off with a French dance teacher). The visionary mode helps Sedgwick explode Calvinist dogma without refuting it logically. Jane, like the Methodist Mary Hall and the Quaker Mr. Lloyd, does not discuss doctrine. She simply is an angel. Crazy Bet provides a surrogate visionary line to the divine, assuring Jane of God's existence and benevolence. When *A New England Tale* was lambasted by some orthodox readers as unfair and malicious, Sedgwick could calmly reply that if anyone "could consider this tale as a designed attack upon the character of any class of christians, such an object would be distinctly disavowed."[23] The visionary mode becomes both a strategic weapon and a shield. By the author's caveat, the heroine is a human angel with a friend who can see God. Supernatural imagery helps to rescue the author from both the burden and the commitment of logical discussion.

In *Redwood* Sedgwick aims the visionary weapon at safer targets—Voltairean skepticism and Shakerism. The novel tells of the misery and final conversion of the skeptical Henry Redwood and his daughter, Caroline, through the ministrations of Ellen Bruce, who turns out to be Redwood's long-lost daughter. In the subplot, Reuben Harrington, a licentious Shaker preacher, abducts a devotee named Emily Allen, whom Ellen finally saves. Ellen is the angel of the piece. Like Jane Elton, she is constantly called an angel, though she is more actively heroic than the earlier heroine. Sedgwick again rhetorically uses a visionary episode, as Caroline Redwood dreams of a celestial being sanctifying the Christian Ellen while ignoring her infidel father. Instructed by her vision, Caroline comes to admire Ellen and to embrace Christianity with her father. The visionary mode also appears in the form of a protective dead relative, as Ellen calls her departed mother a guardian spirit watching over her. Sedgwick requires such visionary devices in this book, for she is attempting to combat "Gibbon, Hume, Voltaire" in the person of Henry Redwood.[24] Redwood is thus the devil of the dream and the main concern of the human angel, Ellen. When he recognizes Ellen's divinity, and when he reads a lachrymose letter left by her guardian spirit, he is converted without question. Again Sedgwick has used the visionary mode to facilitate a nonlogical victory over fearfully logical opponents.

Although it caused less of an uproar than *A New England Tale, Redwood* antagonized some readers, particularly Shakers. Therefore in *Hope Leslie* Sedgwick commissioned two human angels, Hope Leslie and the Indian Magawisca, to redeem less controversially contemporary religionists: early New England Puritans. By retreating to the historical past, Sedgwick could make her case without fearing the obloquy provoked by her portraits of contemporary faith. Indeed, *Hope Leslie* became her most universally applauded work. In the novel Magawisca is unfairly imprisoned by the Puritans and charged with witchcraft. At the end she is rescued by Hope and a virtuous Puritan, Everell Fletcher. Magawisca, whom one reviewer correctly called America's "first genuine Indian angel,"[25] often holds converse with wood gods sent by the Great Spirit. But the greatest number of angelic images are attributed to Hope, who in one scene is actually compared to the Virgin Mary appearing as "a celestial visitant" to "a poor banished son of Eve."[26]

Hope and Magawisca are exemplars of man's potential divinity, viewed by friends as angels and by enemies, particularly a few "stiff-starched Puritans," as witches. They become touchstones for opposing views of human nature. If the mind is filled with guilt and "recollections of sin," then "the ministering angels of Nature are converted into demons" (II, 217); if one is willing to entertain the possibility of human perfectibility, these demons are recognized as angels. As Sedgwick explains: "Nature has her ministers that correspond with the world in the heart of man. The words, 'my kingdom is within you,' are worth all the metaphysical discoveries made by unassisted human wisdom" (II, 217). The visionary assertion again supplants theological discussion. At the end of the novel the Puritan community has come to revere Hope and Everell, whose marriage is sanctified by "celestial spirits . . . from their bright spheres" (II, 256).

Thus, in her first three novels Sedgwick invests the human angel, which in Rowson had remained a background figure, with active redemptive power. At first meekly virtuous (Jane Elton), Sedgwick's angels become increasingly heroic and self-sufficient (Ellen Bruce, Hope Leslie). In *A New England Tale* and *Redwood* the allegorical visionary episodes of pre-1820 novels are replaced by more directly applicable supernatural dreams. The customary recoil following

Crazy Bet's vision is dropped in Caroline Redwood's dream, which symbolizes the central religious message of the book. In each of the three novels, the visionary mode is a convenient rhetorical device for subverting opposing doctrines.

After *Hope Leslie* the visionary mode became less attractive to Sedgwick. Just as William Hill Brown had noted the loss of fairyism in his late novel, so Sedgwick began the second half of her literary career by dismissing the supernatural in a story of 1835: "This is the age of facts and evidence, experience and demonstration, the enlightened age, *par excellence.* Ghosts, apparitions, banshees, phocas, cluricaunes, fairies, 'good people all,' are now departed spirits. The fairies, the friends of poets and story-tellers, the patrons, champions, and good geniuses of children, . . . are gone, exhaled like the dews that glittered on last summer's leaves."[27]

As in the Oriental tale of the period, facts and evidence, experience and demonstration began to take precedence in the religious novelist's mind. In Henry Ware, Jr.'s novel series, *Scenes and Characters Illustrating Christian Truths,* to which Sedgwick contributed *Home* (1835), the divine is interpreted almost totally in terms of the human. A study of Sedgwick's novels after 1830 shows her slow abandonment of the visionary mode.

In *Clarence* (1830) angelic behavior is the result not of supernatural intervention but of the careful nurture of human capabilities. Thus in reference to the infant Gertrude Clarence, Sedgwick writes: "Enfolded in this minute frame are the capacities of an angel. Go forth then, labor, struggle, and knowledge shall fill thy mind with light of thy own."[28] Although several times called an angel, Gertrude is more decisive, less dreamy than Sedgwick's previous heroines. She is described as "a fit heroine for the nineteenth century; practical, efficient, direct, and decided" (I, 239). A potential visionary episode is avoided when Gertrude, mistaken by a friend for an Oriental angel, corrects him: "But you saw none . . . Ours is not the country of enchantments—nature is *merely* nature here" (I, 245). Given to romantic reveries early in the story, Gertrude learns the value of moral duty. Sedgwick explains that Gertrude's future "moralizing" will be "linked to action—a difficult sort of *lay-preaching*" (II, 224). By the end of the novel, domestic bliss and practical piety have replaced supernaturalism.

The Linwoods (1835) shows Sedgwick again puncturing the visionary dream and renewing the dedication to active virtue. Bessie Lee is a half-crazed angelic dreamer whose illusions are shattered by experience. When she views another character as an angel, she is reminded: "Yes . . . But yet, she is pretty well spiced with humanity."[29] In the course of the novel Bessie learns that we must "come down" to humanity and "adapt ourselves to things as they are" (I, 14). At the end she takes up social work. Another character, Isabella, also changes from a dreamer to a realist. She confesses that since youth she has been "groping in mist: now I stand in a clear light—I see objects in their true colours—I am mistress of myself" (II, 191). Sedgwick has allowed her early visionary probings to give way to a confidence in man's self-created goodness.

In Sedgwick's most popular novels—*Home* (1835), *The Poor Rich Man and the Rich Poor Man* (1836), and *Live and Let Live* (1837)—the visionary mode is absent. This trilogy, which William Ellery Channing hailed as the beginning of "an era in our literature,"[30] equates religion with nurture, social concern, and domestic morality. Barclay of *Home* teaches his children "punctuality, order, neatness, temperance, self-denial, kindness, generosity, and hospitality."[31] When someone asks Barclay about "angels and archangels," he declares: "The ladder is knocked down, my friend, we stand on nature's level" (41). The only visionary reference in the other two novels is a paean in *The Poor Rich Man* to moral action: "Well may reflection be called an angel, when it suggests duties, and calls into actions principles strong enough to meet them."[32]

The rejection of visionary devices takes on a slightly more negative coloring in "Second Thoughts Best," a tale Sedgwick wrote in 1840. The story describes a woman who loses her idealism in the "ever-open school of experience."[33] By the end of the story the woman "had extinguished the 'angel light';—she had herself closed the gates of Paradise, and voluntarily circumscribed her vision to this world" (256). By 1840 Sedgwick herself had in large part extinguished the angel light.

In *The Boy of Mt. Rhigi* (1848) social religion is the main emphasis, as Sedgwick depicts the unwarranted imprisonment and eventual conversion of the indigent Clapham Dunn. Sedgwick gently mocks the visionary mode, as the youthful Clap has a "drollish dream" of a "little chubby angel."[34] After Clap has his vision his friend Harry Davis informs him: "The times have gone by, mother says, when God teaches men by dreams" (26). Clap's angel has come not to save him but to teach self-redemption. The cord that the angel throws down is said to symbolize "the help that always comes if you help yourself" (27). This experiential interpretation of the visionary mode is underscored later by the assertion that Clap's "good angel must be the firm resolve, the manly struggle of the boy himself!" (54). Persevering through social ostracism and an unfair jail term, Clap survives to marry well and to form a successful business partnership with Harry. If *Home* knocks down the heavenly ladder and places man on nature's level, *The Boy of Mt. Rhigi* anticipates Horatio Alger by erecting a social ladder that is climbed by the good angel of firm resolve and manly struggle.

The two tendencies of Sedgwick's imagination—the visionary and the secular, the divine and the human—clash directly in a late novel, *Married or Single?* (1857), which contrasts two sisters, Eleanor and Grace Herbert, to show Sedgwick's final rejection of supernaturalism on behalf of humanistic morality. Eleanor has the "holy calm" that comes "from religious aims, moderate expectations, and attainable hopes."[35] Grace is more brilliant, imaginative, "capable of soaring higher" (I, 34); but, as she says, "I . . . have made wings for myself, which *I* know will melt off in the first fiery trial" (I, 23). In the course of the novel Grace learns the value of Eleanor's humble faith. After attending a séance in an effort to commune with otherworldly spirits, Grace is "recalled to the actual world" when the genius loci of a library appears in a vision with the advice to *"work out your own salvation"* (I, 257, 261). In a passage that seems to reflect Sedgwick's own experience with the visionary mode, we are told that Grace had "tried the thousand-times repeated experiment of Icarus, and the wings had dropped in the forbidden element, under the stern law, 'thus far shalt thou go, and no farther' " (I, 261). Sedgwick emphasizes the necessity of exercising mundane duty in the face of calamity. Also, she satirizes metaphysical theology, Transcendentalism, and romantic ideality as quixotic transgressions against actuality. By the end of the novel, Grace has exchanged dreamy philosophizing for "the common events of every day, the little accidents of household life" (II, 195). As Sedgwick's preface indicates, secular affairs have been elevated to a level of sanctity, while religion has been divested of its visionary idealism.

Although temperamentally and artistically different from Catherine Sedgwick, Lydia Maria Child is like her in her attitudes toward religion and in her use of the visionary mode. Like Sedgwick, Child passed from Congregationalism through Unitarianism to an amorphous nonsectarianism. Just as Sedgwick was a borderer, so Child verged on skepticism. As she wrote to her clergyman brother in 1820: "You need not fear my becoming a Swedenborgian. I am in more danger of wrecking on the rocks of skepticism than of stranding on the shoals of fanaticism . . . I wish I could find some religion in which my heart and understanding could unite; that amidst the darkest clouds of this life I might ever be cheered with the mild halo of religious consolation."[36]

Like Sedgwick, Child never found a comfortable religious home. In 1835 she felt that her faith was so weak that she wept like a child. In 1838 she wrote that given the alternatives of infidelity and theology, she would choose the former. Although sympathetic to Transcendentalism in the early 1840s, she came to think that Emerson and Kant had lost themselves in "a bank of fog."[37] In 1857 she confessed to Lucy Osgood that "if I could only find a church, I would nestle into it as gladly as a bird ever nestled into her covert in a storm. I have stayed away from meeting, because one offered me petrifications, and another gas, when I was hungry for bread" (92). She longed to believe rather than to investigate; yet belief constantly eluded her. Relief from spiritual indecision came first in the writing of fiction and later in a dedication to secular faith, as she came to view "the church of the future" as "a church of deeds, not of doctrines of any sort" (185). Just as Sedgwick turned to secular affairs, so did Child find solace in deeds after a struggle against theology and skepticism.

Child's use of the visionary mode reflects these changing attitudes toward religion. Before 1850 references to angels and heaven are common in her fiction. Later, visionary images are relegated to minor characters or are made more concrete. Not only does Child resemble Sedgwick in this overall pattern; she also follows Sedgwick's lead by exploiting the visionary potential of various religions and philosophies: Greek polytheism, Roman Catholicism, American Indian faiths, Islam, Zorastrianism. As in Sedgwick, these religions offer metaphors for an objectification of the divine that New England Protestantism lacked. Child's early novels tend to be meditative, seeking quiescent divine communion; her later fiction is more hurried and forward-moving, as though plot itself has become a substitute for religious reflection.

Like Sedgwick, Child devoted her first novel to an attack on logical Calvinism. *Hobomok* (1824), anticipating Sedgwick's *Hope Leslie* (1827), revisits Puritan times to form a creedless center of natural religion around the Indian Hobomok and Mary Conant, who learns to dislike her father's rigid orthodoxy. Child's main religious point is that in the face of large, permanent things—nature, death, love—quarrels about doctrinal niceties are pointless. Although not as heavily reliant on the visionary mode as is Sedgwick in her first novel, Child does make extensive use of quiet, contemplative moments that are meant to put the lie to jarring creeds. Both Hobomok and Mary hold communion with the divine in ways that are reminiscent of Sedgwick's Crazy Bet and Jane Elton and that contrast with heated theological discussions between several Calvinists in the novel.

In *The Rebels* (1825) and *Philothea* (1836) visionary devices become more prominent. The heroine of *The Rebels,* Grace Osborne, is presented as an angelic medium between other characters' religious excesses; she exerts "an angelic influence" until her death, when "she seemed like a celestial spirit, which, having performed its mission on earth, melts into a misty wreath, then disappears forever."[38] The visionary theme appears in other characters and episodes as well. After a chapter of theological discussion, Child uses a visionary scene that serves as a kind of baptism, purifying the characters of their theological differences and creating a more cooperative feeling among them. By the end of the novel, Child has borrowed visionary metaphors from Catholicism and neoclassicism as well.

Philothea goes beyond the somewhat haphazard probing of visionary alternatives in Child's previous novels to a thoroughgoing investigation of the visionary possibilities of early Greek and Oriental religions. Philothea is a semi-divine heroine who inspires dreams of the spirit world. Throughout the novel she is referred to as a celestial visitant. Philothea's friends take on her divine glow, so that they too have visionary sensitivity. Her husband, Paralus, is subject to a lingering illness during which he often has divine visions. The visionary mode again supplants intellectualism, as when the philosopher Plato claims to have learned more from Paralus' visions than from all other accounts of heaven. When Paralus dies, Philothea constantly dreams of him in paradise. And after Philothea dies, her friend Eudora receives heavenly directives to seek out a Persian who turns out to be her father.

In *Philothea* Child has found visionary relief from the unmediated Protestantism of her background. At one point in the novel an Oriental tells a Greek: "You not only adopt foreign gods, but sometimes create new ones, and admit them into your theology by solemn act of the great council."[39] This statement can be seen as a metaphor for Child's use of the visionary mode. Child's early novels, especially *Philothea,* show her effort to adopt foreign gods in order to create new ones. She borrows, at first randomly and then more purposefully, from a variety of religions and philosophies to creat an aesthetic, objective sense of the divine. It is difficult to say to what extent this is a compensatory infusion of divine validation into a faith that threatened to collapse. But it can be suggested that Child's longing for the halo of religious consolation found at least vicarious satisfaction in the portrayal of characters whose visions of angels and heaven were joyfully real. If Child's own faith came close to wrecking on the rocks of skepticism, the faith of her early protagonists— whether Indian, Persian, or Greek—was confirmed by the power to see God.

Child's attraction to classical divinities persisted through the decades following the publication of *Philothea.* Always enamored of paintings of angels, she described in a letter of 1848 her delight over Correggio's Diana: "If I lived where it was I should make a little golden altar, and burn incense before it. You see there is no washing my Greek heathenism out of me."[40] Charmed by Raphael's Sybils, she wrote again in 1856: "I don't know what it is that draws me so toward those ancient Grecians!"[41] The impulse to adopt foreign gods— particularly gods possessing a consoling visibility and tangibility—thus lasted in the face of criticism from some quarters that in *Philothea* she was flirting with paganism.

Like Sedgwick, Child in time became more interested in the God inside the human soul than in angels outside it. Her *Letters from New-York* (1843) contain Emersonian statements like, "After all, the God *within* us is the God we really believe in, whatever we may have learned in catechisms and creeds," and, "The human heart is like Heaven; the more angels, the more room."[42] In Transcendentalism Child found an appealing correspondence to her belief in man's divinity and her distaste for creed. But at the same time she demanded a more palpable relation to the divine. Thus through both series of *Letters from New-York* (1843 and 1845) she continued her study of the visionary imagery of various faiths. In the first series she sympathetically discusses Islam, Swedenborgianism, and Roman Catholicism. Child states, "Whenever God appears to the eyes of faith as terrible in power, and stern in vengeance, the soul craves for some form of mediation," particularly "a chorus of love from angel voices" (12). This desire for divine mediation is evidenced in an anecdote about a man carried to heaven by an angel to meet Jesus. It surfaces in differ-

ent form in an attraction to the saints of Catholicism and the gods of paganism. In *Letters from New-York. Second Series,* Child transforms Swedenborg's
doctrine of correspondences into a law of angelic intervention: "The angels
. . . are but mediums of the divine love and wisdom of God, flowing through
them into the hearts and minds of men, and transmitted and received according to established laws. This intervention of mediums, this gradation of causes
and effects, pervades all creation."[43] However, Child goes on to combine a plea
for practical religion with eulogies of such secular religious novelists as Sedgwick, Maria Edgeworth, Mary Howitt, and Frederika Bremer. In effect, Child
wants it both ways at once. She seeks to equate man with the angels, but she
holds that celestial mediation is necessary. In sum, the *Letters* show Child
struggling toward earthly analogues to the visionary ideal yet still delighting
in the contemplation of angels.

In *Fact and Fiction* (1846) Child began to deemphasize the religious aspects
of the visionary mode. In this tale collection, the interest in foreign gods remains, as early-Christian, Indian, and Greek religions are invoked. But secular
experience came to dominate Child's imagination, so that she used the supernatural primarily for the purposes of entertainment. The writer who had been
concerned with human and divine angels in her earlier work suddenly preferred to write escapist fiction about haunted waterfalls, endangered lovers,
and activist Quakers. The precise reason for this change is not clear. In *Fact
and Fiction* Child may have tried to cater to public demand for more entertaining, less doctrinal versions of the visionary mode.

But as with Sedgwick, there appears to have been more fundamental reasons for Child's embrace of the secular. In 1856 she wrote her brother, "Ideas
which formerly seemed to me a foundation firm as the everlasting hills, are
rolling away from under my feet, leaving me on a ladder poised on the
clouds."[44] Just as Sedgwick's Barclay had acknowledged that the ladder had
been knocked down, so Child started to feel that her own visionary ladder was
about to topple. In the late 1840s and throughout the 1850s, her letters deni-
grated "foggy" philosophers such as Kant, Carlyle, and Emerson, calling for a
solid, rocky foundation and a church of deeds. The author who had established a universal law of supernatural mediation in 1845 could declare in a letter of 1860 that her mind "will not accept any supernatural mediums between
my soul and its Heavenly Father; whether the mediums be Virgin Mothers, or
Divine Humanities" (144). Increasingly concerned with abolition and social
reform, Child began to value the utilitarian and entertaining, as opposed to
the meditative, qualities of fiction.

That Child had dropped from the height of visionary philosophizing
reached in *Philothea* is suggested by her late abolitionist work *A Romance of the
Republic* (1867), a predominantly secular novel about the period just before
the Civil War. The only vocally religious figure in this novel is the Methodist

slave Chloe, whose visions of dead friends and Jesus give her the confidence that "De good Lord up dar, He hars."[45] Chloe is "a great seer of visions," and "to her they seemed to be an objective reality" (177). She sometimes sees Jesus as a child riding a pony before her in the fields. As opposed to the exotic, rather postured seers of Child's early novels, Chloe is approachable, talkative. She is closer to the visionary bumpkins of Annie T. Slosson's *Seven Dreamers* (1890) than to Child's own Philothea. Her visions of the child Jesus antici-pate portrayals of Christ's babyhood by such later writers as Lew Wallace and O. B. Frothingham. Although this realistic visionary mode had not yet been summoned into the center of white Protestantism, as it would be in *The Gates Ajar* novels, it nevertheless was brought to the level of secular experience. Chloe's visions seem to spring from the earth rather than descend from the sky. They fit comfortably into the nonreligious, primarily experiential out-looks of the other characters. Once fearful of wrecking on the rocks of skepti-cism, Child settled in this novel on the bedrock of objective reality, even as her interest in visionary devices remained.

Unlike Sedgwick and Child, Sylvester Judd had a short literary career, pro-ducing only three imaginative works: *Margaret* (1845), *Philo* (1850), and *Richard Edney* (1850). There are, however, important similarities between Judd and these female novelists. Like them, he was a religious borderer. Raised a Congregationalist, he experienced a crisis of faith in the mid-1830s, after which he became first a skeptic and then a Unitarian. He assumed the Unitar-ian pastorship of Augusta, Maine, in 1840. But like Sedgwick and Child, he remained a nominal Unitarian who attempted to create in his novels, as he put it in 1852, an ecumenical "true, Christian church."[46] Just as Sedgwick and Child made free use of various religions to form an eclectic and variable fic-tional faith, so Judd borrowed widely to fabricate his true church. His aims saw little fruition. His fiction drew more puzzlement than applause, and his efforts in Augusta to found the nonsectarian Birthright Church resulted in re-buffs from more doctrinally precise ministers.

Judd's early use and final dismissal of the visionary mode follows the pattern seen in the careers of the two women novelists. In *Margaret* Judd utilizes vi-sionary techniques to help defeat Calvinism in nonlogical fashion. In *Philo*, a poetic narrative, the visionary mode becomes more extensive yet more pos-tured, as it was in Child's *Philothea*. In *Richard Edney*, which identifies religion with doing good, the mode is rejected. Like Sedgwick and earlier novelists, Judd began by creating fictional gods and ended by portraying socially active humans.

The dialectic between the real and the ideal, which had been implicit in Sedgwick and Child, became a modus operandi for Judd. *Margaret*, as the subtitle says, is *A Tale of the Real and Ideal, Blight and Bloom;* in it the vision-

ary and the secular are mingled so as to define each other. Judd's next two
works expand on the ideal and the real respectively, almost to the exclusion of
each other, settling at last in the real.

Margaret is a classic example of the fictional formation of faith through a
rhetorical use of the visionary mode. In this novel the visionary subversion of
Calvinism, which in the 1790s was benign and indirect, becomes strategically
planned and forthright. The visionary episodes in *Margaret* are carefully arranged, first to familiarize the reader with angelic dreams and then, after the
process is established, to topple orthodoxy through a direct conversation with
Jesus and John. Judd prepares for the novel's central anti-Calvinist dream by
having the young Margaret, who has already had several visions, attend
church one Sunday to hear Parson Welles deliver an Edwardsean sermon on
human depravity. After the sermon Margaret shocks several of the parishion-
ers with her "heathenish" answers to their orthodox drill questions. When
asked how many persons are in the godhead, Margaret replies that she does
not know, but, "I should love to see it."[47]

She gets to see the godhead in the next scene. After climbing a mountain to
contemplate the loveliness of the afternoon, she goes home and falls asleep. In
her dream she sees white statues of Jesus and John, who come to life and smile
at her. Suddenly the scene is disrupted by the appearance of several Calvinists
from Welles's congregation. One of the Calvinists declares that Jesus has
come to doom Margaret to "everlasting destruction" because the girl is "vain,
proud, deceitful, selfish and wholly depraved" (I, 166). Another ridicules
Margaret for thinking that her natural amiability will commend her to Christ.
At this point, John, "the Apostle of Love," intercedes on Margaret's behalf:
"Her natural amiability is pleasing to Christ. He was amiable in his youth before God and man. No human being is sinful by nature" (I, 169). Margaret
takes flowers to Jesus, who accepts them and speaks gently with her. The
reprimanded Calvinists withdraw, leaving Margaret alone with Jesus. He tells
her: "Margaret! . . . The Church has fallen . . . The Eve of Religion has again
eaten the forbidden fruit. You shall be a co-worker with me in its second redemption" (I, 173). Christ and John turn into statues again and disappear.

This dream is the culmination of an anti-Calvinist tendency that originated
in the visionary tales of the 1780s and 1790s. It was now safe for the American fictionist to cast off the camouflage of allegorical indirection and to have
anti-Calvinist dicta come straight from the lips of Christianity's founders.
Also, Margaret's dream exaggerates the tendency of earlier visionary tales to
objectify the divine, to reduce it to the tangible and human. Jesus and John
begin and end as marble statues, as though fashioned by the novelist's own
imagination. They blossom and fructify like the plants Margaret loves so
much. Atonement results not from a sense of sin but from an exchange of
flowers. Thus, Calvinism is ousted not by argument but by a visionary dream
which palatably coalesces the ideal with the real.

After this episode, there is little mention of Calvinism in the novel. Judd's major doctrinal demons appear to have been effectively exorcised through the anti-Calvinist dream. Judd next applies himself to the task at hand: the creation of a new church that combines the aestheticism of classicism and Roman Catholicism with the nonsectarianism of New England liberalism. Such a combination requires tact, so again Judd invokes the visionary mode. He creates a series of additional dreams to validate Margaret's semipagan impulses. In them Margaret sees various neoclassical divinities who are more lovely and less doctrinally concerned than the gods of her previous visions. In effect, aestheticism displaces dogma. Margaret has one more dream of Jesus, but this time he is a weak and weary man who grasps Margaret's arm for support. When Margaret gives him water, he revives and takes on a look resembling "the Transfiguration of Raphael" (II, 233). The visionary dream not only makes Christ reliant on the heroine but transforms him into a work of art. By the end of the novel, all the characters of Margaret's dreams have been objectified. She has statues made of Christ, John, the benevolent lady, the classical divinities. These statues adorn the landscape of Mons Christi, Margaret's new religious community, which is a kind of Protestant Vatican City cum Athenian art colony. Margaret can at last exlaim: "My dreams have gone out in realities! THE CROSS IS ERECTED ON MONS CHRISTI!" (II, 229).

Judd's treatment of religion in *Margaret* raised some eyebrows among reviewers. The *North American Review* charged Judd with intellectual evasion in his use of the visionary mode. Calling Margaret "a visionary enthusiast," the reviewer complained that Judd's idea that "each individual should have miracles and an apocalypse of his own . . . throws the whole process of her conversion into the regions of fable, and destroys all our interest in tracing the influences brought to bear on her mind and heart." The vision of Jesus and John struck the reviewer as particularly offensive, since it "has the same effect, as if, in the history of some difficult wayfaring, the traveller should be represented as borne on the wings of angels over some mountain-pass which was peculiarly difficult to tread."[48] As we have seen, Judd does indeed resort to visions in *Margaret* whenever the religious passage becomes especially difficult.

In light of such objections to visionary devices in *Margaret*, it is surprising that Judd used them even more extensively in *Philo*. It seems that his visionary impulses had not been fully satisfied in *Margaret* and that his interest in objectifying the divine could be extended in verse to imagine conversations with various Christian and pagan divinities. In *Margaret* the visionary mode was restricted to dreams. In *Philo* many spirits and Christ himself hold regular converse with men, accompanying them on celestial flights. The chief visitant is Gabriel, who appears to the pious Philo and the skeptical Charles in order to help them judge and rectify the world. He flies with them around the world, hovering over America to decry theologians. Then he takes them to hell, where demons describe their kinship with hellfire preachers. In the course of the book Philo and Charles meet the classical Graces, the Spirit of Wisdom, the Genius of the Earth, and the Pope of Rome. The main theme is that man has distorted Christ's message through theological exposition and harsh doctrines. At the end several philosophical and religious figures, including Transcendentalists and Catholics, confess their shortcomings to Christ.

In *Philo* Judd continues his subversion of opposing doctrines through the visionary mode. If his target in *Margaret* was Edwardsean Calvinism, it is broadened here to include various denominations and metaphysical theology in general. The overuse of visionary devices suggests a mind that has become voracious for validation of the supernatural. It is no accident that in *Richard Edney,* Judd's novel published later in 1850, the visionary mode is slighted. *Philo* comes perilously close to destroying God by creating too many gods. *Richard Edney,* like the late novels of some other American writers, embraces secular experience as a solid alternative to visionary speculation.

Instead of having celestial visions, Richard Edney heeds "the good angel of common sense and rational hope, that ever attended him."[49] We are told that Richard is "deeply religious" (9), but "religion" here means something quite different from what it meant in Judd's previous works. There is no creation of doctrine in this novel, no attack on religious enemies. There is just honest moral endeavor, with its attendant frustrations and eventual triumph. Tragedy and experience have tempered visionary ideals. Even human love has lost its ideality. Thus, the romance between Richard and Melicent "did not look into the heavens, or the ideal and dreamy alone. It looked upon the world at their feet, at men and things about them, and life as it is" (329–330).

Although at one point Richard weeps for "some long-lost Ideality" (389), he finds relief in ethical duty. His religious model is Pastor Harold, whose Operative Philanthropy aims to solve social problems like poverty, war, and slavery. Exterior angels are transformed into the innate capacity to achieve the chief end of religion—"TO BE GOOD, AND TO DO GOOD" (80). Judd's more circumscribed vision is reflected in one clergyman character's remark: "Nature, like Art, seems to require a border, in order to be finished" (280). This is explained as the "ultimate law" of "Limitation" (283). According to this rule, man should be engaged in "rather the reduction of the Infinite to palpable bounds, than an elevation of the Finite to the immeasurable" (283). Judd's overt discussion of this law is accompanied by a deemphasis of supernaturalism and a concern with various social problems—politics, economics, reform. As Judd says at the end of the book, he is now turning to "the actual and the real" in order to show "that a man is what he makes himself . . . by his own inherent energies" (370). The abandonment of the visionary mode has made Judd more aware of suffering reality yet also more optimistic about man's ability to endure it without the aid of angels.

Summing up his literary output in a closing address to *Richard Edney,* Judd writes: " 'Philo' is as an angel of the everlasting Gospel; you and 'Margaret,' one in the shop, and the other on the field, are practical Christians" (468). As we have seen, this appraisal is only partly correct. If any generalization can be made, it is that *Margaret* is half angel, *Philo* is all angel, *Richard Edney* is practical moralist. Whether any of them are Christian in any meaningful sense is open to question. More central to Judd's consciousness is the redemption sought by an erstwhile Calvinist in fictional reproductions of what he called the ideal and the real.

Other Examples of the Visionary Mode after 1820

The overall visionary-to-secular pattern found in Sedgwick, Child, and Judd appears, to varying degrees, in the careers of some other pre-Civil War novelists: Sarah J. Hale, Charles Sealsfield, William Gilmore Simms, and Robert M. Bird. Because these writers are not centrally concerned with religion, their careers need not be reviewed. But it should be noted that these writers' first works—Hale's *Northwood* (1827), Sealsfield's *Tokeah* (1829), Simms's *Book of My Lady* (1833), and Bird's *Calavar* (1834)—all use visionary devices which are minimized in their later fiction.

But this pattern cannot be considered a universally applicable key to religion in early-nineteenth-century American fiction. The careers of Caroline Hentz and Harriet Beecher Stowe suggest that in some cases the visionary mode was invoked only after a period of literary apprenticeship. Hentz's first novel, *Lovell's Folly* (1833), endorses creedless piety in a nonvisionary account of rural domesticity. It is not until *Aunt Patty's Scrap Bag* (1846) that Hentz begins to show the reliance on visionary devices that continues to buttress religious discussion in her later work. Similarly, Stowe's *A New England Sketch* (1834) and *The Mayflower* (1843) contain neither the angelic heroines nor the visionary episodes of *Uncle Tom's Cabin* (1852), *The Minister's Wooing* (1859), and *Oldtown Folks* (1869). Yet within the last three novels, which are Stowe's central works, we see a semblance of the visionary-to-secular pattern. In these novels the ladder to heaven that Stowe said had been destroyed by Jonathan Edwards was increasingly reconstructed with materials from nature and humanity. Thus, in the visionary heroines of these works, Stowe passes from the ethereal angel (Little Eva) through the stronger "Catholic Puritan" (Mary Scudder) to the earthbound nature lover (Tina Percival).

The post-1820 works that I have discussed to this point reveal shifting uses of the visionary mode in the course of several novelistic careers. At the same time that these career patterns were being established, other writers were experimenting with visionary devices in individual works. The "dreamy and visionary" hero of Thomas Gray's Biblical *Vestal* (1830) is converted to Christianity; he learns that "the loved and the lost from their unseen state, are yet permitted to watch around our earthly steps, and, unseen and unheard, to sympathize in our earthly enjoyments and sufferings."[50] A story in Caroline Gilman's *Tales and Ballads* (1839) describes a young man's vivid dream of joining his departed family members in heaven. The anonymous author of *Ella V——* (1841) gives a detailed account of heaven as a comfortable society where we will meet all our old friends and make many new ones, including the patriarchs and apostles. The conversion of the Roman hero of Harriet V. Cheney's *Confessions of an Early Martyr* (1846) is spurred by the assurance that for Christians the dead are "ministering spirits, ever around us, as sacred links to bind us to the unseen world, where we are told, 'Their angels do ever behold the face of their Father in heaven.' "[51] Fanny Forester's "Angel's Pilgrimage," a tale in *Alderbrook* (1846), is a *Philo*-like celestial flight aimed at undermining sectarianism. The indigent heroine of Elizabeth O. Smith's *Newsboy* (1854) dreams that Jesus welcomes her to heaven while forbidding entrance to several rich people. The visionary mode thus became a variegated phenomenon applied to such different ends as Biblical drama, domestic piety, and social commentary.

Cornelius Mathews' "Parson Huckins' First Appearance" (1838) and George Rogers' *Adventures of Elder Triptolemus Tub* (1846) show that visionary techniques could even be used for religious satire. Mathews' John Huckins falls to sleep while preparing a sermon to learn in a dream the folly of his Calvinist doctrines. He sees "two more than mortal beings," who are self-parodying caricatures of Calvinist preachers.[52]

The Universalist George Rogers mocks orthodoxy more extensively in a visionary dream. Triptolemus Tub is a self-satisfied Calvinist who one day has a vision of Shadrack Paddle, a spirit from the afterlife. Through Paddle, Rogers comically deflates the Calvinist doctrine that good works do not insure salvation. Paddle reports that hell is full of worthy types (for example, Shakespeare, Dryden, Pope, Franklin) who while alive had supposed that "God is good enough to take care of all the souls he has made."[53] In contrast, "Some very scurvy souls have gone to heaven," including John Calvin and the horse thief Anthony Pimp, who "got religion before he graced the gallows" (27–28). Like Judd in *Margaret*, Rogers here replaces the indirection of earlier anti-Calvinist visionary tales with an overt attack on orthodoxy.

Although primarily an anti-Calvinist vehicle, the visionary mode came to be used by a few orthodox fictionists, particularly writers who valued feeling over logic. The anonymous author of *Lucretia and Her Father* (1828) crowns the conversion of a repentant gambler with a deathbed view of heaven. The protagonist of B. R. Hall's *Something for Everybody* (1846) has a dream in which an angel lifts him from hell and drops him into a Presbyterian church pew. In the controversial temperance tale "Deacon Giles' Distillery" (1835), the Presbyterian George B. Cheever portrays manlike demons who produce large quantities of rum in barrels marked with invisibly inscribed words of death and damnation that blaze forth when the liquor is sold. In John P. Brace's

Tales of the Devils (1846) a libertine dies, becomes a demon in hell, and is commissioned by other devils to implant sinful thoughts in the mind of his son, who remains virtuous despite the literally hellish plot. Cheever's and Brace's works, which are early examples of the dark visionary mode, suggest that the Calvinist imagination could summon up fictional devils as readily as the liberals could call forth angels.

This dark mode was not confined to Calvinist fiction. For example, it appeared in George Lippard's *The Quaker City; or, The Monks of Monk Hall* (1844–1845), in which Devil-Bug has an apocalyptic vision of an "orthodox mob" of demons causing a "massacre of judgment" that destroys Philadelphia.[54] This disastrous vision symbolizes Lipard's literary technique, which consists of exposing religious and political enemies through violent, lurid portraits of corruption.

Orestes Brownson's *The Spirit-Rapper* (1854) shows that the dark visionary mode could appear even in Roman Catholic fiction. Although there is no vision in the novel, there is a long series of table liftings, rappings, and suggestions of demonic presence. By the end of the novel, Brownson has suggested that devil possession or mesmeric illusion is behind all philosophies and religions opposed to Catholicism. One of Brownson's main targets is American liberalism, which is said to deny God by denying Satan. The Roman Catholic Church is singled out as the glorious example of good angel possession. In this novel proving the devil becomes an obverse way of praising God.

Brownson's novel, however, was an exception to the rule; most Catholic fiction of the period was determinedly intellectual, avoiding the visionary mode as if it were merely an irrational gimmick. Generally, religious novels containing extensive logical discussion of doctrine eschewed visionary devices. Therefore, such devices were normally absent from novels by Roman Catholics and by strict New England Calvinists, who could invoke solid traditions of theological intellectualism.

The visionary mode was also minimized by novelists on the opposite end of the religious spectrum—those who mistrusted both angelic revelation and doctrinal logic while favoring secular morality. The Unitarian minister Henry Ware, Jr. is a case in point. Like other liberals discussed above, Ware devoted his first novel, *The Recollections of Jotham Anderson* (1824), to an attack on orthodoxy. But unlike less establishmentarian liberals such as Sedgwick and Judd, Ware made his argument with portraits of moral behavior rather than with angelic heroines or dreams of heaven. The visionary mode was not used in the series of novels commissioned by Ware in 1835–36, *Scenes and Characters Illustrating Christian Truths*. Another liberal who avoided visionary techniques was Henry's brother, William Ware, whose three novels stressed religion in experience. Even the Biblical miracles of *Julian* were stripped of clearly supernatural meaning.

The visionary mode, therefore, was a rhetorical device used primarily by religious borderers—writers who were not wholly satisfied either with doctrinal tradition or with merely behavioral religion. As suggested above, several writers invoked the visionary mode in early works to imagine direct communication to God and to subvert opposing doctrines without refuting them inductively. Then in later works many of them put aside both visionary devices and doctrinal controversy, finding in common morality a kind of secular redemption. No single decade can be clearly established as the period when American writers as a body rejected the visionary mode. Rather, the visionary-to-secular pattern was an ongoing dialectic within individual careers.

On the other hand, one may point to the 1830s as the time when vociferous complaints about allegorical versions of angels and heaven began to be heard. In 1831 John Greenleaf Whittier wrote: "The days of faery are over. The tale of enchantment—the legend of ghostly power—of unearthly warning and supernatural visitation, have lost their hold on the minds of the great multitude."[55] William Cullen Bryant's compilation of *Tales of Glauber-Spa* (1832) contains a story in which an invisible spirit touches, as opposed to merely appearing to, the protagonist. The tale is designed to contravene "all the idle and silly stories of ghosts and apparitions," to present "palpable truth, or truth demonstrated by touch."[56] Two years later Catherine Sedgwick penned her sweeping dismissal of angels and fairies as departed spirits. At the same time that Sedgwick called for facts and evidence, experience and demonstration, Henry and William Ware began to write notably nonvisionary religious fiction,. as did several Catholics and Calvinists.

The visionary mode did not die out in the 1830s. Rather, supernaturalism began to be subsumed under the imperatives of human experience. The allegorical distance of earlier visionary fiction was abrogated on behalf of more realistic visions and more human angelic characters. This process of secularization resulted in four overall changes in the visionary mode during this period.

First, the angelic revelations and celestial vistas that before 1820 had seemed startlingly majestic gave way to a kind of offhand familiarity with the supernatural. In 1785 Celadon had been amazed that an angel would condescend to visit the world. Nearly all the protagonists of the early tales had revered their angels and heavenly views with obeisant awe. After the modifications of the 1830s, visions elicited equal reverence but less shock. Thus, Judd's Margaret is a familiar traveler in the world of dreams, and her visions of Jesus, John, and other divinities are presented as perfectly natural. Ellen Montgomery of Susan Warner's *The Wide, Wide World* (1851) can respond to the death of a friend with the blithely confident remark: "Well, I will see him in heaven!"[57] The humanized visitants of "Deacon Giles' Distillery," "Parson Huckins' First Appearance," and *Triptolemus Tub* similarly reflect this growing familiarity with the divine.

Second, the visionary mode after 1830 became more concrete and domestic. The distance and vagueness of the early tales was replaced by more terrestrial visions. In *Ella V——* we learn that in heaven we will possess the same powers of thinking, feeling, and making friends that we have on earth. In *Margaret, Philo,* and "The Angel's Pilgrimage," we are introduced to various genial divinities who talk of earthly heavens. A late work by George Lippard, *Adonai* (1851), contains an episode on "The Other World" in which the hero has "a vision—rather a clear sight—not so much of the gorgeous complete of Eternity, as of some single home of the Other World."[58] Lippard explains: "Not vague, nor vain, nor transitory, is the life of the Other World. It is no dream, but a reality . . . There are voices sounding now which we heard in old times, when we were of the lower earth; our hands are grasped by hands, that we thought long ago were chilled by Death, forgetting that [in] *God's universe there is no such thing as Death;* but in its place only a transition from one life or state of life to another" (70).

Third, the visionary mode became more varied and complex. The oblique attack on Calvinism was transformed in works by Mathews, Rogers, and Judd into more overtly anti-Calvinist dreams. Visionary devices were borrowed from a variety of non-Christian religions to fashion a fictional faith that verged on creedal relativism. Also Presbyterians, as well as a few Catholics and Methodists, began to experiment with the visionary mode. In some works a darker, more horrific version of the supernatural appeared. In fiction by George Cheever, William Cambridge, and Elizabeth O. Smith, social problems such as temperance and poverty were resolved through visionary devices.

Fourth, angelic characters became more actively redemptive. Whereas the pre-1820 characters had generally been the passive recipients of divine instruction, after 1835 many protagonists possessed the capacity to struggle and endure, to rescue others and teach them. This is particularly true in the late novels of Sedgwick, Child, Stowe, and Hentz. In a novel such as Judd's *Margaret* the pattern of the eighteenth-century visionary tales is reversed: when Margaret revives the feeble Jesus in her last visionary dream, the divine is made dependent on the human. This shift was encapsulated in a comment by the Universalist Sarah E. Mayo in a letter of 1838: "Angels in elder times came down to earth; would that mortals in later days might go up to heaven! And may they not—and do they not sometimes? We have some beings in our world who seem indeed to walk with God—so pure and holy, that we gaze upon them and love them as if they were visitants from the 'Father-land.' "[59]

The process of secularization would culminate in post–Civil War religious fiction, which was rarely visionary even when dealing directly with heaven. In Elizabeth Phelps Ward's *Beyond the Gates* (1883) and *The Gates Between* (1887), the passage to the afterlife is converted to a pleasant journey with departed friends to a place combining the bucolic beauty of Kansas with the cultured domesticity of Boston. Annie T. Slosson's *Seven Dreamers* (1891) portrays various vernacular seers who prove that "dreamin' awake's about as common's dreamin' asleep . . . And as long as the dreams are pleasant, comfortable ones—not nightmares, o'course—why, I sometimes think the people that lives in 'em are about as happy as other folks, and maybe happier."[60] A year later in *The Heresy of Mehetabel Clark* Slosson described heaven as the White House, regulated by the President and his son Jesus; the narrator gets a firsthand look at the smiling President. Similarly terrestrial pictures of heaven are found in Louis Pendleton's *The Wedding Garment* (1894), G. H. Hepworth's *They Met in Heaven* (1894), and Rebecca Springer's *Intra Muros* (1899). The genre became significant enough to draw fire from Mark Twain, whose Captain Stormfield finds the earthly heaven to be a dull place indeed.

Surveying the multitudinous versions of the visionary mode in nineteenth-century American fiction, one looks back to Jonathan Edwards' cautions against imagined heavenly vision and angelic converse. By asking simple questions about the afterlife in 1746, the author of the visionary Oriental tale "Cassim" had initiated a sizable school of fiction that would have startled Edwards, the man who had tried to knock out the earthly rungs of the ladder to heaven.

II

Doctrinal and Illustrative Fiction

*A*S WE HAVE SEEN, for a wide variety of American writers between 1785 and 1850, the Oriental tale and the visionary mode provided a vehicle for avoiding strict theological debate, for subverting religious opponents, and for advancing a predominantly anti-Calvinist religion of hope. Oriental and visionary tales prepared the way for more familiar types of religious fiction by transplanting popular religious discussion from logical and doctrinal to imaginative and secular receptacles.

But the shifting approach to religious debate and consolation during this period was not confined to such distanced fiction. It also appeared in an increasingly large body of fiction that dealt more directly with American religion and with Biblical history.

The pattern of secularization noted in Oriental and visionary tales was apparent within each of the four schools of doctrinal or illustrative fiction: Calvinist, liberal, Biblical, and Roman Catholic. Calvinist fiction written between 1795 and 1825 tended to be doctrinal, minimizing plot on behalf of polemical dialogues derived from orthodox tradition. Later Calvinist fiction evidenced a growing interest in such matters as romantic and filial love, reform, and poverty. Liberal fiction, although never as doctrinally precise as Calvinist fiction, similarly moved from early experimentation with polemics to almost entirely secular exempla. In the 1830s this secularizing tendency gave rise to Christian martyr and New Testament narratives, which retold the early history of Christianity in dramatically human terms. Even that venerable bastion of religious intellectualism, Roman Catholicism, began in the 1830s to produce some American authors who turned to the novel to fashion earthly buttresses for old beliefs. Taken together, these four fictional schools formed a link between Oriental and visionary fiction, which modified received doctrine obliquely, and well-known post-1850 religious best sellers, like *The Lamplighter, Norwood,* and *Ben-Hur,* in which religion became virtually identified with secular morality, romantic ideality, or heroic action.

There is no type of later religious fiction that was not explored before 1850. In several senses the early fiction was more complex and significant than the popular post-1850 works, many of which were mere variants on earlier patterns. Doctrinal debates on such issues as predestination versus free will, innate depravity versus perfectibility, election versus universal salvation were still heated and significant during this transitional period. Liberalism had not yet broadened into the genial mainstream Liberal Protestantism of the 1870s, New England orthodoxy was not yet relegated to the seminaries, and evangelicalism had not yet hardened into fundamentalism. Roman Catholicism, although growing rapidly, was not yet the preeminent force it would become and was still primarily on the defensive. As a result, writers of various denominations discovered in doctrinal and illustrative fiction a convenient vehicle for religious discussion during a time of intense controversy and religious change.

This fiction often contained interesting paradoxes. Because fiction was still widely decried, many writers felt compelled to include denunciations of novel reading in their novels. Aware of the doctrinal tradition they were rejecting, several authors tried to maintain a pretense of intellectuality and respectability in the face of the sentimental, secularized piety to which they were instinctively attracted. Writers of different faiths often used similar plots and characters to endorse their views. Moreover, many Protestants, alarmed by the increasing divisiveness of American sectarianism, tried to fabricate a fictional faith of universal love and active virtue that might nevertheless retain some measure of doctrinal distinctiveness. This problem provided fodder for the Roman Catholic novelist, who invoked the grand unity of the True Church as the panacea for the fragmentation of American Protestantism. Another kind of unity was offered by the Biblical novelist, who circumvented doctrinal issues by illustrating the precreedal origins of Christianity.

Despite differences in outlook and style, all doctrinal and illustrative writers of the period faced the common dilemma of popularizing religion without reducing it to the level of what Jonathan Edwards had called "mere nature." The tensions resulting from this dilemma yield much of the interest of the fiction these writers produced.

3

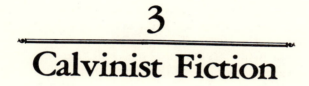

Calvinist Fiction

There is something of a scholarly consensus that members of the Calvinist establishment frowned upon novels and that their antipathy diminished only with religious liberalization and the rise of proper fiction. This generalization belies the complexity of early Calvinist attitudes toward fiction. Although complaints about fiction were heard from some conservative quarters well into the 1840s and beyond, a growing number of Calvinist authors came to be attracted to fictional devices that might help convert orthodox doctrine into popular entertainment. Often this attraction was mingled with guilt and self-laceration over the abandonment of traditional theology, as evidenced in Calvinist novels containing vilifications of novels.

Though not as comfortable with fiction as rationalists or liberals, Calvinists began to write novels quite early (the first appeared in 1795) and continued to produce them in increasing quantity throughout the next five decades. Until Harriet Beecher Stowe, Calvinist efforts in fiction were sporadic and artistically primitive in comparison to the works of such prolific liberal writers as Catherine Sedgwick, Lydia Child, Sylvester Judd, and William Ware. Moreover, respectable Calvinists involved in the Unitarian controversy were not as ready to espouse fiction as were their liberal opponents. But a significant body of Calvinist fiction was produced between 1795 and 1850, so that there was ample precedent for the mixture of plot, characterization, and doctrinal discussion that occurs in Stowe's novels. A study of early orthodox fiction reveals that the common critical assumption about Calvinism's unilateral hostility to the novel must be qualified.

Joseph Morgan and Joseph Alden, Calvinist authors who wrote, respectively, before the beginning and at the end of the period in question, may be said to represent the poles of doctrinal and secular fiction between which other orthodox novelists moved. In *The History of the Kingdom of Basaruah* (1715) Morgan allegorizes covenant theology in terms of the chronicle history of an imaginary kingdom. Every character and every event in Morgan's kingdom is linked to some aspect of the elaborate, rigorously precise covenant system. Despite Morgan's typically Puritan proclivity toward homely and concrete imagery, secular experience in the work is totally subordinated to doctrine.

In contrast, in Joseph Alden's pious novels of the late 1840s secular experience controls doctrine and impels conversion. The heroine of Alden's *Alice Gordon* (1847) learns about human frailty and divine omnipotence from family deaths and social ostracism. Theology in the novel is relegated to a minor character, Pastor Beals, who discourses briefly on "the entire alienation and enmity of the natural heart to God."[1] Alden's main concern is the conflict between virtuous poverty and irreligious wealth, a conflict which is resolved when the indigent Alice marries the fashionable Newall to create "The Family Altar" (196). Alden's reduction of religion to the imperatives of romantic love and social position is equally evident in his other novels, particularly *Elizabeth Benton* (1846) and *The Lawyer's Daughter* (1847).

Joseph Morgan's God is the inscrutable and arbitrary King Pancrator who issues edicts directing Arminians, antinomians, and heathens to fiery lakes. Joseph Alden's God of Orphans is, in contrast, a kind of sympathetic witness to the emotional and financial vicissitudes of the protagonists. Morgan fabricates a mythical kingdom that symbolizes covenant theology in all its complexity; Alden finds relatively uncomplicated spiritual meaning in the economic and physical landscape of nineteenth-century America. Morgan's fictionalized faith is monarchical and logical; Alden's is democratic, emotional, and domestic. Even though the Congregationalist Alden was trained at Princeton Theological Seminary and wrote fiction while holding a professorship at Williams College, his novels have none of the rigorous intellectuality of *The Kingdom of Basaruah*. Both Morgan and Alden engaged in the objectification of orthodox belief. But the doctrinal serviceability of Morgan's concrete symbols had by Alden's time been replaced by a fascination with quotidian experience which threatened to eclipse doctrine altogether.

The movement of Calvinist fiction from Morgan to Alden occurred in three general stages. Between 1795 and 1825 some Calvinists wrote novels that retained the logical and semiallegorical nature of previous orthodox literature while cautiously exploring the dramatic potential of secular situations. Between 1825 and 1835 northern Calvinists were joined by frontier evangelists in rejecting theological strictness on behalf of sentimental narratives that were often designed to attack such social evils as gambling and intemperance. After 1835 this reformist instinct began to be absorbed into a more wide-ranging interest in other behavioral aspects of American life—courtship and marriage, adventures at sea and on the frontier, the plight of orphans, domesticity. This pre-1850 Calvinist fiction never managed the sophisticated combination of romantic feeling, vernacular humor, and religious commentary that the post-Calvinist Harriet Beecher Stowe would achieve in novels such as *The Minister's Wooing* (1859) and *Oldtown Folks* (1869). Nor did it subordinate piety to plot to the extent that Susan Warner would in *The Wide, Wide World* (1851). But the early fiction does reveal the Calvinist imagination escaping its doctrinal shackles and moving toward more secular forms of religious expression. Once the bridge between Joseph Morgan and Joseph Alden had been formed, the female writers of the 1850s were free to write popular religious fiction with few serious qualms about the theological tradition that had been left behind.

Cautious Beginnings

Calvinist fiction in America before 1825 was scarce but significant. We have seen that pious fiction during this early period was dominated by Oriental and visionary tales, many of which were written by religious outsiders with the intent of indirectly subverting received doctrines and traditional literary modes. Also, some sentimental novelists distributed throughout their stories Calvinist snippets on depravity, predestination, and religious affections in order to lend an air of sacredness and depth to the topic of seduction.

But while orthodoxy was being attacked in Oriental and visionary fiction and cheapened in the sentimental novel, some serious Calvinists were beginning to write fiction. One story collection and four novels written between 1795 and 1824 were devoted to the advancement of orthodox beliefs. The Reverend Ebenezer Bradford's *The Art of Courting* (1795) and the Reverend Elijah R. Sabin's *The Life and Reflections of Charles Observator* (1816) betrayed tension between the obeisance to logical homiletics and an attraction to sentimental anecdote. Edmund Botsford's *The Spiritual Voyage Performed in the Ship Convert* (1814) and Aaron Lummus' *The Life and Adventures of Dr. Caleb* (1822) put aside concern for logic while modifying Puritan allegory to suit the contemporary taste for adventure. The longer *Justina; or, The Will* (1823) wove doctrinal proof into a complex story involving filial devotion, courtship, and quarrels over a legacy. Although all of these works satirized religious opponents while endorsing orthodoxy, the concern for doctrinal specificity diminished during the period as a whole. Increasing attention to plot development was coupled with a decreasing interest in the theological exactitude that had characterized Morgan's *Kingdom of Basaruah*.

Ebenezer Bradford's *The Art of Courting* opens in a conservative manner befitting the earliest Calvinist story collection. Chapter 1 is broken into standard sermon divisions of text, exposition, and improvement. But a shift in emphasis is apparent from the start. The Puritan homiletic structure is used not to explain such ideas as predestination or sanctification but rather to distinguish sacred marital love from "whoredom and adultery."[2] Having sanctified his romantic interests in the sermonic introduction, Bradford presents eight fictional sketches of different love relationships, some exemplary and others cautionary. The most interesting feature of these tales is an implicit conflict between theology and fiction, between the rational defense of doctrine and the sentimental illustration of it.

This tension is evident throughout *The Art of Courting*, as Bradford feels conflicting attractions to doctrinal exposition and diverting narrative. The latter wins a clear victory in the story of two irreligious party goers, Bragadotius and Numskuldia, who are described "not for the example, but for the amusement of the American youth" (129). On the doctrinal end of the spectrum is the tale of Damon and Harriet. In this sketch the author uses a love relationship to defeat religious opponents in semilogical fashion. Damon experiments with various anti-Calvinist views—deism, Arminianism, Universalism—before he is persuaded by Harriet to accept the orthodox doctrines of predestination and total depravity. Rescued both by his love for Harriet and by God's "free and sovereign grace," Damon at last marries Harriet and becomes a Congregationalist minister (214).

The other six stories in *The Art of Courting* fall between the amusing Bragadotius sketch and the doctrinal story of Damon. Lacking a consistent fictional voice, the author essays various balancings of theology and narrative in a primitive effort to locate a comfortable equilibrium. At times, divine grace becomes virtually identified with the social graces, as when the lovers Emilius and Olivia take on *"many embellishments which served to heighten their mutual esteem,"* including polite manners, elegant clothes, and "real religion" (110, 113). More typically, romantic love becomes a vehicle for lambasting rationalists, liberals, and Roman Catholics and for promoting orthodox beliefs in an entertaining way. Although he was unsuccessful artistically, Bradford initiated a radical revision of doctrinal discussion in American literature. By mingling Calvinism and courtship, he summoned orthodox exposition into the realm of human emotion and manners.

A similarly palatable mixture of the divine and the human is attempted in Elijah R. Sabin's *Charles Observator* (1816). Sabin's hero learns that if children "are *religious,* they ought not to be *rude;* but polished in their behavior." Charles' father explains that "as citizens of the world, and candidates for eternity, it concerns them to be pious, learned, and polite."[3] As in *The Art of*

Courting, social and spiritual improvement begin to be combined. In Sabin's novel several doctrinal sermons, delivered by various clergymen characters, are connected by a story of Charles's religious education and worldly advancement. A slim love plot is developed, mainly because Charles's beloved Prudentia is the daughter of a Calvinist minister. Though piously reared, Charles becomes indifferent to religion. In time, he rationally weighs the various claims of Arminianism, Pelagianism, antinomianism, deism, and modified Calvinism, finally deciding in favor of the last. Charles's conversion results from extensive theological debate, which teaches him the reasonableness of orthodoxy.

Throughout the novel runs a tension between fiction and traditional homiletics. Like Bradford, Sabin seems instinctively drawn to the former but morally obligated to the latter. He fulfills both impulse and obligation by portraying first an entertaining storyteller and then a rigorously doctrinal clergyman. The fictionists's *"strange* and *uncommon* stories" make Charles feel "divided between mirth and astonishment" (16, 17). The clergyman, who operates as a Puritan superego, counters with a logical sermon in which fabulists are consigned to hell. Trying to bring his novel into the realm of propriety, Sabin has the minister repeat antifictional orthodox attitudes: "If you cannot read but one book, let *that one* be the Bible. Never read *love novels,* and *common fictions;* for they will corrupt your minds. Sermons, books of experience, histories, &c, may be read with profit. But let much of the Sabbath be taken up in study of the Scriptures. Here you will meet with entertainment and instruction" (36-37). Sabin appears to fear that he is flirting with Satan by writing fiction, so he loudly denounces fiction and implies that his novel is in the Puritan tradition of sermons, books of experience, histories. At the same time that he elevates his work in this way, he accommodates the Bible to his fictional interests by reducing the Bible to Sunday entertainment and instruction.

This theology-fiction dialectic continues through the rest of the novel, as various sermons appear amidst anecdotes and conversation. At times Sabin attempts doctrinal discrimination, as when he complains "that among those who claim the *sacerdotal* character, there may be found the *lazy antinomian,* who is always singing, *why me;* or the *workish outsided pharisee,* who spurns the Grace of God; or the *uninstructed* pelagian, who undervalues the blood of Christ; . . . or the easy latitudinarian, who cries *yes, yes,* to every form of worship, and system of doctrine" (153). Elsewhere, fictional exemplum becomes a rhetorical way of resolving doctrinal difficulties. For example, after a long formal sermon, Charles's father assures the youth that he need not worry about "doctrines, modes and forms" and then proves the "evident clearness" of religion by telling three love stories (40).

The balancing of theology and narrative found in *The Art of Courting* and *Charles Observator* also characterizes Edmund Botsford's *Spiritual Voyage*

(1814) and Aaron Lummus' *Dr. Caleb* (1822). Considered superficially, these allegories seem closer to Puritan literature than Bradford's and Sabin's narratives. *Spiritual Voyage* is clearly intended to be a nautical *Pilgrim's Progress,* while *Dr. Caleb* describes a symbolic religious quest in early Christian times. Yet the modifications of traditional literary models initiated by the other writers are in fact accelerated in Botsford's and Lummus' works, which reveal that the secularizing tendency was beginning to alter even the old genre of religious allegory. Not only are these works more religiously liberal than former Calvinist allegories, but Botsford and Lummus manifest an interest in adventurous plot that such earlier allegorists as Bunyan and Morgan would have deemed excessive. Bunyan's caution against an overemphasis on the outside of his dream contrasts with Botsford's and Lummus' evident delight in portraying stirring sea battles and early Christian warfare. The illustrative allegorical narrative, which for strict Puritans had been merely a window to divine truth, begins in *Spiritual Voyage* and *Dr. Caleb* to assume an objective importance of its own.

As a South Carolina Baptist minister, Edmund Botsford would seem an appropriate person to initiate such revisions of allegory. By 1814 evangelical Calvinism had already brought about widespread changes not only in the content but in the style of popular orthodoxy. In its appeal to the masses, evangelical pulpit eloquence was turning increasingly from the old standards of logic and theological subtlety to simpler appeals to the heart, often through vivid examples from common life. Such changes are reflected in Botsford's account of the exciting journey of a ship called *Convert* to the Haven of Felicity. Commissioned by an admiral and his prince, the *Convert* is maintained by Captain Godly-fear and his pious crew in the face of various enemy fleets and shoals that threaten to destroy the ship.

This allegorical journey is notable for its modification of Calvinism and its preference for entertaining anecdote over theology. A vernacular perspective distant from Bunyan's formality is evident in Botsford's portrayal of Christian salts waging war on the likes of Will All-joy, Harry Fair-speech, and Jack Rest-on-prayer. Although the sailors realize they are "in a bad condition, under the frowns of our Admiral," in a genial dinner conversation, the Admiral assures them that "if we paid a strict attention to our directions, and the management of our ship, he doubted not but we should do well."[4] Indeed, Botsford's placable Admiral remains far more responsive to human effort than Morgan's stern King Pancrator, who is wont to denounce the "filthy rags" of good works. An even more fundamental departure from Morgan is signaled in Botsford's valuation of narrative over doctrine. At one point in the journey, the *Convert* approaches the Doctrinal and Practical islands; Godly-fear steers a middle course between the two. Botsford introduces various tars who are more adept at spinning yarns than at explaining theology. Botsford jettisons the involved doctrinal disputes that had preoccupied Morgan. Theological exposition and authoritarian divine rule have given way to a milder mixture of piety and anecdotal persuasion.

Aaron Lummus' *Dr. Caleb* shows another moderate Calvinist revising traditional allegory even while professing to imitate it. Lummus praises Bunyan in his preface and goes on to describe Dr. Caleb's allegorical journey from Egypt to Jerusalem in a manner vaguely reminiscent of *The Pilgrim's Progress*. But as in Botsford's work, theological exactitude becomes compromised by an interest in secular adventures designed to underscore the efficacy of human exertion. To be sure, Lummus essays doctrinal precision by having Caleb reject antinomianism, Arminianism, and Arianism while lauding a mediating faith of grace and works. But because this doctrinal discrimination seems to locate no single creedal certainty, Lummus resolves theological difficulties by advancing a code of Christian heroism that stands outside of creed. Upon his arrival in Jerusalem, Caleb is given arms that enable him "to carry on both offensive and defensive warfare."[5] Thus he joins a group of "faithful ones, that do their duty like heroes, and . . . are as rugged as young giants" (30). Caleb battles the likes of Self, Vanity, and Carnal-Wisdom. The allegory ends by emphasizing the muscularity of three exemplars—Holyman, Fightwell, and Perseverance—who ward off besieging demons. Just as Botsford had represented Godly-fear's followers as sailors combating Satan's fleets, so Lummus portrays various warriors for Christ.

Treated allegorically by Botsford and Lummus, this theme of heroic redemption is more directly applied to actual experience in a slightly later Calvinist novel, *Justina; or, The Will*. Raised a moderate Calvinist, Justina Melross feels "so strong in the Lord, and in the power of his might, that she thought there was no proof of faith she could not stand; no trial she could not undergo—indeed, with the enthusiasm of early converts, she almost longed for trials and reproaches, that she might prove herself worthy to suffer for the Lord."[6] Suffer she does, enduring her father's death, a difficult relocation from England to America, and the prolonged advances of a rationalist suitor who wants her money.

At the same time that heroism is more practically illustrated in *Justina* than in previous Calvinist novels, the defense of orthodoxy is more tightly wedded to secular situations. To be sure, a large measure of doctrinal content remains: an attempt at validating Calvinism intellectually is seen not only in the protagonist's refutations of liberal religion but also in the author's citing pro-Calvinist Biblical texts at the end of each volume of the novel. But in the Calvinist works studied above, such exposition was rarely connected to complex sentimental plots, which might spoil the purity of doctrine. In *Justina* doctrine begins to be dependent on plot. A dying Philadelphian named Cavendish, distressed by his nephew Ferdinand's infidelity, believes that Ferdinand would espouse orthodoxy if he were to marry the exemplary Justina. Cavendish persuades Justina to sign a pledge not to refuse Ferdinand's marriage proposals during the six months immediately following his death. Also, he revises his will to grant $400,000 to Ferdinand and Justina jointly, provided they marry within a year. After Cavendish dies, Ferdinand woos Justina with the sole intention of gaining funds to support his dissolute habits. Justina is willing to accept him, provided he becomes "awakened to a sense of sin, and prompted by divine grace to believe in Jesus" (I, 212). She ends up foregoing the legacy as a result of Ferdinand's refusal to embrace Calvinism. After teaching Sunday school for a while, she marries the pious scholar Arlington.

The fiction-theology tension seen in previous Calvinist novels is evident throughout *Justina,* but narrative is clearly beginning to gain ascendancy. The sweeping condemnation of fiction that occurred in *The Art of Courting* and *Charles Observator* is replaced by the admission that while theological works are always preferable to imaginative literature, some novels may belong to "the higher order of literature, which even the friends of religion and morality may peruse with pleasure and instruction, and put into the hands of their children without a caution" (II, 141).

Having inferentially sanctified her work as part of a higher order of literature, the author is freer than former Calvinist novelists to enforce doctrine through sentimental plot. The strongest attacks on liberalism and infidelity are reserved for moments when the reader is apt to be emotionally sympathetic to the virtuous characters. For example, Cavendish's denunciation of "that baneful creed, which dethrones the Saviour, robs him of his divine sonship" is presented as the lamentation of a bedridden Calvinist (I, 155). Liberals, the ailing Cavendish says, are evasive, falsely optimistic, and finally atheistic. The sentimental heightening of antiliberalism culminates with Cavendish's dying injunction to Justina: "Oh! bid them cease from building the Babel of their own works, as the means of reaching heaven; teach them the true way" (I, 165). Secular sentiment continues to endorse orthodoxy throughout the rest of the book. We are invited to admire Justina's uncompromising devotion to Calvinism in the face of Ferdinand's blandishments and of the prospect of instant wealth through marriage to the infidel. Liberals in the person of the Medway and Grafton families are portrayed as frivolous people who would have the Bible "judiciously abridged and altered" to be made more entertaining (II, 150). Although Justina tells them reasonably that liberalism is nothing more than cold morality, the conversion of the Medways and Graftons comes not as a result of arguments but rather of their tearful admiration of their pious children, who have been well schooled by Justina. At the end, Justina's marriage to Arlington is made sacred by their mutual devotion to orthodoxy.

In sum, the author of *Justina* has initiated subtle yet significant revisions of the Calvinist novel. In *The Art of Courting* and *Charles Observator,* theological discussion and sentimental narrative had been either separated altogether or else ineptly combined. In *Spiritual Voyage* and *Dr. Caleb,* martial adventure and anecdote made attractive meeting places for theology and fiction. In *Justina* a more comfortable union of the two extremes begins to be fashioned. The idea of heroic redemption, presented allegorically by Botsford and Lummus, is more realistically figured forth in a young woman's enduring actual physical and spiritual hardships. Romantic love, deathbed emotion, and parental affection—all of which had been largely distinguished from theology in *The Art of Courting* and *Charles Observator*—contribute in *Justina* to doctrinal argument and conversion. Calvinist fiction had begun to turn slowly away from the allegorical precision of Joseph Morgan toward the secularized piety of Joseph Alden.

Toward the Post-Calvinist Novel

After 1820 this secularization of Calvinist fiction was accelerated by a widespread reformist tendency in American religion. This was a period when many American ministers turned from metaphysical speculation to social action. Spiritual infirmities became, in several circles, identified with earthly habits such as intemperance, dancing, gambling, and dueling. To alleviate such ills, a wide variety of social panaceas were offered, including temperance reform and universal education. Between 1810 and 1830 the Benevolent Empire, an evangelical network of reform groups led by New School Presbyterians, prompted the growth of tract, Bible, and Sunday school societies. At the same time, other religious and secular groups—particularly Unitarians, Quakers, and Owenites—were active in social reform. After the decline of the Benevolent Empire in the early 1830s, group reform gave way increasingly to the idea of individual conversion as the source of social change. Reformist religion was not inward and contemplative; rather, it was fervent, puritanical, and Christianly militant, particularly in its evangelical manifestations. Although serious theological debate continued in the seminaries, normative Calvinism began to forge an ethos of clean living and zealous proselytizing.

Calvinist fiction after *Justina* did not suddenly become reformist or nontheological. Indeed, it was not until *Uncle Tom's Cabin* (1852) that reformist Protestantism produced a novel of great impact. But a significant number of Calvinist novelists between 1825 and 1850 paved the way for Stowe by dramatizing the interdependency of social behavior and spiritual regeneration. Unlike the pre-1825 novelists, these writers paid little attention to bygone intellectualism and conventional literary models. The restrained emotionalism of the early novels gave way in the later fiction to a sentimentalism springing from painfully real crises.

Although God's omnipotence and man's frailty were still common themes, greater emphasis was placed on the protagonist's ability to confront tragedy with pious resolve. Such holdovers of Puritan tradition as homiletic structure, allegorical strictness, and exegetical proof—all of which had influenced the pre-1825 novels—were abandoned in favor of plots illustrating the operations of orthodoxy in daily life. In the words of one evangelical writer, Anne Tuttle Bullard, the novelist's aim was to encourage *"the holy activity,* which the present state of religion throughout the world, seems to demand of the rising generation."[7]

Two novels published in 1825, Sarah Ann Evans' *Resignation* and the anonymous *Triumph of Religion,* signaled such changes in Calvinist fiction. Evans' work carries to an extreme the rhetorical use of emotional crisis begun in *Justina.* The fifty-seven deaths that occur in the novel underscore Evans' view of the world as "a scene of probation, of discipline" which is best faced with "the unyielding firmness of virtuous resolve."[8] This theme of Christian courage is enacted in a plot that would become a staple for popular female novelists of the 1850s: an orphaned heroine survives a series of calamities through submission to God and self-reliant effort.

Even more than Justina, Evans' Elizabeth Ellison is forced to recognize life as a battle—against disconcerting solitude, against seducers, against poverty, against bereavement over the loss of loved ones. "From the assaults of discouragement," the author tells us, Elizabeth "defended herself with 'the shield of Faith'" (I, 389–390). The military metaphors tentatively posed by earlier orthodox novelists are extended to create a definition of human experience as a turbulent arena for spiritually muscular, if sometimes physically frail Christians. The experiential interpretation of faith is evidenced not only by the heroine's dauntlessness but also by Evans' attacks on slavery and on Catholicism. The abstract arguments against opposing ideologies made in such earlier works as *The Art of Courting* and *Charles Observator* are humanized through descriptions of a slave and a Catholic who achieve redemption.

In the process of becoming more activist and secular, the Calvinist novel here begins to deemphasize theological niceties. Some doctrinal discussion does remain. The death of Elizabeth's mother, for instance, is said to show that "grace is more powerful than nature" (I, 32). Elizabeth's Uncle Harlington is a believer in natural religion who learns "the darkness of devious, self-depending, human virtue" (II, 64). But such references to doctrine are rare in the novel. The author's antitheological outlook is suggested in her account of Mrs. Ellison, who in schooling Elizabeth "had indeed *implied the existence of sin,* . . . but . . . had not perplexed her infant conception by the slightest breathing of *metaphysical speculations"* (I, 43). Instead of terrifying the girl with pictures of divine wrath, the dying Mrs. Ellison assures her that "the orphan's God is a God of love" (I, 32). Elizabeth learns that a simple *"spirit of piety"* is more essential for survival and reward than a complex intellectual religion (I, 44). The close doctrinal discriminations of *Charles Observator, Dr. Caleb,* and *Justina* are replaced here by a more amorphous code of pietistic prowess in the face of earthly tribulation.

Like *Resignation,* the epistolary *Triumph of Religion* is less concerned with creed than with showing how "the spirit of our Holy Religion" can lead to the "glorious triumph over every difficulty."[9] The preacher hero of the novel, George Tracy, reminds his listeners of depravity and damnation, but he knows that "the truths which he thus preaches must be the matter of his own individual experience, and not a creed imprinted on the memory" (75). The nephew of a reformist foreign missionary, Tracy effects the conversion of several other characters through pious example and a forceful pulpit manner. The central difficulty of the novel is the skepticism and dissipation of Sophia Forbes, the woman Tracy loves. As in *Justina* and *Resignation,* deathbed emotion heightens the religious message, as the failing Sophia is led to recognize "the dark stains which polluted [her] soul" and to accept grace (135). Another sentimental endorsement of Calvinism occurs at the deathbed of the young poet William Ker, who tearfully admits that he is a "condemned sinner" threatened by "the awful gulph of ruin, which yawns beneath him" (57).

Although simple and sentimental, the piety of the novel is neither defeatist nor feeble. Like Evans, the author of *Triumph of Religion* rhetorically exploits the pathos of secular tragedies while avoiding an effeminate faith. George Tracy possesses a "most exquisite meekness," allowing him to be sympathetic to sinners; but he constantly endorses strength in the face of adversity (72). In Tracy's eyes, the prototype for muscularity is Jesus, who "did not shrink from sharing with us the sad calamity of our nature, but girding himself with strength . . . travelled through the dark valley, mighty to conquer, and now has returned to guide and guard, through its terrors, the feeblest spirit that is willing to trust to his rod and his staff for comfort and support" (35). Tracy's personal model for Christian courage is his mother, whose spirit, "strong in faith, fainted not under a Father's chastening," but who faced life with "unshrinking steadiness" (63). Initially mocked by his uncle as being too weak for the ministry, Tracy proves to be an example of hardihood to characters like Sophia Forbes and William Ker. In sum, the old orthodox notions of depravity and affectionalism have been accentuated by sentimental portraits of doomed sinners; at the same time, these human crises have formed an affecting backdrop highlighting the hero's Christian resolution.

In *Lucretia and Her Father* (1828) this combined theme of sentiment and heroism takes on a reformist coloring. Whereas sin in most previous Calvinist novels was linked to innate depravity or to an adherence to opposing religious views, in *Lucretia* it is associated with immoral behavior. What the anonymous author calls "melancholy evidences of the deep depravity of our fallen state" are merely the bad habits of Mr. P., who drinks and gambles, to the chagrin of his wife and his daughter, Lucretia.[10] This behavioral outlook is reflected in the author's warning "that he who would be *useful,* who would be the instrument of the greatest good to his fellow men, must be *consistent* in his *life*—must let his *actions* prove his words sincere" (8). Because his intemperance makes him socially unuseful, P. is branded a sinner. Contrasted to the idle P. is the active Reverend M., the local minister who heads missionary organizations and Sabbath schools. Significantly, the author makes Lucretia, rather than M., directly responsible for P.'s conversion. Awakened by M. to a sense of sin, the renewed Lucretia assures her wayward father that "there is a fountain, which can make the vilest sinner clean; and its waters must be applied by the hand of Grace, or it will be of no avail" (55). The reason for the use of the child as the saving agent becomes clear when Lucretia becomes mortally ill. Parental love, coupled with admiration for the child's heroic endurance of pain, speeds P.'s conversion. P. abandons his cards and his bottle shortly after his daughter's death, becoming aware of "the *loveliness* of Jesus as a Saviour" (77). Exaggerating the familiar device of reinforcing doctrine with sentiment, the author allies conversion with emotional response to a family tragedy.

In the works of two orthodox writers of this period, Anne Tuttle Bullard and George B. Cheever, the new reformist theme of Calvinist fiction is propounded with increased fervor. In *The Reformation* (1832) and *The Wife for a Missionary* (1834), Bullard pits evangelical activism against, respectively, Roman Catholicism and idleness. In the first novel she characterizes Catholicism as a repressive system which encourages vice by prohibiting free inquiry. The military imagery of previous evangelical novelists takes on an anti-Catholic tone when Bullard writes that "we [Protestants] have free access to the panoply of the gospel, and may gird ourselves, unrestrained and unreproved, with the whole sacred armor by which we may 'fight the good fight of faith,' and come off 'more than conquerors through him that loved us.' "[11] This resolute tone gathers force in the course of the novel, culminating in a call for youthful, enterprising persons to distribute Bibles and tracts throughout the West to prevent the Pope's armies from conquering the American frontier.

Just such an enterprising person becomes the focus of Bullard's next novel, which describes a missionary's search for a wife who will share his interest in group reform. Rejecting several frivolous women, Everett Lacy at last selects Helen Scott, a social worker engaged in distributing tracts among the sick and the poor. The truest Christians, in Lacy's eyes, are *"active* and *efficient"* ones. Helen is chosen as a result of her willingness to make "a living sacrifice in active, every-day hearty service."[12] While creating a love plot to attract interest to her activist faith, Bullard, like several Calvinist novelists before her, betrays guilt about writing fiction. Thus she assures us that Helen "had not indulged herself in *novel reading*—that pernicious practice which has unfitted so many *for a life of real usefulness*" (137). The denial of fiction here has different implications than it did in *The Art of Courting* or *Charles Observator*. In the earlier works fiction was found to be antithetical to the intellectual contemplation of doctrine. In Bullard's novel both fiction and theological meditation are anathema, since both threaten to prevent real usefulness in daily life. Thus we see orthodox fiction beginning to merge with Oriental and visionary fiction, which turned during the 1830s from private contemplation to secular action.

Bullard's use of fiction to attack religious enemies and to endorse social change was emulated in the 1830s by the controversial minister George Cheever. After studying divinity at Andover, Cheever worked with the revivalist Charles G. Finney before establishing the conservative Church of the Puritans in New York. According to his biographer, Cheever was continuously active in "temperance, anti-slavery, anti-popery, Sabbath, social, and political reforms."[13] Cheever epitomized the growing Calvinist tendency to equate sin with social misbehavior. His widely-read stories, "Deacon Giles' Distillery" and "Deacon Jones' Brewery," "made an era in the temperance reform"[14] The careful balancing of doctrinal commentary with reformist recommendations seen in such earlier works as *Lucretia* and *The Reformation* is absent from these tales. Cheever's deacons are linked with the devil not so much because of their liberal views as because of their rum selling. The inchoate combativeness of some earlier Calvinist fiction has turned into pugnacity; the Calvinist fictionist has become the scourge of social wrongdoing. Fiction is exploited for self-protective reasons, as the author, when brought to trial for libel, could declare that "Deacon Giles' Distillery" was "the mere creation of fancy," a "purely imaginary" portrait of a very real evil. More significantly, religion is interpreted almost entirely in terms of secular action. Implicit in the temperance tales, this outlook comes to be expressed more overtly in Cheever's lecture of 1843, "The Religion of Experience, and That of Imitation": "The world is to be saved, if saved at all, by the religion of Experience, and not that of Imitation. The religion of imitation is that of forms; the religion of experience is that of realities. The religion of imitation is *Churchianity*. The religion of experience is *Christianity*. The religion of imitation, except when it oppresses, is that of profound quiet and weakness; the religion of experience is that of conflict and power."[15]

Even Cheever's most doctrinal fiction reflects this experiential interpretation of orthodoxy. In his Bunyanesque "Hill Difficulty" (1849) Cheever converts traditional allegory into an indictment of several American denominations and an endorsement of muscular faith. Earlier allegorists such as Botsford and Lummus, despite their modifications of convention, had at least followed Bunyan in equating sin with such inward failings as pride, worldly wisdom, and lust. In Cheever's allegory, sin is connected with hostile religious and secular groups—liberals, Jews, Roman Catholics, Fourierists. Even certain evangelical and orthodox sects come under fire, such as Baptists, Methodists, and Edwardsean Calvinists. Cheever's special targets are formalism, theology, and excessive brooding. The activist note struck in the temperance tales is echoed in Cheever's praise of a group of sedulous Christians: "Their combined intensity and perseverance was the effect, under God's grace, of continued, strong, steady, Christian habit. It was like the impulse of a swift skater, the application of whose muscular energy has given him such power of impetus, that if he should attempt to stand still, the very habit of motion will carry him swiftly forward."[16]

Bullard's noncontemplative piety has been transformed by Cheever into an almost obsessive need for perpetual activity. *"No good ever comes of brooding!"* Cheever emphasizes in regard to some Christians who *"stumbled* up the hill rather than climbed" (14). The way up the hill is full of "conflict and trial," demanding "labor, intense labor" (4). Cheever satirizes denominations that circumvent this labor, whether through a belief in universal salvation or through perfectionism or through rites and pardons. Both in his life and in his fiction, therefore, Cheever epitomizes the tendency of Calvinist authors of this period to put aside theoretical metaphysics on behalf of "muscular energy" and "strong, steady Christian habit."

In the third stage of Calvinist fiction, between 1835 and 1850, the reformist theme of Bullard and Cheever was at first modified and then slowly incorporated into a less political notion of pious activism. After 1850 the popular religious novel most commonly focused on a young orphan's surviving personal tragedies and social ostracism through Christian endurance. Often the protagonist would effect the conversion of dissolute or skeptical characters, making redemption the result of individual example rather than of reform organizations. Just as American orthodoxy after the end of the Benevolent Empire stressed personal regeneration as the basis of social change, so Calvinist fiction increasingly centered on individual sinners and individual saviors. Even so seminal a work as *Uncle Tom's Cabin* would spark the northern cause not so much by advocating abolition societies as by portraying the miseries of particular families as a result of slavery. It would not be until the Social Gospel novel of the 1880s that group Christian reform would again be strongly endorsed, and even then the emotional dramas of individual social workers would be emphasized.

Between 1835 and 1850, of course, Emerson and Thoreau were endorsing, respectively, self-reliance and civil disobedience, sometimes to the detriment of reform groups. At the same time, lesser writers began to promote self-reliant piety as a panacea for such social ills as gambling and intemperance. In some novels between 1838 and 1845 this individual emphasis was coupled with direct ridicule of reform societies. More typically, growing attention was paid to personal wretchedness caused by social misconduct. Also, the attack on intellectual theology begun during the second stage of Calvinist fiction was amplified, as creedal distinctiveness was replaced by a simple sentimental ethic of feeling right and doing good. Sin came to be seen less as the inescapable basis of human nature than as a troublesome but avoidable aspect of the secular environment. The religious pilgrimage was not so much an inward struggle against spiritual demons as an outward battle against harsh social realities and bad habits.

Five novels and one story collection published between 1835 and 1841 reflect these changing notions of orthodox activism. Phoebe H. Brown's *The Tree and Its Fruits* (1836) consists of separate sketches of four wretched men that illustrate the sinfulness of infidel reading clubs, gambling, and alcohol. *A Blossom in the Desert* (1838) shows how the establishment of a Sunday school in a frontier village brings about spiritual and physical improvements among certain families. The Reverend George A. Raybold's two novels of 1838, *The Fatal Feud* and *Paul Perryman,* recommend the conversion of individual sinners as the catalyst of social change. In Robert C. Waterson's *Arthur Lee and Tom Palmer* (1839) a clean-living seaman sets a good example for his foulmouthed mate, who eventually espouses both orthodoxy and temperance. *The Temptation; or, Henry Thornton* (1841), "By a Minister," warns that the first sip of alcohol must not be taken, depicting the fatal effects of drinking on an initially pious, happy couple.

In several senses, this fiction harks back to the religious themes of the pre-1835 works. The noncontemplative activity advocated by Bullard and Cheever is enacted in the characterization of several warriors for Christ battling spiritual infirmities evidenced by worldly waywardness. For example, one of George Raybold's heroes, a Revolutionary War veteran who converts his frontier cottage into a religious center, is described in military images common in orthodox fiction: "His habits as a soldier had given him a firm boldness, unconnected, however, with any appearance of affectation. He had manfully contended for his country's rights, and, now that her independence was obtained, with other weapons, and another spirit, he was zealous in the cause of God."[17]

And yet, though clearly linked to earlier fiction, these post-1835 evangelical works begin to make subtle variations on thematic and stylistic patterns. The later works describe more comprehensively than the previous novels the details of concrete, daily experience. Phoebe Brown stresses that her stories derive "not from the imagination of the writer, but from real life; and that they are, in every important particular, FACTS."[18] In contrast to Cheever, who had fabricated fictional devils and allegorical exempla to promote his "religion of experience," the post-1835 writers tried to duplicate religious experience itself, as embodied in preachers and missionaries, hardy sailors, miserable alcoholics, and long-suffering wives. Bullard had praised *"active* and *efficient"* Christians but had actually spent little time describing missionary activity. In contrast, later authors such as Brown, Raybold, and Robert Waterson detailed the actual tribulations and victories of Christian activists at work. In this connection, the plots and settings of the later works tend to be more complex, attending to a broader range of psychological factors and scenes from nature than those of the earlier works. This is particularly true of Raybold's *Fatal Feud,* in which the idea that "human nature is totally depraved" is objectified in a long account of a sanguinary battle between rival clans (81).

While orthodox fiction became more experiential during this later period, it also turned even less theological than before. Stirring examples and anecdotes illustrating a simple, emotional Calvinism were widely preferred to logical proof of doctrine. In *A Blossom in the Desert,* for example, a clergyman convinces a frontier town of its need for a Sunday school through a sermon which is not a theological discussion but rather a story of a young boy relating what he has learned in Sunday school to his dying grandmother. "Often," the preacher has the grandmother comment, "have I heard the minister preach, but I have never heard it so *plain* before; it never came home to me as it does now. . . . I am a sinner—an old one."[19] The most effective preacher of Raybold's *Paul Perryman* is a pathetic blind girl who "never was instructed in the schools of theology—had neither parchment nor diploma,—but was poor and uneducated."[20] Tom Palmer, the sinful sailor of Waterson's *Arthur Lee,* is converted when he hears a minister tell two sentimental stories, one "a graphic description of sea life" and the other an account of a mother praying tearfully for her child.[21]

Similarly, salvation and the recognition of sin became more closely tied to secular sentiment and behavior than in the pre-1835 novels. A family in *A Blossom in the Desert* shows evidence of saving grace by sweeping the cottage floors and doing the laundry. Mrs. Brown's Gregory, in *The Tree and its Fruits,* reveals "a strange depravity of heart" by attending a reading club and taking up cards and liquor (10). The preachment against swearing and alcohol in Waterson's *Arthur Lee* is dramatically heightened by the dying outcries of the inebriated Dick Stanley. All the novels mention human depravity and redemption through grace. But depravity becomes localized in individual cases of immoral conduct, and grace is less arbitrary, more responsive to human conduct than in earlier Calvinist fiction.

Most of these authors equate being saved with abandoning bad habits. In the process, the reformist message is highly individualized. Bullard's two novels of the early 1830s could have been used as tracts for the Benevolent Empire, since they conclude with demands for widespread social work through established organizations. Similarly, Cheever had generalized the message of his Deacon stories by ending each with an account of people throughout the entire nation drinking devil-produced rum. His court defense of "Deacon Giles' Distillery" had consisted primarily of statistical evidence accentuating the need for nationwide reform. The post-1835 novels, in contrast, turn to individual victims of habit and infidelity: Brown's Gregory, who reads Paine and takes to the bottle; Raybold's Paul Perryman, whose exposure to Volney and Voltaire leads to profligacy and death; the couple in *The Temptation,* whose happiness is ruined by the husband's drinking; Waterson's doomed Dick Stanley. Social improvement is customarily seen to be the result of personal regeneration.

In Bayard Rush Hall's *Something for Everybody* (1846), the rejection of group reform is coupled with a more general discussion of the folly of liberalism, the pros and cons of fiction, and the value of common sense in religion. Both evangelical reformers and liberals are charged with a naïve belief in perfectibility. Hall says that group reformers "whine about the dignity of that human nature which my Bible says is 'deceitful above all things and desperately wicked' . . . about the efficacy of persuasion, irrespective of a divine efficiency, . . . about the grandeur of our morals and good works, when we are often 'whited sepulcres without,' and filthy graves within."[22] Liberals, in Hall's eyes, are even more dangerous than reformers, since they use light literature insidiously to subvert orthodoxy. In poems and magazine fiction, Hall notes, liberals betray a cowardly fear of directly mentioning God or Christ.

On the surface, *Something for Everybody* seems an anomaly among post-1835 Calvinist novels. Unlike such writers as Raybold, Gilman, and Brown, Hall does not describe evangelical soldiers waging war on spiritual and secular evils. Rather, he records the epistolary correspondence between the Reverend Charles Clarence and his friend Robert Carlton, who reflect on the American religious scene. In this sense, the book recalls the expository discussion of doctrine in such early Calvinist novels as *The Art of Courting* and *Charles Observator*. But Hall's novel is quite different from early doctrinal fiction, and its incongruity with other post-1835 works is significant. Hall subordinates theological exposition to a discussion of more secular issues such as reformism and religious fiction. Not only has doctrinal discussion become more closely tied to cultural analysis, but its early sobriety has been replaced by a more emotional, at times humorous tone. Whereas Sabin includes a logical sermon in *Charles Observator* to contest Arminianism, in *Something for Everybody* Hall has Clarence exclaim, "Human dignity, thou art often a great—Strut!" (100). Rather than rationally refute infidelity as Matilda tries to do in *The Art of Courting*, Clarence caricatures it as "a ferociously grand little worm! . . . an active skipper in a cheese, trying to prove to the other mites, that their *habitation of curds* was an eternal cheese, from which they, like the Athenians from the earth, had sprung by the laws of nature!" (101). Thus emotional coloration and refutation through metaphor came to characterize even that most conventional aspect of Calvinist fiction, theological commentary. In this sense, Hall presages Harriet Beecher Stowe, who gently parodied the "logic trap" of traditional Calvinism through characters possessing vernacular wit or engaging personality quirks.[23]

Something for Everybody does not achieve the relatively sophisticated balancing of personality and doctrine, cultural analysis and theological commentary, attained in Stowe's best novels. On the other hand, Hall does point toward Stowe while questioning the group reformism advocated by Bullard and

Cheever. In several ways, Hall's novel is as thematically confused as its title might suggest; but this confusion signifies that the Calvinist novel in 1846 was in a state of transition. Hall can have his hero mock liberal storytellers and yet advise an intellectual friend that composing "light articles, histories, tales, poetry, prose" would have "enlarged his organ . . . of common-sensitiveness, and destroyed the bigness of his other organ, gummabilitiveness." Elsewhere he muses: "If literature, when merely playful, is not decidedly religious, must it of consequence, become immoral? There is unquestionably a common ground where moralities of the world and of the church may stand; or where *externally* good men may meet, and with what they hold in common."[24] Such reflections seem to conflict not only with Hall's earlier aspersions of liberal fiction but also with his denunciation of reformers as externally moral but inwardly flawed. Hall wants it various ways at once; he indeed gives something for everybody. He mocks religious philosophers, but he discusses faith expositionally. He damns reformers, but he prizes noncontemplative religion. He laments and extols light reading by turns. His tone is playful, serious, cynical, and reflective at different moments. It would seem that the Calvinist novelist is struggling toward redefinition, rejecting previous attitudes while failing to place full confidence in new ones.

The rather fragmented state of Calvinist fiction during this transitional period is reflected in three other works of the mid-1840s: Charles T. Torrey's *Home* (1845), John P. Brace's *Tales of the Devils* (1846), and Elizabeth Allen's *Sketches of Green Mountain Life* (1846). Unlike Calvinist fiction published between 1795 and 1820, or between 1835 and 1841, these works do not form a homogeneous group. Torrey traces the religious history of a fictional New England town called Home, lamenting the rise of liberalism and immorality while lauding the decline of strict logic. Brace describes the futile attempts of demons to implant sinful thoughts in the mind of a victim of seduction and her son. Allen's eight short stories include "The Effects of Indulgence," a sketch of a youth who passes from novel reading to intemperance and infidelity, at last being converted to Calvinism when he sees God's frown in the moon above.

Though disparate and uneven, the orthodox novels and stories of 1845–46, when taken together, can be said to form a pathway between the seven works of 1835–41 and the novels of later writers such as Joseph Alden, Susan Warner, and Harriet Beecher Stowe. Hall, as we have seen, transforms the increasingly individualist emphasis of Calvinist fiction into an overt dismissal of group reform; thus he sets the stage for the prevalent concentration on the individual exemplar in the post-1850 works. Also he tests out new voices in doctrinal discussion—for example, wit and satiric hyperbole—which in later works would come to take shape as fictional characters, particularly the idiosyncratic vernacular priests of Stowe's later novels.

Torrey, recreating seventeenth- and eighteenth-century village life in New

England, initiates an interest in the kind of orthodox retrospection and historicism that would become central in such novels as *The Minister's Wooing* and *Oldtown Folks.* Just as Hall makes explicit the suspicion of organized reform, so Torrey looks forward to later novelists by combining the praise of experiential religion with forthright attacks on logic. In words that anticipate Stowe's "logic trap" discussion, Torrey writes: "To fight the logical battle respecting the relation of God's mind, will, and decisions to our theoretical freedom, is of little avail to the mass of minds. In logic, the masses will reject your truth. Preach it with a single reference to faith, submission, and humility and they will love it."[25] We have "ten thousand volumes of logical proof that Christ is God" and "as many more that he is Man," and "both are true." What we need, Torrey says, are "practical" works which vivify "the hopes, fears, struggles, doubts, temptations, trials, joys, triumphs of the Christian life on earth and in heaven" (192). This passage expresses baldly the abandonment of theology that was implicit in most previous Calvinist fiction. To say that Trinitarians and Socinians are equally right but equally misled is to confess the failure of one of the longest doctrinal controversies in New England history. To invoke hopes, fears, struggles, doubts, and so forth as the basis of faith is to open the way for the sentimental piety of the post-1850 religious novel. Doctrine is made relative rather than absolute; it becomes like other aspects of experience a thing to be molded and crafted by the novelist. It is a short step from Torrey's blithe dismissal of the Trinitarian controversy to the studied creedal impartiality of Stowe as expressed in her prefatory explanation of *Oldtown Folks:* "Though Calvinist, Arminian, High-Church Episcopalian, sceptic and simple believer all speak in their turn, I merely listen, and endeavor to understand and faithfully represent the inner life of each. I myself am but the observer and reporter, seeing much, doubting much, questioning much, and believing with all my heart in only a very few things."[26]

If Torrey helped to rid orthodox fiction of its guilty nostalgia for bygone logic, Stowe took the further step of becoming a judicious observer and reporter of several doctrines she disbelieved. If Torrey theoretically grounded faith in such earthly vicissitudes as hopes and trials and triumphs, Stowe revealed the inner life of many characters who struggle and love, debate and emote.

John P. Brace's *Tales of the Devils* and Elizabeth Allen's *Sketches of Green Mountain Life* are also anticipatory. By describing the resistance to the devil on the part of Lucy Woods and her illegitimate son, Robert, Brace is weaving the web of orphanage and self-reliant piety which becomes central in the novels of Joseph Alden, Augusta Evans Wilson, and others. Like Elizabeth Ellison of Evans' *Resignation,* Brace's Lucy Woods keeps her faith in the face of social ostracism and sinful inclinations. But more acutely than the earlier Elizabeth, the wandering Lucy is forced to feel the agony of loneliness in what Susan Warner would call "the wide, wide world." Lucy is closer to such homeless heroines as Gertrude Flint (*The Lamplighter*) and Ellen Montgomery (*The Wide, Wide World*) than to Evans' character.

While preparing for the post-1850 religious heroine in this way, Brace also keeps alive the interest in individual reform, the repudiation of theology, and the muscular faith seen in previous Calvinist fiction. Doomed to Brace's realm of demons are a libertine, a drunkard, a reader of infidel works, a Catholic, and a metaphysical theologian. In contrast, heaven is promised to the nonreflective, diligently moral Lucy and Robert Woods. Robert is guided by "a principle within that impelled to action, not an imagination that excited to romance."[27] A "strong, powerful, athletic man," Robert passes from poverty to political power as result of *"strength of body, steadiness of nerve, and coolness of judgement"* (220, 205). Robert's "manliness of character" and "energy and determination" earn him a congressional seat, vast wealth, and the hand of a woman of society (220). More explicitly than any previous orthodox writer of fiction, Brace couples energetic Christianity with social advancement. He thus anticipates the post-1850 religious novel, in which, as Henry Nash Smith says, "both worldly success and divine grace merge into a single mythical process."[28] The "scribbling women" of the 1850s would dispense with Brace's darkly visionary subplot while exaggerating his connection between salvation and social climbing. By the time of E. P. Roe, the popular religious novel would be virtually reduced to a tract on getting ahead.

While Hall and Torrey are important for their redefinition of reform and theological commentary, and Brace for his social interpretation of Christian activity, Elizabeth Allen is interesting for her restatement of an old paradox: the orthodox novelist's denunciation of fiction. In such early Calvinist works as *The Art of Courting* and *Charles Observator,* the self-lacerating guilt about writing fiction had been expressed in terms of nostalgia for traditional theology. Allen's work shows that in the mid-1840s the orthodox writer's guilt about fiction writing persisted while concern for doctrinal exactitude was being left behind. In "The Effects of Indulgence," a story in *Sketches of Green Mountain Life,* Allen calls novel reading one of several luxuries that contaminate young minds. Like some previous Calvinist authors, Allen writes fiction in which fiction is vilified. But gone is Sabin's quibbling over common fictions, love fictions, sermons, histories, and so forth. By 1846 sermonizing had become sufficiently interwoven with storytelling to allow the Calvinist novelist to dispense with pretended nostalgia for doctrinal tradition. In the novels of the 1850s the self-conscious indictment of fiction, which had been made quite seriously in *The Art of Courting, Charles Observator,* and *The Wife for a Missionary,* would become little more than a perfunctory orthodox tic. For example, Susan Warner's Ellen Montgomery concurs with a friend's advice to "read no novels" but shows little respect for Puritan logic.[29] In fact, though occasionally decrying novels, later fiction would often champion sentimental anecdote as the ideal alternative to theology.

Taken together, the four works of 1845–46 set the stage for Joseph Alden's novels of the late 1840s, which combine individualist reform, democratic and sentimental religion, and social commentary. Significantly, Alden became the first Calvinist novelist to produce a small corpus of fiction. Most orthodox writers before Alden had made only sporadic efforts in fiction; the only Calvinist writers before 1845 who published more than one novel were Bullard, Cheever, and Raybold, none of whom wrote more than three novels. Alden wrote five between 1846 and 1848. He was followed in the 1850s and 1860s by several moderate Calvinists who produced either large bodies of fiction or a small number of long works: Susan Warner, Harriet Beecher Stowe, Josiah Gilbert Holland, and Elizabeth Phelps Ward are prominent examples.

Alden's novels preach a simplified Calvinism through plots involving poor, pious orphans, frivolous rich folk, active ministers, and converted skeptics. More secular than the novels of previous orthodox writers, Alden's works usually show social outcasts or nonbelievers being forced by human events (rather than by intellectual investigation or self-scrutiny) to admit their depravity and their reliance on God. Conversion in Alden's fiction is always sped on by romantic love, and regeneration is consummated by marriage and social advancement. *Elizabeth Benton* (1846) and *Alice Gordon* (1847) typify this mixture of spiritual and social redemption in Alden's novels.

While gathering such disparate elements of previous Calvinist fiction as democratic religion, love, and social betterment into a fairly unified whole, Alden introduces an overt exaltation of aesthetics and imagination in religion which most orthodox writers before him would have deemed excessive. A balanced view of Christianity, says Elizabeth Benton after her conversion, "would show that it had the power to beautify as well as to save."[30] Considering "the culture of the imagination a religious duty," Elizabeth declares, "The fact that so large a portion of the Bible is addressed to the imagination in the shape of poetry and fiction, is enough, of itself, to show the error of those who would proscribe the cultivation of this power" (144–145). When the girl whom Elizabeth is addressing exclaims, "Fiction!" Elizabeth replies: "Yes, fiction . . .; what else are the parables of the New and Old Testament, and probably the whole book of Job?" Elizabeth goes on to say that the Bible is full of "magnificent appeals to the imagination" (145). Alden is quite distant not only from Timothy Dwight, who had emphasized the broad gulf between the Bible and novels, but also from previous Calvinist novelists, who were wont to offer only guarded paeans to fiction. The old Calvinist proscription of the imagination, attacked indirectly in many Calvinist novels between 1795 and 1845, is intentionally overturned by Alden, who goes so far as to call the Bible a masterpiece of imaginative literature.

It was left to later writers to transform the devices and themes of orthodox authors from Joseph Morgan to Joseph Alden into best-selling fiction. The

Presbyterian Susan Warner, for example, in *The Wide, Wide World* (1851) inspired thousands of international readers with her portrayal of Ellen Montgomery, a poor girl separated from her pious mother and placed in the hands of a cruel aunt. The religion of Warner's novel is determinedly nonintellectual and plain. God is a Divine Friend always ready to help, even in the most trifling crisis. Religious action, in the novel's controlling image, is letting one's "rush-light burn bright."[31] Though Ellen reads *The Pilgrim's Progress* and evangelical hymns about depravity, the novel is Calvinist only in the most attenuated sense of the word. Both sin and salvation are interpreted in secular terms. Getting lost in a snowstorm, being mistreated by an aunt, losing a pony, not going to school—such earthly events cause misery, which in turn calls for divine remedy. Like the protagonists of Brace and Alden, Ellen is awarded in the end with wealth and social position. Thus the book epitomizes tendencies in Calvinist fiction that had begun in *The Art of Courting* and that had been gaining momentum in the 1840s.

Such post-Calvinist novelists as Warner, Harriet Beecher Stowe, and Henry Ward Beecher praised religious storytelling and decried strictly intellectual faith with a confidence unseen in earlier evangelical novelists. Ellen Montgomery denounces novels and abashedly confesses: "I wish I warn't so fond of reading stories" (337). But fond of stories she is, and her dismissal of fiction is belied by the fact that she responds warmly to entertaining religious discussion while aspersing theology.

Similarly, several of Stowe's characters—Uncle Tom, Little Eva, James Marvyn, Sam Lawson, Harry and Tina Percival—prefer pious anecdote to doctrinal exposition. Despite her profound interest in the theological controversies of the past, Stowe often lamented the clinical precision and undeveloped aestheticism of Puritan logicians. In *The Minister's Wooing* she derides a minister whose faith is "all logical, not in the least aesthetic," lacking "those attractions by which the common masses are beguiled into thinking."[32] Elsewhere in the novel she asserts that "there is as much romance burning under the snow-banks of cold Puritan preciseness as if Dr. Hopkins had been brought up to attend operas instead of metaphysical preaching, and Mary [Scudder] had been nourished on Byron's poetry instead of 'Edwards on the Affections' " (123). This hopeful conjecture, aptly expressed through the image of thawing or melting, reflects Stowe's attempt in several novels to revisit colonial times in order to dissolve rigorous logic with the humanizing warmth of fiction. "Another and better day is dawning," she announces in her preface to *Uncle Tom's Cabin,* when "the great principles of Christian brotherhood" can be placed "under the allurements of fiction."[33] In 1869 Stowe could contrive a fictional persona who frankly "preferred stories, history, and lively narrative" to theology.[34] In the same novel Stowe describes a vernacular religionist, Sam Lawson, whose mind "was a boundless world of narrative and dreamy suggestion" (184). By 1871, in her preface to *My Wife and I,* Stowe could make the generalization—one that would have been labeled heresy a century earlier—that American clergymen of all denominations were popularizing doctrine through stories, often using similar plots and characters, despite their differing outlooks.

It took Stowe's brother, Henry Ward Beecher, to communicate this growing interest in pious anecdote not only to novel readers but to mainstream ministers as well. In Beecher's *Norwood* (1868) the attraction to religious narrative has been transformed into an almost overwhelming desire for fiction. "Story-hunger in children is even more urgent than bread hunger," Beecher writes, so that "scores of times [Dr. Reuben Wentworth] had been wont to weave fables and parables for Rose;—fictions that under every form whatsoever, still tended, in his child's imagination, to bring Nature home to her as God's wonderful revelation, vital with sentiment and divine truth."[35] Throughout *Norwood* Beecher satirizes the logical Calvinism of Parson Buell while extolling the imaginative and anecdotal propensities of Wentworth, his daughter Rose, Pete Sawmill, and Tommy Taft. In his widely published sermons and discussions of homiletic theory, Beecher would attract millions to his view that imaginative illustrations and anecdotes are more congenial to true religion than logical proof.

The post-1850 interest in fiction as an ideal method of religious instruction was accompanied by increased secularization of religious novels. As early as 1848 an alarmed Orestes Brownson, discussing religious fiction, declared that "the secular order . . . has the right to exist as a servant, no right to exist as a master." In Brownson's eyes, religious novelists "secularize the spiritual, while we would spiritualize the secular." In 1869 Brownson was disturbed by such tendencies in Beecher's *Norwood:* "The author, though nominally a Christian, and professedly a Congregational preacher, is really a pagan, and wishes to abolish Puritanism for the worship of nature."[36] Indeed, Beecher—along with many other late-nineteenth-century religious novelists—tipped the stylistic and thematic scale so far away from traditional doctrine toward the anecdotal and human that the divine came to be interpreted almost wholly in terms of the secular.

As we have seen, neither Warner nor Stowe nor Beecher can be called the first to secularize Calvinism in the novel. These and other post-1850 novelists developed naturally out of a long line of authors running from Joseph Morgan to Joseph Alden. What Stowe called "the snow-banks of cold Puritan preciseness" were beginning to be melted by fiction when Ebenezer Bradford, the author of *The Art of Courting*, put pen to paper in 1795.

4

Anti-Calvinist and Liberal Fiction

An initial difference between early liberal and Calvinist fiction is suggested by the fact that, despite some anti-Calvinist passages in a few novels of the 1790s, liberalism was not overly promoted in American fiction until 1812, nearly two decades after the publication of the orthodox *Art of Courting*. The relatively late origin of liberal fiction resulted not only from Unitarianism's tardy development but also from the early liberal preference for such oblique vehicles as Oriental tales and the visionary mode. To study Unitarian fiction is to take up where Oriental and visionary stories left off: after 1810 the indirect subversion of Calvinism became direct attack; the distanced allegory became practical exemplum; exotic settings and characters were replaced by familiar indigenous ones. Oriental and visionary devices were not abandoned after 1810; rather, they either became more complex and secular, or else they began to be absorbed into more realistic liberal fiction. For example, the evil Calvinist family of *The Parent's Counsellor* (1825) is said to be "barricadoed by rules and regulations numerous as the chains of an Algerine captive."[1] In the same novel, a liberal father illustrates his distaste for constrictive orthodoxy by entertaining his children with a Sabbath story of a Baghdad mechanic who escapes a sultan's tyranny. Such Oriental metaphors appear in several liberal novels of the period. Similarly, the visionary mode was exploited by such liberals as Sedgwick, Child, and Judd. Thus, writers of liberal fiction had a tradition of oblique anti-Calvinism in Oriental and visionary tales, a tradition they could invoke to reinforce the precepts of divine benevolence and human perfectibility that they wished to endorse in a more practical and readily applicable manner.

A second difference between early Calvinist and liberal fiction lies in the fact that among Unitarians there emerged a relatively homogeneous literary culture that was lacking among Calvinists. Unlike Calvinism, liberalism produced several writers between 1785 and 1845 who wrote three or more novels: Sarah A. Savage, Catherine Sedgwick, Lydia Child, Lucius M. Sargent, Susan A. L. Sedgwick, Hannah F. Lee, Eliza Buckminster Lee, William Ware, and Sylvester Judd were the most prolific. In many cases liberal novelists were not, like the Calvinists, minor or tangential figures but rather established, well-known ministers or churchgoers. The widely admired Henry Ware, Jr., for instance, began to write religious fiction while he was the pastor of Boston's First Church, and in 1835–36 he coordinated the efforts of six liberal novelists to produce the popular novel series *Scenes and Characters Illustrating Christian Truths*. There was a widespread interest in fiction even on the part of those who did not write it. William Ellery Channing, the venerable leader of Boston's Unitarians, met regularly in the late 1820s with Charles Follen, Wendell Phillips, and other ministers to discuss fiction. In the words of the liberal historian Octavius Brooks Frothingham: "The Unitarians were the first . . . who adopted art, humanity, and literature as expressions of the divine mind . . . Secular culture came up in their generation."[2] Despite many individual efforts, orthodoxy would not produce a comparable body of novelists until the 1840s and 1850s, when theological differences were dissolving and Calvinism itself was softening into a liberalized mainstream.

Committing Nobody, yet Taking All

A more fundamental distinction between early Calvinist and liberal novelists lay in their contrasting reasons for espousing fiction. Calvinist writers between 1795 and 1825 were wont to include in their novels some amount of doctrinal exposition, exegetical proof, or homiletic structure which recalled orthodox tradition. Liberals, in contrast, were more doctrinally imprecise from the start. More determinedly than Calvinists, liberals saw in fiction an opportunity for gaining victory in a time of intense theological discussion. Fiction answered a widespread liberal impulse to avoid theoretical controversy on behalf of practical application.

The liberal tendency to doctrinal caution or evasiveness was noted by Calvinists and liberals alike. Liberals, declared the orthodox Jeremiah Evarts in 1815, "generally conceal their religious opinions . . . with particular care," while Calvinists "generally avow their religious opinions with the utmost frankness."[3] A character in the Calvinist novel *Justina* (1823) mocked liberals who "boast that the tendency of their doctrines could not be discovered in the sermons of their preachers; they fear to shock the ears of their . . . hearers by advancing what they know will at first appear to them to be blasphemy; they unfold themselves gradually as they think will best ensnare."[4] B. R. Hall's *Something for Everybody* (1846) lamented "prudent" liberal writers who show "a cowardice, which we term caution" in works that are "crafty, and catch with guile."[5] Throughout the Unitarian controversy, according to Eliza B. Lee, liberals were charged with "a disingenuous concealment of opinions, arising from a spirit of indifference to the purity of doctrine, and an attachment to worldly advantages."[6] Lee explains that liberals, afraid of "dogmas and polemics," were told "that they did not come out and make proclamation of their opinions upon certain points, and of their disagreement with the dogmas of Calvinism" (328, 329). Even the comparatively outspoken Channing was decried for subverting orthodoxy "in a cunning, deceitful, hypocritical way."[7]

Liberals often answered such charges by calling themselves peace loving and Calvinists disputatious. By "avoiding controversy," Channing declared, "we have thought that we deserved, not reproach, but some degree of praise for our self-denial. Every preacher knows how much easier it is to write a controversial than a practical discourse."[8] The more pragmatic Charles Follen argued that "in many cases an entire disclosure of one's own faith could be of no use to others, while it is apt to destroy the usefulness, and means of living, of him who holds these opinions."[9] Priding themselves as practical rather than theoretical, peaceful rather than contentious, many liberals found in poetry and fiction a convenient nondoctrinal shelter from the storm of controversy that raged about them.

This caution and evasion, which had influenced the common liberal choice of Oriental and visionary fiction between 1785 and 1815, became increasingly apparent as time passed. *The Soldier's Orphan*, a liberal novel of 1812, lauded a minister who preached "by artifices, which experience had taught him were more effectual than dull sermonizing."[10] Several protagonists of prominent liberal novelists—Catherine Sedgwick's Jane Elton, Harriet V. Cheney's Miriam Grey, Sarah J. Hale's Sidney Romilly, Eliza B. Lee's Edith Grafton— are reluctant to enter the lists of controversy, believing, in Hale's words, that "dexterity and *tact*" are necessary in religious matters.[11]

Nearly all liberal novelists valued example more than exposition; in some instances this preference was coupled with the explicit intention of concealment. In 1824 Catherine Sedgwick's brother praised her for choosing the novel as a means of opposing Calvinism, commenting, "If brought forward professedly as a controversial article . . . it will not be so useful as it would be if considered simply as a literary effort."[12] Sedgwick was the first of several liberal novelists, including Henry Ware, Jr., and Sylvester Judd, who tried to conceal their authorship of anti-Calvinist novels. Another important liberal, Jacob Abbott, stated that Christianity should be "conciliatory and unobtrusive."[13] Abbott wrote scores of children's novels in the 1830s and 1840s in which dogma was totally subsumed to practice. In some cases, the proclivity for concealment resulted in the deletion of overtly religious references from the titles of liberal magazines and books. Sarah E. Mayo wished to exclude the word "universalist" from the title of a literary journal, confessing, "I am as much— yes, *more* a Universalist than ever—but I will have the whole world to range through if I wish, and be limited by no walls of party."[14] Likewise, Henry Ware, Jr., advised his brother William to omit "Christian" or "Christianity" from the title of his second novel. "I have a feeling of reluctance at seeing this Christian purpose stuck upon the title page," Henry wrote in a letter of 1838. The nonreligious *Probus; or, Rome in the Third Century* is "euphonious and significant, and committing nobody, yet taking all."[15]

Viewed as the product of liberal indirection and caution, early liberal fiction can profitably be studied as a strategy for committing nobody, yet taking all. If obliquity was characteristic of Oriental and visionary fiction between 1785 and 1810, after 1810 it was even more apparent in works that were pointedly experiential, practical, nonspeculative.

To be sure, liberal fiction made the general doctrinal-to-secular movement seen in Calvinist fiction. Thus, between 1820 and 1825 some liberal novels— particularly Catherine Sedgwick's *A New England Tale,* Lydia Child's *Hobomok,* and Henry Ware, Jr.'s *The Recollections of Jotham Anderson*—contained explicit theological debate that was largely absent from later liberal fiction. But liberal works identified secular moral action as the proper alternative to creed far earlier than did the Calvinist ones. As we have seen, Calvinist fiction went through a long and rather tortured process of secularization, passing from modified doctrine to social reform to individual activism. Liberal fiction, in contrast, became secular quite rapidly and painlessly. *The Soldier's Orphan* (1812) and Sarah Savage's three novels of 1814–1821 dramatized the creedless piety of orphaned protagonists, a theme that would not be fully developed in Calvinist fiction until Joseph Alden's novels of the late 1840s. Such liberal writers of the 1820s as Sedgwick, Child, and Ware rapidly abandoned the theological emphasis of their early works, turning to ethical behavior in their later novels. *Scenes and Characters Illustrating Christian Truths,* the novel series edited by Ware in 1835–36, was more secular than Calvinist fiction would ever become.

It would seem that while Calvinists were clinging to the powerful American tradition of doctrinal debate and metaphysical theology in their early works, liberals were gladly embracing quotidian experience as part of a quiet rebellion against this tradition. "The WORLD is the theatre on which you are to prove yourself a Christian," stated Henry Ware, Jr., in his seminal *On the Formation of the Christian Character* (1829). "We must enter the crowd and distractions of common life. We must engage in common and secular affairs."[16] The novel facilitated entrance into the world of "common and secular affairs" for many liberals who wished to leave controversy and metaphysics behind.

Liberals were more eager to adopt fiction than Calvinists, not only as a result of their literary propensities, their caution, and their secular outlook. Another factor was the potential public boredom with liberalism in a time when mass appeal and persuasion were becoming vital to American religion. A major cause of the remarkable growth of evangelical Calvinism between 1800 and 1840 was revivalism's stirring, emotional, even theatrical quality. Unitarianism, lacking both revivalist fervor and the dramatic dualities of heaven and hell, grace and depravity, verged on being dull. According to the Calvinist Timothy Dwight, the liberal minister "urges ... a Religion, in which both his hearers and himself have little interest. His addresses to them are naturally made up of cold, commonplace morality ... They of course become dull and lifeless." The Calvinist, in contrast, underscores "the solemnity and importance of Religion, and presses upon his hearers the necessity of embracing it." There is drama, Dwight stressed, there is climax and denouement built into the Calvinist system; when this drama disappears, other forms of entertainment must be found to attract the listener.[17]

Liberals themselves were aware of the potentially boring tendency of their faith. "The majority of men preferred Calvinism with its mysticism and fervor," remarks O. B. Frothingham, who points out that liberalism's "denial of the most irrational yet most fascinating and impressive doctrines—the depravity of human nature, atonement, election, substitution, everlasting punishment—was precisely the cause of its rejection by the mass of mankind."[18] Henry Ware, Jr., went so far as to declare that Unitarian public worship was frequently "formal, monotonous, and deficient in excitement."[19] As if concurring with Dwight that liberalism needs exterior props to enhance its appeal, Ware declared that religion must be "made inviting" and that public "attention must be roused and maintained by some external application."[20]

For many liberals fiction was the most convenient external application. Sedgwick, Child, Abbott, and the Ware brothers, all of whom spoke of Unitarianism's lack of drama, stressed the importance of lending emotion and crisis to their religion through sentimental plot. For doctrinal reasons, early liberal fiction was customarily more staid than Calvinist fiction of the period. Never did liberal fiction duplicate the emotional dramas of Sarah Evans and George Raybold or the militantly evangelical stories of Anne T. Bullard and George Cheever or J. P. Brace's combined portrait of devils in hell and orphans on earth. Yet liberals turned more often than Calvinists to fiction during this period. If liberal fiction was more sedate, it was also ubiquitous, suggesting that liberalism's abandonment of orthodoxy's fascinating and impressive doctrines was accompanied by a compensatory need for narratives to replace them. Only when, after 1845, American Calvinism itself became

highly liberalized did it begin to produce novelists as prolific as the early liberal writers. After the Civil War, mainstream Protestantism would become
more genial and optimistic, yet also more theologically vacuous and un-
dramatic; as a result, an increasing number of Calvinists would resort to such
external applications as professional hymn singing, homiletic anecdotes,
poetry, and fiction. In each of these areas, but especially in fiction, these later
Protestants were following the lead of the literary liberals between 1810 and
1850.

Fictional Versions of Liberalism

Before 1810 liberal fiction was generally confined to Oriental and visionary
tales, many of which were designed to subvert enigmatic, tyrannical, or intellectual Christianity while affirming God's fairness and man's perfectibility.
But it should also be noted that early American sentimental novelists, even
while exploiting Calvinism for melodramatic effect, usually ended up on the
side of good works and reason. Sentimental heroines ordinarily earned salvation by keeping pure in the face of God's wrath and man's wiles, and depraved
rakes often proved capable of reformation. In sum, Oriental and visionary
tales, and to a lesser extent the early sentimental novel, had Arminian implications.

The oblique fictional answers to orthodoxy were in some other pre-1810
works complemented by more overt anti-Calvinist statements. Enos Hitchcock's Bloomsgrove (1790), for instance, wakes from his dream of benevolent
angels on a visionary ladder to assure his children that "fear and gloominess
are neither the offspring, nor the companions of religion: Pleasantness and
peace are her inmates."[21] In the religious education of their children, both
Bloomsgrove and a later Hitchcock hero, Charles Worthy, prefer storytelling
to more traditional methods of instruction. Another pre-1810 work which
directly satirizes orthodoxy is Susanna Rowson's *Reuben and Rachel* (1798), in
which Calvinists are presented as bigots. The most extended, overt anti-Calvinist commentary in American fiction before 1810 occurs in Royall Tyler's
The Bay Boy (1797), which satirizes a community of intolerant Massachusetts
Congregationalists. After mocking the severe theology and convoluted polemics of several Calvinists, Tyler goes on to praise the reasonable Reverend G.,
who delivers "a good sound moral discourse" instead of "musing on some
knotty point of divinity," and a pious blind boy who knows that religion is
simply "Love to God and good will to man."[22]

In sum, liberal tendencies in pre-1810 American fiction were generally restricted to the following areas: the oblique advancement of optimistic religion
in Oriental and visionary tales; equally indirect suggestions of Arminianism in
the sentimental novel; and overt, if sporadic and undeveloped, attacks on Calvinism in novels by Hitchcock, Rowson, and Tyler. In a broad sense, the ad-

vocacy of ethics and experience in these works anticipated the Unitarian fiction of the 1820s while it stood opposed to Calvinist metaphysics and logic. The rigid Edwardsean differentiation between natural virtue and true virtue was either parodied directly or more commonly blurred by fictional situations in which love of God and man, decent living, and reason insured salvation. In a time when Calvinist fiction was struggling to retain some connections to orthodox tradition, liberal fiction was abandoning tradition, usually covertly and benignly, but sometimes explicitly and satirically.

The large number of more overtly liberal novels and stories that began to appear after 1810 can be attributed, as I have suggested, to several interrelated aspects of the Unitarian outlook: the preference for literature over dogma, the inclination to circumvent doctrinal debate, the rejection of metaphysical or otherworldly faith for practical morality, and the desire to overcome the potential dullness of a hopeful religion.

A literary culture among Boston's liberals emerged quite rapidly. In 1804, a year before Henry Ware's historic assumption of the Hollis Professorship at Harvard, Joseph S. Buckminster and other Unitarian leaders formed the Anthology Club, the first of several liberal groups aimed at drawing connections between religion and polite literature. The publication of the *Monthly Anthology* (1810–1811) initiated a series of Unitarian literary periodicals that would come to include the *Christian Disciple* (1813–1823) and the *Christian Examiner* (1824–1869). The English romantic poets were admired and discussed, as were such foreign religious novelists as Hannah More, Maria Edgeworth, Mary Howitt, and Frederika Bremer. Freed from doctrinal tradition by their pre-1810 literary forerunners, New England liberals ranged widely through imaginative literature to find entertaining and inspiring replacements for the dramatic Calvinist system they were leaving behind. More than seventy important liberals began to write religious verse, a representative sampling of which would be made by A. P. Putnam in *Singers and Songs of the Liberal Faith* (1875). And a good number of them essayed the traditionally suspect mode of fiction. More determinedly and comprehensively than any other single religious group of the period, the New England liberals shifted the focus of religious discussion from dogma to literature, from polemics to illustration, from strict logic to controlled imagination. Displaying an "overwhelming tendency toward literature," as O. B. Frothingham could generalize in 1890, these liberals ushered in "a new era whose end is not yet," an era in which doctrine was replaced by "the lyrical view of religion."[23]

The Soldier's Orphan (1812), the first American novel to promote liberal values overtly, directs patriotic sentiment and the themes of orphanage and romantic love, as well as an Oriental tale motif, to anti-Calvinist ends. The anonymous author opposes both religious and political tyranny by portraying first a liberal minister, Young, and then a sea captain, Morris, the latter having recently returned to America after being held in captivity in Algiers for several years. Both men are dedicated to the religious education of an orphan, Emily Thompson, whom Morris has raised. Young, a liberal and tolerant Harvard graduate, teaches Emily that God has "created us free agents and accountable beings, to be punished or rewarded according to our deserts."[24] Young's anti-Calvinist beliefs are enhanced by his preference for moral example over rigid logic. As the author explains, "The life of such a professor of religion gives almost irresistible force to his doctrine; and thus turns many away from the ways of sin to eternal joys, who would never be convinced by elaborate arguments, or terrified into belief by fearful denunciations" (36).

The author enforces his liberal views by appealing to the patriotic code of religious freedom in America: "Every man has an equal right with his neighbour to form a creed for his own observance; but when he attempts to impose it upon another, he infringes the rights of a free and accountable being" (32–33). This egalitarian view is also underscored by the description of Morris' escape from Algerian slavery, which is accompanied by excoriations of despotism in society and in religion.

This brief novel is notable for its transformation of the Oriental devices of earlier liberal fiction and for its exploitation of secular reinforcements to liberalism. Like Tyler in *The Algerine Captive,* the author treats Orientals with a paradoxical mixture of love and loathing: when praising religious toleration, he says that any believer in human perfectibility, "whether he is a Jew, a Musselman, or a Christian, may rely on the mercy of God"; later, when denouncing Oriental slavery, he asks God to extirpate "this accursed race" of "vile barbarians" from the face of the earth (35, 148). Apparently contradicting himself, the author is in fact reiterating the bifurcated technique of all-embracing toleration with opposition to tyranny which was apparent in Oriental tales by Tyler, Munford, and Sherburne. Moreover, since by 1812 the explicit fictional treatment of religion had become permissible, the author feels free to introduce various American characters who can advance liberalism more directly and at greater length than the protagonists of Oriental tales. In doing so, he borrows from the sentimental novel of the 1790s such figures as the orphaned heroine, the dying foster mother, and the sturdy war veteran. To cast a religious light over all, he transforms the clergyman character, who in earlier novels was ordinarily a quiet background figure, into a vocal, central one. Friendship, compassion, deathbed emotion, and romantic love become components of a piety that is at once benign and heroic, creedless and consistent. By combining the Oriental tale and the sentimental novel and adding elements of his own, the author creates a religious work that responds to changing popular tastes. The writer himself has also become a free and accountable being able to form a creed for his own observance, a creed more secular than divine, more literary than dogmatic.

Sarah A. Savage, the next American writer of overtly liberal fiction, has a

special importance for several reasons: she was the first liberal writer to produce a small corpus of fiction; she was selected by Henry Ware, Jr., to write
the first novel of *Scenes and Characters Illustrating Christian Truths* in 1835; and
her first three novels, published between 1814 and 1821, continued the modifications of liberal fiction begun in *The Soldier's Orphan*. Savage wrote a total of
four novels of an increasingly secular nature: *The Factory Girl* (1814), *Filial
Affection* (1820), *James Talbot* (1821), and *Trial and Self-Discipline* (1835). In
the interest of chronological continuity, I shall postpone analysis of *Trial and
Self-Discipline,* the novel commissioned by Ware, until my discussion below of
the *Scenes and Characters* series.

Sarah A. Savage's first novel, *The Factory Girl,* shows the somewhat retro-
spective literary devices of *The Soldier's Orphan* giving way to a more contemporary brand of religious fiction. The recollection of Oriental motifs is still
apparent, as Savage has a character return from Algiers to denounce tyranny
and slavery. But in contrast to *The Soldier's Orphan,* Savage's novel leaves the
brief Oriental episode undeveloped and unconnected to religious commentary. At the same time, it more fully develops the indigenous characters and
scenes tentatively explored in *The Soldier's Orphan.* Savage's orphan, Mary
Burnam, follows Emily Thompson's example by learning well from a liberal
minister and a pious protector. But Mary, unlike Emily, is forced to validate
her liberalism through active service: she works in a cotton mill, where she
heroically endures the gibes of unbelievers, and she goes on to teach Sunday
school. Whereas Emily nostalgically recalls the Revolution, Mary prays to "be
blessed with healthful activity, and persevering diligence in the discharge of
her duties."[25]

In becoming more active, the heroine has also become more redemptive. To
be sure, the clergyman of the novel, Seymour, is, like Young of *The Soldier's
Orphan,* a vocal anti-Calvinist who strongly influences the heroine. Hostile to
dogma and gloom, Seymour endorses cheer, religious entertainment, and
good works. But the ministerial role begins to be assumed by the heroine herself, as moral example predominates over preaching. Thus Nancy, a friend of
Mary's at the factory, learns "that you can be cheerful, and yet be religious"
not from anything Mary says but from the way she behaves (22). When Mary
does speak of religion, she invariably uses diverting and pathetic stories or descriptions of the divine beauty of nature. The novel's chief alternative to polemic tradition, therefore, is secular example. "Example," Mary explains, "is
the most efficacious way of giving advice. That silent lesson, like the noiseless
dew which does not agitate the tenderest plant it fertilizes, can give no of-
fence. Not being particularly directed to any one, it does not excite the alarm
of a direct admonition" (74).

Like many liberal authors before and after her, Savage attempts a silent lesson that will give no offense. This liberal caution, interpreted by some Calvinists as Machiavellian strategy, had surfaced in the Oriental tale as allegorical

indirection; Savage was the first major liberal writer to discover opportunities for oblique anti-Calvinism in contemporary life. Relegating Oriental devices to a minor episode, she turns to active duty in more realistic settings to advance her optimistic views. The liberal author's doctrinal evasiveness is just as apparent here as it was in the Oriental tale, as the author utilizes secular example for fear of exciting the alarm of a direct admonition. But the evasion has become less obvious, since Oriental dervishes and peasants have been replaced by more familiar American clergymen and factory girls.

The shift away from Oriental techniques is even more evident in Savage's next two novels, *Filial Affection* (1820) and *James Talbot* (1821). Unlike *The Factory Girl,* these novels do not contain an Oriental episode. Nor do they contain an important clergyman figure like Seymour. The heroines of these novels increasingly take on the function of lay preachers: Phoebe Unwin learns from her grandfather liberal precepts that she enacts in daily life, and Lucy Talbot is fully responsible for the religious education of her brother, James. The silent lesson of *The Factory Girl* is manifested in these novels by an almost complete reliance on earthly example. Phoebe's grandfather is praised for "the persuasive eloquence of his example" and "the force and simplicity of his illustrations"[26] "Nothing of gloom or terror," Savage explains, "had ever mingled with his religion" (8). From him Phoebe learns the value of "active exertion," as she dedicates herself to "religious, social, and domestic duties" (42, 162). Lucy Talbot, a combined instructress and exemplar, concentrates, like Mr. Unwin, on "all that was cheerful, animating, and happy."[27] The amusing religious stories she tells her brother conduce to his commercial success and pious benevolence as an adult. In both novels, such physical sciences as geology, botany, and astronomy are posed as avenues to religious knowledge. Having praised the efficacy of example in *The Factory Girl,* Savage now invokes a broad range of secular experiences while continuing to minimize the emphasis on theoretical religion.

Savage's early novels are so reflective of the liberal temperament that it is small wonder that even the least religious of them, *James Talbot,* was widely praised in liberal periodicals and that Savage would be selected as the first contributor to the *Scenes and Characters* series. In 1851 William Ware would recall that early Unitarians "discarded in great measure the peculiar language of theology, and uttered tones familiar to the minds of men. They stripped religion of its stern and gloomy aspect, and vindicated its affectionate character, and showed, more fully than had been done before, its intimate connection with the duties of common life."[28] The typical Unitarian sermon, said Ware, was "simple and practical, rather than speculative and metaphysical" (267). Like Frothingham, Ware described the early liberals as doctrinally cautious, anecdotal, cheerful, and actively moral. Savage became the first of several liberals to amalgamate these characteristics and take them to their predictable literary conclusion: secularized religious fiction. Unlike Calvinist novelists of the period, who were trying to keep alive theological debate and proof, Savage blithely sidestepped tradition and concentrated on the duties of common life. The fact that her portraits of ethical orphans resemble the post-1845 novels of Joseph Alden and Susan Warner is telling: it would take the Calvinist novelist three decades of escaping bygone polemicism to reach the confident secularism of the liberal novelist in 1820.

Between 1820 and 1850 fiction, even while it was damned in some quarters, became an established literary form among many New England liberals. Five distinct though often interrelated subgenres of religious fiction emerged during this period.

First was the historical novel about either Puritan times or the eighteenth century. Typical examples of this kind of fiction are Harriet V. Cheney's *A Peep at the Pilgrims* (1824), Lydia Child's *Hobomok* (1824), Catherine Sedgwick's *Hope Leslie* (1827), Hannah F. Lee's *Grace Seymour* (1830), Eliza B. Lee's *Delusion* (1840) and *Naomi* (1848), Sylvester Judd's *Margaret* (1845), and John L. Motley's *Merry-mount* (1849). In these novels, admiration for the heroism of the New England forefathers was usually qualified by a distaste for their intolerance, gloom, and logical rigidity. Fictional history enabled the liberal writer to resolve theological dilemmas of the present by rewriting the past. Unlike Nathaniel Hawthorne, who would exploit Puritan gloom to contravene optimistic views of human nature, the liberal historical novelist typically portrayed a cheerful, ethical protagonist (often a young woman) who wins either a moral or an actual victory over dour Calvinist antagonists. The liberal rebellion against tyranny and enigma that earlier had been veiled in Oriental guise became in these novels more directly anti-Calvinist. Threatened with imprisonment or death by stern Puritans, the protagonist customarily survived by adhering to a simple outlook of good works, aesthetic imagination, and hope.

This conflict is typically seen in Eliza B. Lee's comparison of a group of Puritan inquisitors with the victimized Naomi: on one side, "the metaphysical subtleties, culled from ponderous tomes of the later fathers and the stern authority of their own church. On the other side, the orphan girl, ignorant of all but the wisdom of truth and honesty, unlearned in all but the love of the heart."[29] Though kind and cheerful, the protagonist is rarely weak or timid. Naomi, for example, possesses "a courageous, an almost lion-hearted independence" (230). The redemptive protagonist of these novels is a paradoxical combination of gentleness and strength, sentiment and reasonableness, toleration and firm adherence to principle.

A second type of liberal fiction that appeared after 1820 was the anti-Calvinist novel about contemporary times, as exemplified by Sedgwick's *A New England Tale* (1822), Henry Ware, Jr.'s *The Recollections of Jotham Anderson* (1824), the anonymous *The Parent's Counsellor* (1825), and Sarah H.

Downer's *The Contrast* (1837) and *Triumph of Truth* (1837). The comparatively small number of such novels suggests that liberals wished to eschew open debate with contemporary Calvinists, favoring historical anti-Calvinist portraits or noncontroversial modern stories. The uproar created by Sedgwick's and Ware's early novels seems to have validated the liberal tendency to evasion and indirection in the subversion of orthodoxy. Ware tried to conceal his authorship of *Jotham Anderson* for several years, and when he resumed writing fiction in the 1830s, he carefully avoided mentioning Calvinism. Like Ware, such writers as Sedgwick, Child, Hale, and Judd openly parodied Calvinism in their early works and then retreated to the safer ground of moral exemplum in their later works. Though atypical, the early anti-Calvinist novels are significant examples of liberals' use of fiction to defeat their opponents rhetorically. The fundamental conflict of the anti-Calvinist novel of contemporary times was similar to that of historical novels: a variety of fanatical and rigid Calvinists were pitted against a mild, moral protagonist.

A third and more common type of liberal fiction after 1820 was a variation of *The Soldier's Orphan* and Savage's novels: noncreedal secularized stories of practical religious duty in contemporary settings. Many of the later works of the important liberal novelists were of this type, as were most entries to the *Scenes and Characters* series. Having experimented with open anti-Calvinism in their early works, often with the aid of the visionary devices described earlier in Chapter 2, many liberal writers turned to common ethical experience in their later works. For example, Hannah Lee, having opposed Calvinist theory in the historical *Grace Seymour* (1830), had the heroine of *The Backslider* say that we may "more properly consider action than *belief* as the great end of Christianity."[30] Similarly, in *Three Experiments of Living* (1837), Lee described religious duty as "the language of action, of example."[31] In the eyes of another liberal novelist, Susan A. L. Sedgwick, practical piety consisted of "the union of precept and example," the adherence to morality in "every-day life, and ordinary duties."[32] Often there was little mention of creed or even of God or Jesus in these novels. Believing in man's self-sufficient morality, liberals found in contemporary illustrative fiction an appropriate vehicle for equating faith with proper earthly behavior.

The growing popularity of secular moral stories was accompanied by a fourth kind of liberal fiction, the reformist tale. Although Unitarians were not as universally active in reform as evangelical Calvinists, some liberals of the period were interested in helping the poor, abolishing slavery, and fighting intemperance. Sarah Hale's first novel, *Northwood* (1827), waged war not only on Calvinism but also on slavery. Many of the secular liberal novels of the 1830s borrowed from Calvinist reform novels the device of identifying error with bad habits such as drinking and swearing. For instance, the villain of Eliza C. Follen's *The Skeptic* (1835) is attracted to freethought and whisky; he gives up both after reading Channing at his wife's suggestion.

The most prolific liberal reform novelist of the period was Lucius Manlius Sargent, who wrote twenty-one temperance tales between 1833 and 1843 to prove that the temperance cause was more than just something "gotten up by the Orthodox, the Trinitarians."[33] Sargent was a forerunner of the more popular and less didactically religious Timothy Shay Arthur, whose temperance novels would make up over 5 percent of all American fiction written in the 1840s. In keeping with his liberal views, Sargent noted that such historical foes of alcohol as Mohammed and Samuel Dexter were not Trinitarians. Far from being a sectarian thing, Sargent wrote, temperance is "a broad ground of neutrality" transcending creedal lines (35). Despite his professed generosity to other sects, Sargent was hard on Calvinists and even harder on Irish Catholics, who were usually the drunkards of his novels. Sargent, along with some other liberal reformist novelists of the 1830s, significantly interpreted liberalism's union of precept and example to mean that sin and salvation could be measured in behavioral terms.

The fifth type of post-1820 liberal fiction—allegory—is represented by just one work, D. J. Mandell's *The Adventures of Search for Life* (1838). As we have seen, three Calvinist writers between 1810 and 1840—Botsford, Lummus, and Cheever—attempted imitations of Bunyan, making modifications in the process. But the revisions made by these orthodox writers pale in comparison to Mandell's ironic version of *The Pilgrim's Progress.* Mandell calls his allegory a "Bunyanic Narrative," but he turns both Bunyan and his American imitators on their heads by arguing that the road to heaven is straight and narrow only where it is made so by various types of Calvinists and evangelicals. Bunyan's Slough of Despond is transformed by Mandell into the town of Partialism, where God's wrath and man's total depravity are law. Mandell's liberal protagonist escapes Partialism and makes a perilous journey past the Halls of Methodism, at last reaching the town of Universalism on Mount Everlasting. Because it is allegorical and explicitly anti-Calvinist, Mandell's work may seem an anomaly among post-1830 liberal fiction, which was becoming increasingly more realistic and noncontroversial. But in fact *Search for Life* is as much a product of its time as the secular novels of Sedgwick or Sargent; the liberal disregard for orthodox tradition had gone so far that even Puritan allegory was subject to a Universalist revamping.

In the broadest sense, these five types of post-1820 liberal fiction represent the attempt to make liberalism palatable through entertaining narratives designed to subvert metaphysical theology. At times the attack on contemporary Calvinism was direct and satirical (as in *A New England Tale* and *Jotham Anderson*). But cautious and fearful of heated controversy, many liberals found appropriate modernized replacements for the highly indirect Oriental and visionary tales of the late eighteenth century. In some cases there was an absorption of Oriental and visionary devices into more realistic kinds of fiction: such writers as Savage, Sedgwick, Child, and Judd used such devices in studied attacks on bigotry and gloom. In such anti-Calvinist novels as *The Parent's Counsellor,* direct references are made to Oriental motifs. More often, such devices were translated into more contemporary, secular terms, providing updated analogues to earlier metaphorical conflicts between tyranny and freedom, gloom and joy. Thus, the enslaving Oriental potentate was transformed into the cruel Calvinist stepmother or the repressive Puritan magistrate. The genius bringing assurance of God's benevolence either reappeared in the dreams of the anti-Calvinist protagonists or else were embodied in the angelic heroine herself. In *Search for Life* the allegorical religious journey of Oriental and visionary fiction was made openly anti-Calvinist. More often it was transmuted into determined struggles against persecution, poverty, and grief.

The stamina needed for such religious tests carried overtones of Arminian heroism.[34] To move, as one critic has done, from an account of "the timid exploits of innumerable pale and pious heroines" through a description of liberal writers as either sentimental women or "delicate, even sickly, homebound little boys" to the generalization that American culture was "emasculated" by literary liberalism is to misinterpret the intention and achievement of Unitarian writers.[35] The argument that a strong, masculine Calvinism gave way to a shrinkingly feminine liberalism is almost a reversal of fact. Many prominent liberals saw Calvinism as a repressive system which not only thwarted human effort but created a timid languor and listlessness. William Ellery Channing declared that the doctrines of predestination and human depravity were "destructive of the sense of moral responsibility, degrading man into a chattel slave of Power" rather than elevating him to "a freely obedient son of Love."[36] Orthodoxy, said Channing, nurtures "a slavish spirit of fear." "All is passive," he went on, "both the sin and the deliverance of sin" (245). Upset by Benjamin Constant's definition of religion as "a sigh of weakness," Channing called Christianity *"the spirit of martyrdom,"* "the Courage of pure Love, which is man's strength and special inheritance from God the Father" (190, 5). A great admirer of "powerful delineations of heroic virtue and martyrdom," Channing never wrote a novel but voiced the interests of other liberal authors by composing "imaginary romances . . . in his reveries" which "always had for the hero some one born in adversity and struggling into victory over obstacles" (267). William Ware and O. B. Frothingham made similar remarks about Calvinism's enfeebling repressiveness and Unitarianism's liberating belief in human perfectibility.[37]

A principal literary manifestation of this heroic Arminianism was fiction in which despotic Christianity and pressing daily problems were overcome through persistent confidence in oneself and in God. This theme, which would not be fully developed in Calvinist fiction until the 1840s, appeared in such early liberal fiction as *The Soldier's Orphan* and Sarah A. Savage's pre-1825 works, in which displaced and calumniated orphans heroically endured as a result of cheerful moral activity. Teaching Sunday school for factory workers,

Savage's Mary Burnam is linked to "a general directing an immense army," to "kings" and "military heroes."[38] Another Savage heroine, Phoebe Unwin, emulates "that courageous Peter" by ministering to a sick friend.[39]

After 1820 the heroic theme gathered force and came to be coupled with overt or indirect anti-Calvinism. Orthodoxy, wrote Catherine Sedgwick in her first novel, makes men "languid, and selfish, and careless of their most obvious duties."[40] Sedgwick went on to draw fictional protagonists of growing independence and moral competency. Harriet Cheney's Miriam Grey warns her meddling Puritan father that she is "not so very weak," displaying her "strength and resolution" by marrying the liberal he despises.[41] Sidney Romilly of Sarah Hale's *Northwood* learns that active duty is worthier than fruitless theological contemplation. The heroine of Louisa J. Hall's *Alfred* (1836) is compared to women who "have fortified citadels, and led armies, and commanded empires."[42] Eliza Lee composed her historical novel *Delusion* "to show how circumstances may unfold the inward strength of a timid woman" and to pit "firm integrity against the overwhelming power of the delusion of the period."[43] Another of Lee's female warriors against Puritan tyranny, Naomi, proves that "women have often succeeded in enterprises so dangerous or delicate that men have shrunk from attempting them."[44] In Henry William Herbert's *The Fair Puritan* (1844), the children of a rigid Calvinist are described as "mere passive, listless, senseless, almost soulless, agents of a will to which they bowed."[45] Herbert contrasts these weak products of orthodoxy to two women who are "thinking, active, energetic, and impulsive creatures" who can "support trials . . . better and with more fortitude than sterner and more hardy characters" (30, 198).

One must be careful not to overstate this heroic theme by positing a theory of the masculinization of American religion. It is essential to recognize that liberals were intent on dissolving Calvinism in many ways at once: the theme of heroic Arminianism was aimed specifically at the gloomy, predestinarian, tyrannical side of Calvinism. The logical or excessively intellectual nature of orthodoxy was attacked from a different angle—that of emotionalism and sentimentality. The protagonists of liberal novels had the courage and independence necessary to enact their creators' faith in perfectibility and self-determination; yet they also exhibited a simple, affectionate love of God and his creation which reflected the liberal distaste for logical precision. Proponents of the "feminization" theory exaggerate the latter quality of the liberal imagination while minimizing the former.

In reality, the liberal protagonist was often a paradoxical amalgam of sturdy courage and winning gentleness, reasonableness and warmth, firm adherence to principle and doctrinal caution. As an opponent of such doctrines as depravity and predestination, the protagonist exhibited such "masculine" qualities as strength and perseverance; as a foil to polemical rigidity he or she showed a "feminine" inclination to simplicity and warmth.

Often this paradoxical combination of values resulted in mixed character descriptions. Mrs. L. Larned, for example, tells us that "in Geraldine Sanford were united many rare and almost opposite qualities—to a dignity of mind and nobleness of sentiment much like her mother's, she united a simplicity that was almost infantine."[46] Cheney's Miriam Grey, Sedgwick's Gertrude Clarence, and many other liberal heroines similarly embody almost opposite qualities such as resolve and tenderness. Unlike their theological antagonists, they intuit God's presence with childlike clarity; yet they hold to a belief in human dignity with iron fortitude. The best-known intentionally balanced portrait of the liberal heroine is that of Gertrude Flint in *The Lamplighter* (1854) by the Unitarian Maria Cummins. Gertrude approaches life "with the simplicity of a child, but a woman's firmness; with the stature of a child, but a woman's capacity; the earnestness of a child, but a woman's perseverance." Gertrude possesses "calmness and fortitude," sensitivity and "heroic resolve."[47]

Significantly, as liberal fiction became more realistic and secular and the obstacles to victory more complex and agonizing, the protagonist became accordingly tougher. In eighteenth-century Oriental and visionary tales, the hero had rather passively received the promise of salvation through good works and divine fairness. In the historical and contemporary anti-Calvinist novels between 1815 and 1835, the protagonist had to prove himself through some independent action; but often the author's rhetorical use of such devices as the visionary mode lessened the hero's responsibility. In the increasingly secular and activist novels of the 1830s and 1840s, the protagonist became almost totally self-reliant. By the time Cummins conceived Gertrude Flint, religion in liberal fiction was barely distinguishable from self-help. Experiencing a series of terrible tragedies, Gertrude continues "to experience more and more the power of governing herself ... with each new effort gaining new strength" (131). The benign, passive expectation of angelic comfort on the part of such early liberal heroes as Cassim and Moclou had by 1854 been transformed into the active braving of seemingly insuperable misfortune. In many novels of the 1850s, feeble or ethereal characters like Stowe's Little Eva become incapacitated and die, while equally sensitive but stronger characters like Gertrude Flint survive by observing the code of Arminian heroism in the secular sphere of daily experience.

The combined theme of pious strength and intuition was enhanced in several liberal novels by another anti-Calvinist device, the advocacy of storytelling and poetic embellishment in religious discussion. As we have seen, Calvinist fiction, even though it implicitly opposed logical tradition quite early, never confidently lauded pious storytelling until the 1840s. Liberal fiction, in contrast, heightened its attack on polemical theology almost from the start with praise of imaginative and literary religious instruction. Enos Hitchcock's heroes of the early 1790s, Bloomsgrove and Charles Worthy, make extensive use of religious narrative. Bloomsgrove, convinced that "fear and gloominess" should be excluded from religion, illustrates "the excellence of virtue and religion" to his children by amusing them with "entertaining stories and anecdotes, suited to catch the ear and reach the heart."[48] The stories Bloomsgrove uses to teach religion include a modernized version of the Good Samaritan parable, various anecdotes about good boys and girls, and a Turkish tale with a Christian moral. Worthy also finds stories the "most pleasing, as well as useful" way to communicate religion to his children, "because they interest the feelings of the heart, while the narrative inclines them to read."[49]

Following Hitchcock's lead, Sarah Savage in *The Factory Girl* (1814) portrayed several characters attracted to entertaining rather than theological forms of instruction. When speaking of God or morality, Savage's Mary Burnam "redoubled her exertions to be entertaining, told all the amusing anecdotes her memory would furnish, and, when those failed, had recourse to singing."[50] In this Mary imitates her minister, Seymour, who believes that in religious teaching "the manner and language should be easy and natural; never made wearisome by long lecture, (for it is difficult to keep the attention of a child fixed on one subject,) but instilled by striking, frequent, and incidental hints" (33). Young retells, among other Biblical incidents, "the beautiful and pathetic story of Joseph" in order to make it "more entertaining" (30–31).

Three years after the publication of Savage's novel, Samuel L. Knapp in *Extracts from the Journal of Marshal Soult,* a fictional comment on the Unitarian controversy, praised the general liberal espousal of imaginative religious writing. In Puritan times, Knapp says, a "narrow and rigid" Calvinism had "quenched every poetical spark, and chilled the flow of fancy, and of soul." Knapp was thankful that with the rise of liberalism "this thraldom of mind . . . is now passing, or has passed away, and the powers of taste and imagination are becoming prominent."[51]

Historical and contemporary anti-Calvinist fiction after 1820 amplified this changing emphasis by contrasting anachronistic logical Calvinists with characters preferring amusement to polemics. Cheney's Miriam Grey, who collects colored ribbons and tells pretty stories, is an imaginative foil to the intellectual Puritans who persecute her. Catherine Sedgwick also uses the antithesis in *A New England Tale,* in which the rigidly orthodox Mrs. Wilson is contrasted with a character who declares, "I shall never addict myself to divinity, till Ann Ratcliffe writes sermons, and Tom Moore warbles hymns."[52] The anti-Calvinist heroine of Sedgwick's *Redwood* is taught by a woman who "insinuated moral, and it may be added, religious principles into her mind, in the form of winning stories."[53] Later Sedgwick protagonists such as Hope Leslie, Magawisca, Gertrude Clarence, and Mr. Barclay are similarly fond of narrative religious style, reflecting Sedgwick's own antipathy, as we have seen, to "the splitting of . . . theological hairs" and "utterly useless polemical preaching."

Like Cheney and Sedgwick, the anonymous author of *The Parent's Counsellor* (1825) distinguishes between logical orthodox and imaginative liberal methods of instruction. In the Calvinist Clifford family, "narrative was generally thrown aside by their rigid instructors. Biography was looked upon as rather doubtful. The treatises usually preferred, were wholly didactic."[54] The liberal father of the Newton family, on the other hand, regales his children on the Sabbath with Bible parables, amusing illustrations, and religious stories, including an Oriental tale about the wages of despotism. The choice of the Oriental tale results from the children's Sunday project of "selecting any interesting narrative which they met with in the course of their reading, and proposing it as a subject of general conversation" (65). Combined with the earlier reference to the orthodox Cliffords as being enslaved like "an Algerine captive," their selection of the Baghdad story suggests that the liberal writer is still interested in anti-Calvinist Oriental devices. But the post-1820 liberal author's readiness to subvert orthodox theology through more realistic fiction is shown by the Newtons' next choice for Sunday reading, a long contemporary tale about a pious blacksmith taken from the *Christian Observer*. By 1825 the fictional scope of the liberal author had broadened to include not just Eastern fiction but any "tales from history, or biography, or narrative written in humble imitation of the parables of Christ" (12).

By 1830 pious storytelling was so prevalent a feature of liberal fiction that it would be tedious and redundant to recount all appearances of the theme. Timothy Flint, Sarah Hale, Susan Sedgwick, and Eliza Lee were just a few of the authors who sympathetically depicted imaginative protagonists dismayed with Puritan logic. As early as 1824 the Congregationalist Lydia Hunt Sigourney stated that "the writer of novels" had taken over the department of "Sunday reading."[55] Slightly more conservative than other novelists, Sigourney expressed her fear "that days are coming, when sound doctrine must be stinted, both in weight and measure; and when it will be thought necessary so to refine and gild truth, as to destroy its specific nature" (166).

Indeed, many liberals were devoted to refining and gilding truth through fiction. By 1843 Harriet Beecher Stowe could remark in her preface to *The Mayflower* that the time when to "the religious world, *novel reading* was almost as much an interdicted amusement as dancing and card-playing" had passed, and that "now we can find novels as a part of the clergyman's library, and novel writers publicly eulogized by some of the most influential among our clergy and theological professors."[56]

Although, as we have seen, Calvinist novelists were engaged in freeing themselves of logical restraints, liberal writers made the earliest and most radical departures from polemical tradition. Once Hitchcock's Bloomsgrove and Worthy had essayed to dispel Calvinist gloom through pleasant narrative persuasion, religious storytelling was firmly planted in the liberal imagination.

Henry Ware, Jr., and Fiction

While more could be said about common techniques and themes of early liberal fiction as a whole, it is helpful to trace more closely the career of a single writer, Henry Ware, Jr., to show how the interest in fiction emerged within the Unitarian establishment. In Chapter 2 an analysis of the careers of three typical liberal novelists—Sedgwick, Child, and Judd—revealed a steady process of secularization, epitomized by the progressive dismissal of visionary and anti-Calvinist devices on behalf of practical morality. In this chapter, the process has been connected in both Calvinist and liberal fiction to an overall movement away from the style and the content of traditional orthodox literature.

To turn now to the career of Henry Ware, Jr., is to study manifestations of this secularizing tendency in the writings of one of New England's important liberal ministers before 1850. Although Ware produced only one novel and several short stories, this fiction, as well as the material in Ware's private journals and letters, follows the polemical-to-secular pattern. Perhaps more importantly, the popular novel series commissioned by Ware, *Scenes and Characters Illustrating Christian Truths,* reveals both Ware's and the entire liberal community's interest in secular fiction by the mid-1830s.

Historians have generally overlooked Henry Ware, Jr., while concentrating on his father, the celebrated Hollis professor at Harvard and participant in the famous "Wood 'n' Ware" debate during the Unitarian controversy. Literary scholars, if they study any of the Wares, usually mention Henry's brother William, America's first author of popular Biblical novels. Few have recognized the importance of Henry, who maintained a continual dialogue with his father, his brother, and several liberal novelists of the period about Unitarianism's increasingly secular literary aims. Ware had constant contact with Emerson; he left his pastorship of Boston's Second Church to Emerson in 1829, wrote a poem celebrating Emerson's ordination, and then in 1839, rather dissatisfied with his former comrade, published a rebuttal to the Divinity School Address. Ware's career, at first similar to Emerson's and then quite different from it, therefore provides a convenient Unitarian paradigm in light of which the Transcendentalist revolt may be more fully understood.

Ware's letters and journals reveal his increasing repugnance to polemics and his search for imaginative and practically illustrative replacements for metaphysical theology. As a youth Ware restricted himself to writing within the conventional genres: sermons, poetry, and biography. By 1812 his desire for greater literary latitude was suggested in his comment to his father that Andrews Norton's *General Repository and Review* "ought to have more entertainment and less abstruseness."[57] Like others of the period, he was beginning to fear that liberalism was too dull to be popular. He attributed the wide circulation of a Calvinist periodical, the *Panoplist,* to its "long, and wondrous, and dolorous accounts of conversions, revivals, etc." (I, 47). No friend to orthodoxy, he nevertheless envied its emotional appeal for the masses.

An indication of Henry's search for more diverting liberal genres is his father's warning of 1813 that he curb his "poetic mania" and confine himself to "sober prose" (I, 63). Henry's defensive overreaction to his father's charge is equally telling: Henry felt compelled to explain that he was not "so fond of what is light and entertaining, as to be disgusted with whatever is not of this character," and that "I am not such a simpleton as to expect entertainment merely in the study I am pursuing" (I, 64). Henry's actual feelings became more apparent when his concerned father sent him an outline for a strictly logical sermon. Does not an effective sermon, Henry asked his father in a reply of 1814, depend more "on the skill with which any topic is wrought up, on striking passages, than on the general connexion of the whole?" Does not the traditional homiletic format "leave too little room for that free play and range of thought and imagination, which can give a flow and fascination that nothing else can give?" (I, 69). The elder Ware answered bluntly that Henry was letting his imagination get the best of his logic. Undeterred, Henry went on to complain that in conventional religious writing "there is nothing to *stick* to the fancy,—no entertainment,—no interest" (I, 75). Religion must somehow be made "attractive and forcible" (I, 87).

By 1822 Henry's preferences had become clear. Most people, he wrote William, "really are vastly more pleased to hear even a common-place explanation of an important or curious passage of Holy Writ, than a very logical, philosophical, and elegant discussion of a topic in morals or metaphysical divinity, the use of which they cannot fathom" (I, 161). As a result, Henry developed a strong interest in popular literary genres—extemporaneous preaching, inspirational verse, and fiction.

The fiction Henry wrote between 1824 and 1840, while he was pastor of the Second Church and then professor of Pulpit Eloquence at Harvard, followed the customary liberal pattern of an early attack on Calvinism followed by secular exempla. His only novel, *The Recollections of Jotham Anderson* (1824), a determined attack on orthodoxy, was followed by a series of noncontroversial short pieces on self-culture which appeared sporadically through the 1820s and 1830s.

Jotham Anderson, like the first novels of many other liberals, was purgatively anti-Calvinist. In 1819 Ware had written Channing of his agreement with the latter's idea that America needed "good books and tracts, exposing the errors of Calvinism" (I, 133). But Ware's intrinsic fear of controversy led him to treat the topic with delicacy. His one objection to Catherine Sedgwick's *A New England Tale* was that the wicked Mrs. Wilson was too glaring a caricature of orthodoxy. Sedgwick's representation of Calvinist ideas "in their most bold and pernicious form" through Mrs. Wilson is "very well, and doubtless a picture to the life," Ware commented in his review of the book.[58] But more effective than such open attack would have been the portrayal of a moderate Calvinist whose "barren notions" are "neutralized by the great and essential principles of religion" (206). This would show "how the simple and essential truths of Christ, when made living principles of action, are capable of triumphing over those dangerous dogmas, crushing their powers, and destroying their poison" (207).

A year after this review Ware gave Sedgwick and other liberals a lesson in anti-Calvinist strategy in *Jotham Anderson.* In the novel Ware converts Sedgwick's intractable Mrs. Wilson into more receptive Calvinists, Mr. and Mrs. Hilson, who come to admire Jotham's equanimity while learning to despise the orthodoxy they once held dear. Ware portrays other educable Calvinists who discover in themselves an underlying repugnance to Trinitarian theology. Jotham himself, educated to view Arminianism as a "monstrous thing," after close study finds, to his "inexpressible surprise," that "I was not, and never had been, a Trinitarian."[59] Jotham asserts that "the large majority of those educated in the orthodox faith are no more truly Trinitarian than I was, though they imagine themselves to be." Most Calvinists "have been Unitarians all their lives without knowing it" (57).

By adopting the redeemed Calvinist persona in Jotham, Ware is able to neutralize orthodox dogma from within rather than lashing it from without as Sedgwick had. This strategy in turn enables Ware to depict sentimentally the tragic results of an adherence to false doctrine. At one point Jotham feels "most distressingly bewildered in the contradictions about depravity and accountability, irresistible grace, involuntary faith . . . It was a wilderness to me; I turned on every side, and could find no relief" (21). Besides describing Jotham's perplexity, Ware has a Calvinist preacher, Dunbar, miserably drink himself to death and a layman, Garstone, lose all faith, becoming "anxious, melancholy, fitful, unsettled; an unbeliever, yet longing to believe" (65). In addition, Ware presents several victimized Arians, poor virtuous people who remain cheerful despite the calumny of Calvinists. In short, Ware attacks intellectual religion with the rhetorical devices of nonintellectual sentimental fiction. While we hear that Jotham studies two "long and painful" years to validate Unitarian theory, we are given no samples of his scholarship on this pivotal subject. Ware simply has Jotham say, "It would take too much room to detail the progress of my experience at this time" (57). Ware has neutralized Calvinism with weapons other than logic, proving himself both sentimental and cautious.

A year after the appearance of *Jotham Anderson* in *Christian Register* installments and in bound form, Ware wrote a friend: "I hear that it is reported at Martha's Vineyard, that I wrote 'Jotham Anderson.' Do you know anything about it? . . . My impartial judgement would lead me to decide it can't be I; for I don't see how in the world I could find time for it now, while I am writing tales for children, and carrying a volume of sermons through the press. My impression, therefore, is that the folks at Edgarton Old-town must be a little mistaken."[60] This curious statement, whether playful or serious, reveals Ware's inclination to sidestep controversy by hiding anonymously behind the mask of fiction. In 1811 his father had advised him "to treat all persons and opinions on religious subjects with great delicacy,—and be deliberate, cautious, and conscientious in forming your own" (I, 38). After years of mild contretemps with his father over entertainment in religion, Henry took his father's advice to its natural literary end—strategically crafted religious fiction whose authorship he could deny. By 1838, as we have seen, an even more cautious Henry would be extolling to William the opportunity in fiction for committing nobody, yet taking all.

After *Jotham Anderson,* Ware made a further retreat from controversy by writing wholly secular stories of pious poor boys and self-determined families. Next to tales like "Robert Fowle" (1825), "How to Spend a Day" (1838), and "David Ellington" (1839), *Jotham Anderson,* as sentimentally circuitous as it may appear, is forthrightly intellectual. Anti-Calvinism, or indeed theoretical discussion of any sort, is excluded from Ware's later fiction. As a professor of homiletics during this period, Ware was stressing the preacher's need for "making experiments, trying new combinations, arrangements—*artifices,* if you will," for "bringing to [religion's] service all subjects of human interest; . . . you cannot go too far, nor gather too widely" (II, 138, 260). This experimental outlook was directed toward the discovery not of divine truths but of earthly illustrations. While calling as a professor for an interest in "all subjects of human interest," as the author of *On the Formation of the Christian Character* (1829) Ware was recommending entry into common and secular affairs. The metaphysical subtleties that had bewildered Jotham Anderson and Ware himself were being overcome by a return to daily experience and practical activity.

Reflecting this increasingly secular tendency, Ware's fiction after *Jotham Anderson* concentrates on morality and self culture. "Robert Fowle" anticipates Horatio Alger by showing a poor boy's rise to respectability and wealth. In "A Sabbath with My Friend" the effectiveness of Sunday worship is said to rely not on the content of the sermon but rather on a family's preparation for and follow-up to the sermon. On the Sabbath the pious Benson family rises early, eats a light breakfast, reads together, goes to church, and then returns home to "improve" the sermon in familiar conversation. This "wise arrangement of the day" makes Sunday service, which otherwise might be "commonplace, dull," seem "both pleasant and sacred."[61] Religious truth has become dependent on secular behavior. This theme is even more apparent in Ware's five stories of 1838–40 about a hardy young mechanic, David Ellington. Indifferent to dogma, Ellington is concerned solely with moral practice. In one story a friend confesses to him, "I don't know that all the sermons I have ever heard, have done me the least good in the world."[62] Ellington smilingly agrees and goes on to say that rather than worry about a sermon's doctrinal content, we must "turn its advice into real practical rules" (75). In another story Ellington gives a shiftless acquaintance a copy of Channing's "Self-Culture," recommending manly diligence and constant activity. Elsewhere Ellington exhibits industrious and frugal habits which help him get on in the world. What is most notable about these tales is their complete lack of theological discussion or otherworldly speculation. Having disposed of Calvinism in *Jotham Anderson,* Ware finds in his later fiction the safest answer to theoretical dilemmas: religious practice.

By the 1830s, therefore, Ware's early quest for entertaining and practical replacements for metaphysical theology had brought him to a confidence in fiction. His high regard for the genre was evidenced by his proposal in 1834 that a religious story collection be written by several liberal novelists and distributed widely. In this "series of narratives, between a formal tale and a common tract," he wrote in a letter to Catherine Sedgwick, religion would be promoted "more efficiently than in many sermons."[63] This proposal resulted in *Scenes and Characters Illustrating Christian Truths,* which came to include the following works: Sarah Savage's *Trial and Self-Discipline* (1835), Catherine Sedgwick's *Home* (1835), Eliza Cabot Follen's *The Skeptic* (1835), Hannah Farnhum Lee's *The Backslider* (1835), and Louisa J. Hall's *Alfred* (1836). These novels, heralded by Channing as the initiators of a new era in literature, were quite popular in the Northeast. They indicated a concerted effort on the part of Boston liberals, under the direction of one of their most respected leaders, to produce a body of fiction that would illustrate liberal principles in entertaining, noncontroversial, and secular fashion. If, as O. B. Frothingham said, Ware's *On the Formation of the Christian Character* was the *Imitatio* of American Unitarian essays, his *Scenes and Characters* may well be called the *Pilgrim's Progress* of liberal fiction.

Ware's stated object for the novels was "to present familiar illustrations of some of the most important practical principles of religion, and to show, by an intermixture of narrative and discussion, how they operate in the government of the heart and life."[64] Seemingly vague, this statement in fact prepares for the entire series by setting forth the combined themes of liberal fiction since 1810: practical principles of religion are to predominate over theology; a mixture of narrative and discussion is to supplant logic; the operation of faith in the heart and life will sentimentalize and secularize religious commentary.

Ware's regulations were observed by the five writers, most of whom were practiced liberal novelists. Significantly, the least experienced author, Follen, contributed the most polemical piece; *The Skeptic* is an extended effort to refute freethought through Unitarian argument coupled with pietistic sentiment. The other writers, having done away with religious opponents in their early novels, entered the less controversial arenas of domestic culture and pious social effort. The most common plot was analogous to that which had been introduced by Savage before 1820 and which would be repeated by later novelists: a young protagonist, through self-confidence and submission, triumphs over such potentially devastating calamities as the death of loved ones, poverty, and the moral degeneracy of friends.

As in previous and later Unitarian fiction, there is in these novels little sickly or feeble religion. Ware's *On the Formation of the Christian Character* had set the stage for the heroic theme of these novels by castigating Calvinism's tendency "to supersede human exertion" and to provide "a reason for indolence and religious neglect."[65] Instead of complaining of human weakness and awaiting God's grace, Ware wrote, one must realize "that a man's own labors are essential to his salvation" (30). Religion for Ware was not a matter of listless retreat but rather of soldiership and action. Thus, Ware converted meditation into "the surveying and burnishing of the warrior's arms" and religious practice into "the daily drill of the soldier" (80, 149).

This code is enacted in *Scenes and Characters* by various resolute protagonists. Sarah Savage's heroine comes to prize "the struggles of the good," holding that "the harder they are, the more strength a person gains."[66] Hannah Lee's Anna Hope calls Christianity "a state of watchfulness and warfare," emphasizing that "we have weapons given us and instructions how to use them, and it is because we are unfaithful to ourselves, if we do not gain the victory."[67] Witnessing a friend's tragic backsliding into infidelity and crime, Anna faces "affliction with the high hopes and unfailing strength of a Christian" (83). Similarly, Louisa Hall's Matilda Brinley, who is compared to women who have "led armies," resolutely endures a brother's dissipation and advises him that "strength alone" will save him.[68]

The praise of human effort in these novels is accompanied by a deemphasis of creed, of church, and even of God and the Bible. Again, Ware's *On the Formation of the Christian Character* had anticipated the novelists' priorities by pointing out the deficiencies of theology and public worship while extolling self-created doctrine and individual activity. Critics of Unitarianism from Catholics to Calvinists often charged liberals with a disbelief in God and an overconfidence in man; Orestes Brownson once remarked that Channing had made man a little God and God a little man. God and Christ are sometimes mentioned in *Scenes and Characters,* but usually they are presented as last resorts for imperiled characters rather than as omnipotent determinants of human life. The novelists are more interested in the strength created by the God within the human soul than in the dependency resulting from the operation of the divine from without. As Hall puts it, the "creative power" of religion "not only arouses dormant energies, it not only awakens deep, powerful, permanent feelings; it is the Deity himself stirring within" (77). In *The Backslider,* Lee declares "that religion is not mere belief in God or in the Scriptures, but is the putting that belief into effective operation in the constant and daily concerns of life" (29). The devaluation of belief, God, and the Scriptures trembles on the edge of relinquishing the central tenets of Christianity.

It is perhaps no accident that so much space is devoted to the discussion of freethought in *Scenes and Characters*. Ostensibly designed to refute infidelity, such novels as *The Skeptic* and *The Backslider* verge, consciously or not, on agreeing with deism's disparagement of Biblical miracles, revelation, and the need for salvation through Christ. When Follen's Ralph Vincent, an afficionado of Paine and Fanny Wright, calls Biblical miracles absurd, the Christian heroine does not confidently deny his claim; rather, she equivocates by pointing to the ongoing miracle of nature. When Ralph denies Christ's divine authority, the pious blind girl, Fanny, circumvents the issue by saying that we may simply admire Jesus "because he was so good."[69] Likewise, Lee's Anna laments a skeptic's disbelief in the afterlife yet stresses an earthly faith of active morality, as if she tacitly agrees with the skeptic.

It is a small step from the religion of *Scenes and Characters* to Emerson's dismissal of historical Christianity on behalf of self-reliance, nature, and the view of Jesus as an expression of divine humanity: a small step, perhaps, but a momentous one that most Unitarians were not prepared to take. Follen could value natural more than Biblical miracles without surrendering herself to the currents of Universal Being described by Emerson in the "transparent eyeball" passage in *Nature* (1836).[70] Hall and Lee could displace creed with human effort without reaching Emerson's triumphant assertion of individual capabilities in "Self-Reliance" (1841). All the novelists could oppose tyrannical orthodoxy without moving, as did Emerson in his Divinity School Address (1838), from an indictment of "this eastern monarchy of a Christianity, which indolence and fear have built" to a sublime exaltation of man as wonderworker.[71] Their ministerial mentor, Henry Ware, Jr., had placed a high premium on individual discovery of religious truth in *On the Formation of the Christian Character*. But Ware, like the novelists themselves, was not ready to repudiate tradition altogether by moving toward Emerson's original relation to the universe. Although engaged in overturning religious and literary norms, Ware and his followers refused to translate this quiet rebellion into Emersonian nonconformity and self-reliance.

It is understandable, therefore, that Ware, the early colleague of Emerson, would in the late 1830s criticize the Divinity School Address and would write the sober David Ellington tales, whose focus on small daily activities contrast strikingly with Emerson's exuberant flights into the Oversoul. Ware became one of several liberal writers to complain of Transcendentalism's foggy nature. Indeed, the entire movement of American liberal fiction was away from visionary fantasy toward the portrayal of the sort of earthly activity that Emerson would consign to the accidental world of the Understanding. In the

1830s, when Emerson and Thoreau were beginning to contemplate truths transcending selfhood and factual experience, lesser writers were awakening from the visionary dream into a world in which quotidian reality was imbued with divine meaning.

The old question of why Transcendentalists avoided novel writing may thus in part be answered by the fact that native religious fiction was moving progressively toward the earthly precisely when Transcendentalism wished to reaffirm the metaphysical. Commenting in 1841 on "The Unitarian Movement in New England," the Transcendental organ, the *Dial,* disparaged liberalism as part of the post-Lockean "sensuous philosophy" which "recognizes no source of ideas but the senses."[72] Significantly, one of the rare short stories in the *Dial,* "The Two Dolons" (1842), contrasts a misled materialist with his dreamy son. Criticizing his son as "visionary and romantic," the elder Dolon does "not see that the so-called visionary was as real to the inner sense, as the so-called real is to the outer sense."[73] In spite of his father's demands for "practical" endeavor, the boy devotes himself to "quiet and passive" contemplation of nature, nurturing an "instinctive quiet consciousness, as if God had put into his soul a celestial flower-plant on which were little fairies" (121).

This story mirrors Emerson's desire to become a transparent eyeball in Nature, as well as Thoreau's withdrawal from the practical world of human society to Walden. At the same time, it recalls the liberal visionary fiction of the 1790s while contrasting markedly with the increasingly activist liberal fiction of the 1830s and 1840s. While "The Two Dolons" describes quiet and passive visionary musing in semi-Transcendental fashion, liberal fiction of the period dramatized constant moral activity in home and in human society.

In light of the secularizing pattern of both orthodox and liberal fiction, it is understandable that two major best-sellers of the 1850s—*The Wide, Wide World* by the Presbyterian Susan Warner and *The Lamplighter* by the Unitarian Maria Cummins—are religiously similar. To be sure, Warner places slightly greater stress on depravity and conversion than does the liberal Cummins. But both authors show that denominational affiliation had by the 1850s become inconsequential for the Protestant novelist. The large differences between earlier orthodox and liberal fiction—between *The Art of Courting* and *Bloomsgrove* or between *Charles Observator* and *The Factory Girl*—have given way in the later novels to a commonly nonsectarian piety of love, emotion, and endurance. The choice of metaphors for religious activity in both novels is virtually identical: Warner's Ellen lets her rush-light shine just as Cummins' Gertrude lights the lamp of faith in the darkness of the world. The briefly sketched settings and minor characters of most earlier religious novels have been expanded into a complex tapestry of shifting scenes and psychological influences which demand both sensitivity and self-sufficient strength on the part of the pious heroine. Static visionary contemplation and logical exposition have been almost entirely left behind. The orthodox and the liberal novelist, after all their previous differences in literary intention and performance, in the 1850s at last make a common entry into the wide, wide world of common and secular affairs.

5
Biblical Fiction

Because Biblical fiction has become so prominent a feature of American popular culture since the Civil War, it may be difficult to imagine the time before 1845 when such fiction represented a radical departure from traditional treatments of the Bible. In this chapter, I shall consider the emergence of American Biblical fiction from its exploratory beginnings to its growing popularity after 1835.

I use the term "Biblical fiction" to include two separable but closely related types of stories: those based on the experiences of Christ's early followers, usually Christian martyrs in Rome up to A.D. 3, and those based on the Bible itself. Within the latter kind of Biblical fiction, New Testament narratives figure most strongly in my discussion, since Old Testament fiction did not become important until Joseph H. Ingraham's last two novels, which were published after 1855.

As a result of Christians' deeply rooted view of the Bible as sacred and inviolable, Biblical fiction appeared later and in lesser quantity than other kinds of religious fiction. Some Biblical novels and stories were written between 1825 and 1835, but it was not until William Ware's novels of the late 1830s that such fiction gained a wide audience. Yet the inclination to fictionalize the Bible was evident in America as early as the 1780s; and though it took several decades for this impulse to reach literary fruition, the fiction itself cannot be fully understood without an account of the shifts in Biblical interpretation during this preparatory period.

The fact that Biblical fiction was a relatively late outgrowth of New England liberalism gives further proof of the progressive secularization of pre-1850 religious fiction in general; only after the pioneering efforts of Oriental-tale writers, followed by the more contemporary fiction of Calvinists and liberals, did American writers dare to begin the conversion of the sacrosanct Christian text into mass entertainment.

Polishing God's Altar

O. B. Frothingham called Boston Unitarians the first Americans who took "a poetical instead of a dogmatical view" of the Bible.[1] This statement, which Frothingham did not fully explain, is only partly accurate. Unitarians did become the first significant religious body to deemphasize dogma on behalf of poetics, but they were preceded by several Americans, ranging from the Calvinist Timothy Dwight to the deist Benjamin Franklin, who experimented with poetical Biblical interpretations well before the rise of Boston liberalism. Thus, the Unitarian embellishments of the Bible constituted neither a sudden nor a wholly innovative break with the past; rather, they were part of a shift in some religious quarters from Biblical hermeneutics to Biblical aesthetics, a movement that began in the late eighteenth century. The liberals were the first to make a concerted shift from the modifications of earlier writers to the creation of Biblical fiction. In the 1850s they would be joined by orthodox Biblical novelists.

Before the American Revolution, it was generally considered sacrilegious either to tamper with the Bible or to heap excessive praise on its stylistic merits or its sentimentally appealing qualities. As the Word of God, the Bible needed no improvement. The editors of *The Bay Psalm Book* (1640) were careful to attempt an accurate literal translation of the Psalms in order to avoid taking "liberty or poetical license to depart from the true and proper sense of David's words in the Hebrew verses." As John Cotton explained, "we have respected rather a plain translation, then to smooth our verses with the sweetness of any paraphrase, and so have attended conscience rather then elegance, fidelity rather then poetry." As a result, the verses of *The Bay Psalm Book* are intentionally simple, unadorned, and, on occasion, a bit awkward:

> The Lord to me a shepherd is,
> Want therefore shall not I.
> He in the folds of tender-grass,
> Doth cause me down to lie.[2]

The Bay Psalm Book's prohibition against Biblical embellishment was widely accepted by orthodox clergymen at least until the Revolution and was complemented by other calls for respect for the Bible. In 1739 George Whitefield voiced the typical conservative attitude by asserting that the Bible is "the grand Character of our Salvation" and by stressing "the Danger, Sinfulness, and Unsatisfactoriness of reading any other than the Book of God."[3] Jonathan Edwards, to counteract an Arian tendency to glorify the human Jesus, stated that to overemphasize the history of Jesus' life was to reduce the Bible to the level of tragic romance and to remain in the realm of unregenerate nature. Edwards' followers, particularly Nathaniel Emmons and Samuel Hopkins, amplified this attitude into a vehement condemnation of Arians who desired greater latitude in Biblical interpretation.

Edwards' grandson, Timothy Dwight, was one of the first prominent American ministers to shift the emphasis to a more literary understanding of the Bible. In "A Dissertation on the History, Eloquence, and Poetry of the Bible," delivered at his Yale commencement in 1772, Dwight studied the Scriptures as a poetic, imaginative piece of "fine writing" comparable to the best works of classical and English authors.[4] In the Bible Dwight found consummate examples of pastoral poems, odes, elegies, epics, and allegories. The Bible, in Dwight's eyes, is full of "the boldest metaphors, the most complete images, and the most lively descriptions" as well as "an endless variety of incidents and characters" and "every embellishment of human nature" (546, 548–549). Words like "pathetic," "charming," "engaging," "fanciful" occur often in the "Dissertation," as Dwight focuses on captivating Biblical scenes and passages. Unlike Edwards, who decried external imagination while lauding inward religious affections, Dwight finds that the writers of the Bible "sensible that the Imagination is the principal inlet to the Soul, and that it is more easily enkindled than the Passions ... passed by no occasion for engaging its assistance" (548).

Although in the 1790s a more conservative Dwight would qualify his youthful innovations by calling for more traditional readings of the Bible, his "Dissertation" symbolized the late eighteenth century's growing fascination with those entertaining and secular Biblical features that Puritanism had tried to underplay. Because Dwight was a moderate Calvinist, he was more prepared than previous orthodox leaders to accept the view that the Bible was written by men who made rhetorical use of common literary devices.

More than this, Dwight went on to indicate that the contemporary author could emulate Biblical writers in poetry of his own. By modernizing the Book of Joshua in *The Conquest of Canaan* (1785), Dwight again evidenced distaste for the Puritan proscription of Biblical improvements. Not only did Dwight revise the story of Joshua's military adventures to make it more exciting and heroic, but he also transformed the plain Biblical text into ornate verse with a regular meter and rhymed couplets. While Dwight stressed the wide "gulf" between novels and the Bible, he initiated the kind of aesthetic appreciation and poetic refurbishment of the Bible which eventually would help give rise to American Biblical fiction.

Attempts to adapt the Bible to late-eighteenth-century literary tastes were made by other writers as well. In 1786 Joseph Lathrop followed the example of Dwight's *Canaan* by translating passages from the Old and New Testaments into smooth rhymed verse. In contrast to the authors of *The Bay Psalm Book,* Lathrop did not shrink from adding rhythmic elegance to the original, even if it meant a slight change of meaning:

> God is my shepherd, by whose care
> I'm safely kept, when danger's near;
> He, with unweary'd goodness, grants,
> Constant supplies to all my wants.[5]

Soon a few more familiar authors, not all of them known for their religious fervor, joined the move to Biblical embellishment. Before beginning his "Rhapsodist" series, the young Charles Brockden Brown sharpened his writing skills by reworking a part of the Book of Job and some of the Psalms. Benjamin Franklin wrote a rationalist imitation of the Lord's Prayer. In the 1790s Thomas Jefferson worked on a simplified version of the New Testament in an attempt to retrieve the "unsophisticated doctrines" of "the unlettered Apostles."[6]

Brown, Franklin, and Jefferson—like Dwight in his youthful period—were applying Enlightenment optimism about man's capabilities toward a new approach to the Bible. Whereas colonial thinkers like Whitefield had held that totally depraved man had neither the right nor the power to improve on "the grand Character of our Salvation," these later writers began to suggest that the Bible sometimes needed abridgement or alteration and that man was fully capable of getting the job done.

Enos Hitchcock's two novels of the early 1790s, which as we have seen were seminal instances of anti-Calvinism through the visionary mode and anecdotal religious instruction, carried the tendency to embellish the Bible a step further toward Biblical fiction. Hitchcock's Bloomsgrove and Worthy emphasize to their children the Bible's entertaining qualities. They also retell scriptural incidents in familiar language. The Bible, says Bloomsgrove, is "filled up with such a variety of incidents and interesting events, as to combine in one view, all the advantages of character and sentiment, description and precept; to paint the different shades of virtue and vice in real life and genuine character. All the human passions, with their various operations, are unfolded in the numerous scenes exhibited, and the picture presented to the heart through the medium of the imagination." Through "the agreeableness of the narrative and its instructive tendency," the Bible "cannot fail to entertain, to please, and ennoble the mind of the attentive reader."[7] Bloomsgrove's pleasure in interesting events, human passions, and agreeable narrative verges on an exclusion of the Bible's divine meaning and an exaltation of its human attractions. Hitchcock virtually reduces Holy Writ to a sentimental novel with moral overtones.

Hitchcock's next hero, Worthy, outdoes Bloomsgrove by fabricating amusing descriptions of the daily life and physiognomy of Biblical characters. This method "afforded [Worthy's children] amusement, while it conveyed useful sentiments to the heart."[8] Although Hitchcock did not write Biblical fiction, he came closer than any other writer before 1800 to placing the Bible in the realm of sentimental amusement and fictional imagination.

After the turn of the century, the emphasis on the Bible's aesthetic and human appeal was amplified. In his Oriental tale *Letters of Shahcoolen* (1801), Benjamin Silliman compared the Hindu Gitgovinda to the Song of Solomon in order to point up the poetic elegance and sensuous richness of effective religious texts. In *The Asylum* (1811) Isaac Mitchell became the first of several American authors to defend novel writing by citing the use of diverting stories by Old Testament prophets and by Jesus himself.

Six years later, a contributor to the Unitarian *Christian Disciple* felt compelled to designate "Popular Reasons for Studying the Scriptures." According to the essayist, the Bible can be exciting for "the mass of readers" as a result of its entertaining miracles, its easy style, and its practical anecdotes, all of which will "awaken the curiosity of the most sluggish mind."[9] In 1819 the *American Monthly* ran a review of a work identified as *"Conversations on the Bible—By a Lady"* that flatly stated that "the Bible . . . requires something besides its intrinsic value, something besides its multiplied commentaries to make it entirely intelligible." In the reviewer's eyes, "Much remains to be done, to make this venerable volume yet more interesting, and to diffuse its spirit more widely, by rendering its narrative more clear."[10] The reviewer admits that the Bible "cannot be touched without mutilation" and "that any altered representation must be tarnished by comparison with the inimitable, and perfect beauty of the original" (180). But the review's respect for the original becomes lost in an attraction to the anonymous author's use of pathos and incident to make the Bible "more interesting." Praising the author's sentimental retelling of the Joseph story, the reviewer calls the Bible a well-written but potentially unexciting work which can use the assistance of literary "stage effect" (181).

After 1820 praise of the Bible's entertaining features and acceptance of Biblical paraphrase came with greater frequency and from increasingly respectable sources. The novelist John Neal as a youth had learned to equate Bible stories with "the stories I met with in a score of other books."[11] In *Seventy-Six* (1822) Neal had a character define a novel as "any tale . . . like the parables of our Saviour—the fables of men."[12] In 1827 the *American Quarterly,* reviewing "Early American Poetry," dismissed *The Bay Psalm Book* as homely, common, and unnatural, recommending the more polished versions of Biblical poetry by recent British and American writers.[13] Two years later the same magazine damned "the dull quaintness, and grotesque fustian" of Puritan Biblical poetry as "sheer nonsense," praising the smooth lyrics of several Boston liberals.[14] Samuel L. Knapp in his landmark *Lectures on American Literature* (1829), arguing that an elegant style could help free Americans "from the fetters of bigotry and the prudery of excessive puritanism," identified the Bible as the paradigm of "every species of writing from the simplest narrative to the most affecting tragedy."[15]

In the 1830s Jacob Abbott brought the spirit of Biblical improvement into the heart of the Boston establishment. His *The Young Christian* (1832), which became a widely read manual of liberal nurture, recommended a practical as opposed to a theological reading of the Bible. In defense of his own heavy reliance on secular anecdotes to illustrate religion, Abbott wrote: "This book is not more full of parables than were the discourses of Jesus Christ. I shelter myself under his example."[16] The Bible, Abbott noted, can be extremely problematic for those who study it from the vantage point of theology or strict historicism. Theorists must expect "difficulties, insuperable difficulties" in the Gospels, so that it is better "to repose quietly in . . . acknowledged ignorance" and concentrate on the simple morality advised by Jesus (109). Not only is the Bible difficult, Abbott continues, but it can become boring for those who are too familiar with it: "Every phrase comes upon the ear like an oft-told tale, but it makes a very slight impression upon the mind" (226). To remedy both the theoretical inconsistencies and the potential dullness of the Bible, Abbott advised imagining *"the real scene"* of the Gospels and describing this scene in striking, familiar terms. In this way the creative father can take "his family to some elevation in the romantic scenery of Palestine, from which they might overlook the country of Galilee," which "will probably make a much stronger and more lasting impression than merely reading . . . the simple language of the Bible" (228). For Abbott, as for some Americans who were beginning to write Biblical fiction in the 1830s, revisiting the real scene of the Bible helped to resolve complex theological questions by evading them and to alleviate the possible dullness of hackneyed passages.

Therefore, by the time such novelists as Sylvester Judd and Harriet Beecher Stowe called for literary interpretations of the Bible, the movement to Biblical paraphrase was well under way. In an essay on "The Dramatic Effects of the Bible" (c.1845) Judd noted that the Bible "contains all that is sublime in tragedy, terrible in guilt, or intense in pathos." With "a magnificence of plot all its own," said Judd, the Bible makes "the ravings of Lear, and the agonies of Othello" seem pale.[17] Closer to the spirit of the times was Stowe, who in her preface to her brother Charles's *The Incarnation* (1849) expanded on Abbott's idea that the Bible needed secular embellishment to be made interesting. Stowe wrote: "One of the principal difficulties realized by those who wish to bring themselves under the influence of the Bible . . . is that want of freshness and reality which is caused by early and long-continued familiarity with its language."[18] Describing those who find reading the Bible a "wearisome task," Stowe went on: "In vain they ponder its pages; nothing is suggested; and while words known by heart from childhood pass under their eye, their mind wanders in dreamy vacancy." What is needed, said Stowe, is a creative "blending together [of] the outlines of truth and fiction," as well as imaginative "appliances of geographical, historical, and critical knowledge" (iv). Stowe would have the novelist stop short only at minute descriptions of Jesus' physical person.

In sum, the path was broken for Biblical fiction. While many Americans, particularly evangelical Calvinists and New England seminarians, maintained the traditional notion of the Bible as inviolate and sacrosanct, a growing number of liberals and litterateurs were modifying this notion. For some, the Bible was a high example of such common genres as poetry, drama, and fiction, an example to be followed in contemporary imaginative literature. For others, the Bible had become clay in the hands of the creative writer.

Several theological and cultural changes contributed to this view of the Bible as poetic and pliable. The decline of the strict Calvinist doctrine of God's otherness and man's depravity resulted in an increasing faith in man's ability to judge and even improve the Bible. The rise of Arianism and Socinianism was accompanied by an admiration for the human, historical Jesus, an admiration which Edwardsean Calvinists had called idolatry of mere nature. Attacks on the Bible by skeptics like Voltaire and Paine—coupled with the historical criticism of Hermann Reimarus, David Strauss, and Ernest Renan—weakened traditional assumptions about the Bible as the Word of God above human history. In Jacob Abbott's words, "insuperable difficulties" had arisen which could be best overcome by the imaginative recreation of Biblical times. Combined with the widely favored Common Sense outlook that practical experience was more reliable than metaphysical inquiry, such a recreation could summon up the real scene of the Bible while setting aside troublesome theoretical questions. Also, there were complaints from some quarters that the Bible was antiquated and dull. Some adapted the Bible to modern demands by defending its entertaining features; others thought sentimental and historical stage effect was needed to make the Bible more interesting.

In the hands of an Emerson or a Bushnell, such tendencies would help engender original, truly aesthetic interpretations of the Bible as a poetic artifact. In the hands of lesser thinkers, it gave rise to polished Biblical verse and fiction which refurbished the Bible in the interest of making it more engaging and real. In short, Biblical fiction provided a creative outlet for believers in human dignity, a short cut for historians, a solace for baffled theorists, and a diversion for bored Bible readers.

The Rise of Biblical Fiction

The earliest Biblical fiction in America—New Testament and Christian martyr narratives—began to appear in the late 1820s and increased in number through the 1830s and 1840s, to be joined by the more secular Old Testament novel in the 1850s.

Before 1825, however, there was a precursor to these familiar types of Biblical fiction—that is, imaginary dialogues about the Bible between parents and their children. Such dialogues were an exploratory way of introducing free interchange and relaxed discussion of Biblical topics without contravening Puritan propriety through actual fictionalization of the Bible. At first, the dialogues took the inchoate form of small episodes in novels of domestic culture. The familiar Biblical conversations that Hitchock's Bloomsgrove and Worthy had with their children are the earliest instances of these episodes in American fiction. A few of Susanna Rowson's novels written between 1795 and 1815 also contain dialogue scenes, as does Sarah Savage's *The Factory Girl* (1814).

After 1815 the dialogue episode was expanded to a book-length format which permitted more detailed Biblical discussion while offering greater opportunity for embellishment of the original. The *American Monthly* review of *Conversations on the Bible* (1817) noted that such long dialogues had been published in England since 1770 and asked American writers to follow the British example. In response to growing demand, in 1822 the novelist and teacher Susanna Rowson published a massive volume entitled *Biblical Dialogues Between a Father and His Family: Comprising Sacred History, From the Creation to the Death of Our Saviour Christ . . . The Whole Carried on in Conjunction with Profane History.*

Rowson's two-volume work epitomizes the various impulses to embellish the Bible that would lead to the writing of Biblical fiction. The book is a prolonged effort at improving the Bible—improving it by mixing sacred and profane history, by smoothing over potentially crippling contradictions and problems, by adding local color through geographical descriptions and scientific data. In her preface Rowson explains that she undertook this "herculean labor" as result of her students' bewilderment with the Bible and her own secular preferences. She recalls "the time, when to my own uninformed mind the world of the Bible, and the world of which I felt myself an inhabitant, were two distinct worlds."[19] She describes her dialogues as an effort to draw the divine and human worlds together in a mutually dependent center. She confesses that many of her students were wont to read the Bible "with perfect indifference," remaining "bewildered and confused in their ideas" (I, iv). Besides making the Bible more entertaining, dialogues are of "infinite benefit to the young, the ignorant, or weak-minded, . . . for answering the objections of skepticism, and turning aside the shafts of self-confident wit" (v).

Rowson is here stating explicitly what would become the tacit basis of later American Biblical fiction. Because the spiritual seems incomprehensible or distant, the profane world can be consulted for the assurances of secular additions. Because the Bible may seem dull, a lively interchange between a father and his children can add emotion and interest. Because skeptics have threatened to invalidate the Bible, a simplification of the Bible for these "young" and "weak-minded" readers can help the writer evade serious intellectual debate on thorny theoretical issues.

Rowson's dialogues consist of a series of conversations about the Old and New Testaments between Justinian Alworth, a Connecticut gentleman of modest fortune and aristocratic manners, and his five children: Horatio, the eldest and most critical; Amy, the youngest and most faithful; Charilea, the oldest daughter; and John and James, pious twins. The dialogue format permits Rowson to establish a respected authority on the Bible, Alworth, and occasionally his wife, who can answer difficult questions with ease for the adoring children. Issues like the incompatibility of the Gospels or the nature of the True Church—issues which would perplex such minds as Strauss and Feuerbach—are here presented through the innocent probings of receptive children who come to be thoroughly satisfied with their father's answers.

The children are both pseudoinquirers and moral evaluators who pronounce various Biblical characters as either good or wicked. Infidelity and Biblical criticism are embodied in Horatio's schoolmate, George Walker, who is dubbed "a very naughty boy" at the start and who, represented only at second hand by Horatio, is refuted easily by Alworth. Thus, skepticism is overcome without being granted full voice in the discussion. Sentimentalism often heightens the religious message, as when the children cry at Adam's fall and at the crucifixion of Christ. Evidence from nineteenth-century life is often invoked to explain apparently miraculous Biblical occurrences. For example, when the children ask how Noah's group could survive a raging storm in a frail ark for forty days, Alworth cites studies of the survival of cave savages as well as the longevity of modern steamships. He explains that "sacred and profane history are so intimately connected, that to doubt the authenticity of one, is to destroy the credibility of the other" (I, 244). Theologically the book is ambiguous. Original sin is mentioned, but mainly to account for aberrant or criminal behavior in the Old Testament. Predestination is used to explain some miracles; elsewhere human agency and morality are emphasized. Although sectarianism is denied in the preface, the last several dialogues aim to establish Rowson's religion, Episcopalianism, as the ideal via media between Roman Catholic despotism and American Protestant divisiveness.

Viewed unsympathetically, Rowson's book might be called a rhetorical, facile, and theologically muddled rewriting of the Bible in which large questions about Biblical authority are glossed over with the aid of sentimentalism and superficial scholarship. Designed for the young and the ignorant, the book points up the exploitation of children's literature as a repository for adult anxieties about religion. Rowson could pretend to solve religious problems for the young and in the process overlook the fact that such problems were beginning to create a crisis of faith among greater minds than hers. And yet, when seen in the context of later Biblical improvements in America, the book seems relatively ambitious and intellectual. Rowson at least tussles with weighty questions, and her facile solutions are perhaps preferable to Jacob Abbott's advice to forget theory and return to the real scene. Also, the work is far closer to the Bible and less dependent on secular props than the later Biblical fiction by William Ware, Joseph Holt Ingraham, and Lew Wallace. In fact, Rowson's serious effort to be historical and scientific seems to have prevented the book from attaining the popularity of her lachrymose *Charlotte Temple.* Perhaps the greatest irony about the book, then, is that in spite of its extensive rhetorical use of domestic sentiment and earthly reinforcement, it stands as the most intellectually solid fictionalization of the Bible that American literature produced before 1850.

Despite increasingly widespread interest in Biblical embellishment throughout the 1820s, the first long piece of American Biblical fiction, Thomas Gray's *The Vestal; or, A Tale of Pompeii,* did not appear until 1830. As if the Bible were still too sacred to be readily converted into fiction, Gray chose the less direct Christian martyr narrative. The tale is a first-person manuscript by Lucius Diomedes, a skeptical nobleman of Naples, who is converted to Christianity and who is condemned to death and at last killed, along with his fellow Christians and his pagan persecutors, by the eruption of Vesuvius.

In this brief novel Gray establishes the themes and devices that typify the Christian martyr story. Gray's identification of Christianity with heroic action and martyrdom, his imagined victory over skepticism, his linking of conversion with romantic love, his replacement of theological inquiry with martial adventure—all of these ideas would be repeatedly used by later writers of Christian martyr narratives. The stirring conflict between early Christians and their pagan oppressors strips religion of its theoretical complexities, reducing it to easily distinguished poles of good and evil. The story of a Roman's conversion from anguished paganism to confident Christianity gives a central dramatic movement to the plot, and adds emotional point to the subversion of infidelity. The destructive skepticism that Rowson had feared is disposed of by being embodied in easily hated Romans whose main pastime is watching lions devour Christians in the arena. Christianity is made more appealing by being represented in the Vestal Lucilla, whose charms speed Lucius' conversion.

The secular embellishment that Rowson felt compelled to defend expositionally has in Gray's novel become the unspoken basis of religion. Some guilt about the rhetorical use of sentiment remains, as when Gray has Lucius apologize, "Blame me not . . . that a spice of earthly love quickened and mingled with my holiest aspirations," and repeat later, "Blame me not, I say, that while the door of my heart was opened for devotion and religion to enter, love crept in unheeded behind them."[20] But Gray is more than willing to put aside even such guarded apologia in the interest of recreating the real scene of early Christian conversion and persecution.

Indeed, the entire novel moves from fruitless otherworldly speculation to dramatic earthly action. Lucius emulates his courageous fellow martyrs by changing from a feebly introspective pagan to a Christian of "sublime firmness" (113). His friend Flavius Piso undergoes a similar transformation: "Tried in the fiery furnace, the gentle and retiring boy had yielded to the grave, stern, and decided character, which fearful trials had wrought" (168). Not only does the emphasis on heroic martyrdom reflect Gray's belief in human dignity and strength, but it also deflects serious theological discussion. Piso stresses the "superior excellence" of "practical piety . . . over jarring creeds and wrangling sectarism" (155). The Christian martyr framework permits Gray to turn away from strict discussion of jarring creeds to an enactment of practical piety in its most diverting and muscular form.

There was little deviation from Gray's formula in later American Christian martyr fiction, which in the three decades after *The Vestal* came to include William Ware's *Probus* (1838), Edward Maturin's "The Christians" in *Sejanus* (1839), John W. Brown's *Julia of Baiae; or, The Days of Nero* (1843), the anonymous *The Roman Exile* (1843), and Eliza B. Lee's *Parthenia; or, The Last Days of Paganism* (1858). The portrait of a weak, confused pagan who becomes a heroic Christian martyr is repeated in most of these works. Maturin introduces the Biblical Paul, whose crucifixion in Rome inspires a Roman senator to espouse Christianity. Brown's Julia is the first female protagonist to assume the central role of the heroic convert, to be followed by Acelia of *The Roman Exile* and Lee's Parthenia. Maturin and Brown anticipate many post–Civil War Biblical novelists by contrasting sturdy Christians with the effeminate emperor Nero. The creedless, determined practical piety dramatized by Gray is amplified by all the later authors, who portray the fortitude of Christians on the rack and in the arena. Skepticism continues to be defeated through the depiction of despicable pagans.

At the same time, the oblique anti-Calvinist contrast between tyrannical oppressors and their dignified captives that characterized some Oriental tales becomes highly exaggerated. The liberal view of Calvinism as a morbidly determinist, enslaving system of superstition and bigotry is translated into descriptions of Roman emperors who use every means in their power to attempt to crush the Christians' faith in religious tolerance and human perfectibility. By granting moral victory to the Christians, the authors—most of whom were liberals—could imaginatively defeat the gloomy, authoritarian religion they disliked. Moreover, the conflict between pagan polytheism and Christian monotheism provided a convenient analogue to the war between Trinitarians and Unitarians. Thus, for instance, when the polytheist Acelia of *The Roman Exile* realizes at last that "there is only *one* God" who is best worshipped by "a blameless life," she is voicing the standard Unitarian outlook.[21]

And yet, even while devoted to overcoming such religious enemies as skeptics and Calvinists by depicting hateful pagans, these Christian martyr novels betray such a fascination with the glittering pageantry of pagan life that the Christian message is sometimes lost in the secular landscape. *Probus*, as will be seen in the discussion below of William Ware, contains extensive descriptions of the metalwork and statuary of Roman artisans, descriptions that unconsciously verge on the pagan interest in physical icons that Ware's Christian characters denounce. Brown's *Julia of Baiae* is full of lavish descriptions of the trees, gardens, and statues around the heroine's villa, so that the reader often goes for pages without any sense of the spiritual faith the author ostensibly endorses. *The Roman Exile* contains extravagant accounts of the gilded, embroidered trappings of the court of Marcus Aurelius. In *Parthenia* the author revisits fourth-century Greece to depict a "Paganized Christianity . . . arrayed in the gorgeous and attractive forms of the Grecian mythology."[22] She takes the interest in gorgeous and attractive forms to an extreme, describing jewel-encrusted altars, boudoirs filled with dazzling mirrors, and a multitude of marble and alabaster figures. Whereas Rowson in *Biblical Dialogues* had tried to achieve a staid balance between the spiritual and secular worlds, these later novelists come close to allowing the surface glory of the secularized paganism they intend to decry overwhelm altogether the spiritual. In the twentieth century, Cecil B. de Mille and other Hollywood directors would translate this fascination with pagan trappings into magnificent Roman stage sets which mesmerized moviegoers as surely as the Christian heroes inspired them. Thus, in Christian martyr fiction the idea of polishing God's altar took on a more literal, concrete meaning than it had in other types of religious fiction. Simply by closely describing the physical details of pagan settings, American authors could temporarily enjoy the lush aestheticism their native Protestantism lacked.

This seemingly ambiguous mixture of explicit dislike and veiled admiration of early paganism is in fact perfectly consistent with the largely secular priorities of the Christian martyr authors. In order to avoid intellectual debate with religious opponents, the writers transformed religious conflict into a fast-paced, sensational war between tyrants and Christians. Exposed as gloomy polytheists who wrathfully determine the fates of their victims, the oppressors become further vehicles for the indirect anti-Calvinism that had originated in the Oriental tales of the 1790s. Characterized as materialistic attackers of Jesus and the Bible, they also embody the skepticism Rowson had tried to defeat.

At the same time, though, this search for earthly analogues to creedal discussion leads several of the authors to a fascination with the materialistic splendor of pagan religion. Thus, the love and the loathing are paradoxical products of a single effort to reduce the spiritual to the physical.

As might be expected, New Testament fiction appeared later in America than did Christian martyr narratives. To fictionalize the Bible itself was potentially more sacrilegious than to dramatize the experience of Christ's early followers. A long New Testament novel of the Lew Wallace or Lloyd Douglas variety did not appear until 1837, when in *Zerah, the Believing Jew* an anonymous author described a contemporary of Christ who went on to proclaim the Word among pagans. After *Zerah* came William Ware's *Julian* (1841), Charles Beecher's *The Incarnation* (1849), Maria T. Richards' *Life in Judea* (1855), and Joseph Holt Ingraham's *The Prince of the House of David* (1855). In addition, fictional versions of the New Testament occurred as novelistic episodes or as short stories in Harriet Beecher Stowe's *The Mayflower* (1843), George Lippard's *Washington and His Generals* (1847), and James Gallaher's *The Western Sketch-Book* (1850). But all this New Testament fiction was preceded not only by Rowson's *Biblical Dialogues* but also by a curious novel written in 1832 by the Reverend John Hewson called *Christ Rejected: or The Trial of the Eleven Disciples of Christ, In a Court of Law and Equity; as Charged with Stealing the Crucified Body of Christ out of the Sepulchre.*

Though not Biblical fiction in the familiar sense, Hewson's book is notable as a prenovelistic, semiexpository attempt to revisit the New Testament period with the aim of answering charges of modern infidelity. Dedicated "to Jews and Deists," the book tries to refute the skeptical notion that the Resurrection did not actually happen but was a stunt staged by Christ's disciples, who stole Jesus' body from the tomb and buried it elsewhere. To disprove this idea, Hewson assumes the persona of a New England sailor, Captain Onesimus, who calls a court trial of all the parties involved, including Biblical characters. Several modern witnesses, especially followers of Paine and Voltaire, dismiss the Resurrection as absurd hearsay, arguing that Christ's body was stolen by his deceitful disciples. But their evidence proves to be slim, and testimony by the guards of Christ's tomb prove beyond a doubt that the tomb was closely watched and unassailable. Thus, Hewson vanquishes "Jews, Deists, and Atheists, and profound Philosophers," all of whom are at the end sent to join their father, Beelzebub, in hell.[23] Later Biblical novelists would often share Hewson's goal of rhetorically conquering skepticism by resurrecting eyewitnesses to Christ's miracles. But the later writers would go beyond Hewson's clumsy courtroom format to a full recreation of New Testament times. Hewson's awkward artistry, like Rowson's in *Biblical Dialogues,* results from an attempt to disprove skeptics with some amount of logic and serious argument. Of course, like Rowson, Hewson resorts to fictional devices to facilitate the task. And yet his professed intention to "forcibly rebut [Judaism and skepticism] by sound argument" is borne out by his long chapters of debate between modern critics and Biblical witnesses of divine revelation (iii). Later writers would circumvent such debate simply by allowing the real scene to speak for itself.

Five years after the publication of Hewson's book, the author of *Zerah, the Believing Jew* showed how the refutation of cavils against Christianity could be achieved less expositionally than in *Christ Rejected*. Hewson's separate logical arguments against skepticism and Judaism are drawn together and sentimentalized in the portrait of Zerah, a skeptical Jew who becomes a Christian after meeting Jesus and witnessing various miracles.

Just as Jacob Abbott had identified the imaginative return to the physical landscape of Palestine as the best solution for frustrated theorists, so the author of *Zerah* indicates that the five senses of his fictional protagonist absolutely disproves skepticism. By recording the enthusiastic outpourings of a single skeptic turned believer, the author can swiftly accomplish what Hewson took hundreds of pages of cumbersome expository discussion to prove. To insure the defeat of skeptical critics, the author invokes the familiar Common Sense equation of religious truth with factual experience. Zerah declares: "What dreams suggest or *heated imagination* while awake presents, it is possible might deceive age or youth; but what men saw, heard, experienced while in perfect mind, and bodily health, *can* they deny? Can *facts* so witnessed be other than *facts?* . . . What eyes, ears, senses attest, must men believe when themselves give testimony. Now or hereafter, should other men doubt the testimony of *one* witness, a body of collective evidence *never* may be disputed. Sceptics may cavil, but they cannot *disprove.*"[24] Hewson's courtroom debate between various Jews, deists, and Christians has become supplanted by the exuberant testimony of a single eyewitness to the physically real "facts" of Christ's miracles.

Significantly, however, the New Testament novelist still avoids dealing too freely with the Bible. A fictional eyewitness, Zerah, can be created with due propriety, but the author is careful not to revise Jesus' words or to invent new miracles to make a point. As the preface states, "Extracts from the Scripture are carefully marked in italics between commas, so that not the smallest interpolation therewith or subtracting therefrom, is even shadowed in the narrative of the Believing Jew" (3). The author also avoids minute accounts of Jesus' appearance, vaguely noting that Jesus "shed all around ineffable benignity—an elder brother's tenderness, and friendship's generous confidence" (15). Hewson, of course, had been even more cautious than the *Zerah* author, resurrecting only "safe" Biblical figures like tomb guards while eschewing any direct account of Jesus. The writer of *Zerah* has taken a momentous step toward more secular New Testament fiction but has tried to maintain reverence for the Bible by adhering as closely as possible to the original. The chronology of Jesus' life, Crucifixion, and Resurrection, as well as the ministry of Peter and Paul after his death, is quite close to that found in the Bible.

Later New Testament novelists became progressively more daring in their embellishments of the Bible, though some vestiges of the early caution lasted until the Civil War. In *Julian* William Ware gave American readers their first glimpse of the human Jesus; but at the same time, Ware's characteristic indirection was manifested by several hundred preparatory pages describing Judean political struggles unrelated to the Bible story. Harriet Beecher Stowe's *The Mayflower* contains an episode in which an anecdotal farmer, old Father Morris, transforms the Bible into "a gallery of New England paintings," presenting such "graphic minutiae of an eyewitness" as Mary and Martha *"frying fritters and making gingerbread."*[25] As we have seen, in the introduction to her brother's *The Incarnation* Stowe explains that the dull Bible needs enlivening, though, like the author of *Zerah,* she feels that Christ's person should not be described and that his words should be copied "without paraphrase, dimunition, or addition."[26] Heeding Harriet's advice, Charles was careful to transcribe exactly and to italicize Jesus' words. But unlike *Zerah, The Incarnation* is full of lavish descriptions of the geography and people surrounding Jesus, who is virtually buried under a blazing surface of burnished language.

George Lippard, vitriolic foe of elitists and religious hypocrites, gave Biblical paraphrase an egalitarian coloring in an episode on Jesus' life in *Washington and His Generals; or, Legends of the Revolution* (1847). In the process of envisaging Jesus as a lowly workman and friend of the poor, Lippard created the freest variations on the Bible yet to appear in American fiction. In a long central chapter of *Legends,* several Bible scenes—including Christ's childhood, the temptation in the desert, and the preaching in the temple—are retold in sentimental terms to show Jesus as a representative poor man fighting wealthy hypocrites.

Lippard returns to Nazareth, to "the rude hut of a Carpenter, with the sound of a hammer and saw, echoing from the solitary window."[27] Out of the window peeps a face: "It is a young face—the face of a boy—but O, the calm beauty of that hair, flowing to the shoulders in waving locks—mingling in its hues, the purple of twilight with the darkness of midnight—O, the deep thoughts of those large, full eyes, O, the calm radiance of that youthful brow!" (405). The conventionality of this description does not detract from its significance as an effort, not evident in most earlier New Testament fiction, to describe the physical Jesus. Furthermore, Lippard takes far greater liberty with the Christ story than previous writers. He portrays the adult Jesus bent over a workbench and "thinking of his brothers—the Brotherhood of Toil! ... of the Workmen of the World, the Mechanics of the earth ... the Poor man from immemorial ages!" (405). Such familiar portraits of the poor Jesus at work would become common in certain kinds of late-nineteenth-century Biblical novels after the rise of Christian Socialism. But in 1847 they were quite new and ambitiously secular. Making Jesus "resolved to redress the wrongs of the Poor," Lippard revises the story of Christ's refusal of Satan's kingdom in the desert to create a critique of moneyed classes (406). Similarly, casting out the moneychangers becomes equivalent to spearheading a poor man's revolt. Unlike previous Biblical novelists, Lippard does not seem to fear adding extensively to the original.

We might be tempted to dismiss Lippard as a peculiar case, a radical who stood outside the mainstream of Biblical embellishment in America. But while uniquely daring among pre-1850 authors, Lippard was engaged in the same recovery of the real scene that earlier writers from Rowson through Beecher attempted. Like the others, he proves to be fearful of skeptical attacks on the Bible. Thus, shortly after he gives the portrait of Jesus quoted above, he calls Paine's *Age of Reason* a "polluted . . . Manuscript of Falsehood" (440). Like several authors before him, Lippard answers the skeptical critique in sentimental and literary-aesthetic terms:

> Let me at once confess, that if the Bible is a Fable, it is a Fable more beautiful than all the classics of Greece and Rome . . . Search your Poets for scenes of that quiet pathos which at once melts and elevates the soul—search your Homer, your Shakespeare; search them all, the venerable Seers of the Ages, and I will point you to a single line that puts them all to shame! [When Christ rises from the grave and tearfully says, "Mary" . . .] that one scene, sublime in its very simplicity considered as a mere composition, is worth all the pathos of Greek and Rome (441–442).

Though coming closer than previous writers to admitting that the Bible may be a fable, Lippard follows the lead of authors such as Knapp and Judd by pointing to the diverting pathos of the Bible. Coupled with his free rendering of the Christ story, this passage places Lippard in a group of important popular authors who posed practical and sentimental solutions to difficult Biblical problems.

After 1850, New Testament novels underwent changes that were the predictable result of the increasing secularization of earlier Biblical fiction. A growing number of conservatives and evangelical Calvinists began to fictionalize the Bible. In 1855 the Episcopalian minister Joseph Holt Ingraham wrote the most popular New Testament novel to date, *The Prince of the House of David*. Ingraham combined a stirring conversion drama, eyewitness accounts of miracles, guarded physical descriptions of Jesus and his followers, and lavish passages on the Judean countryside and on pagan rites to produce a best seller. In his next two novels, *The Pillar of Fire* (1859) and *The Throne of David* (1860), Ingraham dared to deal with the pre-Christian world of the Old Testament. In 1855 the American Baptist Publication Society, the perennially conservative publisher of evangelical tracts, offered to the public Maria T. Richards' *Life in Judea,* which was followed in 1857 by her *Life in Israel.* A Midwestern Methodist minister, William P. Strickland, wrote the Biblical *Astrologer of Chaldea* (1855), which contained in its preface a long paean to the imagination in religious writing.

Traces of guilt about rewriting the Bible remain in these works, as evidenced by Richards' hope "If aught has been written presumptuously or irreverently, that [*Life in Judea*] may be caused to fall powerless to the ground."[28] But in the 1850s such cautious statements were rare and perfunctory obeisances to tradition. A more typical expression of the aims of the later writers was given in Ingraham's appendix to *The Pillar of Fire:* "The intention of the author in writing these works on Scripture narratives is to draw the attention of those persons who do not read the Bible, or who read it carelessly, to the wonderful events it records, as well as the divine doctrines it teaches; and to tempt them to seek the inspired sources from which he mainly draws his facts."[29] Once denounced by Whitefield as a genre wholly antithetical to "the grand Character of our Salvation," fiction had come to be viewed as an effective embellishment of the Bible, manmade bait for indifferent readers of God's Word.

William Ware: From Pulpit to Popularity

Taken together with the career of his brother Henry, William's experience suggests that the younger Wares were not wholly satisfied with the more traditional, doctrinal Unitarianism of their father. William's shift was even more dramatic than his brother's. After a long pastorship at New York City's First Church, from 1823 to 1836, William resigned as a result of his dissatisfaction with preaching and went on to devote himself to writing historical fiction. By the time of his death in 1852 he had written *Zenobia* (1838), *Probus* (1838), and *Julian* (1841), popular novels about early-Christian and Biblical times.

William left the ministry for a variety of related reasons: he was a rather uninspiring preacher; he was doctrinally cautious and indirect; he came to prefer free artistic expression and historical example to stricter forms of religious discussion. His closest friend in New York, Orville Dewey, reported that William wrote moving letters confessing "a fatal mistake in his choice of a profession." Dewey attributed such complaints about a "mistake for life" to Ware's "essentially artistic" nature and "a certain delicacy and shrinking in his nature that made it difficult for him to pour himself out freely in the presence of an audience."[30] In a letter of 1832, his brother Henry complained of William's dull sermons and asked: "Why won't you write sermons in precisely the brief, pithy, broken, dialogue style of this letter of yours? It would be prodigiously taking and lively, and would inevitably do good to your delivery."[31]

In attempting to heed his brother's advice, William soon found himself more inclined to write novels than sermons. When applied to religious compositions, the familiar dialogue style of his letters became transformed into epistolary fiction. Combined with his artistic inclinations and his delicacy and shrinking, this stylistic shift led to Ware's espousal of fiction-writing as a full-time career in 1837.

Ware's turn to fiction resulted not only from his ministerial shortcomings but also from his growing interest in historical fact as the proper alternative to metaphysical inquiry. His reliance on experiential historicism first surfaced in an essay on *The Antiquity and Revival of Unitarian Christianity* (1832), and extended through his three novels to his works of 1851, *Sketches of European Capitals* and *American Unitarian Biography*. In none of these works is Ware theologically ambitious or original; indeed, he is determinedly the opposite. His main point about the numerous Unitarians that he studies in *American Unitarian Biography* is that they replaced Calvinist polemics with a practical morality advanced through a literary and anecdotal sermon style. Like several of the liberals he describes, Ware found special solace in illustrating this earthly religion through the recreation of Biblical history. The return to Biblical times answered Ware's impulse to avoid theological controversy, offering the assurance of a primitive era before creeds and sects had developed. The Biblical novel provided not only an entertaining replacement for Ware's dull sermonizing but also a means of portraying historical incident and human emotion while indirectly suggesting his religious preferences.

Ware's *The Antiquity and Revival of Unitarian Christianity,* his first major publication, bears a similar relation to his novels as did Hewson's *Christ Rejected* to New Testament fiction or Rowson's *Biblical Dialogues* to American Biblical fiction in general. It is a mainly expository statement of the fundamental ideas that are later dramatized in his fiction. *Antiquity and Revival* shows Ware attacking Trinitarian theory with an argumentative boldness and precision unapproached in his later works. Ware begins by showing, through exegetical analysis, that a belief in the Trinity is scripturally unsound. He records key references to "the One God" in the Gospels and notes that Luke and Acts make no mention of the Trinity. After this, Ware traces chronologically the history of Unitarian thought from early-Christian to modern times. The villains of this history are "tyrannical persecutors" from Roman emperors to John Calvin and his American followers who have tried to crush liberalism. The heroes are liberals like Arius, Socinus, Servetus, and Boston Unitarians, who have brought to the world "the light of free inquiry, enlightened reason, and sound scriptural interpretation."[32]

In the novels that Ware began to write three years after *Antiquity and Revival,* the explicitness and theory of the essay were replaced by indirection and secularism. In these novels, as Orville Dewey remarked, "there is a certain staidness, a measured step, from which [Ware] never departs."[33] The ideas of the essay were safely transmuted into fiction that permitted relaxed dialogue as opposed to strict exposition, emotional character struggles as opposed to open sectarian controversy, colorful dramatization of history as opposed to a dry, logical ordering of it. The central conflict of the essay—vicious Trinitarians versus victimized liberals—is converted in each novel into the attempts of a tyrant to defeat Christians who believe in practical morality and one God. In *Zenobia* this conflict is seen in the siege and invasion by Aurelian's forces of Palmyra, a town in the eastern Roman provinces ruled by a rebellious queen who is entertaining several Christians. In *Probus* it becomes Aurelian's persecution and torture of Christians in Rome. In *Julian* the conflict is traced to the New Testament period, when Herod tried to stamp out Jesus and his followers. The superstition, bigotry and prejudice argumentatively opposed in the essay is enacted by the pagan or Jewish oppressors of the novels, who are often referred to as gloomy, superstitious, bigoted, and so forth.

The essay's bold intellectual effort to survey all Biblical and historical instances of Trinitarian error is replaced in the novels by a highly objectified expansion of localized scenes in ancient times. The honest—if sometimes emotionally colored—religious history of the essay gives way in the fiction to a rhetorical mixture of piety, sentiment, action, and scenic description. By the time he began writing fiction, Ware had learned to put aside dull sermons and combative anti-Calvinist essays. He had internalized his brother's advice to use calculation in developing a dialogue style. Having openly endorsed Unitarian Christianity in the title of the early essay, Ware became willing to delete the mention even of the inoffensive word "Christianity" from a novel title. At his brother's behest, he had become more adept at committing nobody, yet taking all.

This indirection is manifested by the chronology of Ware's choice of fictional modes. He began with the Oriental tale (*Zenobia*), the most oblique vehicle of anti-Calvinism in American fiction. Then he moved to the Christian martyr narrative (*Probus*), the least daring or sacrilegious form of Biblical fiction. By the time he wrote *Julian,* with his literary apprenticeship behind him, Ware could safely experiment with the New Testament story. In a sense, then, Ware backed into Biblical fiction through the Oriental tale. We have seen how traditional liberal novels such as *The Soldier's Orphan, The Factory Girl,* and *The Parent's Counsellor* redirected Oriental devices to more contemporary religious matters. Ware used the Eastern story as an established means of entering the more delicate area of Biblical embellishment. But even after he had worked his way through the Eastern tale and the Christian martyr narrative to the very nexus of Christianity, Ware remained cautious. Much of *Julian* consists of reporting Judean politics and Jewish expectation of the Messiah. Most information about Jesus—until the middle of the second volume, when we are at last offered a distant glimpse of him—takes the form of secondhand reports to the traveling Julian.

This caution appears in the novels themselves, as Ware endorses adaptable Christian characters and indicts excessively vocal ones. In this matter Ware had a slight problem: in keeping with his Arminian belief in the efficacy of good works, he wanted to extol heroic strength and determination; but in keeping with his Unitarian caution, he wished to reward silent benevolence and doctrinal timidity. To accommodate both tendencies, each of his novels contains fiery characters who fight tyranny with admirable courage but who fail in the end and are outlasted by the less aggressive figures. Thus Zenobia nobly opposes Aurelian but is at last defeated, while the more moderate Piso, Fausta, and St. Thomas survive. Likewise Macer, the Christian zealot of *Probus,* brashly derides paganism and champions Christianity before Roman leaders; but he is tortured on the rack and is outlived by more secretive Christians. In *Julian* Philip, the militant Christian denouncer of Herod, dies early in the novel; Julian describes Philip as "overhasty," with "virtue in its excess— in such excess that it was changed almost to a vice."[34] Macer and Philip are purists whose failure to be diplomatic exacerbates opposition and precipitates their downfall. As Piso says of Macer, "In his stern and honest enthusiasm he believed all prudence cowardice; all calculation worldliness; all moderation and temperance treason to the church and Christ."[35]

Those qualities Macer dislikes—prudence, calculation, moderation, temperance—are the ones Ware, having left behind the outspoken assertiveness of *Antiquity and Revival,* had come to prize. This does not mean that Ware extolled passivity or feebleness. On the contrary, several of his Christian spokesmen underscore the necessity of steady activity and manly resolution. Rather, prudence and moderation refer more specifically to Ware's request for caution and compromise on doctrinal questions. Thus he sympathetically portrays various Christian characters, or "half-Christians," who simply live morally without risking their lives for questionable theological issues. As Macer's daughter learns, "Our duty is to go on the even tenor of our way, worshipping God after our own doctrine and in our own manner, and claiming and exercising all our rights as citizens, but abstaining from every act that might rouse [the Romans'] anger, or needlessly irritate them" (265). Those who will survive Aurelian's purge are "an invisible multitude . . . who do not openly profess [Christianity], but do so either secretly, or else view it with favour and with the desire to accept it" (279). In *Julian* this call for indirection is repeated in Ware's account of Jesus, who "gives himself out, though not plainly, but obscurely and covertly as it were, for Messiah" (II, 171). Similarly, John the Baptist's "speech has indeed been ambiguous and obscure"; he "utters oracles, by himself not clearly understood" (II, 46).

There is repeated evidence in Ware's novels that this doctrinal caution is connected to a suspicion of any religion outside of common moral practice. Ware regularly denounces doctrines and creeds, often suggesting that any sort of logical explanation or even supernatural validation of Christianity is unnecessary. As Probus explains: "With the Christian, the highest service only commences when he leaves the Church. Religion with him is virtuous action, more than it is meditation or prayer."[36] In all the novels, Ware approves virtuous action on the part of seemingly incompatible believers—stoics, Platonists, atheists, Jews, Christians. It is understandable, then, that in *Julian* he emphasizes Jesus' humanity, questioning his divinity and concentrating on his good deeds. He contrives a scene in which the doubting Julian visits Jesus' family, who deny that Jesus is divine. When Julian at last sees Jesus, his doubts about the teacher's divinity are confirmed: "I saw that the language of his countenance was not that of an angel, nor of a God, but of a man, bound like myself, by the closest ties to every one of the multitudes who thronged him."[37] By humanizing Jesus, even to the point of having the Holy Family doubt him, Ware makes him imitable by every one of the multitudes.

By continually dismissing the importance of doctrine and church, Ware indicates that expository discriminations between Trinitarians and Unitarians like those he essayed in *Antiquity and Revival* have minimal importance. Like many religious novelists before and after him, Ware turned from early polemics to secular fiction, in which virtuous action becomes the center of faith.

Accompanying this secularized religion is the heightened interest in pagan spectacle and human drama that characterized other Biblical fiction of the period. In his early essay Ware strictly excluded all mention of the physical backdrop to religious history. In his novels, the emphasis is reversed, as concrete description predominates over religious discussion. If humanity has displaced God at the religious core of the novels, the secular landscape threatens to crowd out religion. The *North American Review,* in an analysis of Ware's novels, commented that readers would find Ware's religion pedestrian but his descriptions expert. The reviewer lauded "the gorgeous scenes and stirring adventures" of *Zenobia,* and said of *Probus:* "In description of external scenery it becomes ornate, and sometimes highly colored. In presenting scenes, which involve human actions and passions, it is warm, brilliant, and animated." In an apt phrase, the reviewer referred to Ware's style as "realities reduced to writing."[38]

Indeed, in the process of turning from otherworldly religion in his novels, Ware has exaggerated the gorgeous features of the realities he transcribes to the page. While doctrinally vague and brief, he is eloquently specific on such realities as Zenobia's blazing armor, the golden cup of Livia, dazzling Roman artwork, and Herod's luxurious palace. His tolerance of some non-Christian characters is often related to an admiration for paganism's aesthetic objectification of faith. In the opening scene of *Probus* he has his epistolary spokesman Nichomachus abjure Christian theory and yet praise towering alabaster statues of Moses and Jesus. In the same novel Ware favorably portrays the Greek artisan Demetrius, who has completed a silver Apollo statue and is working on a gold Christ figure. "Do you know," Demetrius asks Probus, "the Christians have some sense of what is good in our way? they aspire to the elegant, as well as others who are in better esteem." The Christian Probus, an admirer of Roman sculpture, later concurs with Demetrius: "Christianity condemns many things which by Pagans are held to be allowable; but not everything."[39] Likewise, the protagonist of *Julian,* believing that "truth ... should be clothed with beauty," writes, "The useful and ornamental arts I would have common to all, and by no means confined to one people or one faith."[40]

It is overstating the matter to say that Ware revisits early-Christian times to place faith in what Eliza Lee would call "Paganized Christianity." A fairer appraisal is that Ware, having rejected metaphysics on behalf of experiential faith, becomes hypnotically engaged with the physical reality surrounding the secular figures he depicts. His novels are full of such descriptions as the following account of Livia's jewelry: "Gold is doubly gold in her presence; and even the diamond sparkles with a new brilliancy on her brow or sandal."[41] In *Sketches of European Capitals* (1851) this fascination with the physical leads Ware to praise the "dazzling beauty" and "unapproached magnificence" of St. Peter's Cathedral in Rome.[42] In *American Unitarian Biography* it is faintly echoed in Ware's advocacy of colorful illustrations and graceful diction in the pulpit.

In conclusion, the career of William Ware further illustrates the pattern of secularization found in the careers of many other religious novelists of the period. In the novel he could resolve the conflicts of his earlier essay in a manner that was religiously indirect and humanly appealing. When his three novels are placed beside those of the other major pre-1860 Biblical novelist, Joseph H. Ingraham, the secularizing pattern becomes even more apparent. Taken together, the two writers produced, in chronological order, an Oriental tale (*Zenobia*), a Christian martyr novel (*Probus*), two New Testament narratives (*Julian* and *The Prince of the House of David*), and two Old Testament novels (*Pillar of Fire* and *Throne of David*). This succession of novels shows a scale of descending obliquity and ascending freedom with the Bible. The liberal Ware found a convenient passage to the writing of Biblical fiction through the Oriental tale, a familiar liberal vehicle; the Christian martyr narrative was likewise an appropriately safe method of experimenting with the fictional devices that would lead him to the New Testament. A decade later, beginning where Ware left off, the conservative Ingraham wrote an extremely popular New Testament novel and then became the first major popular novelist in America to venture into the pre-Christian realm of the Old Testament.

Along with a host of other American novelists of the period, Ware and Ingraham showed that polishing God's altar could signify the transformation of Holy Writ into entertaining fiction.

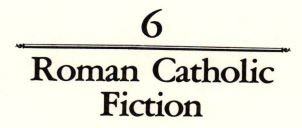

6

Roman Catholic
Fiction

Unlike Protestant novelists, who wished to find diverting, sentimental replacements for the rigorous theology of the Puritan past, Roman Catholics generally devoted their novels to attacking what they saw as Protestant divisiveness, theological evasion, and lack of logic. The free Biblical interpretation
and privately formed faith that Protestant novels increasingly extolled were
ultimate heresy for the Catholic writer, who tried to validate the authority of
the historical True Church as a cure for contemporary Protestant corruption.
While Protestant fiction was generally nontheoretical, much Catholic fiction
before 1850 attempted to be intellectual and polemical.

This emphasis on reasoned debate was designed as both a foil to Protestant
sentimentalism and a pointed reply to the growing number of Americans who
dismissed Catholics as illiterate slum dwellers enslaved by the "Beast of
Rome." Accordingly, most Catholic novels of the period include an account
of a Protestant character who, after years of Catholic baiting and smug self-sat-
isfaction, becomes miserably aware of Protestantism's shortcomings, often
through the agency of a rational Catholic priest or lay person. And yet, despite
this stress on reason and tradition, Catholic fiction made rhetorical use of sentimental devices which became progressively more prominent as time passed.
Thus much of the interest of early Catholic fiction lies in the way its vaunted

intellectualism was reinforced, with growing frequency, by secular props similar to those found in Protestant fiction of the time.

Logic and "Arms of the Flesh"

Protestantism, which had been called fragmented and confused by Catholics since the Reformation, was particularly vulnerable to Catholic criticism in nineteenth-century America. The right to private conscience and religious freedom guaranteed by the Constitution resulted in the proliferation of Protestant sects which were often doctrinally or politically antagonistic. In her preface to *Redwood* (1824) Catherine Sedgwick said that she wrote "at a period, and in a country of constant mutations, where old faiths are every year dissolving, and new ones every year forming."[1] As we have seen, the author of *The Soldier's Orphan* (1812) had claimed that every "free and accountable being" in America "has an equal right with his neighbour to form a creed for his own observance" (32). This democratic ethic placed renewed emphasis on private inquiry and toleration in religious matters, as external authority was seen as antithetical to individual freedom. Five new denominations of major importance would be founded by American Protestants in the nineteenth century; by 1960 the number of different Protestant sects would total more than two hundred. Thus, the century immediately following the Revolution saw a paradoxical combination of increasing theological similarities with growing sectarian schisms in American Protestantism.

The Catholic novelist capitalized on this post-Revolutionary religious ethic, converting into vices those values lauded by Protestants. The Catholic writer represented Protestant diversity as self-mocking fragmentation, private interpretation as the seedbed of religious chaos, toleration as theological relativism. Whereas Protestant authors, from writers of Oriental tales to Biblical novelists, attacked tyrannical authority on behalf of individual freedom, the Catholic novelist was quick to point out that without the guiding hand of authority, freedom can lapse into unregulated license, engendering mutually exclusive doctrines. The Catholic argument was an old one: there can be just one True Church derived from Christ, and the Catholic church is the only existing denomination that can justifiably lay claim to a link with early Christian times through a continuing tradition of ecclesiastical leaders, saints, and scholarly commentators. By definition, according to this view, Protestantism is merely an offshoot or modification of Catholicism, so that Protestant pretenses to originality are inaccurate. The corruptions Luther attributed to the Catholic church have been exceeded by those of Protestantism itself, which has created a battlefield of jarring sects each claiming to be the True Church. This familiar Catholic argument had special import in a period when the Unitarian controversy was raging, when the Plan of Union between Presbyterianism and Congregationalism was collapsing, when evangelical Calvinism was spawning many different sects.

In a sense, Protestant fiction of the period constituted a massive effort to fabricate a meeting place for schismatic religionists. Usually minimizing sectarian differences while endorsing universal religious principles, Protestant writers offered such commonly acceptable ideas as morality, goodness, and social activity to a religiously diversified nation. The Biblical novel provided, among other things, a surrogate connection to the early-Christian past that most American Protestants lacked; William Ware, for example, could imaginatively consummate his search for a Unitarian apostolic succession in his early essay by returning directly to Biblical times in his novels. To be sure, the doctrinal controversies of the period were reflected in the Protestant novel, as evidenced by such works as *Charles Observator, Justina, A New England Tale,* and *Jotham Anderson.* But most controversial Protestant novels were written before 1830, as writers of all sects tried to fabricate a unity in diversity in fiction that placed virtuous action at the center of faith.

The Catholic novel, which began to be written in America around 1830, tried to expose Protestant attempts at unity as fraudulent, ahistorical, and ephemeral. There is just one unity, the Catholic novelist stressed, the unity of the Church founded by Christ through the authority of Peter and maintained by the Holy Fathers for eighteen centuries. Protestants offer only pale copies of this grand unity and usually must resort to tricks or to false hope to do so.

The pre-1850 Catholic novelist faced a uniquely difficult task: to win the sympathy of predominantly Protestant readers who were apt to dislike not only Catholicism but authoritarian religion of any sort. To accomplish this task some writers stressed features of Catholicism that would be naturally attractive to Americans, such as the patriotism of Catholic soldiers during the Revolutionary War or the social work of groups such as the Sisters of Charity. More typically the Catholic novelist tried to defuse Protestant objections by portraying a vehement hater of Catholicism who comes to see the error of his prejudices. To oppose the common Protestant view of Catholicism as a sensuous religion of forms, the Catholic novelist deemphasized material emblems of faith. Indeed, the extensive concrete descriptions of statues and icons in such Protestant novels as William Ware's *Probus* and Eliza B. Lee's *Parthenia* were generally avoided by the Catholic writers on behalf of more expository presentation of ideas.

Yet the Catholic novelist used common fictional devices to underscore rhetorically his religious message. For instance, a narrow and hateful Protestant preacher was often compared to a learned, urbane Catholic priest. Such a contrast cleverly overturned the normal conflict in Protestant novels—gloomy bigot versus tolerant protagonist—to make a case for Catholicism. Also, the Catholic writers of the period often invoked domestic sentiment and romantic love, which were standard features of Protestant fiction. Though the Catholic's final message was that the individual cannot create his own creed, all the authors borrowed the central Protestant premise of a restless individual protagonist seeking religious truth; exactly reversing the religious journey in Protestant novels, the Catholic writers showed a character emerging from the bigotry of Protestantism into the reasonableness and secure authoritarianism of the Catholic church. Some Catholic writers used the visionary mode to sanctify this journey. Combined with the increasing reliance on secular sentiment as time passed, these features of Catholic fiction suggest that in the process of appealing to a generally hostile audience, the Catholic novelist was forced to adopt several of the fictional techniques popularized by his Protestant opponents.

Catholic fiction in America before the Civil War was principally the product of the following novelists: Charles Constantine Pise, John Boyce, John T. Roddan, Hugh Quigley, Charles James Cannon, George Henry Miles, Jedediah Vincent Huntington, Anna Hanson Dorsey, Mrs. James Sadlier (formerly Mary Anne Madden), and Orestes Brownson.[2] Besides the fiction written by these authors, there were individual efforts by other Catholics, including Mary Hughs's *The Two Schools* (1836), the anonymous *Father Oswald* (1843), and John D. Bryant's *Pauline Seward* (1847).

We find in this early Catholic fiction further evidence of the secularizing pattern apparent in much other religious fiction of the period. The earliest important novelists—Pise, Boyce, Roddan, and Quigley—were priests whose fiction passed from primarily intellectual defenses of doctrine to largely sentimental narratives illustrating practical Catholicism. In the 1840s these priest-novelists gave way to several Catholic lay persons—Cannon, Miles, Huntington, Dorsey, Sadlier—who increasingly deemphasized logic on behalf of pathos and adventure. Like many of the Protestant scribbling women of the 1840s and 1850s, these later Catholic writers were generally professional novelists trying to make a living through writing religious fiction: Cannon and Miles were determined to gain popularity, and Dorsey and Sadlier each wrote more than thirty Catholic novels between 1845 and 1890. The best novelist of the group, Huntington, was also the most worldly; an avid reader of English and French romantic fiction, he was often praised and occasionally damned for the sensuous richness and realism of his descriptions. Much of the early Catholic fiction was reviewed by Orestes Brownson, who found several novels lacking in intellectual rigor but who nevertheless recognized the importance of fiction in promoting Catholicism. Brownson tried his hand at writing fiction, outdoing the reasoned argumentation of his Protestant *Charles Elwood* (1840) in his Catholic *The Two Brothers; or, Why Are You a Protestant?* (1847), after which he resorted to a more sensational approach in *The Spirit-Rapper* (1854). The general movement of popular Catholic writing was away from theology toward sentimental fiction. In the 1840s novels displaced doctrinal works as the most lucrative product of Catholic publishers, and in 1845 Edward Dunigan of New York inaugurated his Dunigan's Home Library Series of Religious and Moral Works for Popular Reading, which was composed largely of novels.

The Catholic novelist faced the delicate task of disproving Protestantism logically while appealing to the emotions in ways the American novel reader expected. More acutely than Protestant novelists, who were often willing to abandon dogma happily, Catholics felt the painful paradox of the question: How does one write an intellectual religious novel? The Catholic novelist wished to invoke the powerful scholarly tradition of his church and to contrast his own reason to the evasive tactics of his Protestant enemies. At the same time, he did not want to put his readers to sleep with dull polemics.

This tension was most explicitly expressed in Brownson's literary articles of the late 1840s. In an 1847 article on religious novels Brownson declared that the novel was "the most convenient literary form which can now be adopted."[3] The age demanded entertainment with its religion, and the novel was by far the most entertaining of popular genres. But Brownson was deeply disturbed by the failure of most religious novels, which he called "literary hybrids" combining "the sentimental story, and the grave religious discussion" (144). Brownson established the general rule that "they who are seriously disposed would prefer taking the theology by itself, and those who are not so disposed will skip it. The one class will regard the light and sentimental as an impertinence; and the other, the grave and religious as a *bore*" (144). Noting the prevalence of religious fiction in nineteenth-century America, Brownson declared that "we respect the rigidness of our Puritan ancestors more than we do the laxity of their descendants" (178). In an essay of 1848 entitled "Novel-Writing and Novel-Reading," denouncing J. D. Bryant's defense of religious novels as the proper response to public demand, Brownson noted, "Study any age or nation, and you will find its peculiar heresy to have originated in the attempt to conform the church to its dominant ideas and sentiments, or to incorporate them into her teaching and practice" (223). Moreover, said Brownson, religious fiction is usually a literary monstrosity, since "the interest of a story is diverse from the interest excited by a logical discussion, and not compatible with it. The one demands action, movement, is impatient of delay, and hurries on to the end; the other demands quiet, repose, and suffers only the intellect to be active. It is impossible to combine them both in one and the same piece so as to produce unity of effect" (226). Religious novelists, Brownson went on, are wont to combine "profane love with an argument for religion," and "no two interests are more widely separated, or less capable of coalescing, than the interest of profane love and that of religion" (226). In the final analysis, religious novelists assume "that nature, as nature, nature without elevation or transformation by grace, may be pressed into the service of God" (230). In another essay of 1848, "Catholic Secular

Literature," Brownson reiterated that religious novelists "secularize the spiritual, while we would spiritualize the secular" (299).

The fact that Brownson wrote four pieces of fiction in spite of his great reservations about religious novels points up the general problem of the Catholic novelist in nineteenth-century America. To overlook fiction altogether would be to risk losing the attention of an American public that was buying Protestant novels by the thousands. To write fiction was to risk debasing the sacrosanct tradition of Roman Catholic logic. If he tried too hard to be popular, the Catholic novelist might be dismissed as theologically flawed. If he tried to be intellectual, he might be called artistically inept. In a sense, the Catholic novelist, like the logical Calvinist of the period, was backed into a corner. He wanted to be entertaining but respectable, popular yet precise. He wanted to endorse divine grace and strong intellect through the avenues of nature and secular sentiment. The literary hybrids produced by Catholics between 1829 and 1855 reflect the plight of a logical religionist in a secular culture. By 1855 it had become apparent that the Catholic novelist had decided to conform to the culture he had been wooing for nearly three decades.

America's first important Catholic novelist, Charles Constantine Pise, wrote three novels that were pointedly reasoned and intellectual. Each of his novels is a doctrinal conversion drama mildly seasoned with domestic sentiment. The first, *Father Rowland* (1829), traces the conversion to Catholicism of Virginia Wolburn, a Baltimore Episcopalian who at first derides Catholics, through conversations with her parents, her sister Louisa, and particularly the refined Father Rowland. In *The Indian Cottage* (1830) the Unitarian Elizabeth Preston adopts Catholicism after talking with Charles Clermont and his sisters. *Zenosius; or, The Pilgrim-Convert* (1845) allegorizes a young man's religious pilgrimage from a chaotic country, Sectarianism, to Rome.

Pise's basic story of a bigoted Protestant who comes to be convinced of Catholicism's reasonableness through careful deliberation epitomizes the most staid, conservative type of Catholic fiction. Strongest emotion in Pise's novels is directed to doctrinal matters, as when Father Rowland exclaims that American Protestantism is "the prolific parent of a thousand creeds, each contradicting each; all disagreeing; none admitting anything like a tribunal to decide their controversies; all appealing to the Bible, the Bible, the Bible!" Protestant Bible societies, Rowland continues, merely "scatter abroad the seeds of error: each individual interprets for himself, and forms a religion for himself," so that he can "make the scripture speak any language he pleases."[4] In each novel Pise depicts a learned authority, a priest or an educated lay person, who can explain the precepts and history of Catholicism to the searching Protestant. Pise avoids both lively adventure and romantic love in an effort to attain the quiet and repose that Brownson found essential to logical argument. Except for the allegorical Zenosius, Pise's characters are wealthy southern families who have leisure to discuss doctrinal niceties while enjoying peaceful Maryland sunsets.

But Pise, like most religious novelists, adopted fiction for rhetorical reasons, and secular sentiment often creeps into even his determinedly logical stories. Despite his pose of sobriety and equanimity, Pise discovers in fiction some anti-Protestant weapons which would be used by later Catholic novelists: appeals to American patriotism, contrasting personal descriptions of Protestants and Catholics, winning anecdotes, sorrowful deathbed scenes, and to a lesser extent, the visionary mode. By making the father of Virginia Wolburn a distinguished veteran of the Revolution, Pise plays on the democratic sympathies of Protestant readers. More significantly, by contrasting a handsome, forthright priest with an ugly, evasive Protestant minister, he plays on the average reader's sense of attraction and revulsion. While avoiding romantic love, Pise portrays the priest of his first novel as a pious young bachelor whose "unaffected gracefulness . . . could not but conciliate the prejudices of any company" (28). Rowland's history of the Catholic church is "interspersed with several amusing anecdotes," showing that the priest, "though grave, was facetious and lively, presenting a living picture of a truly pious man" (39). In contrast, his Episcopalian opponent, the Reverend Mr. Dorson, is "a tall, spare . . . person with a bald head, and a stern sanctimonious countenance" who makes certain "to allude in all his sermons to the *ignorance,* and *superstition,* and *idolatry,* of the Catholic worship. Rome he styled Babylon. The Pope the beast. The Church the mother of corruption" (86). While Rowland desires honest discussion, Dorson tries "to evade it most dextrously," relying on vitriolic name calling (90). Louisa Wolburn is struck by the "difference between the calm, dispassionate reasoning of Mr. Rowland, and the vapid vituperation of Doctor Dorson" (98).

Pise repeats the contrast in *Indian Cottage:* the Catholic Charles Clermont is "elegant in his manners, and refined by the most polished education," while the Unitarian Alton is emotionally biased.[5] By embodying standard obloquies against Catholicism in disagreeable Protestant figures, Pise can overcome them through his appeals to the bourgeois values of his readers in his depictions of polished Catholic gentlemen.

Pise does not just use Protestant patriotism and anti-Catholic preconceptions to his own ends; he skillfully reverses common devices of Protestant fiction. This reversal is most apparent in the full title of his second novel, *The Indian Cottage: A Unitarian Story.* In 1830 the typical American reader might have picked up the book with expectations of another Unitarian Indian tale along the lines of Child's *Hobomok* or Sedgwick's *Hope Leslie.* The fact that the reader may have been disappointed to discover that "Indian Cottage" is simply the name of a Maryland mansion housing a Unitarian family that turns Catholic probably did not worry Pise; he at least caught the reader's eye and, perhaps, made him consider Catholicism. In his novels Pise often directs devices from Protestant fiction—deathbed sentiment, vernacular perspective, anecdotal persuasion, and even the visionary mode—to Catholic ends.

Pise masks his reversal of Protestant literary devices with conventional Catholic paeans to logic. His outlook is summed up by a priest in *Zenosius:* "Error should, certainly, be combated: but not with the arms of the flesh: not with impetuous abuse, not with passionate declamation against one another. If the Protestant believes one faith erroneous, let him confine himself to argument, to solid reasoning, to scriptural authority."[6] However, as we have seen, Pise, even while establishing himself as the most logical Catholic novelist America would produce, made subtle use of arms of the flesh in his novels. It was left to later Catholic writers to exaggerate the secular devices Pise had strategically covered with the guise of sober reason.

Mary Hughs's *The Two Schools* (1836) leaves behind Pise's doctrinal priorities and advances a creedless Catholicism of social action and feeling. The restrained domestic affection of Pise's Wolburn and Clermont families is replaced by Hughs's emotional portrait of the Monkton family, Anglicans who leave England for Baltimore, where they discover that a poor Catholic orphan, Mary McDonald, is in fact their long-lost daughter, Aline Monkton. The basic plot of Pise's novels—Protestant conversion to Catholicism—is echoed in Hughs's account of how the Anglican Augusta Monkton and her father adopt the Catholic faith as a result of their growing disaffection with Protestantism. But the reflective stasis of Pise's novels gives way in Hughs to dramatic movement as the Monktons wander from England to Baltimore and Wilmington in search of religious truth. Moreover, Pise's logical Catholic preceptors are replaced by secular exemplars: the Sisters of Charity, whose social work the Monktons come to admire, and the angelic Mary, who retains her peaceful faith in Catholicism despite poverty and solitude. Like a number of Calvinist and liberal novelists of the mid-1830s, Hughs finds in social activity and perseverance ideal alternatives to doctrinal religion.

Catholic fiction might have continued in Hughs's quietly noncontroversial vein had it not been for the increasingly rancorous anti-Catholicism that swept America between 1835 and 1850. The influx of Irish and European Catholics in the 1830s and 1840s caused great alarm in many Protestant circles and helped give rise to such nativist groups as the Know-Nothings. Several Protestant authors wrote vicious anti-Catholic novels that represented nunneries as whorehouses run by rum-drinking priests (see Chapter 7). Such Protestant criticism deserved stronger reply than staid, reasoned novels like Pise's or innocuous social-working dramas like Hughs's. At the same time, Catholics did not wish to lose their intellectual superiority by descending to the mud-slinging tactics of their opponents. Therefore, they opted for fiction that combined solid Catholic argumentation with more sensational anti-Protestant devices. Catholic novelists after 1840 were more willing than Pise to take up arms of the flesh in the defense of their church.

As a result of the rising opposition to Catholicism in America, a new tone of defensive vindictiveness characterized several of the post-1840 works. *Father Oswald* (1843) was written, according to its preface, in reply to the anti-Catholic "Father Clement and many similar productions" since 1835. Presented as "an antidote to the baneful production of Father Clement," the book promises to answer all charges made in the anti-Catholic novel, "although they have been previously refuted a hundred times."[7] In his preface to *Harry Layden* (1842) Charles Cannon explains that the book "has been written—but with no controversial spirit—for the purpose of saying something in favour of that portion of the Christian family which every dabbler in literature feels himself at liberty to abuse."[8] Likewise, Hugh Quigley's *The Cross and the Shamrock* (1853) is prefaced by the assertion: "The corruption of the cheap trash literature, that is now ordinarily supplied for the amusement and instruction of the American people . . . calls for some antidote, some remedy."[9]

In keeping with such aims, post-1840 Catholic novelists gave new satiric point to their attacks on Protestantism. Unlike Pise, who had selected Episcopalian or Unitarian characters to outreason, the later writers often coupled their attacks on such mild characters with sharp caricature of more sensational Protestants—evangelical revivalists, Millerites, and so forth. In *Father Oswald* the dying William Smith is converted to Catholicism partly as result of the callous inattention of his Methodist pastor, Ebenezer, whose religion seems harsh and narrow. After Smith's death his antievangelical sentiments are repeated by a Catholic character who notes the "frightful spectacle" of "so many swarms of new sects, that rise up daily around us. In every village new meeting-houses are erected, and every illiterate fanatic quits the loom or the anvil, and, with all self-sufficiency, mounts to the pulpit to explain to the stupid crowd the deep mysteries of revelation." Such evangelism places the Bible in the hands of "every *unlearned* and *unstable* mechanic" who wishes to address "the gulled and gaping multitude."[10]

Charles Cannon similarly capitalizes on evangelical excesses. In *Harry Layden* he mocks the "great scandal" of Methodist camp meetings, where "the Christian heaven is described in the glowing colors of a Mahometan paradise; the praises of the 'Lamb' are sung with the frenzied ardor of Bacchanals; and even the Holy Name is mouthed with the most impious familiarity, to the horror of every right thinking man or woman present."[11] Cannon continues the attack in *Mora Carmody* (1844) and *Father Felix* (1845). Cannon's Mora is shocked by "the miserable jargon" of an itinerant who denounces the Pope as "the Son of Perdition, the Man of Sin, the Anti-Christ, foretold by the prophet."[12] In *Father Felix* a Millerite revival brings about the derangement of Julia Baldwin, whose former placidity is replaced by frenzied ravings which lead to her death.

Thus after 1840 Catholic novelists raised their voices in response to the clamorous vituperation that was coming from the Protestant press. The lascivious priest of the anti-Catholic novel was parodied by the ignorant, wild revivalist of the Catholic novel. But the Catholics did not wish to give themselves over to sheer emotionalism, for to do so would be to sacrifice their most dependable ally, logic. Thus, they presented their novels as reasoned refutations of unreasonable Protestant slander. Cannon, for example, denounced "those flagitious attacks upon the professors of the Catholic faith, with which the American press has lately teemed, that make up in abuse what they lack in argument."[13] Nearly every Catholic novel before 1850 contains a priest who defends such doctrines as transubstantiation, the Virgin Birth, and apostolic succession with cool wisdom. The priest normally stresses that Protestantism is hopelessly fragmented and that the final destination for the Protestant is either bewilderment or atheism.

And yet the Catholic novelist was fully aware that these were old arguments that might without sentimental refurbishment bore American readers. Accordingly, those secular arms of the flesh Pise had subtly used came to be utilized more explicitly and frequently by the post-1840 writers. Priests were not only learned but also well dressed and handsome, in contrast to their slovenly Protestant opponents. The domestic emotion Pise had tried to restrain became the key to conversion in several of the novels, and romantic love was a common theme. The Protestant couple of *Father Oswald,* for instance, separates when the wife adopts Catholicism and reunites when her husband follows her into the True Church. Cannon's orphaned Harry Layden wins love and wealth along with religion. The Protestant narrator of *Mora Carmody,* at first dismayed that Mora is a Catholic, is eventually won over as much by her winning demeanor as by her logic. In *Father Felix* Cannon connects Protestantism to seduction, madness, and murder while linking Catholicism to social advancement. A similarly sentimental scheme informs Bryant's *Pauline Seward* and nearly all the novels of Anna Dorsey. In many of the novels, deathbed scenes enforce the need for salvation in the Catholic Church. In short, the Catholic novelist after 1840 was using sentimental devices that had been standard features of Protestant fiction since the 1820s.

In addition, this later Catholic fiction, while always more doctrinal than its Protestant counterpart, relied increasingly on anecdotes and illustrations of religious truth. The priest figure was usually a good storyteller as well as a careful logician. *Father Felix* contains several interpolated religious legends, ranging from a story of medieval knighthood to a visionary tale, which dramatically accent the intellectual disquisitions of the main characters. In some novels an effort is made to reduce doctrinal references while extolling secular illustration. In the interest of "supplying the younger portion of the Catholic community with a source of mental recreation," Anna Dorsey emphasizes that she has merely "touched lightly on a few doctrinal points."[14] Indeed, her novels, which resemble those of the Calvinist Joseph Alden written during the same period, concentrate more on the tears of orphans than on the talk of priests. Likewise, in *Harry Layden,* Charles Cannon is willing to sidestep a key doctrinal discussion in the interest of getting on with the story:

> We are not writing a treatise on education, nor a volume of controver-
> sial divinity and will therefore, neither trace step by step, the progress of
> Harry in the path of learning, nor go over all the arguments made use of
> by Redmond in his conversations with Agneta, to prove that Catholi-
> cism—the religion of some of the wisest and best men the world has
> ever known—might have some claim to be considered Christianity. Nor
> will we describe the struggles of the ingenuous Agneta with herself,
> when obliged to abandon, one by one, the prejudices she had cherished
> as truths, until she was forced to admit, that, notwithstanding all she
> had heretofore heard and read, all that is essential to salvation may be
> found in the Church of Rome [35].

Evasion of doctrinal exposition had always been common in Protestant fiction in America; even relatively cerebral works such as *Jotham Anderson* and *A New England Tale* contain several passages that, like Cannon's, relegate vast intellectual inquiries to a vague sentence or two. But such circumvention was new to the Catholic novelist of the 1840s, who was now eager to avoid the appearance of writing a volume of controversial divinity.

After 1850 this movement to the sentimental and anecdotal was accelerated and was underscored by a minimizing of tedious argumentation that might alienate Protestant readers. Jedediah Vincent Huntington, an Anglican who was converted to Roman Catholicism in 1849, voiced the sentiments of many later novelists when in the mid-1850s he distinguished between "controversial" and "poetic" Catholic fiction. Echoing Brownson, Huntington wrote, "The modern controversial Catholic novel . . . is liable to the fatal objection of mixing things in themselves heterogeneous and incompatible." Dismissing the controversial novel as "essentially inartistic," Huntington declared that Catholic fiction should aim "to create the beautiful imitation of real human life, not to convince, not to refute even the most real and the most lamentable errors."[15] Huntington's interest in real human life was reflected in his five novels, which were more notable for their vivid realism and romantic adventure than for otherworldly contemplation or doctrinal subtlety. This secular emphasis sometimes angered Huntington's reviewers. In 1850 the *North American Review* found in his *Lady Alice* an "irreverent flippancy with which things sacred and things secular are constantly intermingled."[16] The *Review* lamented Huntington's "thoroughly licentious" and "voluptuous" accounts of concubinage, nude art models, and mixed public bathing, voicing its "solemn protest against the intrusion upon English literature, under the garb of religious purism, of the vilest forms and worst features of modern French fiction" (237).

In response to such criticism, Huntington tried to tame his impulse to graphic sensuous description, though it did surface in each of his four Catholic novels of the 1850s. For example, Huntington was condemned by several critics for allowing the heroine of *The Forest* (1852) to camp for a time with her lover in the North woods. Each of his Catholic novels made courtship prerequisite to conversion. *Rosemary* (1860), which dealt with such lively topics as clandestine marriages and reanimated corpses, was explained by the author as follows: "This is not a prayer-book, but a story written expressly to win the attention of those who will read nothing but stories, and sensational ones at that."[17] Mirroring this anecdotal propensity, Huntington's novels contain several storytelling characters and interpolated narratives. Alban of *Alban* (1853) and *The Forest* "can repeat whole novels from beginning to end."[18] In *The Forest* the Catholic heroine's long sentimental tale of the placidity of convent life effects the conversion of a Protestant girl, while Alban's intellectual cerebrations during a monastic retreat are dismissed with Huntington's statement that "it is not our intention to follow our hero through the course of this celebrated discipline" (277).

Other Catholic novelists after 1850 manifested this antitheological secularism in different ways. Such works as Anna Dorsey's *Woodreve Manor* (1852) and Charles Cannon's *Tighe Lyfford* (1859) have little Catholic content. Mrs. James Sadlier, adopting the favorite formula of Protestant domestic novelists, wrote numerous novels of displaced Irish orphans enduring Protestant obloquy and gaining money and marriage through firm adherence to simple Catholic principles. George Henry Miles's *Loretto* (1851) was "severely handled" by critics because it contained "no good solid arguments in it, extracted from standard theological works."[19] The heroine of Miles's *The Governess* (1851) brings about the conversion of a Protestant family not by argument but rather "by the force of example," giving rise to another evasion-of-exposition passage: "The winter passed in religious controversy, which we do not mean to repeat: there are so many better reasoners than Mary, that it is quite unnecessary to record her instructions."[20] Similarly, the Irish priest of Hugh Quigley's *The Cross and the Shamrock* (1853) shows "reluctance to enter into a theological discussion" with a Protestant character.[21] Quigley's sensational interests are reflected in this book, *The Cross and the Shamrock,* which associates camp meetings with sexual promiscuity and Protestantism in general with dissolution and suicide, as well as in his *Prophet of the Ruined Abbey* (1855) and *Profit and Loss* (1873), in which farcical anti-Protestant satire and stirring Irish legends predominate over logic.

This growing resistance to intellectual doctrine is most clearly illustrated in John Boyce's *Mary Lee* (1860). Boyce's special target is Orestes Brownson, who appears in the novel as Dr. Horseman-Henshaw, a recent convert to Catholicism whose ponderous logic contrasts with the simple emotional piety of the Irish heroine and a fun-loving priest. Like several other Catholic novelists of the day, Boyce had reason to be upset with Brownson. Although Brownson had lauded Boyce's *Shandy M'Guire* (1848), he had qualified his praise by stating, "We object to novels in general, because they are sentimental, and make the interest of their readers centre in a story of the rise, progress, and termination of the affection or passion of love."[22] Brownson had blasted Boyce's second book, *The Spaewife* (1853), calling it "too grave for fiction, and too light for history.[23] Boyce responded with his caricature of Henshaw, who "as a polemic and logician . . . has very few equals" but who is coldly distant from practical, human Catholicism.[24] One of Boyce's Irish Catholics complains that Henshaw "wields theology like a sledge-hammer, and sends all Protestants to misery everlasting" (182). Another, noting that Henshaw "reviews every book he can lay his hands on—stories, novels, poetry, every thing," declares: "I think so little of his literary criticisms I don't care to read them" (165). In contrast to Henshaw, who believes that "intellectual men need intellectual treatment," Mary Lee wins over a Protestant girl "not by dosing her with dogmas, anathemas, and philosophy," but "by the mere example of her every-day life" (325, 324).

Thus post-1850 Catholic novelists, following a pattern similar to the one seen in the works of orthodox and liberal Protestant novelists, increasingly embraced quotidian example and noncontroversial piety, rejecting the more logically reasoned argumentation used by Pise and other priest-novelists before 1845.

Orestes Brownson's Attempted Reformation of Catholic Fiction

In light of this movement toward the sentimental and anecdotal, it is not surprising that Orestes Brownson wrote several essays in 1847 and 1848 emphasizing the need for stricter logic in Roman Catholic fiction. The increasing use by Catholic novelists of the themes of love and adventure alarmed Brownson, who wished to reverse or at least retard the secularizing trend. But Brownson offered no real alternative to the writer of Catholic fiction. As we have seen, he could note that religious novelists "secularize the spiritual, while we would spiritualize the secular"; but how was such equivocal advice to be practically applied? He could declare that novelists "overlook the essential incongruity between nature and grace"; but how was intangible grace to be reproduced in fiction? He attacked J. D. Bryant's request for an adaptation to cultural tastes. Yet not only did he admit that the popular novel was "the most convenient form which can now be adopted," but he tempered his criticism of Anna Dorsey's *Conscience* (1856) by writing: "Let every man, every woman, old or young, that can write a passable book, write it. Even trash is better than noth-ing."[25] On the matter of religious fiction, Brownson was torn between the demands of culture and those of conscience, between popular appeal and doc-trinal purity. Brownson's love affair with religious fiction was as painful as had been his infatuations with Presbyterianism, Unitarianism, socialism, and Tran-scendentalism—but it was much longer, as it began in the early 1840s and continued long after his conversion to Catholicism.

Both fascinated and repelled by religious fiction, Brownson made four ef-forts at writing fiction: *Charles Elwood* (1840), *The Two Brothers* (1847), "Uncle Jack and His Nephew" (1854), and *The Spirit-Rapper* (1854). In this fiction we see Brownson, first from a Protestant and then from a Catholic standpoint, struggling to locate a proper fictional voice. After mingling senti-ment with argument in his first novel, he ascends to almost pure logic in his second and third tales, and then experiments with sensationalism in *The Spirit-Rapper*. The inconsistency in tone of these works suggests that even one of the most acute Roman Catholic thinkers in nineteenth-century America had extreme difficulty in discovering a fictional equipoise between religion and nature in the popular religious novel.

Many of Brownson's apprehensions are captured in his introductory apolo-gia to *Charles Elwood:* "It may be objected that I have introduced too much fiction for a serious work, and too little, if I intended a regular-built novel."[26] His later novels and essays would constitute a prolonged attempt at deciding what was too much or too little fiction. In *Charles Elwood* Brownson essays a balanced combination of logic and emotion. He describes Elwood's painful passage from gloomy skepticism to piety as a result of his love for the dying Elizabeth Wyman and his intellectual dialogues with two progressive Protes-tants, Morton and Howard. Clearly Brownson in the novel is trying to ex-punge the frivolous in favor of the serious. He carefully records the cerebra-tions that lead Elwood from atheism to Protestantism. Basically, the argument is a fully developed version of the theme of most American Protes-tant novels of the period: that the religious sentiment beneath changeable creeds can be apprehended through free individual inquiry. Instead of resort-ing to indirect secular analogues like the Biblical novelist's Roman tyrant, Brownson directly attacks the "ecclesiastical tyranny" of Roman Catholicism and Calvinism, championing "individual reason" and every man's "right and power to form his own creed" (251).

And yet, despite this rational emphasis, Brownson does bend to the senti-mental requirements of popular fiction. Branded a pariah by religionists, frus-trated in love, finding no stoic or existential pleasure in life, Elwood before his conversion is a restless Wertherian seeker tailored to suit the romantic tastes of the reading public. He cries despondently over his disbelief and his lover's death and joyfully over his new-found faith. Even after his long talks with Morton and Howard, he is as much swayed by their benevolent example as by their logic. He can thus conclude: "As a general rule would you gain the reason you must win the heart. This is the secret of most conversions. There is no logic like love" (241).

In his effort to please both the sentimentalist and the logician Brownson pleased neither. *Charles Elwood* did not have popular success, and reviewers wrote contradictory evaluations of the book according to their doctrinal preferences. The *Christian Examiner* dubbed Brownson a "logic-grinder, without heart and soul, or at best with nothing but a gizzard."[27] The conservative *Boston Quarterly Review,* arguing that Brownson resorted to "a subtler influence than logic" in the novel, said precisely the opposite:

> Abstract the personal interest taken in Charles himself, the aesthetic effect of his conversation with his betrothed, and of the moral beauty of Mr. Howard's life and generous friendship, and the life and force of the argument would be greatly impaired, and nearly all the efficacy of the work would be lost ... Abstract the deep, earnest feeling, the passion even, that [Brownson] mingles with his arguments, to an extent perhaps little expected, and we apprehend his logic would be by no means remarkable.[28]

Thus, Brownson included in *Charles Elwood* both too little and too much fiction to satisfy anybody.

After he was converted to Catholicism in 1844, Brownson went through a period, roughly between 1847 and 1851, in which the logical side of *Charles Elwood* was exaggerated to fuel an antipathy to anyting tinged with secular sentiment. The kind of intellectualism used by Elwood's teachers to support Protestantism was transformed in this later period to expository defenses of Catholicism and attacks on Protestantism in *Brownson's Quarterly Review.*

It was at this time that Brownson wrote the aridly logical *The Two Brothers; or, Why Are You a Protestant?* (1847). The novel consists of prolonged debates between John and James Milwood, brothers who were raised as Presbyterians and who have made adult choices, respectively, for Catholicism and Protestantism. In the face of his brother's spurious, emotional argumentation, John coolly performs dizzying intellectual feats to prove that Protestantism is a confused array of nonreligions which change God into a liar. Protestants, John says, are wont "to assume a bold and daring tone, to make broad and sweeping assertions, and to forego clear and exact statements, and close and rigid logic"; Catholics, in contrast, "speak to sober sense, to prudent judgement, and aim to convince the reason, instead of moving the sensibility and inflaming the passions."[29] John's logic is pointed in the opposite direction from that of the Protestant thinkers of *Charles Elwood.* The individual creation of religion recommended by Howard and Morton becomes, in the eyes of Brownson's Catholic spokesman, the cause of religious anarchy and relativism.

In Protestantism, says John, "there is a multitude of sects, indeed, sometimes arranged under one common name, but without any common faith of principles, except that of hostility to the [Catholic] church" (268). Brownson keeps romantic love out of his novel; the two brothers are sexless mouthpieces for an inductive refutation of Protestantism. Even the conventional happy ending is eschewed, as James remains a hardened Catholic hater and John enters a monastery at the end.

While trying to offer a model of disinfected fiction to the Catholic novelists he was attacking in his essays of 1847–48, Brownson nevertheless does use a subtler influence than logic even in this highly intellectual novel. He has gotten rid of profane love here, but domestic and deathbed sentiment remains in the person of the brothers' mother, who, while dying, is tearfully converted to Catholicism. John is given the emotional advantage from the beginning by receiving his mother's blessing and by acting on her last request that he reconsider his childhood Presbyterianism. Brownson borrows from other Catholic novelists not only the deathbed scene but also the device of placing vehement anti-Catholicism in the mouth of a Protestant straw figure. James's first defense of Protestantism is a self-parodying torrent of vitriol: "I am a Protestant because the Romish Church is corrupt, the Mystery of Iniquity, the Man of Sin, Antichrist, the Whore of Babylon, drunk with the blood of the saints, a cage of unclean birds, cruel, oppressive, tyrannical, superstitious, idolatrous" (248). The reader is prepared by this outburst to agree with the later statement that Protestants are "far abler demogogues than logicians" (263). Furthermore, Brownson cleverly creates a devil in the ranks in his portrait of Wilson, a Presbyterian friend of James's who comes to criticize his own religion even more sharply than does John. "The time is not far distant," admits Wilson to James, "when you will have no Protestantism to defend, but each man will have a gospel of his own" (267). In sum, even while writing what is possibly the most studiously reasoned religious novel in American literature, Brownson makes rhetorical use of characterization and sentiment.

If *Charles Elwood* had been treated roughly by the public and by reviewers, *The Two Brothers* suffered an even worse fate: indifference. There is little evidence that the novel had a readership outside of regular subscribers to *Brownson's Quarterly Review*, in which it appeared serially. Brownson could intellectualize at length about what elements religious fiction should and should not contain, but he was finding the writing of such fiction difficult. The problem was really one of genre: to be theologically successful Brownson had to restrict himself to the essay; but to be popular he felt compelled to attempt fiction.

Criticized or ignored by reviewers and unsure of himself artistically, Brownson decided in *The Spirit-Rapper* (1854) to defy his critics by leaping over the boundary of genre altogether: "If the critics undertake to determine, by any recognized rules of art, to what class of literary productions the following unpretending work belongs, I think they will be sorely puzzled. I am sure

I am puzzled myself to say what it is. It is not a novel; it is not a romance; it is not a biography of a real individual; it is not a dissertation, an essay, or a regular treatise; and yet it perhaps has some elements of them all, thrown together in just such a way as best suited my convenience, or my purpose."[30] By now accustomed to both giving and receiving unfavorable reviews in his search for the ideal Catholic novel, Brownson invites his critics "to bestow upon the author as much of the castigation which, in his capacity of Reviewer, he has for many years been in the habit of bestowing on others, as they think proper" (1). The confident tone of the essays of 1847–48 has been replaced by a defensive, slightly cynical humor. The firm discrimination made in 1848 between the sentimental story and the grave religious discussion, between nature and grace, have given over to an ironic confession of literary puzzlement and possible failure. The issue is no longer a clear-cut conflict between too much and too little fiction; rather, it is a complex jugglery of genres and voices, none of which can be wholly accepted as the ideal ingredient of successful Catholic fiction.

As its preface indicates, *The Spirit-Rapper* is a potpourri of fiction, autobiography, history, satire, and theology. In several senses the book is notably different from Brownson's previous novels. Inductive logic has been replaced by flexible sentiment, a limited cast of characters by a multitude of religious voices, a nonadventurous plot by wide-ranging movement and even melodrama. Brownson's narrator, a liberal Protestant who is dabbling in mesmerism and spiritualism, meets the lovely Priscilla, a socialist despiser of despotic religions, who persuades him to join her World-Reform movement to overthrow the Catholic church. Along with Priscilla's husband, James, the two travel through Europe, where for six years they try to incite revolt against the Pope through a combined strategy of mind control and exhortation. Their attempts fail, as Pius IX causes a Catholic revival which crushes organized anti-Catholicism. Returning to America, the three reformers enter more troubled waters. The narrator becomes a gloomy atheist and is stabbed by James, who jealously suspects him of trying to steal his wife. The narrator becomes an invalid who is visited regularly by friends of various philosophical and religious outlooks. Meanwhile Priscilla, frustrated in love with the narrator, has been converted to Catholicism, which has been taught her by an erudite Franciscan monk whose brutal murder Priscilla later witnesses. The narrator follows a different road into the church. After trying to establish a rival religion to Christianity, a mixture of freethought and spiritualism, he at last espouses Catholicism because it is the only religion that distinguishes between "genuine and counterfeit spirit-manifestations" (191). Recognizing Satan, the narrator is forced to recognize Christ.

In this novel Brownson throws aside his earlier concern for strict logic and tightly regulated characterization and plot. He portrays many idiosyncratic characters who would have been banned from his previous fiction: Increase

Mather Cotton, an Old Light Calvinist who mocks nineteenth-century liberalism's disbelief in devils; Edgerton and the American Orpheus, counterparts of Emerson and Alcott: Thomas Jefferson Andrew Jackson Hobbs, a populist demagogue; Rose Winter, a Jew who damns the New Testament; and various spiritualists, mesmerists, and radical reformers. Methodists are mocked as "so many bedlamites or howling dervishes" (11), and Joseph Smith is called "ignorant, illiterate, and weak" (99). In contrast to Brownson's novels and essays of the 1840s, this novel makes an allowance for profane love, borrowing from the popular sentimental novel the device of a love triangle that triggers a murder attempt. The narrator, despite his intelligence, is closer to the stormy, soul-searching protagonists of French romantic novels than to previous Brownson heroes such as John Milwood.

But the most thoroughly exploited area of sensationalism in the novel is spirit rapping and devil possession. Writing six years after the famous Fox rappings in New York, Brownson mentions not only the Fox sisters but also several other reports of spirit manifestations from modern and ancient historical records. Although Brownson's rather chaotic approach prevents him from fashioning a Catholic potboiler like William Peter Blatty's *The Exorcist,* Brownson anticipates Blatty's technique of positing an obverse spirituality through demon possession. One scene, in which Cotton orders a devil to leave a girl's body, presages the climactic moment of *The Exorcist.* Elsewhere, Brownson records instances of table lifting, violent body contortions, speaking in tongues, and Catholic exorcism. Brownson's goal is to destroy "the last infirmity of unbelief, the denial of the existence of the devil" (78). He cites Voltaire's exclamation, *"Sathan! c'est le Christianisme tout entier; PAS DE SATHAN, PAS DE SAUVEUR,"* explaining that "if there was no devil, the mission of Christ had no motive, no object, and Christianity is a fable" (93). Thus, the narrator's conversion comes only when he is convinced that Satan is a powerful being who is best explained and most successfully opposed by the Catholic church.

In *The Spirit-Rapper* Brownson has followed the pattern of those previous Catholic novelists whose foibles he pointed out in his essays of 1847–48. *The Spirit-Rapper* bears a relation to Brownson's earlier novels similar to that which the works of the other post-1840 writers bear to Pise's novels. Like Cannon and the author of *Father Oswald,* Brownson replaces logical refutation of reasonable Protestant denominations with caricature of more floridly emotional sects. He exceeds the other writers in his range of dramatic portrayals, as he describes excitingly radical movements which even the popularly oriented Cannon neglected. The vindictive post-1840 device of containing anti-Catholicism through the depiction of misled Catholic baiters is expanded by Brownson to a complex plot involving Protestant reformers who scheme to subvert the Pope himself. The sentimentalism utilized by Huntington, Quigley, and Boyce is often invoked by Brownson, who heightens his religious dialogue with unrequited love, jealousy, revenge, and romantic ennui. All of these sensational tendencies are epitomized in Brownson's description of spirit manifestations. If *Charles Elwood* and *The Two Brothers* use a subtler influence than logic to endorse Catholicism, *The Spirit-Rapper,* like other Catholic novels after 1840, leaves behind cautious subtlety in favor of more explicitly combative and divertingly secular techniques.

The Spirit-Rapper is in part a sentimental dramatization of a central passage in Brownson's "Uncle Jack and His Nephew" (1854), a story that ran serially in the *Quarterly Review* during the months just prior to the publication of the novel. Among the arguments used by the Catholic uncle to his Protestant nephew is the following summation of Protestant history: "In religion Luther engendered Voltaire, in philosophy Descartes, in politics Jean Jacques Rousseau, in morals Helvetius. In religion you have ended in the rejection of the supernatural, in philosophy in doubt and nihilism, in politics in anarchy, in morals in the sanctification of lust."[31] This condemnation of Protestantism, stronger and more sweeping than any indictment in Brownson's fiction previous to "Uncle Jack," shows Brownson stating expositionally ideas that would be enacted sensationally in *The Spirit-Rapper.* The sanctification of lust here criticized becomes Priscilla's passion for the narrator during her Protestant period. Anarchy surfaces in the portrait of Protestant revolutionists, doubt and nihilism in the narrator's loss of faith before his conversion to Catholicism. Uncle Jack's strongest charge—the rejection of the supernatural—is answered by Brownson's graphic accounts of supernatural occurrences in the novel.

Having completed his secularizing cycle in *The Spirit-Rapper,* Brownson retreated in his later writings to the more conventional genres of unfictionalized autobiography, Catholic essays, and history. Apologetic from the beginning about his fiction, Brownson experimented with various balancings of logic and sentiment only to discover that the most convenient form was also the most artistically elusive.

Brownson stopped writing fiction in 1854, but he continued to review fiction regularly for the next two decades. His views of Henry Ward Beecher's *Norwood* and modern realist novels were predictable: he declared that such non-Catholic works remained in the realm of unsanctified nature and paganism. His attitudes towards what he came to call "Catholic secular literature" were more complex. He continued to treat the Catholic novel as a high ideal rarely realized in practice.

As late as the 1870s, shortly before his death, Brownson was still struggling to define Catholic fiction in a series of essays in his *Quarterly Review:*"Mrs. Gerald's Niece" (1870), "Religious Novels, and Woman versus Woman" (1873), "Catholic Popular Literature" (1872), and "Women's Novels" (1875). In these essays Brownson supported the broadening interest in fiction among Catholics while he lamented the failure of most religious novels. In "Religious Novels" he repeated his argument of 1848 that a mixture of love and doctrine creates "a literary monstrosity, which is equally indefensible under the relation of religion and that of art." "There are," he noted, ". . . very few of our authors of religious novels, even when they know their religion well enough to avoid all grave errors in the serious part of their productions, who have so thoroughly catholicized their whole nature, consecrated their imaginations, and conformed their tastes, mental habits and judgements, sentiments and affections, to the spirit of Catholicity, that when they write freely and spontaneously out from their own imaginations, they are sure to write nothing not fully in accordance with their religion."[32]

To be sure, the Catholic novel is, in Brownson's view, the best antidote to realism, that "most corrupting and infamous school of literature that has ever existed" (573). But in reality the antidote was becoming controlled by the poison, since post-1850 Catholic novelists were descending to realist secularism with disturbing frequency. In an effort to stem the secular tide Brownson reminded his readers: "The object of the Catholic novelist, or cultivator of light literature, is not or should not be to paint actual life, or life as we actually find it, but to idealize it, and raise it, as far as possible, to the Christian standard, not indeed by direct didactic discourses or sermonizing, which is out of place in a novel; but by the silent influence of the pictures presented, and the spirit that animates them" (572).

Instead of clarifying matters for the Catholic novelist, Brownson brought up an old paradox: there is no comfortable via media between direct didactic discourses and portraits of actual life for the Catholic author of popular fiction. Pise had tried to tip the fictional balance to the side of doctrine. Later novelists, such as Cannon, Dorsey, and the post-1850 authors, were more apt to find rhetorical reinforcements for doctrine in actual life.

Brownson himself had utilized first extreme logic and then extreme sensationalism before abandoning the writing of fiction for literary theorizing. By 1873 Brownson was sounding less like a prophetic elucidator of contemporary fictional tendencies than a reactionary purist in search of a genre that never did—and perhaps never could—exist.

III

Debunkers and Extenders

WHILE A POSITIVE, inspirational outlook dominated the fictional discussion of religion before 1850, there was during this period a small number of combative novels whose main goal was to satirize American denominations or religious figures. Between 1790 and 1815 this fiction was relatively staid and attentive to doctrine, concentrating on clever satires on various types of Calvinists. In the four decades after 1815 it became increasingly lurid, melodramatic, and pugnacious. Therefore, even this rather fragmented underground genre of combative fiction followed the overall doctrinal-to-secular pattern.

Although satirical fiction continued into the second half of the nineteenth century and beyond, the most notable feature of the post–1850 period was the rising popularity of affirmative religious novels, as evidenced by such best sellers as *The Gates Ajar, Ben-Hur,* and *In His Steps.*

7

Combative or Satirical Fiction

Several general tendencies can be identified as contributing to early fictional satire on religion in America. Eighteenth-century attacks on established religion, begun by British freethinkers and French *philosophes,* and echoed in America by such moderates as Franklin and such radicals as Paine, created an atmosphere of protest that made churches and clergymen common targets of parody. Despite the demise of deism and the dramatic growth of American religion after 1800, the aftershocks of the eighteenth-century upheaval continued to reverberate in the essays of Robert Dale Owen and Robert Ingersoll as well as in the novels of George Lippard and, later, Harold Frederic and Mark Twain. Also, the English Gothic novels of the 1780s and 1790s summoned sacrosanct religious characters into the fictional world of sanguinary adventure and seduction. While Gothic fiction contained little doctrinal discussion, it sometimes portrayed priests drunk with power and driven by lust. Moreover, in the opening decades of the nineteenth century, sectarian controversy in America was, in some important circles, accompanied by a decreasing emphasis on formal theological debate; fictional caricature became a convenient strategy for some authors who wished to circumvent polemical discussion. Lastly, the post-Revolutionary democratic ethos made American religion the province of homespun humorists who enlivened theology with sardonic wit.

Although vernacular satire on religion would not be fully developed until Mark Twain, such diverse early humorists as the Connecticut Wits and the Old-Southwest writers illustrated the opportunity provided by egalitarian piety for idiosyncratic, ironic interpretations of faith.

The satirical attitudes among which many American writers would choose were established in the eighteenth century by Joseph Morgan, Benjamin Franklin, and Thomas Paine. In *The History of the Kingdom of Basaruah* (1715) Morgan, the allegorist of covenant theology, became the first of several American authors within the religious establishment to resort to the fictional satire of religious opponents on specifically doctrinal grounds. Morgan allegorized typical conflicts involving Arminians, antinomians, deists, and so forth, conflicts that would be dramatized more realistically in much affirmative nineteenth-century fiction.

Franklin and Paine were rationalists who were dissatisfied with orthodox theology but who attacked it in different stylistic ways. The doctrinally prudent Franklin was wont to employ amiable characters—Poor Richard, Polly Baker, an Oriental magician—to advance a system of utilitarian morality and divine goodness that was aligned against New England theology. Particularly toward the end of his life, Franklin reserved his strongest religious opinions for his private letters, and even in these he was vague. Paine, in contrast, baldly expressed his disapproval of theocratic religion, his disbelief of the Bible's divine sanction, and his Socinian view of Jesus in the expository *Age of Reason.* Franklin's public satire was distanced through personae and lightened by gnomic wit. Paine's was direct and combative.

Most early American writers of fictional satire on religion preferred the indirect Franklinian persona to either Morgan's elaborate doctrinal corrections or Paine's frontal assault. In the 1790s, Susanna Rowson's invisible inquisitor, Royall Tyler's Bay Boy, and Philip Freneau's Robert Slender were fictional spokesmen used to retain some of Morgan's theological specificity while capitalizing on the witty detachment offered by the Franklinian device. As seen in Chapter 3, the kind of internecine logical satire initiated by Morgan was increasingly displaced in orthodox and liberal fiction by dramatic parody of religious opponents or else avoided altogether. At the same time, in more overtly satiric fiction the Franklinian commentator of the 1790s became absorbed, as time passed, into melodramatic plots in which sensationalism and caricature predominated over wit or theological exactitude. The figure of the wily clergyman-rake, lightly sketched by a few pre–1820 writers, became exaggerated in the satiric fiction of the 1830s, in which some Protestant and many Catholic characters were shown using heavenly persuasion to sensual ends. The anti-Catholic novel, which often represented priests as pimps and nunneries as brothels, was closer to pornography than any other early American fiction. Thus the porno-gothic style that George Lippard popularized in the 1840s had precedent in earlier American fiction.

Early Fictional Satire on Religion

In the two decades immediately following the Revolution American Calvinism was particularly subject to criticism. Edwardsean orthodoxy had rigidified into the gloomy legalism of Samuel Hopkins, Nathaniel Emmons, and Jonathan Edwards, Jr. Timothy Dwight had created an atmosphere of hostility by denouncing deists and liberals in *The Triumph of Infidelity* (1786). In the late 1790s Dwight was joined by Jedidiah Morse and other anti-Jacobins in calling freethought the product of a Bavarian cult, the Illuminati, which had infected France and which threatened to overthrow all world governments by spreading anarchy and free love. Also, ascendant evangelical religion was introducing a fervid emotionalism that repelled many rationalists and liberals.

In the face of such orthodox and evangelical excesses, the disgruntled writer could reply with Paine-like expository bombardment, with oblique subversion through Oriental or visionary tales, or with satirical fiction that mediated between direct and indirect protest. As we have seen, many writers, perhaps fearing the orthodox censure provoked by Voltaire and Paine, sought protective Oriental and visionary camouflage. At the opposite extreme, some skeptical essayists risked Paine's fate by openly repudiating Christianity. A few writers, balancing indirection and radical attack, chose fictional satire.

It is understandable that American religious satire should be introduced in the 1790s by two Episcopalians, Susanna Rowson and Royall Tyler, and a deist, Philip Freneau. Anglicanism in America had been hurt by the war, and deism was becoming increasingly unpopular. The Anglican and freethinker found in satirical fiction a means of vindictive reprisal which sidestepped the potential obloquy that could result from an inflammatory essay. In *The Inquisitor* (1793) Rowson couched an attack on revivalist Calvinism in the self-protective visionary mode. Her invisible rambler, witnessing an evangelical preacher who publicly damns sinners while privately living in sin, operates as a rational persona who keeps the author slightly distanced from overt satire. Similarly in *The Bay Boy* (1797) Tyler assumed the guise of Updike Underhill to satirize Calvinist polemicism and fanaticism; later in 1797, in *The Algerine Captive,* Tyler sent Underhill to the Orient for the more dangerous task of advancing Arian and Arminian views.

Freneau's *Letters on Various Subjects* (1799), published under the pseudonym of Robert Slender, contains the most extensive ridicule of religion in American fiction before 1800. Like Rowson and Tyler, Freneau takes on the persona of an intelligent, somewhat amused observer of the current religious scene. Robert Slender contrasts the venality and hypocrisy of the established clergy with the unpretentious virtue of American farmers. He then goes on to mock the Illuminati theory as paranoid and self-contradictory. Mentioning Timothy Dwight and Jedidiah Morse by name, Slender constructs a long, witty defense of deism against its anti-Jacobin foes.

Thus, fictional satirists before 1800 presented explicit renderings of anti-Calvinist themes without venturing into the risky area of open expository attack. Rowson's two-faced preacher, Tyler's squabbling polemicists, and Freneau's xenophobic Calvinists were updated versions of comic characters of Fielding, Smollett, and Sterne that had kept Americans laughing since mid-century. The invisible rambler, Updike Underhill, and Robert Slender were lowly but wise characters invented to please a generation reared on Poor Richard. The contrast between fuming religionists and a cool observer reinforced the image of reason and self-possession commonly held during the American Enlightenment. The devices of fictional satire thus enabled three religious outsiders to expose the absurdities of established religion and at the same time to shield themselves behind the conventions of fictional entertainment and enlightened commentary.

After 1810 this rather cautious anti-Calvinist satire was joined first by fiction aimed at liberals and deists and then by a more sensational brand of satirical fiction. The growing diversification of combative fiction was reflected in four novels published between 1815 and 1820: Elijah Sabin's *Charles Observator* (1816), Samuel L. Knapp's *Journal of Marshal Soult* (1817), *The Yankee Traveller* (1817), and *The Life and Adventures of Obadiah Benjamin Franklin Bloomfield, M.D.* (1818). Sabin summoned satirical weapons into the Calvinist novelist's arsenal, explaining in his preface, "The inspired writers have given us some of the *liveliest* and most *cutting* examples of satire; [the author] begs that religious readers would not think him altogether unjustifiable in his method of writing."[1] Despite this announcement, Sabin tried to restrain his caricature of liberals in keeping with his orthodox proclivity to doctrinal discussion reminiscent of Morgan. Knapp too tempered his satire on the tilting match between Unitarians and Calvinists with some compensatory praise of the parties involved; his real animosity toward Calvinist metaphysics did not surface until his Oriental tale *Ali Bey* (1818).

It was left to the anonymous authors of *The Yankee Traveller* and *Obadiah Bloomfield* to introduce extreme caricature and the theme of seduction to fictional satires on American religion. Like Sabin and Knapp, these writers convert the Franklinian persona into a traveling protagonist who comments on current religious tendencies. But the judicious doctrinal debate of *Charles Observator* and *Marshal Soult* gives way in the later novels to more highly charged, adventurous portraits of sinning philosophers and clergymen. *The Yankee Traveller* depicts curiously named freethinkers wooing women and duping men; *Obadiah Bloomfield* shows a Methodist itinerant using his persuasive powers to seduce members of his congregation.

The characters in *The Yankee Traveller* include Hector Wigler, the narrator, who records his skeptical upbringing under the stewardship of his deistical Uncle Humbug; Nihil, an atheist Wigler meets on a stage, who cleverly persuades a fellow traveler, Miss Wimble, to sleep with him in an inn; Squib and Scribble, two Godwinian pranksters who dress up as avenging devils and cause the terrified Nihil to renounce his infidelity; Thomas Conundrum and his aide, Dr. Von Stufflefunk, leaders of a freethinking organization; and a loud Methodist revivalist.

The Yankee Traveller attacks nearly every philosopher of the skeptical and radical Enlightenment, not through reasoned refutation but through comic characterization and plot. For instance, Nihil wins Wimble's favor by referring her to "the writings of Mary Wollstonecraft, Godwin, and Paine, who would teach her to make the best of this life, for hereafter we had nothing to expect; for we should know nothing and be nothing."[2] The satire on infidelity is heightened by the portrait of Conundrum, a "withered up, monkey-faced, lantern-jawed form of a man" (34) whose wall motto reads: *"True Philosophy rising upon the ruins of superstitious, vindictive, and dogmatical theology"* (49). At first dazzled by Conundrum's erudition, Wigler soon learns that the man is "superficial, ostentatious, visionary, whimsical, illiberal, perfidious, and vain" (51). The pimpled Stufflefunk is no better, for he devotes his time to prolix treatises on the length of tadpole tails. Wigler finds affirmative Christianity equally unattractive. The itinerant Methodist he meets has "a bawling sort of eloquence," with a speciality "in groaning" (56).

The abbreviated denunciation of Methodism in *The Yankee Traveller* is expanded in *The Life and Adventures of Obadiah Benjamin Franklin Bloomfield, M.D.,* in which the circuit-riding hero seduces and abandons various women and then leaves the ministry altogether. By name and by temperament this hero is linked to the witty Franklinian persona. By the vicissitudes of his life he is trapped in the stormy domain of the sentimental novel. Renouncing the Presbyterianism of his childhood, Bloomfield learns the art of popular preaching from Mr. Method, an unlearned but successful revivalist. Bloomfield soon gains a great reputation as an itinerant, but his persuasive powers prove his downfall, as he convinces one of his female listeners that she is "a poor, frail, weak sinner" whose carnal desires demand satisfaction. Knowing that he has "polluted the sacred order" by seducing the girl, Bloomfield quits preaching and becomes a doctor.[3] After several love affairs, two painful marriages, a bigamy trial, and a love duel, Bloomfield can still display a pretense of piety, hoping that someday all men will bow down before Christ, who atoned "for the sins—the incalculable sins, of the degenerate descendants of Adam!" (129).

Despite their different intentions, *The Yankee Traveller* and *Obadiah Bloomfield* introduced to American literature that genre of satirical fiction that would eventually produce *Elmer Gantry.* The idea of a religionist who bends theological notions to serve licentious aims would become quite common in debunking novels of the twentieth century; but in 1818 the theme represented a marked break with the past. *The Yankee Traveller,* safely distanced by two decades from the period of deism's greatest popularity, converts the rake of sentimental fiction into the self-parodying villain of the antideist novel. *Obadiah Bloomfield* takes the further step of portraying the moral degeneration of an evangelical preacher. The detached persona of the pre-1800 satiric novel has begun to be drawn into a world of freakish philosophers, conceited clergymen, and willing women.

Through most of the 1820s, as in the period between 1800 and 1815, this sensational type of satire was not being written. Explicit satire tended to appear during relatively troubled moments in American religion, moments when the wave of religious expansionism was checked by a small backwash of disillusionment. The decade of the 1790s was one such moment; American religion was recovering from the devastations of the war, church membership was down, and the religious scene seemed polarized between fearful Calvinists and critical freethinkers. The first fifteen years of the nineteenth century, in contrast, brought a dramatic upsurge of affirmative religion: the Second Great Awakening, the founding of the Benevolent Empire, and the Plan of Union created a general spirit of enthusiasm and cooperation. In a sense, this spirit would not be seriously challenged until the Civil War. But it changed cyclically, and there were times when it was particularly apt to be questioned. For instance, the period between 1815 and 1820 was a time when the start of the Second Great Awakening was far behind and the important tract societies of the 1820s were yet to be formed. Similarly, the 1830s brought the decline of the Benevolent Empire and of the Plan of Union, as well as the sudden influx of Roman Catholics from abroad. Thus, sensational religious satire was an extreme response to periodic religious changes which seemed disturbing enough to be challenged with arms of the flesh.

This is not to say that religious satire disappeared in the 1820s; rather, it temporarily became respectable. The early novels of Catherine Sedgwick, Lydia Child, James Kirke Paulding, and Sarah Hale showed that anti-Calvinist satire could be incorporated into fairly sophisticated novels of American history and manners. Each of these writers produced at least one novel in the 1820s which contained an extensive satiric portrait of an evil Calvinist figure. Orthodox fiction of the period also utilized satire. The allegorical *Dr. Caleb* (1822) and the sentimental *Justina* (1824), for example, caricatured liberal opponents. But the character of the scheming, pious seducer was absent from the novels of this decade. This was a time when religious discussion was not to be taken too lightly and when the distribution of didactic literature was in full force. In New England the Unitarian controversy was at its height, so that writers like Sedgwick and Child were careful to avoid easily dismissed smear tactics in their anti-Calvinist novels. A serious competition among various denominations to win the American public resulted in the establishment of several important religious publishing houses, including the American Tract Society and the American Sunday School Union. It was a period when satire was sober rather than salacious, studied rather than vehement.

The reemergence of sensational satire was signaled by three works published between 1828 and 1835: *Morganania* (1828), an attack on various indigenous and foreign sects; *The Confessions of a Magdalene* (1831), a lurid study of the victim of a Calvinist seducer; and Catherine Read Williams' *Fall River* (1833), an account of sex and murder at camp meetings.

Morganania, though it professes to be a translation of an Arabic manuscript, and though it utilizes a devil figure, is less an Oriental or visionary tale than a lighthearted rationalist satire with a serious intent. The narrator sees, among other things, a dandyish Satan hobnobbing with the Pope, with American Protestant ministers, and with Turkish Muslims. "I have often seen [Satan]," the narrator reports, "at a conventicle and at church in New England, and at a mosque in Turkey, at which places he seems as pious as the most devout, and the ladies have universally paid him the most marked attention."[4] In America "the devil is a particular friend of many religious sects, and very often kindly helps out a parson in preaching" (35). In Turkey, when he denies the special sanctity of Allah and Mohammed, his head is cut off and replaced backwards. Such humorous exposure of religious intolerance is combined with long attacks on Masons throughout the book. Though brief and uneven, *Morganania* is important for the reiteration of the kind of farcical, excessive satire that had characterized some of the works between 1815 and 1820.

In *The Confessions of a Magdalene* the sober anti-Calvinism of most 1820s novels is replaced by a sensational mixture of seduction and satire reminiscent of *Obadiah Bloomfield.* The villain of the piece is Deodat Pidgeon, a hellfire revivalist who seduces the lovely Experience Borgia. At the start, Pidgeon is a "searching" preacher renowned for discoursing "beautifully" upon "election—the secret will of God—the awful depravity of man."[5] Experience at first balks at his strict Calvinism. But he warns her that it is sinful "to indulge in liberal feelings," that "liberal feelings" are "wicked feelings" (5). Overwhelmed with lust for his parishioner, Pidgeon puts a soporific drug into her milk one night and ravishes her while she is asleep. When she awakes, he begs for pardon by saying that "the tempter reigned over me,—I have prayed to God and he has forgiven me" (13). He promises to marry her but frames her in a petty theft case instead. While she is on trial, he escapes to the western frontier, where he becomes a famous revivalist. Well set on the path of sin, Experience goes to the city, becomes a drunken prostitute, and marries a bigamist who later abandons her. Several years later Experience meets a blind beggar on the street who turns out to be Pidgeon. Experience sneers at the "poor boast of the final perseverance of the saints, by those who are themselves the worst of sinners" (23). Soon after this encounter, Experience joins a whorehouse. At the end, however, she reforms and establishes a settlement house where "the vicious" are "reclaimed by gentle means." In this "abode of industry, order and good morals" many wayward women are made "hopefully religious." "No fanatical preacher" is permitted inside (25).

In *The Confessions of a Magdelene* the sensational undercutting of orthodox doctrine is more consistent and more comprehensive than it was in *Obadiah Bloomfield*. Conversion, damnation, original sin, election, and perseverance of the saints are shown to be glibly voiced theories mocked by "Experience." The novel couples lurid anti-Calvinism with a direct attack on tract publishers. Early in the novel Experience writes down an ecstatic conversion experience and gives it to a religious society. Later she recalls cynically: "I have seen it since in tracts and other publications, mutilated and mended, or rather, altered to suit the purposes of the publishers" (9). The entire novel betrays the author's suspicion of both the affirmative didactic literature and the serious doctrinal controversy of the 1820s. Tract biographies of wholesome preachers guiding their congregations are here mocked by the story of a lustful preacher who drugs and deflowers a faithful admirer. The sedate portrayal of the evil Calvinist in the 1820s is pushed to an extreme caricature of a licentious clergyman.

Catherine Read Williams' *Fall River,* published two years after *Magdalene,* tries to ground sensational satire more solidly in fact. In *Religion at Home* (1829) the Episcopalian Williams had lamented the startling growth of evangelical religion in America. After linking Methodism to social disruption in *Religion at Home,* Williams charges it with individual corruption in *Fall River.* The latter novel describes the "disgusting intrigues" of E. K. Avery, a revivalist "of wicked, and revengeful, and persecuting temper" who has "frequent closeting in [his] famous study with females."[6] After one camp meeting, Avery violently ravages the young Maria Cornell, who soon dies of grief. Avery's acquittal at the subsequent murder trial is shown to be a mockery of justice. At the end of the novel, the Episcopalian Fanny Windsor's successful resistance of Avery's advances is posed as a lesson for potential victims of Methodist seducers. In her appendix Williams presents more instances of "the great evils of fanaticism generally, and of Camp-Meetings in particular" (166). Included are several "factual" stories of drunkenness, seduction, and murder at Methodist revivals.

These religious satires published between 1828 and 1833, then, represented a small cynical backlash against the triumphant renewal of affirmative Christianity in the 1820s. *Morganania* assigns self-satisfied American religionists to the devil; *Magdalene* and *Fall River* puncture the pious exteriors of evangelical preachers to reveal wiliness and lust within their souls. The attack on recent popular tracts in *Magdalene* and Williams' attempts at topical historicity suggest that in the early 1830s some American writers were disillusioned with the expansionism of the previous decade. As in the 1790s, the writers of religious satire were outsiders—a freethinker, a vehement anti-Calvinist, an Episcopalian—who could not accept the exuberant optimism of the religious mainstream and who showed evidence of a jealous bitterness over being left out.

In this connection, it is notable that the most notorious outsider of the period, the freethinker Robert Dale Owen, began the decade with the publication of *Popular Tracts* (1830), a collection of essays and stories intended to parody the serious didactic literature that had begun to proliferate in the 1820s. In one of Owen's tales, "Darby and Susan," the contentment of a freethinking couple is destroyed when they attend a revival meeting. Hearing themselves being called sinful worms dangling over a lake of fire, Darby and Susan are driven insane. In another story a boy is made gloomy by his mother's orthodoxy and comes to be gladdened by his father's liberating skepticism. Like the other satirists, Owen used fiction to undercut the preconceptions of the average didactic reader.

After 1833 sensational satire was increasingly channeled away from anti-Calvinism to anti-Catholicism. The lustful revivalist was replaced by the lascivious priest, as the novelist's animosity shifted to the Catholics who were arriving from Europe. But religious satire after 1833 was not restricted exclusively to anti-Catholic fiction. Combative portraits of contemporary religious types continued to be presented in a series of novels: Robert Montgomery Bird's *The Hawks of Hawk-Hollow* (1835), the anonymous *Retroprogression* (1839), *The Hypocrite* (1844) by "Aesop," and Theodore Bang's *The Mysteries of Papermill Village* (1845). Bird's brief sketch of the itinerant Nehemiah Poke subjects Methodism to the charge of ignorance and sanctimony common in satirical fiction. More extensive religious commentary appears in the other novels, which show that some satirists continued to scourge the Protestant mainstream even while most were turning their attention to Catholics.

If the novels of 1828-33 were aimed at tract writers and sober religious figures, *Retroprogression* was aimed at another product of nineteenth-century religious expansion: reform. With the acme of the Benevolent Empire behind, the anonymous author of this novel could note that "moral reformers" tend to "advance backward" and "injure the very cause they are laboring to promote."[7] Among the misled reformers of the imagined town of Jumbleborough are the Reverend John Meanwell, "one of those restless characters, so common now a days, whose zeal outruns their discretion" (9), and, interestingly, Willdo Emerson, who "told his hearers they were gods, and that Jesus Christ was only a 'model man'" (13). Another citizen of the town, Dr. Solomon Grayman Snakeroot, thinks "that one disease could be cured by a universal pill," abolition (15). The most strongly satirized figure is Deacon Inobetter Wronghead, a Benevolent Empire reformer who tries to destroy the great tree of human sin by lopping off the branches of profanity, slavery, intemperance, and war. Wronghead is told by a more intelligent clergyman: "The ministers of CHRIST have been commanded by their master to lay the axe to the *root* of this tree, but, supposing that they had discovered a safer and more effectual procedure, they are, like you, trying to annihilate the tree by cutting off the branches first" (32). Such pruning, Wronghead is warned, in fact gives the tree added vigor, engendering thousands of new shoots. The model man of Jumbleborough is Dr. Stedman, whose Episcopal church is the town's only bulwark against "the headlong torrent of change, falsely called improvement!" (78–79).

Thus in *Retroprogression* we find one more writer outside the religious mainstream, an anonymous Episcopalian, trying through fictional satire to stem the torrent of change raging in American religion. Yet another pseudonymous Episcopalian satirist, Aesop, carried such criticism into the 1840s with *The Hypocrite*. Aesop's novel attacks various forms of popular American religion through the persona of Tristram Slyman, the son of a Presbyterian farmer and his freethinking wife. "In matters of religion," Tristram learns, " 'the true Yankee' will be anything you please, with a very easy conscience. A Churchman, a Calvinist, a Quaker, a Baptist, a Papist, a Methodist, or a Mormon, will suit him equally well, so long as money can be made by his profession of faith."[8] Tristram's father proves to be venal and superstitious, absurdly credulous of the "divine miracles" staged by the playful Tristram. His mother, raised a Voltairean skeptic, opposes the father's Calvinism but finds little solace in her infidelity. As the novel progresses we learn that as a young woman she had been seduced by the Reverend Mr. Bullneck, an orthodox preacher "hypocritically wicked beyond a parallel" (38). The sensuous, canting Bullneck had won Mrs. Slyman's heart by preaching that we must *"become the means of pleasure to others"* (43). Another satirized figure is Calvin Longface, a "miser bigot" who hates Catholics and hoards his wealth without giving to the poor (25). Bullneck and Longface show how "one bad professing Christian will do more harm to the cause of pure piety than ten infidels" (56). The one unblemished character is the Episcopalian clergyman, the Reverend Thomas Goodman, "who was as much like an angel as Bullneck was like a devil" (69). Under Goodman's tutorship, Tristram learns to defend the "true religion" against the corruptions of "base hypocrites" and "Judases" (104).

Retroprogression and *The Hypocrite* suggest that in the 1840s some Episcopalians in America were still suffering from the same cynical alienation that had been manifested by earlier Episcopalian satirists such as Rowson, Tyler, and Williams. Evangelical Calvinism was thriving, liberalism was holding its own, and American religion in general was changing rapidly to meet the demands of an expanding nation. In the face of such changes, the Episcopalian was more likely than other novelists to make satirical sallies at a culture that threatened to exclude him. This embittered attitude was evident not only in the satires cited above but also in the relatively logical *History of a Pocket Prayer Book* (1839), in which the Episcopalian Benjamin Dorr exposes a wide variety of American Protestant sects by posing the Anglican liturgy as a stable standard that puts the lie to changeable sectarian opinion and ministerial talents. Although they had, like Catholics, a strong tradition of intellectual scholarship to support their cause, Episcopalian novelists were more willing than Catholics to resort to caricature and sensationalism. Americans had violently rejected the hierarchy of the Anglican church in the Revolution, and the early Episcopalian novelist felt compelled to take equally violent measures to restore the true religion in fiction.

That the skeptical rationalist also felt alienated from American religion in the 1840s is evidenced by Theodore Bang's *Mysteries of Papermill Village*. Bang attacks various Christian citizens of his fictional Sipsville as slanderous, pugnacious, and intemperate. "RELIGION," Bang notes, "often, too often, is a gilded name; . . . a business of policy, craft and cunning, a regular-built speculation; a dollar-and-cent trade, where the Rev. will read off, on Sundays, say two or three prosy sermons . . . but . . . will not say grace at all without dollars and cents."[9] "Rivers of blood" have flowed because of bigots who use "the annihilating cannon, or the murderous sword" (144). The Sipsville Christians "are DEVOTED; are ZEALOUS; are ACTIVE" to nothing but "*our* cause" (14). Like the freethinking *Morganania* author, Bang conjures up an amiable devil to vivify his satire. The devil says of the town's churchgoers: "Their badge is 'universal love,' but in truth, they fight worse than my little satans ever did" (16). At the end Bang advises a general renunciation of jarring sectarianism and practical observance of the Golden Rule.

The post–1835 fictional satires reveal a broadening critique of American religion that prepares for the comprehensive commentary of George Lippard in the late 1840s. In the 1790s established ministers were charged with fanaticism, narrowness, and intolerance; in the periods from 1815 to 1820 and 1828 to 1833 lust and vanity were added to the list of faults. In the post–1835 works these shortcomings were stressed along with others. Reformers were posed as myopic purveyors of false panaceas. Greed was identified as a common ministerial motivation, as Bang had called religion "a dollar-and-cent trade" conducted by "cunning" entrepeneurs. Proselytizing zeal was equated with self-interested competition, alleged benevolence with shallow ingratiation. The post–1835 satires were neither longer nor more complex than the earlier ones; but their scope was wider, their criticism more severe and sweeping. The earlier studies of such individual sinners as Obadiah Bloomfield, Deodat Pidgeon, and E. K. Avery were replaced by more inclusive portraits of representative towns peopled with sensualists and hypocrites of all sects. The author of the later satire was similar to the pre–1835 writer: he was typically an Episcopalian or freethinker who used fiction to expose mainstream vices. But he was less content than his predecessors to write a farce about an erring individual. He wished to create a satire that was at once engaging and biting, colorfully particularized yet generally applicable.

At the same time that affirmative religious fiction was exalting individual exertion as the key to earthly and heavenly reward, satirical fiction was answering that individuals of all sects are trapped in a maze of earthly desires and ills that bars them from heaven.

Fictional Attacks on Roman Catholicism

Between 1834 and 1850 several American Protestants wrote a series of novels that attributed nearly every sin imaginable to Roman Catholic priests and nuns. Such satires as *Obadiah Bloomfield* and *Confessions of a Magdalene* seem innocent when compared with some of the anti-Catholic novels. Alcoholism, prostitution, flagellation, and infanticide were said to be common within convent walls. Priests were represented as emissaries of the papal devil bent on ruining the virtue of young women. The convent system was branded a malicious threat to democratic ideals. The story of early anti-Catholic fiction is one of increasing xenophobic outrage on the part of nativists who felt that the growth of Roman Catholicism in America must be stopped at any cost.

Before 1830 fictional attacks on Roman Catholicism were not infrequent but were relatively restrained. The comparative mildness of anti-Catholic arguments in pre–1830 American fiction is explained by the fact that most Protestants felt they had little to fear from a denomination that was numerically insignificant. Violent satire, as we have seen, was principally the product of resentment and alienation on the part of religious outsiders; and in the first three decades of the nineteenth century, expansionist American Protestantism was confident that it was the Catholics who would remain on the outside.

As time passed this confidence began to be shaken. A tiny and ignored denomination as late as 1820, by 1850 Roman Catholicism had become the largest church in America. Various foreign catastrophes, particularly the Irish potato famine, caused great waves of Roman Catholics to flood to America's shores betwen 1825 and 1850. The epoch-making Provincial Council of Baltimore, held in October 1829, made it clear that Roman Catholicism was to be an organized and permanent feature of the American religious scene. To be sure, a number of American Protestants were attracted to Catholicism: nearly seven hundred thousand would be converted between 1813 and 1893, including the celebrated Orestes Brownson and Isaac Hecker. But Catholicism's foes became more numerous and vociferous than its friends. Anti-Catholic writings appeared in various native periodicals, most prominently the *New York Observer* (founded in 1823), George Bourne's *Protestant* (founded in 1830), and William Craig Brownlee's *Protestant Vindicator* (founded in 1833). The English Catholic Emancipation Bill of 1829 provoked a large amount of "No Popery" literature which was read widely in America and Canada. The nativist cause was taken up by such noted clergymen as Lyman Beecher, Samuel

Morse, and Horace Bushnell. In Massachusetts anti-Catholic sentiment led to the burning of Charlestown's Ursuline Convent in August 1834 by a group of enraged Protestants. Never, except perhaps during the Communist scare that would be instigated by Joseph McCarthy in the 1950s, was vindictive xenophobia so rampant and strident as it was in nativist circles in antebellum America.

Assured of their supremacy, Protestant novelists before 1830 had frequently made undeveloped and dismissively brief anti-Catholic comments. After 1830 some Protestant writers began to fear that they were exchanging places with Catholics as religious outsiders. Since Protestant fiction was becoming increasingly nontheological, logic was found to be inappropriate for fictional warfare. The combination of embittered alienation and nonlogical fictional technique produced a school of sensational anti-Catholic satire in the 1830s and 1840s the likes of which had not been seen in America before and has not been seen since.

The anti-Catholic fiction of the 1830s began in comparatively intellectual fashion with Anne T. Bullard's *The Reformation* (1832), which in its use of reasoned exposition reflected the approach of the Scottish Grace Kennedy in the popular *Father Clement* (1823). Bullard's book takes the form of a dialogue on the history of the Protestant Reformation between a dignified schoolteacher, Mrs. Athearn, and her female students. Mrs. Athearn carefully defends the justice of Luther's protest and the nobility of his example. Trying to refute Catholicism's claims to infallibility, she says that Christ conferred authority not only on Peter but on all his disciples. She cites the writings of Protestant theologians to support her view that the Bible should be made available to all.

Despite the overall equanimity of the book, Bullard occasionally lapses into the kind of fervid opprobrium that would dominate later anti-Catholic fiction. For example, "the boldness, the fearlessness, and the determined attack" of Luther is contrasted to the "immorality, ambition, fraud, avarice and cruelty" of the priests he opposed.[10] The Pope is called the antichrist, and Catholic rites are said to be infected at the root. In short, Bullard's work is similar to the early novels of many genres of religious fiction: largely expository and intentionally reasoned, it nevertheless summons emotionalism and dramatic embellishment into religious discussion.

A year after the publication of Bullard's book, the anti-Catholic novel began its plunge toward melodramatic sensationalism with the appearance of George Bourne's *Lorette. The History of Louise, Daughter of a Canadian Nun* (1833). Bourne's book became the prototype of the most popular type of post–1835 anti-Catholic fiction—the exposé of convents. Dedicated to several respectable clergymen, Bourne's book presents a lurid record of convent dissipation aimed at displaying "the blasphemy, the wretchedness, the coarse manners, the shameless loquacity, . . . hypocritical sanctity and sensual indulgences" of

Roman Catholic priests.[11] Bourne describes Canadian nunneries as houses of prostitution where sexual perversion and child murder are a way of life. The heroine, a pietistic orphan named Louise, is abducted to a convent. The Protestant God preserves Louise's virtue, but she finally dies of grief.

The expository arguments of Bullard's novel are actively dramatized by Bourne. For example, whereas Bullard theorized that Protestantism was justified in permitting free access to the Scriptures, Bourne's heroine is saved from despoilment as a result of her constant reading of her hidden Bible. Action replaces historical contemplation. At one hurried moment Louise is about to develop the idea that the Pope is "infallible in nothing but impiety and wickedness" when she is forced to add that "this is no time for religious discussion" (38). At moments the novel manifests fascination with the corruption it denounces, as when Louise is told that in convents women may "enjoy every pleasure of life without restraint, unreproached, and exempt from the fear of discovery" (57). Whatever Bourne's secret attractions may be, his anti-Catholicism is unremitting. In his eyes priests are "human monsters," nuns "adepts in every species of vice" (58). The priests "not only kill their children to hide their corruption, but also the mothers of their offspring, rather than their pretended celibacy shall be discovered" (209). They burn babies and Bibles with smirking indifference. Bourne's message is summed up in the following passage: "The interior of a convent is the *sepulchre of goodness,* and the *castle of misery.* Within its unsanctified domain, youth withers; knowledge is extinguished; usefulness is entombed; and religion expires. The life of a Nun is a course of exterior solemn mummery, from which all that is lovely is ejected; and under the vizor dwells everything loathsome and horrible" (124).

Bourne set the pattern for anti-Catholic fiction in America between 1835 and 1845. Some novelists were more lurid than Bourne, some less, and each had a special new "fact" to disclose. All were joined in the denunciation of convents as antidemocratic prisons where grotesque crimes were committed regularly.

The author of *Female Convents. Secrets of Nunneries Disclosed* (1834), using the pseudonym "Mr. DePotter," gave anti-Catholicism a political coloring by stressing the threat to American democracy posed by the convent system. That Bullard's intellectualism has been purposefully abandoned is suggested by the editor Thomas Roscoe's prefatory comment: "Very little reference is made in this work to the theological portions of Romanism."[12] The book aims to show how convents threaten "to subvert the whole fabric of the rights of conscience, and the government and constitution of the United States" (ix). In the novel convents are held suspect for several reasons: they destroy social usefulness by demanding isolation, they encourage sensuality and crime, they inhibit the progress of intelligence, and they subvert true religion.

After 1834, the year of the burning of the Ursuline Convent in Charlestown, increasing emphasis was placed on the veracity of anti-Catholic fiction; to combat what was seen as a very real danger, real proof was needed. As a result, two former nuns, Rebecca Reed and Maria Monk, penned allegedly autobiographical accounts of convent life which became the most popular and most notorious anti-Catholic works of the period. *Six Months in a Convent* (1835), Reed's record of her stay in the Charlestown nunnery in 1832, was heralded by its publishers as a work comparable in importance to Luther's first tract against the Catholic church. Indeed, though Reed's book was rather tame, it took the nation by storm and initiated a two-decade battle about who was responsible for the Charlestown burning. Even more widely read was Monk's *Awful Disclosures of . . . the Hotel Dieu Nunnery at Montreal* (1836), a tale of convent torture and infanticide which sold so well that it earned, as Ray A. Billington says, "the questionable distinction of being the 'Uncle Tom's Cabin of Know-Nothingism.' "[13]

Since they are ostensibly autobiographical, these two works do not appear in most modern bibliographies of early American fiction. But they deserve attention in this discussion because their embellishment of the truth reflects the readiness of anti-Catholics of the period to make reality conform to the preconceptions of the fictional satirist. On this score, Reed's work is the least excessive of the two. The penances Reed describes as common at Charlestown—self-laceration, walking on pebbles until blood flows, never smiling except at recreation period—are harsh but conceivable. The lust of priests is implied but not detailed. Protestant readers were probably attracted to the apparent authenticity of Reed's narrative. The story of a girl who enters a nunnery idealizing priests and nuns, who eventually deceive her, impelling her to escape and to renounce Catholicism, vindicated the suspicions of a readership long accustomed to wily monks victimizing innocent heroines in sentimental and Gothic novels. In light of the nation's growing nativist bias, Reed's seemingly historical work had a natural appeal to Americans who wished to see their fears substantiated by fact.

But it is Maria Monk's *Awful Disclosures* that most graphically illustrates the idea of reality conforming to fiction. Monk was aided in the writing of her memoirs by George Bourne, author of the sensational *Lorette*. When Monk arrived in New York in 1835, allegedly having just escaped the Hotel Dieu convent in Montreal, four anti-Catholic clergymen, including Bourne, helped her transcribe her experiences into publishable form. It is probable that Bourne's group undertook the project for mercenary reasons. By 1835 anti-Catholicism, as one essayist of the time noted, had become "a regular trade, and the compilation of anti-Catholic books . . . a part of the regular industry of the country, as much as the making of nutmegs, or the construction of clocks."[14] After Harper Brothers refused to publish the book because of its scurrilous contents, the four clergymen established a dummy publishing firm to insure themselves a share of the profits from the sale of the book.

Despite its pretenses to originality and truth, *Awful Disclosures* seems suspi-
ciously like a mixture of Bourne's *Lorette* and Reed's *Six Months in a Convent*.
We know that Bourne helped Monk write the book and also that Monk was
reading Reed's report, which fascinated her, in the year before *Awful Dislosures*
appeared. Monk's plot of entering and escaping a convent follows Reed's pattern, and her account of whoredom and infanticide recalls Bourne's work. The
apparent veracity of Monk's book is enhanced by her detailed physical descriptions of the Hotel Dieu and her citation of convent records. The most remarkable feature of the nunnery is a large basement used both as a torture
chamber and a tomb. Monk reports having witnessed priests torturing nuns
and strangling babies in this cellar and then casting them into a deep lime pit.
From the convent log Monk discovers that at least 375 infants had been born,
baptized, and killed in the Hotel Dieu since its founding.

In the five years after the publication of *Awful Disclosures* controversy raged
over the issue of the book's factuality. Prominent anti-Catholics insisted the
book was true, citing such evidence as scars on Monk's body which she
claimed were the result of torture devices used in the nunnery. Catholics replied that Monk was an impostor and her book a vicious novel gotten up by
venal Protestants. Monk's mother testified that the girl had never been in the
Hotel Dieu, saying that the whole story was the product of brain damage
caused when Maria had run a slate pencil through her head as a child. She recalled that Maria had been a wild girl who of necessity was placed in a Mag-
dalen asylum in Montreal.

At last, the obvious solution to the problem, an investigation of the Hotel
Dieu, was hit upon by some ministers involved in the controversy. After one
investigator was called a dupe of the Catholics when he reported that the
nunnery was perfectly safe, another, the respected Colonel William L. Stone,
made a thorough search of the convent with Monk's book in hand to find cor-
roborative evidence of torture chambers, dead babies, and prostitutes. Stone
found no such evidence and declared: "I most solemnly believe that the priests
and nuns are innocent in this matter."[15] Monk's story was largely discredited,
and even her most ardent supporters began to refer to her work as a novel.
Once a public figure pitied as the victim of Catholic wrongdoing, Monk sank
into obscurity. Arrested for picking the pockets of her companion of the moment in a house of prostitution, she died in a New York prison in 1849. But
Awful Dislosures continued to be popular. At least three hundred thousand
copies were sold before the Civil War. If Maria Monk had not told the exact
truth, she had at least produced a fictional satire on religion with wide appeal
in a time when popular fiction was beginning to shape reality.

While Reed's and Monk's books dominated the anti-Catholic literary scene
between 1835 and 1845, other nativist novels also gained currency. Rosamond
Culbertson's *Rosamond* (1836) climaxed an account of the author's love affair
with a Cuban priest by exposing a clerical plot to capture Negro boys, kill

them, and grind them into sausage meat for public consumption. In *The American Nun* (1836) Mrs. L. Larned paradoxically blamed entry into nunneries on novel reading, which was claimed to create a disposition to seclusion and illusory romanticism akin to convent life. An English novelist, Charlotte Elizabeth Tonna, published at least nine anti-Catholic novels between 1841 and 1846 which achieved considerable popularity in America despite their argumentative quality. Benjamin Barker's pseudo-historical *Cecilia* (1845), an American novel about a nun terrorized by a lecherous priest and saved by a valiant soldier, is typical of the most popular anti-Catholic novels of the period. The Charlestown issue was kept alive by Justin Jones, who, in *The Nun of St. Ursula* (1845), attributed the conflagration to a Protestant turned Muslim who rescued his fiancée from the Charlestown nunnery upon his return from Turkey. A similar plot provided the basis of three novels by Charles W. Frothingham published in 1854. Rachel MacCrindell and James M. Campbell were other American authors who attacked convents in several novels between 1845 and 1855.

Predictably, the burgeoning convent genre drew fire from Catholics. Such Catholic novelists as Charles J. Cannon, John D. Bryant, Anna Dorsey, and Jedediah Huntington tried to refute Protestant distortions by portraying nuns as angels, priests as sages, and nunneries as peaceful havens. In *John O'Brien* (1850) John T. Roddan culminated a long tirade against convent novels with a direct parody of Culbertson's *Rosamond* in which Protestant boys were shown being cast into a large meat grinder that produced sausages.

An even more violent means of reprisal was found by Norwood Damon, whose *The Chronicles of Mount Benedict* (1837) satirized convent fiction. Damon reduces the charges of his Protestant foes to absurdities by outdoing them. Presenting a parodic version of the true origins of the Ursuline Convent in Charlestown, Damon revisits sixteenth-century Europe, where the young Maria Ursula is shown being seduced by lustful priests and by the Pope himself. Declaring that he "must plant a sucker of the true vine in America, in that land of future generations," the Pope commissions the ghosts of Ursula and her paramours to travel to Charlestown to establish a convent.[16] Because of delays the spectral band does not arrive in America until 1826. The Charlestown establishment becomes the site of revelry, torture, and child murder until a group of Protestants, disturbed by the smell of roasting flesh, attack and burn the convent. In his ironic conclusion Damon explains that American readers will ignore a story with "plain common sense and truth to recommend it":

But give them some awful, nasty disclosures, by Maria Monk, or some other whorish, wild, improbable, bugbear story, and they will gullup it all down voraciously, and lick their lips with ineffable gusto. Extravagant stories! their extravagance is at this day, their highest recommenda-

tion, it is the very thing that will gain them credence; all the pious
snuff-taking grannies in the nation will crave after this book, as the sand
craves water; they will believe every word of it; they will bring out the
briny rheum from their withered eyes to weep over the sorrows of
Lionel and Maria; then they will wipe their round-eyed, far-sighted spectacles, and pronounce their sage anathemas upon the wicked catholics
[123].

Damon's comment cannot be dismissed as the overreaction of a sour Catholic—it points to the real phenomenon that after 1835 anti-Catholic fiction in
America was especially salable when it was sentimental and scabrous. As an
essayist for the *Freeman's Journal* wrote: "Verily, the hatred of Rome covers a
multitude of sins. Whoever wishes to gain honor, and renown in the United
States need only write a book against the 'Harlot of Babylon.' The blacker he
paints her, the more profitable will it be for him."[17]

In other anti-Catholic novels this multitude of sins came to include more
than just the persecution of nuns. W. C. Brownlee's *Whigs of Scotland* (1833),
J. C. Meeks's *Pierre and His Family* (1841), and Lawrence Bungener's *The
Priest and the Huguenot* (1854) described the sufferings of Protestant martyrs
who faced popish inquisitors. Other novels, notably *Recantation* (1846) and
Helen Mulgrave (1852), recounted the punishments inflicted on converts from
Catholicism by priests who sought their forcible return. More popular than
either of these themes was the notion of a papal conquest of the United States
through the work of Jesuit spies, as evidenced by such works as *The Female
Jesuit; or, the Spy in the Family* (1851) and *Stanhope Burleigh; the Jesuits in our
Homes* (1855). Not all these works were purely sensational; some attempted
reasonable refutation of Catholic arguments. A common point was that Protestantism began with Christ's birth and not, as Catholics claimed, with the
Reformation. Such Catholic doctrines as papal infallibility, transubstantiation,
and purgatory were said to be contradicted by the Bible and mocked by Catholicism's historical corruptions. These novelists often cited the Inquisition as
an example of Catholic intolerance and religious ritualism as mass idolatry.
Still the reliance on melodramatic heightening was always stronger in anti-
Catholic fiction than in Catholic fiction of the period, and the best-selling nativist novels were those which, like Maria Monk's, concentrated on carnal
corruption.

Anti-Catholic fiction might appear to be a departure from Protestant fictional norms, but in fact it was a result of the same secularizing process that
controlled other religious fiction of the period. At the same time that popular
orthodox and liberal fiction was merging in a nonreflective center of virtuous
behavior, satirical fiction in its extreme anti-Catholic form was exposing those
hostile religious forces that threatened to nullify this behavior and replace it
with an obverse moral code. When trapped in a convent, the nun of the anti-

Catholic novel was the precise opposite of the heroine of the affirmative Protestant novel: she was separated from society, the proper sphere of Christian duty; her independence was totally stifled; she witnessed immorality in its most heinous forms. If liberal and orthodox fiction after 1830 increasingly banned such earthly misconduct as profanity and alcoholism, the anti-Catholic novel took a further step in the same direction by painting this misconduct in its blackest shades.

We have seen how affirmative religious novelists transformed the tyrant of Oriental tales into various new characters: the cruel stepmother, the rigid Puritan magistrate, the oppressive emperor of Biblical times. The anti-Catholic novelist added to the list the despotic priest or abbess who inhibits the protagonist's freedom. The main flaw of converts, in the words of Mrs. L. Larned, is that they *"undermine our liberties, and corrupt the sources of our strength and greatness."*[18] "For it is only in society," Larned later explains, "that we can perform the duties enjoined upon us by our divine Master" (133). The Catholic, according to the novelists, is villainous in proportion to the extent to which he prevents those conditions conducive to active piety, involvement in society, access to the Bible, and the free exercise of moral inclinations.

In sum, the typical anti-Catholic novel was a highly secularized enactment of current Protestant values written by those who felt particularly endangered by the rise of Roman Catholicism in America. Like much religious fiction of the time, it was characterized by paradoxes. Its authors often seemed to derive pleasure from the description of those atrocities they professed to decry, just as Biblical fiction sometimes betrayed a fascination with the trappings of paganism. It was wont to call Catholicism materialistic and worldly, but it was not without mercenary motives of its own. It pretended to be factual but was usually embellished. Even at its most intellectual it was more rhetorically sensational than its Catholic counterpart. Also, it provided an outlet for the repressed sexuality of a generation that prided itself on right conduct.

Anti-Catholic fiction did not impede the growth of Roman Catholicism in this country, but it did permit a substantial number of American Protestants to vent their fears and frustrations while secretly indulging their fantasies.

George Lippard and the Rainbow of Corruption

"All that Lippard wrote, talked, or did was so intimately interwoven with [his] religious faith, that we are almost ready to pronounce it the leading trait in his character."[19] Despite this evaluation made in 1855 by George Lippard's most reliable contemporary biographer, little attention has been paid to the role of religion in the novels of this often neglected Philadelphia author. Most Lippard scholars are aware that he was raised by evangelical Methodists, that he trained for the Methodist ministry, and that he left his studies "in disgust

at the contradiction between the theory and practice" of Christianity, report-
edly as result of an incident involving a clergyman who did not offer Lippard a
peach from a bagful he had just bought.[20] It is often noted that Lippard, after
abandoning the practice of law with equal contempt, went on to become a
notorious critic of institutions—religious, political, and social—in his novels
and lectures between 1842 and 1854. But scholars usually focus on a variety of
issues unrelated to his religious views: his acquaintance with Poe, his pioneering efforts in social reform, the sensational nature of his fiction and his
private life, and the great popularity of his novel of 1844–45, *The Quaker City;
or, The Monks of Monk Hall.*

I include Lippard in this chapter on satirical fiction not only because he was
the most forcefully and consistently combative novelist of the age but also because he gathered together various themes and devices that had been used in
American fictional satire on religion since the 1790s. However, he was more
than a satirist. It is appropriate that Lippard's career be the last one to be detailed fully in this study, since his novels were a repository for a large variety
of religious forces, satirical and affirmative, that had been gathering strength
since the 1820s.

We may initially review those aspects of religion Lippard protests against in
his novels and those he endorses. He deplored religious intolerance and persecution, especially on the part of Calvin and his anti-Catholic followers, of the
Roman Catholic Inquisitors, and of all sectarian wranglers; fanaticism, particularly that of Millerites and other evangelicals; sensuality, greed, and hypocrisy, all of which Lippard found to be common among aristocratic churchgoers; modern religious reformism and tract writing, which he saw as finally
indifferent to America's poor and oppressed; and theological dogma, especially
Trinitarianism. Lippard endorsed a creedless religion of love and morality,
hope for the common man, faith in the human Jesus, an egalitarian view of
the Bible, belief in a domestic and tangible heaven, sympathy toward benevolent Catholics, and admiration for Revolutionary War heroes.

The comprehensiveness of both Lippard's protest and his affirmation is evidenced by these groupings. Complaints about intolerance by earlier religious
novelists had usually concentrated on the narrowness of specific sects; Lippard
expanded the attack to include both modern anti-Catholics and medieval
Catholics, both vicious anti-Calvinists and extreme Calvinists. The list of ministerial shortcomings that had been growing in American fictional satire since
1828 lengthened in Lippard's novels to create a wide-ranging critique of
American religion. Lippard's hostility toward creeds mirrors the antitheological tendency of both orthodox and liberal fiction. His democratic emphasis,
his veneration of heroic action, his idea of a tangible heaven, and his humanization of Jesus are equally products of ongoing currents in American religious
fiction discussed throughout this study.

The reason for the scholarly neglect of religion in Lippard can be related to the fundamental process in early American religious fiction that I have been outlining: secularization. Critics have sometimes noted Lippard's pious side but have neglected to emphasize it because of the diverting adventurousness and sensationalism of his fiction. But melodramatic adventure and physicality have as much meaning in Lippard's novels as they did in the works of other American novelists concerned with religion. They are part of a rejection of traditional intellectualism, formal theology, and ineffable otherworldly religion, a rejection that was implicit in many other novelists and overt in Lippard.

If orthodox and liberal fiction of the period was becoming increasingly more crowded with earthly scenes and active characters, Lippard's novels opened the floodgates to a torrent of such scenes and characters. If satirical novelists were giving greater space to criminality and perversity, Lippard borrowed every device from horror literature to make such grotesque activity as graphic as possible. If religious novelists of all genres were depending with greater frequency on sentimentality, Lippard outdid all of them by producing *The Quaker City,* an emotionally turbulent novel that would become, in Lippard's own estimation, "more attacked, and more read, than any work of American fiction ever published."[21]

Where do those benign affirmative religious values mentioned above fit into this rather frenetic and morbid picture? The same biographer who called religion Lippard's chief interest elsewhere referred to "the soft, sweet aspirations that run through his most terrible books, like the delicate filigree of gold upon a warrior's sword."[22] An apter metaphor for the operation of religion in Lippard's novels is suggested by a description toward the end of *The Quaker City* of a rotting corpse. Describing the colors—"blue and red and purple and grey and pink and orange"—on this "mass of decay," Lippard explains that "corruption has its Rainbow" and that the rainbow of corruption can make even the grotesque seem beautiful.[23]

The religion of Lippard's novels is like this rainbow of corruption. The simple dichotomy I have suggested between those aspects of religion Lippard endorses and those he protests against is somewhat misleading, since in his novels the negative and positive religious poles are inextricably connected: the negative always leads to the positive, the satire to the affirmation—the corruption to the rainbow. Like some of Flannery O'Connor's stories, Lippard's fiction is often so radically secular, so forcefully negating, that the negation itself evokes a religious perception of reality. For example, Devil-Bug, the host of orgiastic Philadelphians at Monk Hall, is one of the most monstrously depraved characters in American fiction. Yet he turns out to have the most ecstatic religious experience in the novel, and he heroically saves two endangered women. His cohort in sin, Long-haired Bess, is a similarly grotesque figure who comes to glimpse God and rescue the distressed. Lippard seems to suggest that only those steeped in vice and pushed to the brink of an awareness of evil can see God. Devil-Bug and Bess become the saviors of threatened virtue, forces of demonic reality in a world of pious sham.

In order to comprehend Lippard's religious rainbow it is useful to gauge the forces of corruption in his novels. Lippard's satire on established religion is certainly the most trenchant in American fiction before the Civil War. It is more pointed and topical than the generalized subversion of conventional piety in Hawthorne and Melville and more unrelenting and fully developed than the satire of the pre-1845 novelists.

Critical judgment of Lippard's fiction inevitably begins with *The Quaker City,* though little has been written on the wide-ranging attack on religious hypocrisy in the novel. The setting of the novel is Monk Hall, a monastery turned house of revel where otherwise respectable Philadelphians—clergymen, lawyers, editors, moguls—convene nightly to wine, dine, and seduce under the supervision of Devil-Bug and his helpers. Among the frequenters of Monk Hall are wealthy churchgoers "with round faces and gouty hands, whose voices, now shouting the drinking song, had re-echoed the prayer and the psalm in the aristocratic church, not longer than a Sunday ago" (48). Also present are members of " 'Bible-Societies,' 'Tract Societies' and 'Send-Flannel-to-the-South-Sea-Islanders Societies,' " as well as those who read aloud "a tale from the German on *Transcendental Essences"* (50). By specifically mocking pious aristocrats, evangelical tract writers, and Transcendentalists, Lippard is repeating similar appraisals made in such earlier satires as *Retroprogression* and *The Hypocrite.* At the same time, despite the fact that he would sometimes berate anti-Catholic fiction, Lippard appears to borrow from the anti-Catholic novel. Not only is his subtitle, *The Monks of Monk Hall,* reminiscent of the Maria Monk vogue, but also the hall itself, a former monastery with torture chambers and a large cellar where corpses are thrown, recalls the Hotel Dieu and other convents of nativist fiction. Devil-Bug is a ghoulish version of the leering priest of anti-Catholic novels, and Long-haired Bess brings to mind a bedraggled abbess. The scene of a multiroomed establishment where perversion and seduction reign is also directly reminiscent of nativist fiction, as is the plot of innocent young women entering this establishment and being threatened by pious seeming sensualists.

By creating a kind of urban "Young Goodman Brown," Lippard is able to draw from various satirical genres to produce a broad critique of American religion. His portrait of the lascivious ultra-Protestant Reverend F. Altmont T. (F. A. T.) Pyne is perhaps the strongest caricature of evangelical Calvinism in American fiction before 1850. An advocate of "the Universal American Patent-Gospel School," Pyne preaches "a gospel of fire and brimstone and abuse o' the Pope o' Rome, mingled in equal quantities" (223, 221). With "a tone of spermaceti smoothness," Pyne by day persuades his congregations to give money in support of his tract campaign to convert the Pope, money which by night he applies to the purchase of brandy and opium at Monk

Hall (229). Pyne has a "red, round face, with thick lips, watery grey eyes, and lanky hair, of a doubtful color, mingling white and brown, and hanging in uneven masses around the outline of his visage," which "formed the details of a countenance very sanctimonious and somewhat sensual in its slightest expression" (171). One night Pyne puts a drug in a young woman's coffee with the intent of ravishing her when Devil-Bug enters, ties him to the bed crucifixion-style and tickle-tortures him until "he blasphemed the name of his God, then invoked all the curses of hell upon his head, and then the white foam frothed around his lips" (279). While tormenting this "corpulent representative of St. Andrew's cross," Devil-Bug cries: "I guess I got yo' on the anxious bench that time!" (277).

In his portrayal of Pyne, Lippard is taking to its natural conclusion the antievangelical impulses that had engendered such earlier fictional characters as Obadiah Bloomfield, Deodat Pidgeon, and E. K. Avery. Pyne embodies all the characteristics of these figures: pulpit unction, duplicitous use of theology and social concern, lust, inner feebleness. Lippard's satire, unlike that of the earlier writers, is greatly aided by the presence of Devil-Bug, who can puncture Pyne's pretensions by humiliating the minister.

The frequenters of Monk Hall are only a few of the established religionists satirized in Lippard's fiction. Hiram Barnhurst of *The Empire City* (1850) is another evangelical preacher who, "with the same tongue that had uttered the solemn ritual of the sacrament, whispered infamy into the ears of a sinless girl."[24] Barnhurst "polluted the Sacrament with his touch" by using "the name of the Lord Jesus as a cloak for deeds, whose atrocity would bring a blush to a devil's cheek" (89). A nativist hypocrite like Pyne, Barnhurst publishes an anti-Catholic tract that is "stained with the pollution of lascivious deeds, cankered to the heart, with the same leprosy that poisons the blood of the Profligate of the Brothel" (90).

In *Blanche of Brandywine* (1846) Lippard sharply indicts those "obscene tracts, abusing men of different faith" written "by vagabonds, who escaped perhaps from some European galley, howl[ing] forth their ribald slander, for the greedy ears of bigotry and cant."[25] Another Calvinist Lippard exposes is Calvin Wolfe, leader of the Holy Protestant League in *The Nazarene* (1846). Wolfe, in Lippard's italicized description, is *"a man of strong mind, immense wealth and much outward piety, firmly believing that whatever crime he may commit, whatever blasphemy he may enact, yet still he cannot sin, for he is one of the Elect of God."*[26]

Lippard's most extensive satire on American religion occurs in his little known *The Memoirs of a Preacher* (1849). As in *The Quaker City,* Lippard uses a Gothic mansion in Philadelphia as the site of aristocratic revelry, though he has expanded the list of fraudulent religionists to include Quakers, Millerites, spiritualists, hypnotists, and especially a "Popular Preacher" named Edmund Jervis. Jervis is described as "the man of men, who has given all the women in town love powders, and who frightens our most respectable merchants into fits, with his sermons."[27] Under his shell of sanctity lies "a hollow-hearted Sensualist . . . tainted to the core by perjury, seduction, and slow, cool, calculating Murder" (55). Jervis has seduced and abandoned several women, including one whose brother, Charles Lester, tracks him to his nightly haunt to avenge her death. Charged by Lester with having "the lust of the Sensualist, the cold unbelief of the Atheist," Jervis replies, in what seems to be Lippard's view, that he is the natural product of a society that idolizes its preachers and thrives on sectarian warfare (99). Although he never achieves redemption, Jervis becomes a tragic victim of the religious excesses he has been trained to practice. Using everything from Millerism to mesmerism to gain his lustful goals, he is at last driven to ask, "For me, the Preacher of a creed, which my soul laughs to very scorn—where is there hope, where mercy? Where any future, but despair and hell?" (92).

In light of the corruption Lippard finds almost everywhere in American religion, one would hardly think him capable of making a positive religious reconstruction. Yet Lippard's rainbow is as benevolently lovely as his description of corruption is violent. Though broader than the satire of any popular writer before him, Lippard's critique, in the final analysis, remains restricted to particular sects. He does not allow his complaints about the foibles of churchgoers and clergymen to grow into an all-consuming vision of evil or ambiguity, as did Hawthorne and Melville. His position as a satirist was essentially paradoxical. To promote a nontheological religion of pacifism and brotherhood he resorted to combative techniques which earned him notoriety as an improper author. Despite his religious outlook, his attacks on various sects laid him open to the charges of impropriety and sacrilege.

Lippard's frustrations over what he considered the public's misinterpretation of his religious aims surfaced in a chapter in *Memoirs of a Preacher* where Lippard asks his critics why it seems so "preposterous to you that a Writer of Novels, shall dare to speak of Religion?" He notes that while the public loves farces and chivalric romances, a serious religious writer like Lippard is branded "lamentable, and *eccentric.*" Lippard continues defensively: "The pen which now writes, may do a braver, better work for Humanity, than the pen which merely writes a Sermon in defence of a mere creed, or turns ink into gall again, by putting down on pure white paper, some horrible Dogma of Theology, stolen from the cells of heathen barbarity." Lippard asserts that "he is doing a better work by writing Novels, than he would be doing were he to put himself to making Sermons or tinkering Creed" (59).

Lippard was caught in the predicament of a religious author trying to adopt satirical devices of American fiction for ultimately affirmative reasons. Like many liberal and orthodox novelists he found in fiction an ideal secular replacement for theology. But his antipathy toward dogma carried him to a combative extreme that the more cautious authors of the religious main-stream found distasteful and dangerous.

At times Lippard betrays an awareness of his paradoxical situation. For example, in *The Quaker City* he qualifies his caricature of F. A. T. Pyne with the following footnote: "For the religion of Jesus Christ, our Savior and Intercessor, the author of this work has a fixed love and reverential awe. For the imposture and trickery of the various copies of Simon Magus . . . whether they take the shape of ranting Millerites, intemperate temperance lecturers, or Reverend politicians, the author does entertain the most intolerable disgust and loathing. The first make maniacs, the second make drunkards, the last make infidels" (170).

But instead of explaining himself overtly in footnotes, Lippard more typically allowed his belief in Christianity to emerge through sensational dramatizations of the violent and the unacceptable. He had no tolerance for easily optimistic authors, purveyors of what he called literary "Lollypop-itude." Thus Lippard often forged positive religion from terror or perversity. He contrasted smooth but corrupt clergymen with such grotesque but redemptive religious spokesmen as Devil-Bug, Long-haired Bess, various sorcerers and ritualists, and bloodthirsty soldiers. After an apocalyptic dream of Jehovah's destruction of the Quaker City, Devil-Bug feels God's presence: "For a moment the soul of Devil-Bug was *beautiful* . . . He felt that he, Devil-Bug the outcast of earth, the incarnate outlaw of hell, had one friend in the wide universe; that friend his Creator. He felt in every fibre of his deformed soul that the eyes of the awful being were fixed on him in terrible reproof, yet with a gleam of mercy breaking from their eternal lustre" (287). Similarly, when Bess saves the imperiled Mary and Mabel, Lippard tells us that Bess, "degraded, steeped to the very lips in pollution, cankered to the heart with loathsome vice . . . was a holy thing in sight of the angels" (293). Two of Lippard's mysterious sorcerers, Ravoni of *The Quaker City* and Aldarin of *The Ladye Annabel* (1843–44), are perverse characters who also function affirmatively. Through Ravoni and Aldarin, Lippard indulges his fascination with the trappings of ritualistic religion while fashioning an extracreedal faith "in the name of MAN and for the good of MAN."[28]

In Lippard's patriotic novels this paradoxical use of violence and enigma to endorse humanitarian religion surfaces as battle scenes tinged with pious recommendation. In *Blanche of Brandywine* a Revolutionary War engagement gives rise to the following exclamation: "Here is Poetry, Sublimity, Religion! Here are twenty thousand men, tearing each other's limbs to fragments, putting out eyes, crushing skulls, rending hearts, and trampling the faces of the dying under foot, . . . hewing them down in gory murder, . . . Religion!" (211). Similar passages occur throughout *Washington and His Generals*. In *Paul Ardenheim* (1848), borrowing from the evangelical Protestant doctrine of dispensationalism, Lippard identifies three great epochs for the renewal of true religion: the Epoch of the Apostles, in which the altar of brotherhood is reared in the New World; the Epoch of the Deliverer, ushered in by Revolutionary leaders who "scourge the oppressors of body and soul" from America; the Epoch of the Crowned Avenger, whose "tremendous battles, supernatural glories, and Death sublime in its very isolation, will prepare the world for the approach of the Holiest Epoch, for the Coming of the Universal Liberator," after "an Exodus of incredible carnage."[29]

Encircling all this violence is a religious rainbow as remarkable for its pristine simplicity as the corruption is for its ugliness. Lippard suggests that the world may be full of mountebanks and hypocrites but man remains perfectible and God remains loving. Though Lippard sees evidence of depravity everywhere, in *Paul Ardenheim* he firmly denounces the Calvinist view of man: "If there exists such a thing as Total Depravity on the face of the earth, you will find it in the heart of the man, who has so brutalized his nature, as to be able to believe the Dogma" (388). We admire liberals like Channing, Dewey, and Parker, he declares in *The Empire City,* not "because they are ministers [but] because they are men" (90). In Lippard's novels, righteous warriors from Devil-Bug through Aldarin to Washington are designed to drive the money-changers of theology and sensuality from the temple of love and brotherhood. These warriors are secular counterparts of the Poor Man of Nazareth, who liberated religion from creed and man from his oppressors. Thus, as Paul Ardenheim learns, with just "three words—*The Carpenter's Son*—we can regenerate the world" and teach it that faith has nothing to do with sect:

> We will go to the Poor. We will ask them—not to believe in the Trinity, or in the Unity of God, nor in Catholic, nor in Protestant, nor in Buddhu, nor in Mahommed—we will not waste time in comparing speculations, or analyzing creeds. Armed with this Christ of the Poor, we will say to the Poor, He was a Poor Man, such as you are. Like you he toiled. Like you he hungered. At the graves of Poor Men like you he wept. He lived for you—for you he died. Then listen to his voice, which utters all truth, in simple words—LOVE ONE ANOTHER [316].

Lippard's novels, instead of breaking sharply from literary convention, amalgamate themes and devices common in American religious fiction between 1785 and 1845. We have seen how the subversion of tyrannical religion allegorically stated in early Oriental and visionary fiction was updated by writers of various religions after 1820: by liberals, Calvinists, Biblical novelists, general satirists, and nativists. The rejection of religious despotism, either indirectly or overtly coupled with protests against such tyrannical faiths as strict Calvinism and Roman Catholicism, was often accompanied by a democratic emphasis in the common man's ability to survive misfortune through an Arminian confidence in himself and through trust in God's attentive fairness. Lippard extends this outlook to a violent repugnance toward religious authoritarianism and an affirmation of man's capabilities. Jesus, in Lippard's view, came to oppose "the rich, the proud, the oppressor" and "to redress the wrongs of the Poor."[30] Liberated from despotism by Christ, man has nevertheless been subject to the oppression of ecclesiastical hierarchy and theology for eighteen centuries; only a violent upheaval will renew the egalitarian religion of Jesus.

Translated into modern terms, this upheaval became fused in Lippard's imagination with an overthrow of the moneyed elite, with cataclysmic visions of destruction and divine judgement. If piety in previous American religious fiction was often compared to republican independence, in Lippard it was directly called "the religion of patriotism."[31] If other novelists found social analogues to religious action, Lippard so completely politicized faith that it became almost formulaically dependent on social position. If previous writers experimented with military metaphors to promote an increasingly muscular faith, Lippard described violent battles that were necessary antecedents to the Epoch of the Universal Deliverer.

Perhaps more important in the context of this study than Lippard's amplification of earlier themes is his stylistic abandonment of strict theological discussion. The most significant common tendency of all religious fiction of the period is the movement away from static otherworldly contemplation and polemical precision toward an experiential faith involving sentiment, secular conflict, and objectification. Lippard became a chief spokesman for this overall rejection of theology and sectarian narrowness. In several novels Lippard stressed that creeds have created persecution, intolerance, fanaticism, all of which can be overcome only through an immediate return to primal Christianity. As he expressed it in *Memoirs of a Preacher* Lippard's motivation for novel writing was fundamentally antitheological, as he declared the composition of novels "a braver, better work" than the exposition of "some horrible Dogma of Theology."[32]

This purposeful rejection of dogma is one reason for the notorious emotionalism, sensationalism, and hyperbolic satire in Lippard's novels. In the attempt to divest the historical Jesus of the "dogma of musty parchments, or thesis of monkish schools,"[33] Lippard recreated Biblical scenes with a sentimentalism unparalleled in pre-1850 American fiction. To highlight the cruelty of contemporary factionaries like F. A. T. Pyne, Hiram Barnhurst, and Edmund Jervis, he resorted with unprecedented frequency to the old figure of the pious rake. To accentuate the need for violent heroic action, he described bloody battles and apocalyptic visions with a new interest in graphic physical detail.

Like other American satirists after 1835 Lippard was wont to focus on the more sensational religious denominations and sects of modern and historical times: the Inquisitors, rigid Calvinists, Millerites, anti-Catholics, spiritualists, mesmerists. By doing so, Lippard could make his point against creedal intolerance while enhancing the excitement of his plots. Scholars who have criticized Lippard's overuse of Gothic devices and sensuous description normally neglect to mention that such excess was one outcome of Lippard's strongly antitheological bias. The rapid-fire action, the multitude of freakish characters, the stormy emotionalism all reflect a mind so repelled by logical approaches to doctrine that it tends to be swept up in the drama and physicality it has created. If previous religious novelists had begun to replace the theological with the secular, Lippard enacted his dismissal of theology by granting the secular a sanctity of its own.

In sum, Lippard amalgamated the complex, somewhat contradictory forces of earlier religious fiction into a fictional center containing both vicious satire and benign affirmation, both perversity and inspiration. His vision of ministerial wrongdoing was as penetrating as that of satirists before him; yet his hopes for American religion were as fervently patriotic and pietistically simple as those of the most nonreflective affirmative novelists. Disillusioned with the Methodism of his childhood, Lippard, like several novelists before him, attempted a fictional reconstruction of faith outside church and creed. His artistry was often slipshod, and his religion was compromised by conflicting loyalties and intense secularism. But both his artistic deficiencies and his paradoxical religious views were part of a struggle to locate an appropriate replacement for the theology he wished to eradicate. Acutely aware of depravity, Lippard was prevented by humanitarian piety from achieving the more generalized visions of blackness and ambiguity of Hawthorne, Poe, and Melville. Cognizant of corruption, Lippard was nevertheless in perpetual search of a religious rainbow.

8

Into the Mainstream

Although not at first well received by reviewers, by conventional clergymen, and even by the reading public, religious fiction proliferated in nineteenth-century America, giving rise to such best sellers as *The Gates Ajar, Barriers Burned Away,* and *In His Steps.* At the same time, fictional devices infiltrated the didactic literature of religious publishing houses as well as the sermons and lectures of representative American preachers. Not only did more evangelicals of the mainstream write novels after 1850, but even in circles where fiction continued to be vilified, secular anecdotes and sentimental embellishments were frequently preferred to theological exposition. The subversion of intellectual doctrine through fictional techniques was accompanied by a turning away from tangled metaphysical questions and an embrace of such real aspects of experience as nature, human feeling, and vernacular perspective. In a century when revealed religion was subject to sharp attack, common experience provided both diversion and solace for those who feared that the logical religious approaches of the past might lead to self-criticism and even to skepticism.

Launching the Sable Fleet

In an analysis of Sylvester Judd's *Margaret* in 1846, the *North American Review* declared: "The sable fleet of religious novels, oppressed with their leaden cargo, have shown marvellous alacrity in sinking where they were never heard of more; and the whole history of these experiments proves, that there is an inherent unfitness in this form of communication for any such purposes."[1] This pronouncement was not precisely true, since religious novelists by 1846 had already produced a few best sellers and several novels, such as Henry Ware, Jr.'s *Scenes and Characters* series, commended by established clergymen. However, the complaint that fiction was unfit for religious discussion was widely echoed during this period, even on occasion by religious novelists themselves. Such criticism pointed up real dilemmas faced by the novelist who wished to popularize his views in an increasingly secular culture. Many critics and novelists found themselves faced with Orestes Brownson's paradox: they recognized that fiction was the coming popular genre, yet they also knew that much was being sacrificed in adapting religious discussion to the tastes of the age. Several serious issues were raised by early critics of the religious novel, issues that in later periods would often be glossed over or ignored.

A major complaint was that religious fiction militated against doctrinal purity by creating mental laziness and devaluing logical inquiry. In the words of a tract writer of the 1840s:

> Familiarity with popular fiction gives a disrelish for simple truth. . . . The Bible becomes a wearisome book; spiritual classics, like those of Baxter, Bunyan, Flavel, and Doddridge, though glowing with celestial fire, become insipid and uninteresting; and the influence of the pulpit is undermined, by diverting the attention from serious things, and lessening the probability that truth will take effect upon the conscience; or if it does for a time, the bewitching novel furnishes a ready means of stifling conviction and grieving away the Spirit of God.[2]

Such commentary betrays not only conservative nostalgia for theology but also a fear that novels threatened to make venerable spiritual books, even the Bible itself, seem dull.

Connected to this charge was the ironic recognition that religious novels were likely to be less fascinating than purely escapist fiction of love or adventure. Another tract writer complained: "A few pious persons have written works which are sometimes called novels. But they are too serious for the gay, and too gay for the serious. So they are seldom read . . . They lie, covered with dust, on the shelves of the bookseller, are sent to auction, and used as waste paper."[3] Orestes Brownson voiced a similar sentiment by stressing that the doctrinal portions of religious fiction would disappoint the theologian while boring the regular novel reader.

Another of Brownson's complaints aired by others concerned the fatal mixture of the divine and the earthly in religious fiction, an idea most forcefully pointed up by John Neal in *Authorship* (1830). In Neal's view, religious novels are "among the most pernicious of all the books that appear," because they promulgate materialistic values under the guise of holy inspiration: "Religious novels forsooth! Why, what do they teach but this—*this!*—the very end and aim of all novels; namely, that after a certain portion of suffering, trial and sorrow, marriage comes about,—marriage with the desired accompanied by beauty, wealth, rank, &c., &c., *as the greatest of earthly good!*"[4] Brownson and Neal were not alone in their regrets about the reduction of God to the world in religious fiction. One didactic writer labeled the Irish novelist Maria Edgeworth "the most irreligious writer I have ever read" because she invariably gave material rewards to moral characters.[5] As a result of this secularization of religion in fiction, many critics placed qualifiers such as "allegedly" or "professedly" before "religious novels." For instance, the orthodox *Port Folio* in 1822 said that "a professedly religious novel" commonly showed "bad taste . . . in its selection of incidents and arguments, especially on such subjects as the love of the world, and worldly company, and worldly amusements."[6]

In sum, the religious novelist before 1850 wrote at the risk of being called antitheological, shallow, dull, and impiously worldly. By 1847 the *North American Review* could state: "There is a general distrust of works commonly called religious novels. We usually find in them either an intolerable infusion of doctrinal theology, or a mixture absolutely revolting of earthly passion and spiritual pride; so that it may be deemed lucky, if they are only tedious and uninteresting."[7] In the face of such criticism, some novelists rhetorically denounced fiction in their novels while others guardedly disavowed a predominantly religious intention. The irony of the situation was captured as early as 1805 by Caroline W. Thayer, who began *The Gamesters* by admitting that while novels were becoming clearly preferable to pulpit instruction, "the novelist is seldom greeted with a solitary smile of approbation from the whole regiment of literati," and "even 'the house is divided against itself,' and *novel writers* attribute many of the fashionable foibles of the day, to *novel reading.*"[8]

Some novelists who realized the special problems posed by religious fiction tried to deflect criticism by masking their pious goals. Catherine Sedgwick prefaced *Redwood* (1824) with the comment: "We have not composed a tale professedly or chiefly of a religious nature, as, if left to the bias of our own inclinations, we might possibly have done. We do not think that such attempts have been heretofore eminently successful."[9] While not a religious novel, Sedgwick went on, *Redwood* was meant to illustrate "the religious principle, with all its attendant doubts, hopes, fears, enthusiasm, and hypocrisy" (x). Similar equivocation occurs in the introductory explanation of *True Womanhood* (1859), the final novel of that inveterate questioner of religious fiction John Neal: "Though not properly a religious novel, I trust the reader will find in it enough religious feeling, without sectarianism, for everyday use, and not enough to be troublesome, or obtrusive, or unpalatable; or, in other words, 'none to hurt'—as the man said, when asked if a mutual friend had not grown pious."[10] As late as the 1870s American authors could sense the problems of religious fiction, as seen in Edward Eggleston's prefatory note that his *Circuit Rider* (1874) "is not a 'religious novel,' one in which all the good people are a little better than they can be."[11]

Religious fiction, then, was not universally applauded during a period that was looking guiltily to the theological past and furtively to the secular future. Whatever the mixed motives of antifictional commentators may have been, their complaints did not impede the growth of religious fiction in nineteenth-century America. America's policy of religious toleration was particularly conducive to fiction that attempted to cross sectarian lines while deemphasizing doctrine. At the same time that the Oxford Movement in England was impelling several British novelists to weigh specific creedal alternatives, American Protestants were using fiction to advocate a nonsectarian piety for a nation that prided itself on religious freedom. By 1850 Edward Everett Hale could contrast the narrowness of English religious fiction with the breadth of American novels:

> A host of English books, called "Religious Novels," have been transplanted into this country, and reprinted, "without note or comment."
> It is to be hoped that they have done our young people some good. But it is certain that, in our parish and Sabbath-school libraries, they have greatly puzzled those who read, by their obstinate adherence to close sectarian usages, and by their utter ignorance of the generous spirit which exists in America between Christians of different names.[12]

Sanctioned by established rhetorical theory and Biblical parables, and nurtured by democratic policy, religious fiction was selected by an increasing number of American authors who wished to escape strict intellectualism and metaphysical inquiry. Boston Unitarians, naturally averse to theology, became the first major American religious group to take a communal interest in fiction, but by the 1840s more conservative writers from various parts of the country had taken up fiction writing. After 1850 pious novels were no longer being produced primarily by New England liberals but rather by authors of the evangelical mainstream, by such Congregationalists, Episcopalians, Presbyterians, and Methodists as Harriet Beecher Stowe, Sarah Payson Willis Parton ("Fanny Fern"), Marion Harland, Harriette Newell Baker, Josiah Gilbert Holland, Martha Finley, Isabella MacDonald Alden, Elizabeth Phelps Ward, Edward Payson Roe, Augusta Evans Wilson, Henry Ward Beecher, Lew Wallace, and Charles Sheldon. Once mainstream religious writers followed the lead of the prolific Unitarian authors of the 1820s and 1830s, the American reading public was inundated with novels that placed the halo of piety around narratives filled with sentiment, romance, and social commentary. Not only had early criticism of religious fiction failed to stamp it out, but a variety of respectable writers after 1850 made good livings by writing inspirational novels with great popular appeal. The sable fleet of religious novels did not sink into obscurity after 1850; it sailed triumphantly and rapidly, precisely because it became progressively less sable as time passed.

Contributing to the growing popularity of religious fiction was an acceleration of the secularizing process begun in pre-1850 fiction. Henry Nash Smith has found that in representative best sellers of the 1850s and 1860s, "the boundary between natural and supernatural is abolished; the noumenon is bureaucratized . . . [and] both worldly success and divine grace merge into a single mythical process."[13] Elmer Suderman, in a dissertation on one hundred fifty religious novels published between 1870 and 1900, concludes that "in fact, religion is very often not central to the theme of these stories, merely peripheral."[14] By conforming to the literary demands of the American public, the popular religious novelist after 1850 verged on excluding the divine altogether. Indeed, a brief look at this later fiction shows that visionary, Biblical, and social novels were more secular and correspondingly less theological than most of the novels before 1850.

Writers of visionary fiction made the passage to heaven increasingly more natural and heaven itself more earthlike. George Wood's *Future Life; or, Scenes in Another World* (1858) retained some of the pre-1850 caution while initiating the kind of detailed celestial description that typifies later visionary works. In his preface Wood admits that his celestial account "has been made with many misgivings" and carefully cites such traditional authorities on heaven as Dante, Milton, Jeremy Taylor, and Biblical authors. Yet his novel, though sometimes quoting these writers, is mainly an expansion of the author's stated premise: "All our ideas of the future must be formed out of the present life; nor can we reach outside of a physical theory."[15] In Wood's heaven, two dreaming Americans discuss philosophy with ancient sages, hear new symphonies by classical composers, and meet Rembrandt.

A more updated version of heaven is found in Henry J. Horn's *Strange Visitors: A Series of Original Papers . . . By . . . Spirits Now Dwelling in the Spirit World* (1869). In contrast to Wood, who paid rather formal deference to classical authority, Horn offers written analyses of all aspects of heavenly life by the souls of thirty-eight prominent authors, politicians, artists, and actors who lived between 1750 and 1860. Among these "original papers" are celestial accounts by Margaret Fuller, Napoleon, Nathaniel Hawthorne, John Wesley, Lyman Beecher, and Artemus Ward. Horn disposes of intellectual doctrine by having Margaret Fuller report that in heaven "we have but few works on theology; the nature and essence of God is discussed with us, but not so elaborately as with you."[16] Hawthorne, Fuller writes, "informs me that many of the mysteries that seemed inexplicable to him while on earth are now cleared up" (172). Heaven, we learn from various sources, is a republican nation with libraries, amusement parks, art colonies, and museums. Wesley reports that earthly sects have been replaced by One Church whose sole creed is "the brotherhood of man, and the love of God for his children" (209). Reprobates like Edgar Allan Poe have been placed in comfortable jails to work out their salvation.

Later novelists of heaven became even more ambitious than Wood and Horn. William Holcombe, combining the visionary mode with Biblical paraphrase, had the American protagonist of *In Both Worlds* (1870) discover a first-person manuscript by Lazarus describing his three-day tour of heaven, his recall from the dead by Jesus, and his experiences as a friend of the disciples and as a victim of Roman persecution. The most famous describer of heaven, Elizabeth Phelps Ward, confined herself to hopeful conjecture in *The Gates Ajar* (1868) but freely traveled through heavenly realms in *Beyond the Gates* (1883), *The Gates Between* (1887), and *Within the Gates* (1901). Ward's main contribution to visionary fiction was the complete domestication of heaven and the familiar visualization of Biblical figures, including Jesus. In her three post-1880 visionary novels, hell is reduced to separation from loved ones and salvation to a reunion with them, usually after a genial talk with The Master.

In the 1890s Ward was imitated by various authors, including Ernst von Hummel, Louis B. Pendleton, George H. Hepworth, and Annie T. Slosson. The message of all these writers was the same: heaven, instead of being fearfully ineffable or distant, is an idealized earth. The dreaming hero of Pendleton's *Wedding Garment* (1894) discovers that he is no "thin, vapory, sexless something which floats about in the atmosphere," but "a *man*" with "head, body, hands, and feet" in a heaven where "everything [is] so similar to everything in the natural world."[17] The celestial dreams of the protagonist of Hepworth's *They Met in Heaven* (1894) confirms his clergyman's previous advice: "Give heaven a location, think of it as you think of France or Germany, teach your soul that when it leaves the body it will go to *a place*, will enjoy the companionship of those it loved in this life, and all fear is gone, and in its stead is high anticipation."[18] This naturalization of the celestial was heightened by vernacular commentary. Hepworth's Hiram Golf, a pious shoemaker, laments old-fashioned views by declaring: "It would be pretty dull business for me to set down to a harp, for I hain't got no ear for music" (139). The Baptist writer Annie Slosson, in *Seven Dreamers* (1891) and *The Heresy of Mehetabel Clark* (1892), made heaven fully creedless and tangible by assuming the personae of commonsensical illiterates. The hero of *Mehetabel Clark* visits the White House of the heavenly republic to glimpse not only Jesus but God himself, who passes in the distance "in all his strength and greatness and goodness and pleasantness, . . . solemn yet smily."[19]

Similar tendencies characterized Biblical fiction of the period. In his three novels of the 1850s Joseph Holt Ingraham retained William Ware's traditional epistolary style but made pioneering expansions upon the New and Old Testaments that prepared for later embellishments. In 1870 William Holcombe, as we have seen, took rewriting the Bible to the extreme of a fictional discovery of a new early-Christian document. This device would be used by several twentieth-century novelists, most notably by Irving Wallace in *The Word*. Lew Wallace produced the most popular Biblical novel of the nineteenth century, *Ben-Hur. A Tale of the Christ* (1880), by coupling Christian martyr and New Testament devices in a highly adventurous and mildly pious plot. Despite its subtitle, Wallace's novel focuses not on Christ but on the prolonged rivalry between the Jewish hero and the Roman Messala. Wallace brings together several ingredients from various kinds of religious fiction—heroic action, domestic sentiment, emotional conversion, pagan spectacle—and adds just enough violence to fascinate his religious readers without repelling them.

Ben-Hur spawned a host of Biblical novels in the 1890s which tried to outdo each other in veracity. Florence M. Kingsley's *Titus, a Comrade of the Cross* (1895) was given first place among four hundred entries in a search conducted by a Chicago religious group for a novel that would "make the life and teachings of Christ as real and practical as if he lived and taught in our streets at the present day."[20] Perhaps the special appeal of Kingsley's novel lay in its pictures of Christ as child singing in the garden and telling pretty stories, a variation of a motif used by Lew Wallace in a story of 1889 called "The Boyhood of Christ." Kingsley went on to dramatize the trials of Jesus' followers in *Stephen, a Soldier of the Cross* (1896) and *Paul, a Herald of the Cross* (1897). Other Biblical novelists of the 1890s included Robert Bird, Elbridge S. Brooks, Caroline A. Mason, and Herbert D. and Elizabeth Phelps Ward. While they generally avoided excessively physical accounts of Jesus, these writers took great liberty with the Bible, even to the point of inventing new miracles for dramatic effect. The new attitude was signaled by the Wards' prefatory explanation that since *Come Forth!* (1891) "is not a Scriptural paraphrase . . . the authors have not thought it necessary to confine themselves to the recorded incidents of Gospel history."[21] The Wards leave the Bible behind in their novel of Lazarus' love affair with Zahara, the daughter of the High Priest of Jerusalem. Miraculous occurrences are subsumed to the interests of plot, as when Jesus walks on the water to rescue the drowing Zahara and raises Lazarus from the dead so that he may rejoin his lover.

Some authors of the period became so daring as to summon Jesus into modern life. This variation of Biblical embellishment was generally an adjunct to the Social Gospel movement, as Jesus was pictured as a reformer come to lash modern moneychangers. William Dean Howells' *A Traveler from Altruria* (1894) and Milford W. Howard's *If Christ Came to Congress* (1894) used the device of Jesus' reappearance to expose political corruption and commercial exploitation in American cities. William Stead's best-selling *If Christ Came to Chicago* (1895) extended Milford's approach to a full-scale statistical analysis of urban ills. Jesus was brought to New England in Edward Everett Hale's *If*

Jesus Came to Boston (1895), in which a Syrian visitor applauds Boston's philanthropic agencies. The hero of Olla P. Toph's *Lazarus* (1895) dreams of
Jesus' and Lazarus' appearing in America to help a man named Reform in his
efforts to aid the poor and initiate social legislation; at the end of the dream
Reform dies and joins his Biblical helpers in heaven. Elizabeth Phelps Ward
added to the genre in *The Supply at Saint Agatha's* (1896), in which a New
England preacher dies committing his flock to Christ, who soon appears in
person to deliver an electrifying sermon that unites the rich and the poor.

The secularizing pattern was as marked in novels dealing with religion in
society as it was in visionary and Biblical fiction. The earthly interpretation of
faith was evident in the two successive stages of social fiction: between 1850
and 1885 it appeared in the religious novelist's endorsement of the status quo
and the American succcess myth; between 1885 and 1900 it was transformed
into the Christian advocacy of reform on behalf of the poor and oppressed.
The domestic sentimentalists of the 1850s and 1860s customarily rewarded
perseveringly pious orphans with money and marriage. The protagonists of
Maria Cummins, Susan Warner, Augusta Evans Wilson, and Josiah G. Holland combined a distaste for gloomy theology with hopes for social advancement. In the 1870s Edward Payson Roe, mirroring the wealth through religion ethic of the Gilded Age, wrote several best-selling novels, most notably
Barriers Burned Away, that connected spiritual regeneration to financial security.

The Social Gospel novel of the late 1880s and 1890s endorsed brotherhood
and universal progress under the direction of a fatherly God to establish the
kingdom of heaven on earth. The earthly emphasis of this reformist religion
was captured in Charles S. Daniel's proclamation of the "unreserved recognition of the secular world as containing all sacred things."[22] Sin was usually
equated with exploitative capital, and redemption was aligned with challenges
to upper-class complacency by activist ministers or collective reform groups.
Howells' *Annie Kilburn* (1889) and Albion W. Tourgee's *Murvale Eastman,
Christian Socialist* (1889) showed social-minded clergymen scolding elitists in
their moneyed congregations. Katherine Woods' *Metzerott, Shoemaker* (1889)
and Margaret Sherwood's *An Experiment in Altruism* (1895) emphasized that
heavenly speculation should be dropped on behalf of active philanthropy. In
A Singular Life (1895) Elizabeth Phelps Ward described a Christ-like minister
who helps the poor in a New England fishing village. The most popular Social
Gospel novel was Charles Sheldon's *In His Steps: "What Would Jesus Do?"*
(1897), which appealed to millions of readers with its mixture of romance,
ministerial activism, and group reform.

In all types of late-nineteenth-century religious novels the themes and devices of the pre-1850 works were carried to secular ends. In visionary fiction,
allegorical distancing and careful recoil, which had virtually disappeared by
the 1840s, gave way to relatively painless imaginings of earthly heavens. In

Biblical fiction, guarded paraphrase was replaced by free adaptations, in accordance with contemporary issues. In domestic and Social Gospel novels, virtuous action was endorsed first to support and then to attack the economic status quo. Nearly all the later novels exaggerated the pre-1850 paradoxical mixture of soft creedless sensibility and hard heroic endeavor, with more weight assigned to the latter as time passed. The Arminian rebellion against tyranny continued to be modernized, in domestic orphans' attempts to escape constricting poverty and cruel foster parents, in the resistance to pagan despotism by Biblical heroes, in the denunciation of bureaucrats by reformers. The objectification of religious experience that had begun in Oriental tales was so prevalent in the later novels that metaphysics and theology had become almost wholly replaced by worldly endeavor haloed by romantic ideality. Struggle abounded in the later novels, but it was ordinarily exterior rather than inward struggle. Dramatic human conflicts and trials came to supplant tortured inner probings, as is evidenced by the Great Chicago Fire at the center of Roe's *Barriers Burned Away* or by the famous chariot race in *Ben-Hur* or by the labor warfare in Social Gospel novels. This removal of inward conflict resulted from the continued softening of the belief in human depravity on the part of mainstream religionists. As the novelist William Baker wrote in *His Majesty, Myself* (1880), "The worst men were only bad boys, whom a little spanking would convert into heroes."[23]

Such developments in religious novels would have disappointed pre-1850 critics of religious fiction. Those tract writers who had tried to resuscitate creed in the face of the bewitching novel would have regretted the aspersions on intellectual theology commonly made in the later fiction. The late-nineteenth-century attitude was summed up in Hepworth's *They Met in Heaven:* "Creeds are not necessary to salvation, but Christ is. The one is made by man, and must be changed as research discovers new facts; the other was sent by God, and is the same yesterday, today, and forever . . . I have known men to linger so long in finding out whether this or that theory of God's will was correct, that they had no time to practice the ordinary virtues" (43). Those who had dismissed religious novels as dull would have been surprised by the late-nineteenth-century discovery of various best-selling formulae. Those who lamented the coupling of worldly gain and spiritual growth would have been saddened by most of the domestic and Gilded Age works. As Orestes Brownson thought that no two things were more incompatible than logical religion and romantic love, he too would have been displeased, since most of the later novels contained love affairs pivotal in the conversions of the central characters.

Along with secularization went a growing mercenary motivation on the part of some religious novelists. Pious sentimentalists such as Susan Warner, Fanny Fern, and Josiah G. Holland adopted novel writing with the avowed intention of alleviating their own poverty. Elizabeth Phelps Ward dismissed the didactic Sunday school works of her prenovelistic period as wearisome hack work and confessed that had *The Gates Ajar* not sold well she would have abandoned the writing of religious fiction for more remunerative work. The celebrated author of *Norwood,* Henry Ward Beecher, was given a $30,000 advance for his manuscript. After *Norwood's* serial run in the *New York Ledger,* the *Ledger's* editor, Robert Bonner, estimated that Beecher's novel had brought in $120,000 of new business. In the 1860s and 1870s the Presbyterian Bonner commissioned eleven other clergymen to write one novel each for the *Ledger* in an effort to increase the magazine's profits while enhancing its respectability. Augusta Evans Wilson earned $100,000 in eight years from the sale of her religious novels. E. P. Roe financed a large estate on the Hudson by writing novels of poor Christian boys struggling to succeed, novels that earned him an average of $15,000 annually between 1872 and 1885. Lew Wallace confessed that he was "not in the least influenced by religious sentiment" in writing *Ben-Hur,* indicating that he wanted to write a bestseller.[24] To be sure, religion was never as commercialized in the nineteenth century as it would become in the hands of twentieth-century Hollywood producers, who would find that "Jesus sells almost as well as sex."[25] Still, several novelists between 1850 and 1900 were discovering that pious entertainment could be quite profitable.

In the face of the secularization and occasional commercialization of American religious fiction, there appeared after 1850 some parodic works that extended the line of pre-1850 combative fiction and even began to satirize religious novels themselves. Some religious best sellers prompted direct parodies: Augusta Wilson's *St. Elmo* (1867) was answered by Charles Webb's *St. Twel'mo; or, The Cuneiform Cyclopedist of Chattanooga* (1867), in which Wilson's ostentatious erudition and garbled religion were mocked; *The Gates Ajar* provoked "An Antidote to *The Gates Ajar*" (1870), whose anonymous author mimicked Ward's heavenly speculations; *Ben-Hur* gave rise to *Ben Beor: A Story of the Anti-Messiah* (1891), in which Herman M. Bien adapted Wallace's novel to anti-Catholic ends.

But more remarkable than these minor parodies was the increasing number of works by more serious American novelists who responded negatively to the values advanced in affirmative religious fiction. As a whole, elite nineteenth-century American novelists, while not centrally concerned with religion, were dismayed by the liberalization of the religious mainstream. Hawthorne satirized the facile optimism and mechanized morality of liberals so pointedly in *The Celestial Railroad* (1846) that the work was pirated and distributed as an orthodox tract. Both Hawthorne and Melville showed themselves to be more attracted to the ambiguities and darkness of Puritan Calvinism than to the more hopeful views of the nineteenth century. In *Clarel* (1876) Melville criticized, among other things, the easy overcoming of doubt, the recreation of Biblical scenes, and the accommodation to bourgeois values on the part of mainstream religionists. The popular Henry Ward Beecher was branded shallow and duplicitously worldly by Orestes Brownson and Henry James, Jr. In 1874 William Dean Howells declared that "the tendency of modern liberalism to ignore the chief of the fallen angels" was "one of the most painful spectacles" of the age.[26] In *The Minister's Charge* (1887) Howells dramatized the failure of institutional Christianity to address urban problems; despite his brief flirtation with Christian Socialism between 1885 and 1895, Howells was never as optimistic as most Christian reformers. This is evidenced by his qualified portraits of the Social Gospel in *Annie Kilburn, A Hazard of New Fortunes,* and *A Traveler from Altruria.*

Perhaps the period's most trenchant appraisal of mainstream religion was Harold Frederic's *The Damnation of Theron Ware* (1896), which traced the collapse of a Methodist minister's faith as result of his exposure to Roman Catholic scholasticism, pre-Raphaelite aestheticism, and modern science. Another serious writer who viewed normative religion cynically was Ambrose Bierce. In a typical work, *The Fiend's Delight* (1873), Bierce reversed the message of inspirational fiction in scores of short sketches that advanced such ideas as the following: children are devious and naturally impious; temperance meetings are exercises in futility; a man can have great fun as a sinner and then be converted on his deathbed; tract writers are interested solely in money; liberals are blind optimists; and so forth. Summing up "the average parson," Bierce writes: "Our objection to him is not that he is senseless; this—as it concerns us not—we can patiently endure. Nor that he is bigoted; this we expect, and have become accustomed to. Nor, that he is small-souled, narrow, hypocritical; all these qualities become him well, sitting easily and gracefully upon him. We protest against him because he is always 'carrying on.' "[27]

The most consistent late-nineteenth-century parodist was Mark Twain, who wrote brief but scathing satires of nearly every type of affirmative religious fiction. In "The Story of the Bad Little Boy" (1865) and "The Story of the Good Little Boy" (1870) Mark Twain overturned the message of domestic sentimentalists by portraying the success of an evil child and the frustrations of a pious one. Both of these tales directly mention the religious fiction and Sunday school narratives that had become popular by 1870. The Bible, and seemingly nineteenth-century Biblical embellishments as well, also drew fire from Mark Twain. His "Extracts from Methuselah's Diary" (1876) and "The Diary of Adam and Eve" (1893), gathered in 1962 by Bernard DeVoto as *Letters from the Earth,* presented a sour rewriting of the Scriptures in which the Bible's chronology, deemphasis of sexuality, and invention of hell were acerbically discussed. Another major preoccupation of religious novelists, the earthly qualities of heaven, was reduced to absurdity in "Extract from Captain Stormfield's Visit to Heaven" (1907). Stormfield finds the terrestrial heaven a place of monotonous routine, annoying crowds, and infrequent appearances by Biblical figures. Yet another theme of religious novelists, redemptive visitation by divine agents, was darkened in *The Mysterious Stranger* (1916), in which Mark Twain carried the demonic visionary mode to a portrayal of chaos and moral relativism.

If the religious novel was becoming more secular and more subject to commercialization and parody, it was also being relied upon far more than before by those who wished to regenerate individuals and change society. Both the popularity of religious fiction and the growing number of its elite critics suggest its pervasive influence on nineteenth-century American culture.

Not only were religious novels widely consulted for moral guidance; they had more tangible, if more trivial, effects as well: "St. Elmo," for instance, became the name of numerous American babies and at least thirteen American towns after 1870, and "The Gates Ajar" became the logo of a tippet and collar and even of a popular cigar. Although mocked by serious writers and appraised unfavorably by prominent reviewers, the religious novelist was normally able to bask in the assurance that thousands of readers could not be wrong. For example, Elizabeth Phelps Ward, responding to attacks on *The Gates Ajar* and to Thackeray's dismissal of the public as a jackass, wrote, "If large numbers of intelligent people like a book, one may believe in one's soul that it is the poorest thing one has done, but one is forced to think that there was something worth while about it."[28]

The religious novel after 1850 thus became a popular way of illustrating domestic piety, visualizing heaven, embellishing the Bible, and advocating reform. It became the single most effective literary tool of the Social Gospel author. The popularity of Sheldon's *In His Steps,* which sold nearly eight million copies, shows that religious fiction, a genre that had begun in the 1780s as brief Oriental tales in obscure American magazines, had by 1896 become both a major means of purveying religious inspiration and a significant barometer of social change.

An increasing number of nineteenth-century commentators noted the wide significance of religious fiction; some went so far as to say that the popular press was threatening to supersede the pulpit altogether. As early as 1797 Royall Tyler had mentioned the public preference for novels over theology; and in 1817 the *Christian Disciple* had declared that "the prodigious multiplication of books in this age . . . has either jostled the Bible from its place, or buried it from notice."[29] By 1843 Harriet Beecher Stowe could comment that novels were in every clergyman's library and that American religion was being strongly influenced by "a most enormous multiplication of sketches, tales, novels, and romances, of all sorts and sizes, which, by the agency of cheap magazines and mammoth sheets, have been showered into every hamlet in our land."[30] Stowe asserted that any "attempt to revert to former strictness, and banish all novel reading as a sinful practice" would be *"utterly impracticable,"* since even popular tracts and sermons were taking on fictional characteristics (ix). In light of the growing dependence on fictional devices, said Stowe, "there is no possibility . . . of making rules to exclude novels, because there is no mode of deciding what a novel is" (x). Stowe saw fiction everywhere—in magazines, in Sunday school libraries, in the pulpit. In her introduction to *My Wife and I* (1871) Stowe reiterated that "the world is returning to its second childhood, and running mad for stories."[31] Of special interest to Stowe was religious fiction and its influence on homiletic style:

> Hath any one in our day, as in St. Paul's, a psalm, a doctrine, a tongue, a revelation, an interpretation—forthwith he wraps it up in a serial story, and presents it to the public . . . We have Romanism and Protestantism, High Church and Low Church and no Church, contending with each other in serial stories, where each side converts the other, according to the faith of the narrator.
>
> We see that this thing is to go on. Soon it will be necessary that every leading clergyman should embody in his theology a serial story, to be delivered in the pulpit [ix].

When, in the second half of the nineteenth century, the shower of religious fiction had become a deluge, some writers found the importance of the pulpit diminishing. In 1856 the *North American Review* declared that "modern fictions . . . are expected to do, not only their own legitimate work, but also that of the hard, dry voluminous treatises on philosophy and morals of former times; they are expected to supply the place of legislators and divines, to obviate the necessity for polemical essays and political pamphlets, in short, to perform all the functions which the several departments of literature could scarcely accomplish a century ago."[32] Elsewhere the same journal noted that "people grow more and more unwilling to swallow instruction, and will hardly take it at all, unless it is cunningly disguised" in fiction.[33] Fanny Fern suggested that in the face of ascendant religious fiction the preacher's only viable choice was to burn his theological library. In 1866 Henry T. Tuckerman summed up the situation as follows:

> The press has, indeed, in a measure, superseded the pulpit. No intelligent observer of the signs of the times can fail to perceive that as a means of influence, the two are at least equal. In the pages of journals, in the verses of poets, in the favorite books of the hour, we have homilies that teach charity and faith more eloquently than the conventional Sunday discourse; they come nearer to experience; they are more the offspring of earnest conviction, and therefore enlist popular sympathy.[34]

On the surface, Tuckerman's generalization seems exaggerated, since late-nineteenth-century America produced several figures—Henry Ward

Beecher, T. DeWitt Talmage, Dwight L. Moody and his many imitators—
who were highly successful occupants of Protestants pulpits. But in reality
such preachers accelerated the press-over-pulpit movement Tuckerman and
others were describing. The eastern Princes of the Pulpit and the famous mass
revivalists competed with newspapers and novels for public attention by exploiting the popular press and using fictional devices in their sermons far more
determinedly than had previous American clergymen. Beecher theorized at
length on the value of colorful illustrations as opposed to dry logic in preaching; he put theory into practice by delivering entertaining sermons famous for
their lively anecdotes and stories. Viewing the press as "the miracle of modern
times," Beecher became a master of self-promotion by having his sermons
printed and generally distributed.[35] T. DeWitt Talmage, who openly called
for more "spicery" and "honest Christian sensation" in religion, attracted
swarms of people to his Brooklyn church with his racy narrative accounts of
vice and degradation in New York's gambling dens, saloons, and whorehouses.[36] In 1885 Talmage initiated a worldwide sermon syndicate whereby
his piquant sermons reached an estimated twenty million readers by being reprinted in three thousand newspapers, prompting the *London Times* to comment that "the whole human race was his congregation."[37]

Similarly, Dwight Moody, who regularly told homely pulpit stories on such
topics as dying parents and home life in heaven, saw his sermons published in
many of the urban dailies, and in 1895 established the successful Colportage
Press, which featured low-priced religious works written in "a popular, read-
able style."[38] Other revivalists of the period, such as Benjamin Fay Mills, Reuben Torrey, and Sam Jones, also preached anecdotal sermons that were widely
printed in secular newspapers. In Jones' words, "The secular papers are so
much more alive and aggressive than the religious papers, that when they fall
into line with a good work they are a power we can scarcely know how to
estimate."[39]

At the same time that novels and newspapers were influencing popular sermons and ministerial printing practices, they were also reshaping the millions
of tracts distributed by the major religious publishing houses. As Fred Allen
Briggs has pointed out, American tracts published before 1840 had been primarily doctrinal, harking back to such colonial theologians as Jonathan Edwards and Samuel Hopkins. After 1840, in an attempt to cater to a public that
was becoming increasingly enamored of fiction, the religious houses made a
wholesale shift to the publication of story tracts. By the late 1870s the contents of a typical Sunday school library had become almost wholly either narrative or biographical. As Briggs sums up the stylistic change, "In the early
collections, the chief interest was in books of doctrines and Biblical exposition; in the later examples, the interest was in stories—to a growing extent in
out-and-out fiction," so that "the later Sunday School library was chiefly a collection of stories rather than a repository of moral facts."[40]

In 1872 Henry Ward Beecher could refer to the conventional pulpit as a thing of the past: "Before books were either plenty or cheap; before the era of the newspaper, the magazine, or the tract; before knowledge was poured in, as now, from a hundred quarters,—an era almost flooded with it, the people imbibing it, so to speak, through the very pores of their skin,—the pulpit was the school, the legislative hall, the court of law; in short, the university of the common people."[41] The fact that Beecher, the most visible American clergyman in the late nineteenth century, could affirm the predominance of the press over the pulpit suggests that popular pious writing—in the forms of novels, stories, poetry, and fictionalized sermons and tracts—had more than entered the religious mainstream. It had virtually become the mainstream.

Epilogue: The Embrace of the Real

The broadening use of fictional devices by popular American religionists signified not only an adaptation to secular culture but also a turning away from intellectual doctrine and otherworldly speculation as the result of a fear that logical metaphysical inquiry was doomed to failure. Puritan thinkers such as Cotton Mather, Edward Taylor, and Jonathan Edwards and his followers had ambitiously dedicated themselves to rigorous exposition because of their confidence in the Bible's sanctity, in God's existence and justice, in heaven and hell, and so forth. The skepticism of the late eighteenth century severely challenged such assurances about revealed religion, as did Biblical criticism and Darwinism in the nineteenth century. Although few prominent nineteenth-century American religious figures were skeptics, many were painfully aware of the French *philosophes,* Paine, Strauss, and other questioners of traditional religion. The findings of science were sometimes successfully amalgamated with mainstream religion, as in Liberal Protestantism's incorporation of Darwin through Christian evolutionism. But as several scholars have noted, Biblical criticism provoked frustration and gloom among many American thinkers, and beneath the surface of nineteenth-century optimism lurked a deep crisis of faith.

Religious fiction became an appropriate solace in this time of crisis because it helped writers forget about difficult Biblical or otherworldly dilemmas. To secularize sin and salvation was to make them more manageable, to retrieve them from the doubtful realm of metaphysics, and to anchor them in perceivable reality. Fictional techniques provided an especially effective means of carrying out this anchoring process. In fiction, tangible reality could not just be contemplated as an alternative to intellectual probing; it could, in effect, be actually reproduced on the page.

Many nineteenth-century religious writers found in fiction a solution to various related problems: personal or professional failings, anxiety over the arguments of skeptics, a fearful distrust of intellectual inquiry. The predominant optimism of religious fiction was in large part a call for cheer in the face of potentially annihilating ambiguity. Skeptical philosophers and elite American novelists were sometimes admired but more often feared, since they were apt to investigate those dark, uncertain regions that the popular writers were trying to avoid.

A significant number of those who dealt with affirmative religion in novels were failed ministers or philosophers. No account of early American religious fiction would be accurate without the recognition that its authors were often people with severe personal or spiritual problems. Moreover, the ubiquity of such difficulties among religious novelists suggests that the fiction itself was often part of a process of self-persuasion and compensatory affirmation.

Joseph Morgan, who produced America's first religious novel in *The History of the Kingdom of Basaruah* (1715), had a stormy career as a minister: he was dismissed from two different pulpits because he allegedly engaged in astrology, promiscuous dancing, and drunkenness. Later in the eighteenth century, Royall Tyler, author of *The Bay Boy* and *The Algerine Captive,* dropped his plan of entering the Episcopalian ministry owing to doubts about revealed religion. Two other novelists of the 1790s, Susanna Rowson and Hannah Foster, were so deeply disturbed by both infidel philosophy and Calvinist theology that they essayed a fictional reconstruction of faith in their novels on the basis of moral behavior and polite education.

In the nineteenth century such religious problems became more common among religious fictionists. Timothy Flint, the Congregational minister turned frontier author, had as a clergyman an "uncanny ability to alienate congregations." In 1814 Flint was ousted from his Lunenburg, Massachusetts, pastorship "in an atmosphere of bitterness and recrimination" as a result of "charges of immorality and non-Christian belief"[42]; Flint recalled the situation in *George Mason* (1829), which built a simplified, anecdotal piety on the ruins of theology and established religion. Charles Sealsfield, a defrocked priest who wrote pious novels about the American frontier, was dismissed from a German monastery because of irreconcilable differences with his peers and his teachers. The Unitarian William Ware, as we have seen, confessed to having made a mistake for life in entering the ministry. His congregation found him cold, and he finally abandoned his New York pastorship to write Biblical novels. His brother Henry also left the ministry to devote himself to, among other things, the editorship of the central body of pre–1840 liberal fiction, *Scenes and Characters Illustrating Christian Truths.*

The crisis was particularly acute for those who wrestled less with professional problems or popular disfavor than with doubt. Catherine Sedgwick, who called herself a borderer, took up the writing of religious novels because she was "spiritless and sad."[43] Lydia Maria Child's early fears of "wrecking on the rocks of scepticism" were echoed throughout her career, as seen in her report in 1838 that she had wept like a child about religion and in her outcry of 1859: "I want to believe. Above all things I want to believe."[44] John Neal, who devoted several early years to the study of theology, confessed in 1818: "I have grown afraid of myself, and still more afraid of controversy."[45] Sylvester Judd, after his period of "annihilating suffering," advised a friend in 1834: "Take care that you do not wrap yourself in your subtle abstractions about the nature of things. It may prove the winding sheet of your soul."[46]

The fictional solution to such problems was most commonly a recoil from insoluble metaphysics through optimistic imaginings of practical religion in action. In Lydia Child's words, "As the sad experiences of life multiply," we should read and write "only 'chipper' books."[47] As we have seen throughout this study, most writers used their early novels to exorcise such demons as strict doctrine or skepticism, often with the aid of the visionary mode. Later, they were wont to turn to objective exemplum and morality.

The embrace of the real had special import for troubled religionists. William Ware helped compensate for previous difficulties as a clergyman and metaphysician by fashioning novels dense with realities reduced to writing. Jacob Abbott acknowledged the insuperable difficulties and useless perplexity of theoretical inquiry and then wrote hundreds of secular children's stories by benignly accepting his ignorance: "Let the region of uncertainty and ignorance be circumscribed by a definite boundary. But when this is done, look calmly upon the surface of the deep which you know you cannot sound, and acknowledge the limit of your powers with a humble and quiet spirit."[48] Similarly, John Neal wrote adventure novels after resolving his early doubts by discovering "that we are bound to draw a line between the knowable and unknowable, and the sooner the better, and never try to pass the bounds of the knowable, however tempted."[49] Child and Sedgwick alleviated similar questions through pious novels, and in *Richard Edney* Judd endorsed a Law of Limitation that restricted religion to human experience.

This return to the surface, to the knowable is one reason for the artistic and thematic deficiencies of many religious novels. In this connection, one thinks of Melville's contrast between Protestant "sand sharks" who remain in "shallows worse than any deep," and those "Whales, mighty whales" who "have felt the wound— / Plunged bleeding through the blue profound."[50] The average American religious novelist was not prepared to feel the wound by making Melvillian plunges into the blue profound. Nor was he ready to send a Young Goodman Brown into the woods to perceive universal evil or to contemplate a loon diving below the surface of Walden Pond or to look beyond nature to a transcendent Oversoul. He was generally content, in Abbott's phrase, to "look calmly on the surface of the deep," or, in Neal's words, never "to pass the bounds of the knowable, however tempted."

Accordingly, when confronted with a major literary artist, the religious novelist felt compelled to accommodate or explain away bothersome ambiguities. The case of Melville was fairly simple: his relatively benign early novels, *Typee* and *Omoo,* could be accepted as travel stories, while his more demonic later novels could be ignored. Emerson, Hawthorne, and Poe posed greater problems because they were closer than Melville to the literary mainstream. Commonly the religious novelist admired the stylistic virtues of these writers while lamenting their quixotic flights beyond ordinary reality. In 1844 Child commented that Emerson's essays were "deep and original" but that in them "nothing is real, that everything eludes us" and that we find only "ghastly, eluding spectres."[51] In a letter of 1849 Sedgwick referred to a pious friend who "is not like [Transcendentalists], foggy, but has, 'au fond,' a sound, rocky foundation, and clear atmosphere of good sense."[52]

Poe and Hawthorne, likewise, could be called fine stylists who lost themselves in the dark. In *Strange Visitors* (1869) Henry J. Horn placed Poe in a celestial holding cell to forget his gloom and stated hopefully that Hawthorne's mysteries have been cleared up in heaven. Sedgwick praised the "marvellous beauty in the diction" of Hawthorne's *House of the Seven Gables* but called the book "an affliction" that affected her "like a passage through the wards of an insane asylum, or a visit to specimens of morbid anatomy." The only redemption she found in the book was "Little Phoebe," the "sweet and perfect flower amidst corruption, barrenness, and decay . . . the ideal of a New England, sweet-tempered, 'accomplished' village girl." The purpose of novels, Sedgwick went on, is to relieve rather than reproduce depression, for "as we go through the tragedy of life we need elixirs, cordials, and all the kindliest resources of the art of fiction."[53]

Resistant to the profundities of their more serious literary contemporaries, religious novelists were also dismissive of skepticism, which they usually referred to as "philosophy." In 1836 Orestes Brownson wrote: "Everybody knows, that our religion and our philosophy are at war. We are religious only at the expense of our logic."[54] The logical Brownson regretted this situation, but more typical American religious figures welcomed it. Christianity's long-standing anxieties about philosophy had been exacerbated in America during the Enlightenment, when the French *philosophes* provoked the ire of American ministers.

We have seen how "religion" was explicitly distinguished from theology in American pious fiction for at least a century. A similar discrimination was commonly made between religion and philosophy in popular novels from Susanna Rowson's *The Inquisitor* (1793) through George Lippard's *Paul Ardenheim* (1848) to Elizabeth Phelps Ward's *The Gates Ajar* (1869) and Lew Wallace's *Ben-Hur* (1880).

Rarely in religious fiction was the battle against philosophy waged in intellectual fashion. If Melville in *Moby-Dick* wished in part to throw overboard the "whale heads" of Kant and Locke in order to "float light and right" in the realm of symbolic art, many lesser nineteenth-century writers pitted against philosophy all the fictional forces of sentiment, exemplary heroism, and morality to insure the victory of hopeful religion. Just as elite authors of the American Renaissance had been countered through appeals for solid good sense and virtuous activity, so the best philosophical minds of the eighteenth and nineteenth centuries were rhetorically defeated in novels that posed practical piety as the highest good.

This is especially evident in Augusta Evans Wilson's *Beulah* (1859), in which the opposition to philosophy becomes open warfare against a multitude of European and American thinkers. "Philosophy," Beulah finds, "or, what is now-a-day its synonym, metaphysical systems, are worse than useless . . . Oh, the so-called philosophers of this century and the last are crowned heads of humbugry!"[55] Embracing the real, Beulah abandons the "grim puzzles of philosophy" and learns to draw "from the beautiful world in which she lived much pure enjoyment" (462). Dropping her scholarly studies, she marries with the recognition that domestic duty "is its own recompense" (477).

Often chastened by experience and driven by spiritual anxieties, the American religious novelist made a determined effort to settle comfortably in ordinary reality. Religious fiction provided elixirs and cordials in a time of widespread spiritual uprooting. In the shape of visionary tales, it made the afterlife, which was being questioned by skeptics, joyfully real and tangible. In the form of Biblical fiction, it made the Bible, which was being called nondivine and mythical, inspirationally accessible and entertaining. In domestic novels it summoned piety into the home, away from dangerous metaphysical realms. In combative and satirical fiction it minimized the problem of logical debate by facilitating rhetorical victories over opponents through caricature and parody. In the Social Gospel novel it reduced the problems of an increasingly complex society to a relatively simple construct of Christian workers versus unregenerate employers. In all its manifestations it permitted such large and potentially disturbing concepts as theology and philosophy to be easily distinguished from religion. Religious fiction was thus an exercise in wish fulfillment, in compensatory affirmation, and especially in the evasion of the kind of shattering self-scrutiny and intellectual inquiry which, if carried too far, threatened to bring one up on the side of doubt.

In sum, the phrase "faith in fiction" has a triple significance in relation to the mass religious culture of nineteenth-century America. It points to the widespread treatment of religious faith in fiction, which appeared variously as novels, stories, narrative tracts, and fanciful pulpit anecdotes. Also, it signifies popular authors' and clergymen's deepening faith in fiction as the most appropriate literary mode in an increasingly secular and antitheological age. Lastly, it suggests the painful suspicion, underlying much of these Americans' surface cheer, that the otherworldly religion in which they ostensibly had faith was a fiction.

Selected Bibliography
Chronology of Fiction
Notes
Index

Selected Bibliography

BOOKS AND DISSERTATIONS

Anker, Roy M. "Doubt and Faith in Late-Nineteenth-Century Fiction." Diss. Michigan State, 1974.

Ayers, Samuel G. *Bibliography of Jesus Christ*. New York: Armstrong, 1906.

Barkowsky, Edward R. "The Popular Christian Novel in America, 1918–1953." Diss. Ball State, 1975.

Baym, Nina. *Woman's Fiction: A Guide to Novels by and about Women in America, 1820–1870*. Ithaca: Cornell University Press, 1978.

Bennett, Eugene Ernest. "The Image of the Christian Clergyman in Modern Fiction and Drama." Diss. Vanderbilt Divinity School, 1970.

Billington, Ray A. *The Protestant Crusade, 1800–1860*. New York: Macmillan, 1938.

Bludworth, Rosa. "A Study of the Biblical Novel in America, 1940–49." Diss. University of Texas, Austin, 1955.

Bode, Carl. *The Anatomy of Popular Culture, 1840–1861*. Berkeley: University of California Press, 1961.

Briggs, Fred Allen. "Didactic Literature in America, 1825–1850." Diss. Indiana, 1954.

Brockway, Philip Judd. *Sylvester Judd(1813–1853): Novelist of Transcendentalism*. Orono: University of Maine Press, 1941.

Brooke, Stopford A. *Religion in Literature and Religion in Life*. New York: Crowell, 1901.

Brown, Herbert Ross. *The Sentimental Novel in America, 1789–1869*. Durham, N.C.: Duke University Press, 1940.

Brumm, Ursula. *American Thought and Religious Typology*. New Brunswick, N.J.: Rutgers University Press, 1970.

Buell, Lawrence. *Literary Transcendentalism.* Ithaca: Cornell University Press, 1972.

Burkhart, Jacob P. "Rhetorical Functions and Possibilities of the Parables of Jesus." Diss. Pennsylvania State, 1972.

Burnett, Ernest. "The Image of the Clergyman in Modern Fiction and Drama." Diss. Vanderbilt, 1960.

Burr, Nelson R. *A Critical Bibliography of Religion in America.* 3 vols. Princeton: Princeton University Press, 1961.

Carey, R. A. "Bestselling Religion: A History of Popular Religious Thought in America as Reflected in Religious Bestsellers, 1850–1960." Diss. Michigan State, 1971.

Carter, Paul A. *The Spiritual Crisis of the Gilded Age.* DeKalb: Northern Illinois Press, 1971.

Chable, Eugene R. "A Study of the Interpretation of the New Testament in New England Unitarianism." Diss. Columbia, 1956.

Charvat, William. *Literary Publishing in America, 1790–1850.* Philadelphia: University of Pennsylvania Press, 1959.

Christy, Arthur. *The Asian Legacy and American Life.* New York: Columbia University Press, 1968.

Conrad, Susan Phinney. *Perish the Thought: Intellectual Women in Romantic America, 1830–1860.* New York: Oxford University Press, 1976.

Coplan, Ruth E. "A Study of Predominant Themes in Selected Bestselling American Fiction, 1850–1915." Diss Pennsylvania, 1967.

Cowie, Alexander. *The Rise of the American Novel.* New York: American Book Co., 1948.

Daly, Robert. *God's Altar: The World and the Flesh in Puritan Poetry.* Berkeley: University of California Press, 1978.

Davis, David G. "The Image of the Minister in American Fiction." Diss. University of Tulsa, 1978.

DeGrazia, Emilio. "The Life and Works of George Lippard." Diss. Ohio State, 1969.

Dillistone, Frederick William. *The Novelist and the Passion Story.* New York: Sheed and Ward, 1960.

Douglas, Ann. *The Feminization of American Culture.* New York: Knopf, 1977.

Doyle, Mildred. "Sentimentalism in American Periodicals, 1741–1825." Diss. N.Y.U., 1941.

Drummond, Andrew L. *The Churches in English Fiction.* Leicester, England: E. Backus, 1950.

Dusenberry, Robert B. "Attitudes Toward Religion in Representative Novels of the American Frontier, 1820–1890." Diss. Washington, 1952.

Featherstun, Henry Walter. *The Christ of Our Novelists.* Nashville, Tenn.: Methodist Publishing House, 1904.

Forgie, George B. *Patricide in the House Divided: A Psychological Interpretation of Lincoln and His Age.* New York: Norton, 1979.

Foster, Edward Halsey. *Catherine Maria Sedgwick.* New York: Twayne, 1974.

Frederick, John T. *The Darkened Sky: Nineteenth-Century American Novelists and Religion.* Notre Dame: Indiana University Press, 1969.

Gamble, Richard H. "The Figure of the Protestant Clergyman in American Fiction." Diss. Pittsburgh, 1972.

Gardiner, Harold C., ed. *Fifty Years of the American Novel: A Christian Appraisal.* New York: Scribner's, 1951.

Gerlach, John C. "The Kingdom of God and Nineteenth-Century American Fiction." Diss. Arizona State, 1969.

Hackett, Alice Payne. *Seventy Years of Best Sellers, 1895–1965.* New York: R. R. Bowker Co., 1967.

Hart, James D. *The Popular Book: A History of America's Literary Taste.* Berkeley: University of California Press, 1950.

Holt, Charles C. "Short Fiction in American Periodicals, 1775–1825." Diss. Auburn, 1968.

Hopkins, Charles H. *The Rise of the Social Gospel in American Protestantism, 1865–1915.* New Haven: Yale University Press, 1940.

Howe, Daniel H. *The Unitarian Conscience: Harvard Moral Philosophy, 1805–1861.* Cambridge, Mass.: Harvard University Press, 1970.

Hurley, Leonard B. "The American Novel, 1830–1850: Its Reflections of Contemporary Religious Conditions." Diss. U.N.C., Chapel Hill, 1932.

Hutchison, William R. *The Transcendentalist Ministers: Church Reform in the New England Renaissance.* New Haven: Yale University Press, 1959.

Isani, Mukhtar Ali. "The Oriental Tale in America through 1865: A Study in American Fiction." Diss. Princeton, 1962.

Keith, Philip. "The Idea of Quakerism in American Literature." Diss. Pennsylvania, 1971.

Kendall, Robert D. "A Rhetorical Study of Religious Drama as a Form of Preaching." Diss. Minnesota, 1973.

Kendall, Robert L. "The Prophetic Impulse: The Philosophy of a Liberal Protestant Religious Rhetoric." Diss. Indiana, 1972.

Kerr, Howard H. "Spiritualism in American Literature, 1851–1886." Diss. U.C.L.A., 1968.

Kimball, Gayle H. "The Religious Ideas of Harriet Beecher Stowe: Her Gospel of Womanhood." Diss. University of California, Santa Barbara, 1976.

Kimber, Thomas. "The Quaker as Author and Subject in American Literature, 1825–1840." Diss. University of Southern California, 1941.

Kroeger, Frederick. "The Unitarian Novels of William Ware." Diss. Michigan, 1968.

Liptzin, Solomon. *The Jew in American Literature.* New York: Block, 1966.

Lohmann, Christoph. "The Paradox of Progress: Popular American Literature, 1850–1860." Diss. Pennsylvania, 1969.

Lojek, Helen H. "Ministers and Their Sermons in American Literature." Diss. University of Denver, 1977.

Lowenstein, Michael. "The Art of Improvement: Form and Function in the American Novel, 1789–1801." Diss. Washington, 1971.

Martin, Terence. *The Instructed Vision: Scottish Commonsense Philosophy and the Origins of American Fiction.* Bloomington: Indiana University Press, 1961.

May, Henry F. *The Enlightenment in America.* New York: Oxford University Press, 1976.

Mead, Sidney. *The Lively Experiment.* New York: Oxford University Press, 1976.

Minor, Dennis Earl. "The Evolution of Puritanism into the Mass Culture of Early Nineteenth-Century America." Diss. Texas A. and M., 1974.

Moore, Jack Bailey. "Native Elements in American Magazine Short Fiction, 1741–1800." Diss. North Carolina, 1966.

Moseley, Edwin M. *Pseudonyms of Christ in the Modern Novel: Motifs and Methods.* Pittsburgh: University of Pittsburgh Press, 1963.

Mosher, William Eugene. *The Promise of the Christ-Age in Recent Literature.* New York: Putnam, 1912.

Mott, Frank Luther. *Golden Multitudes: The Story of Best Sellers in the United States.* New York: Macmillan, 1947.

Mueller, Roger. "The Orient in American Transcendental Periodicals." Diss. Minnesota, 1968.

Murdock, Kenneth. *Literature and Theology in Colonial America.* Cambridge, Mass.: Harvard University Press, 1949.

Myrbo, Calvin. "An Analysis of the Character of the Clergyman in Novels for Adolescents." Diss. Minnesota, 1960.

Nicholl, Grier. "The Christian Social Novel in America, 1865–1918." Diss. Minnesota, 1964.

Noel, Mary. *Villains Galore; the Heyday of the Popular Story Weekly.* New York: Macmillan, 1954.

Nye, Russel B., ed. *New Dimensions in Popular Culture.* Bowling Green, Ohio: Popular Press, 1972.

————. *Society and Culture in America, 1830–1860.* New York: Harper and Row, 1970.

O'Connor, Leo F. "The Image of Religion in Selected American Novels, 1860–1920." Diss. N.Y.U., 1972.

Papashvily, Helen W. *All the Happy Endings: A Study of the Domestic Novel . . . in the Nineteenth Century.* New York: Harper, 1956.

Pedigo, Francis. "Critical Opinions of Fiction, Poetry, and Drama in *The Christian Examiner,* 1824–1869." Diss. University of North Carolina, Chapel Hill, 1953.

Petter, Henri. *The Early American Novel.* Columbus: Ohio State University Press, 1971.

Phy, Allene Stuart. "The Representation of Christ in Popular American Fiction." Diss. George Peabody, 1971.

Redden, Mary M. *The Gothic Fiction in American Magazines.* Washington, D.C.: Catholic University Press, 1939.

Reynolds, David S. *George Lippard.* Boston: Twayne, as yet unpublished.

Robbins, Jack Wayne. "A Theological Critique of Christ Figures in the American Novel." Diss. Southwest Baptist, 1972.

Roberts, Millard G. "The Methodist Book Concern in the West, 1800–1850." Diss. Chicago, 1942.

Rudolf, JoEllen S. "The Novels that Taught the Ladies: A Study of Popular Fiction Written by Women, 1702–1834." Diss. California, San Diego, 1972.

Sears, Donald A. *John Neal.* Boston: Twayne, 1978.

Selby, Thomas Gunn. *The Theology of Modern Fiction.* London: C. H. Kelly, 1897.

Schneider, Louis and Sanford M. Dornbusch. *Popular Religion: Inspirational Books in America.* Chicago: University of Chicago Press, 1958.

Shuck, Emerson C. "Clergymen in Representative American Fiction, 1830–1930." Diss. Wisconsin, 1943.

Smith, F. L. "Man and Minister in Recent American Fiction." Diss. Pennsylvania, 1969.

Smith, Henry Nash. *Democracy and the Novel: Popular Resistance to Classic American Writers.* New York: Oxford University Press, 1978.

Smith, Leslie. "The Popular Novel in America, 1850–1870." Diss. Michigan State, 1972.

Smithline, Arnold. *Natural Religion in American Literature.* New Haven: Connecticut College and University Press, 1966.

Staehelin-Wackernagel, Adelheid. *The Puritan Settler in the American Novel before the Civil War.* Bern, Switzerland: Francke Verlag, 1961.

Steinberg, Abraham H. "Jewish Characters in the American Novel to 1900." Diss. New York University, 1956.

Stewart, Randall. *American Literature and Christian Doctrine.* Baton Rouge: Louisiana State University Press, 1958.

Stigen, William L. *The High Faith of Fiction and Drama.* Garden City, N.Y.: Doubleday, 1928.

Stowe, Lyman Beecher. *Saints, Sinners, and Beechers.* Indianapolis: Bobbs-Merrill, 1934.

Stroupe, H. S. *The Religious Press in the South Atlantic States, 1802–1865.* Durham, N.C.: Duke University Press, 1956.

Suderman, Elmer F. "Religion in the American Novel, 1870–1900." Diss. Kansas, 1960.

Tassin, Algernon. *The Magazine in America.* New York: Dodd, Mead and Co., 1916.

Ulbricht, Armand H. "The Trend Toward Religion in the Modern American Novel, 1925–1951." Diss. University of Michigan, 1953.

Wagenknecht, Edward. *Cavalcade of the American Novel.* New York: Holt, 1952.

———, ed. *The Story of Jesus in the World's Literature.* New York: Creative Age Press, 1946.

Walker, Franklin. *Irreverent Pilgrims: Melville, Browne, and Mark Twain in the Holy Land.* Seattle: University of Washington Press, 1974.

Wegelin, Oscar. *Early American Fiction, 1774–1830.* New York: Smith, 1929.

Welter, Barbara. *Dimity Convictions: The American Woman in the Nineteenth Century.* Athens, Ohio: Ohio University Press, 1976.

Williams, Virginia. "Religion and Church as Motifs in American Fiction." M.A. thesis, Vanderbilt, 1930.

Woodell, Charles H. "The Preacher in Nineteenth-Century Southern Fiction." Diss. University of North Carolina, Chapel Hill, 1974.

Wright, Lyle Henry. *American Fiction, 1774–1850, A Contribution Toward a Bibliography.* San Marino, Calif.: Huntington Library, 1957.

Wright, Robert G. "The Social Christian Novel in the Gilded Age, 1865–1900." Diss. George Washington, 1968.

Ziolkowski, Theodore. *Fictional Transfigurations of Jesus.* Princeton: Princeton University Press, 1972.

ARTICLES

Aldridge, A. O. "A Religious Hoax by Benjamin Franklin." *American Literature,* 36 (May 1964), 204–209.

Antush, J. B. "Realism in the Catholic Novel." *Catholic World,* 185 (July 1958), 276–279.

Arrington, L. J. "Image of Mormonism in Nineteenth-Century American Literature." *Western Humanities Review,* 22: 243–260.

Avni, Abraham. "The Influence of the Bible on American Literature: A Review of Research." *Bulletin of Bibliography,* 27 (1970), 101–106.

Baker, Carlos. "The Place of the Bible in American Fiction." *Theology Today,* 17 (April 1960), 53–76.

Baskette, Floyd K. "Early Methodists and Their Literature." *Emory University Quarterly,* 3 (December 1947), 207–216.

Billington, Ray A. "Tentative Bibliography of Anti-Catholic Propaganda in the United States, 1800–1860." *Catholic Historical Review,* 18 (January 1933), 492–513.

Boynton, P. H. "The Novel of Puritan Decay from Mrs. Stowe to John Marquand." *New England Quarterly,* 13 (December 1940), 626–637.

Buell, Lawrence. "Calvinism Romanticized: Harriet Beecher Stowe, Samuel Hopkins, and *The Minister's Wooing." ESQ: Journal of the American Renaissance,* 24: 119–132.

Cameron, K. W. "Defining the American Transcendental Novel." *American Transcendental Quarterly,* 20 (1973), 114–122.

Dart, John. "Producers Find 'Jesus Sells Almost As Well As Sex.' " San Francisco *Chronicle,* August 1, 1976, p. 19.

Davies, W. E. "Religious Issues in Late Nineteenth-Century American Novels." *Commentary,* 35 (July 1963), 34–42.

Detweiler, Robert. "Christ and the Christ Figure in American Fiction." *Christian Scholar,* 17: 111–124.

Douglas, Ann. "Heaven Our Home: Consolation Literature in the Northern United States, 1830–1860." *American Quarterly,* 26 (December 1974), 496–515.

Hart, James D. "Platitudes of Piety: Religion and the Popular Modern Novel." *AQ,* 6 (Winter 1954), 311–322.

Ingles, J. W. "The Christian Novel and the Evangelical Dilemma." *Christianity Today,* 4 (1960), 3–5.

Jones, Howard M. "Literature and Orthodoxy in Boston after the Civil War." *AQ,* 6 (Summer 1954), 149–65.

Kay, Carol M. "American Literary Periodicals from 1790 to 1830." *BB,* 29 (1972), 126–127.

King, D. R., "Emerson's Divinity School Address and Judd's *Margaret." ESQ,* 47: 3–7.

Loomis, Emerson R. "The New Philosophy Satirized in American Fiction." *AQ,* 14 (Fall 1962), 490–495.

Miller, Perry. "Jonathan Edwards to Emerson." *NEQ,* 13 (December 1940), 589–617.

Nicholl, Grier. "The Christian Social Novel and Social Gospel Evangelism." *Religion in Life,* 34 (Autumn 1965), 548–561.

Paton, Alan, and Liston Pope. "The Novelist and Christ." *Saturday Review* (1954), 15–16, 56–58.

Pitt, A. Stewart. "The Sources, Significance and Date of Franklin's 'Arabian Tale.' " *Publications of the Modern Language Association,* 57: 158–168.

Reynolds, David S. "The Feminization Controversy: Sexual Stereotypes and the Paradoxes of Piety in Nineteenth-Century America." *NEQ,* 53 (March 1980), 96–106.

—— "From Doctrine to Narrative: The Rise of Pulpit Storytelling in America." *AQ* (forthcoming).

—— "Shifting Interpretation of American Protestantism, 1870–1900." *Journal of Popular Culture,* 9 (Winter 1975), 593–603.

Schuyler, David. "Inventing a Feminine Past." *NEQ,* 51 (September 1978), 291–308.

Siegel, Ben. "The Biblical Novel, 1900–1950." *BB,* 23 (1961), 88–90.

Smith, Henry Nash. "The Scribbling Women and the Cosmic Success Story." *Critical Inquiry,* 1 (September 1974) 47–70.

Streeter, R. E. "Mrs. Child's *Philothea:* A Transcendental Novel?" *NEQ,* 16 (December 1943), 648–654.

Strout, Cushing. "Radical Religion and the American Political Novel," *Clio,* 6: 23–42.

Sutcliffe, Denham. "Christian Themes in American Fiction." *Ch. S.,* 64: 297–311.

Suderman, Elmer F. "Jesus as a Character in the American Religious Novel." *Discourse,* 9 (1966), 101–115.

Thorp, Willard. "Catholic Novelists in Defense of their Faith, 1829–1865." *Proceedings of the American Antiquarian Society,* 78: 25–117.

—— "The Religious Novel as Best Seller in America." In *Religious Perspectives in American Culture,* ed. James W. Smith *et al.* Vol II. Princeton: Princeton Universitiy Press, 1961, pp. 195–242.

Trensky, Anne T. "The Saintly Child in Nineteenth-Century American Fiction," *Prospects,* 1 (1975) 389–413.

Voight, Gilbert P. "Our Evangelical Clergymen Novelists." *Religion in Life,* 22 (1953), 604–615.

White, Dana F. "The Early Social Gospel Novel." *South Atlantic Quarterly,* 67 (1968), 469–485.

Winams, Robert. "The Growth of a Novel-Reading Public in Late Eighteenth Century America." *Early American Literature,* 9 (Winter 1975), 267–275.

Wright, Lyle H. "Propaganda in Early American Fiction." *Papers of the Bibliographical Society,* 33 (1939), 98–106.

Chronology of Fiction

ORIENTAL AND VISIONARY FICTION THROUGH 1845

1746   "The Meditation of Cassim the Son of Ahmed; or, An Emblematical Description of the Resurrection," *American Magazine and Historical Chronicle*, 3 (December 1746), 546–548.

1774   "Hamet; or, The Insufficiency of Luxury to the Attainment of Happiness. An Oriental Tale," *Royal American Magazine*, 1 (May 1774), 173–175.

1779   Franklin, Benjamin. "An Arabian Tale." In *The Complete Works of Benjamin Franklin*, ed. John Bigelow. Vol VI. New York: Putnam's, 1888. Pp. 261–262.

1784   "The Discontented Man," *Gentleman and Lady's Magazine*, 1 (October-November 1784), 253–256, 281–284.

       "The Happiness of a life regulated by the Precepts of Virtue," *Gentleman and Lady's Magazine*, 1 (December 1784), 323–325.

       "Zaman," *Gentleman and Lady's Magazine*, 1 (June-July 1784), 47–48, 96–98.

1785   Celadon [pseud.]. *The Golden Age; or, Future Glory of North America Discovered by an Angel to Celadon, in Several Entertaining Visions*. No place or publisher cited.

       "An Oriental Tale," *Boston Magazine*, 2 (February 1785), 57–58.

1786   "The Contemplant," *Columbian Magazine*, 1 (November 1786), 130–133.

       "The Honest Viceroy: A Tale," *Boston Magazine*, 3 (November-December 1786), 422–424.

1787   "The Complaint of Iman; or, the False Appearances of Happiness and Misery," *Columbian Magazine*, 1 (October 1787), 690–694.

       Markoe, Peter. *The Algerine Spy in Pennsylvania; or, Letters Written by a Native of*

Algiers on the Affairs of the United States of America, from the Close of the Year 1783 to the Meeting of the Convention. Philadelphia: Prichard and Hall.

1788   "Moclou; or, The Dreamer. A Politico-Philosophical Tale," *Columbian Magazine,* 2 (April-May 1788), 190–194, 247–251.

"Solyman and Ossmin. An Oriental Tale," *American Magazine,* 1 (May-June 1788), 363–367, 435–438.

1789   "An Eastern Apologue," *Massachusetts Magazine,* 1 (January 1789), 48–50.

T., Dr. "The Visions of Aleph," *Columbian Magazine,* 3 (January 1789), 19–22.

"Temperance and Content—A Tale," *Columbian Magazine,* 3 (December 1789), 733–734.

1790   "Almerine and Shelimah: A Fairy Tale," *Massachusetts Magazine,* 2 (September-October 1790), 539–541, 549–551.

J. "The Story of Hafez. An Eastern Tale," *New York Magazine,* 1 (May 1790), 298–301.

"Orasmin and Almira," *Massachusetts Magazine,* 2 (November 1790), 644–646.

S., B. "Timur—An Eastern Tale," *American Museum,* 8 (September 1790), 105–111.

Sabina [pseud.]. "Louisa—A Novel," *Massachusetts Magazine,* 2 (February-March 1790), 78–82, 147–150.

1791   "Abu Taib: An Eastern Tale," *New York Magazine,* 2 (August 1791), 431–432.

"Mahomet: A Dream," *New York Magazine,* 2 (September 1791), 506–507.

"Nouradin and Fatima: An Eastern Tale," *Massachusetts Magazine,* 3 (July 1791), 417–419.

"The Paradise of Schedad: An Arabian Tale," *New York Magazine,* 2 (September 1791), 417–419.

"The Talisman of Truth," *Massachusetts Magazine,* 3 (October 1791), 614–617.

Wieland [pseud.?]. "Zohar: An Eastern Tale," *Massachusetts Magazine,* 3 (April-May 1791), 235–237, 273–275.

1792   "The Angel of Intelligence: An Eastern Tale," *Massachusetts Magazine,* 4 (July 1792), 436–437.

"Firnaz and Mirvan: An Eastern Tale," *New York Magazine,* 3 (October 1792), 628–630.

Hopkinson, Francis. "An Extraordinary Dream." In *The Miscellaneous Essays and Occasional Writings.* Vol. I. Philadelphia: T. Dobson. Pp. 3–11.

"Prosperity and Adversity: An Allegorical Tale," *American Museum,* 11 (March 1792), 68–70.

1793   "Alcander and Mira," *Massachusetts Magazine,* 5 (March 1793), 156–158.

"Benefits of Adversity," *Massachusetts Magazine,* 5 (July 1793), 411–414.

"An Eclipse of the Moon," *Massachusetts Magazine,* 5 (June 1793), 339–342.

"The Friend: A Chinese History," *New York Magazine,* 4 (November 1793), 682–686.

"Ismael: A Moorish Tale," *New York Magazine,* 4 (November 1793), 687–695.

"Lessons of Sadi," *Massachusetts Magazine,* 5 (December 1793), 715.

"Salah; or The Dangers of Habit," *Massachusetts Magazine,* 5 (January 1793), 45–48.

"A Vision," *Massachusetts Magazine,* 5 (November 1793), 694–695.

"The Vision of Almet the Dervise," *Massachusetts Magazine*, 5 (May 1793), 273–277.

1794 "Memorialist" Column (untitled visionary tale), *Massachusetts Magazine*, 6 (May 1794), 289–290.

Rowson, Susanna. "Uganda and Fatima." In *Mentoria; or, The Young Lady's Friend*. Vol. II. Philadelphia: Robert Campbell. Pp. 82–101.

1795 "The Enchanted Rose," *Massachusetts Magazine*, 7 (October-November-December 1795), 405–410, 483–486, 544–545.

"The Lawsuit against an Unjust Deity," *Massachusetts Magazine*, 7 (December 1795), 551–552.

"The Traveller: An Oriental Apologue," *Massachusetts Magazine*, 7 (April 1795), 38–40.

1796 "The Choice of Abdala, an Oriental Apologue," *Massachusetts Magazine*, 8 (February 1796), 82–86.

J. J. "Sadak—An Oriental Tale," *Massachusetts Magazine*, 8 (May 1796), 267–270.

1797 *The American Bee: A Collection of Entertaining Histories, Selected from Different Authors.* Leominster, Mass.: Charle Prentiss. Contains five Oriental tales.

"The Dervise in Contemplation: An Arabian Apologue," *South Carolina Weekly Museum*, 1 (March 1797), 371.

Tyler, Royall. *The Algerine Captive; or, The Life and Adventures of Doctor Updike Underhill, Six Years a Prisoner among the Algerines.* Walpole, N. H.: David Carlisle.

Munford, William. "Almoran and Hamet." In *Poems and Compositions in Prose on Several Occasions.* Richmond: Samuel Pleasants, Jr. Pp. 25–107.

1800 Sherburne, Henry. *The Oriental Philanthropist; or, True Republican.* Portsmouth, N. H.: William Treadwell.

1801 *Humanity in Algiers; or, The Story of Azem. By an American, Late a Slave in Algiers.* Troy, N.Y.: R. Moffitt.

1802 Silliman, Benjamin. *Letters of Shahcoolen, a Hindu Philosopher, Residing in Philadelphia; to his friend El Hassan, an inhabitant of Delhi.* Boston: n.p. Rpt., Gainesville, Fla.: Scholars' Facsimiles and Reprints, 1962.

1806 "Amorvin: A Tale," *Polythanos*, 2 (July 1806), 225–234.

1810 Fowler, George. *The Wandering Philanthropist; or, Lettres from a Chinese. Written during His Residence in the United States.* Philadelphia: Bartholomew Graves.

1812 "Hamet: A Tale," *Port Folio*, 3rd Series, 8 (August 1812), 184–189.

1813 "The Fortunate Hindoo," *Polythanos*, n.s., 2 (August 1813), 269–274.

Fowler, G. *A Flight to the Moon; or, The Vision of Randalthus.* Baltimore: A. Miltenberger.

1814 "Edmorin and Ella," *New York Weekly Museum*, 1 (September 1814), 161–163.

1815 L., H. R. "The History of Aden: An Allegory," *Port Folio*, 3rd Series (June 1815), 561–568.

"Sered and Tekah; or, The Two Dervises: A Persian Tale," *New York Weekly Museum*, 1 (April 1815), 385–387, 393–396.

1816 "Cassim and Hamid; or, An Emblematical Description of the Resurrection," *New York Weekly Museum*, 3 (April 1816), 401–403.

1818 Knapp, Samuel Lorenzo. *Extracts from a Journal of Travel in North America,*

Consisting of an Account of Boston and Its Vicinity. By Ali Bey. Boston: Thomas Badger, Jr.

1819   "Barkas and Liberat: An Allegorical Tale," *Ladies Literary Cabinet,* n.s., 1 (November 27, 1819), 18–19.

1821   Z., L. G. "Mahmut; or, The Folly of Discontent, An Oriental Tale," *Port Folio,* 5th Series, 11 (April 1821), 437–442.

1822   *The Templar. To Which Is Added the Tales of Passaic.* Hackensack, N.J.: J. Spencer and E. Murden.

1825   Paulding, James Kirke. "The Eve of St. John." In *The Atlantic Souvenir ... 1826.* Philadelphia: H. C. Carey and I. Lea.

1827   Hamlet [pseud.]. "Sadi and Zuleika: An Oriental Eclogue," *Casket,* 2 (September 1827), 358.

1828   "A Morisco Story," *Casket,* 3 (May 1828), 205–209.
        "The Two Garlands," *New York Mirror,* 6 (August 1828), 37–39.

1831   Paulding, J. K. "Jonathan's Visit to the Celestial Empire," *New York Mirror,* 8 (June 1831), 393–395.

1832   Paulding, J. K. "Day and Night; or, The Water-Carrier of Damascus," *New York Mirror,* 10 (December 1832), 201–202.
        ——— "Selim the Benefactor of Mankind." In *Tales of Glauber-Spa,* William Cullen Bryant, ed. Vol. II. New York: J. and J. Harper, 1832. Pp. 156–220.
        W. "A Vision," *New England Magazine,* 3 (July 1832), 63–64.

1833   Paulding, J. K. "Musa or the Reformation," *New York Mirror,* 11 (July 1833), 1–2.
        "The Two Dreams: A Fable," *New York Mirror,* 11 (August 1833), 61.
        "The Vision of Sadak," *Godey's,* 8 (March 1834), 162–164.

1836   Spring, Samuel. *Giafar al Barmeki: A Tale of the Court of Haroun al Raschid.* New York: Harper and Brothers.

1837   "The Rabbi and the Mendicant: A Tale of Jerusalem," *New York Mirror,* 14 (March 1837), 297–298.
        "The Vision of Agib," *Southern Literary Messenger,* 3 (December 1837), 735–739.

1838   Osborn, Laughton. *The Dream of Alla-ad-Deen.* New York: S. White.
        Ware, William. *Letters of Lucius M. Piso, from Palmyra, to His Friend Marcus Curtius at Rome [Zenobia].* New York: C. S. Francis.

1839   "Amram; The Seeker of Oblivion," *Southern Literary Messenger,* 5 (November 1839), 734–741.
        Smith, Richard Penn. "Bator, The Dervise," *Godey's,* 19 (September 1839), 118.

1840   Hentz, Caroline Lee Whiting. "The Abyssinian Neophyte," *Godey's,* 20 (February 1840), 61–68.
        "The Pleasures of Imagination," *New York Mirror,* 18 (July 1840), 9–10.

1841   "Abou Hassan, The Recluse of the Mountain," *Southern Literary Messenger,* 7 (November 1841), 754–759.

1844   Paulding, J. K. "Murad the Wise," *Graham's,* 25 (September 1844), 100–103.

1845   Stephens, Ann S. "The Hindoo Slave," *Peterson's,* 7 (February 1845), 62–64.

1846   Paulding, J. K. "The Vision of Hakim," *Columbian,* 5 (March 1846), 113–115.

1847 Paulding, J. K. "Musa; or, the Pilgrim of Truth," *Graham's,* 30 (January 1847), 28–32.

DOCTRINAL AND ILLUSTRATIVE FICTION THROUGH 1850

Calvinist Fiction

1795 Bradford, Ebenezer. *The Art of Courting, Displayed in Eight Different Scenes.* Newburyport: William Barrett.

1814 Botsford, Edmund. *The Spiritual Voyage, Performed in the Ship Convert, under the Command of Capt. Godly-Fear . . . to the Haven of Felicity on the Continent of Glory. An Allegory.* Charleston, S.C.: J. Hoff.

1816 Sabin, Elijah R. *The Life and Reflections of Charles Observator, in which are Displayed the Real Characters of Human Life.* Boston: Rowe and Hooper.

1822 Lummus, Aaron. *The Life and Adventures of Dr. Caleb . . . An Allegory.* Boston: Lincoln and Edmands.

1823 [DeWitt, Susan?] *Justina; or, The Will. A Domestic Story.* New York: Charles Wiley.

1825 Evans, Sarah Ann. *Resignation: An American Novel.* Boston: John B. Russell. *Triumph of Religion.* Savannah: S. C. and J. Schenk.

1828 *Lucretia and Her Father.* By a Clergyman of New England. Hartford: D. F. Robinson.

1832 Bullard, Anne Tuttle. *The Reformation: A True Tale of the Sixteenth Century.* Boston: Massachusetts Sabbath School Society.

1834 Bullard, A. T. *The Wife for a Missionary.* Cincinnati: Truman, Smith, and Co.

1835 Cheever, George Barrell. "Deacon Giles's Distillery." In *Deacon Giles's Distillery, and Other Miscellanies.* New York: John Wiley, 1853. This volume also contains the following tales and allegories: "The History of John Stubbs. A Warning to Rum-Selling Grocers," "Deacon Jones's Brewery," "The Hill Difficulty: with The Jewish Pilgrim's Progress," "The Two Ways and the Two Ends," "The Two Temptations," and "The Lake Among the Mountains."

1836 Brown, Phoebe H. *The Tree and Its Fruits; or, Narratives from Real Life.* New York: Ezra Collier.

1838 *A Blossom in the Desert: A Tale of the West.* New York: Scofield and Voorhies. Raybold, George A. *The Fatal Feud; or, Passion and Piety.* New York: T. Mason and G. Lane.

———— *Paul Perryman; or, The Unhappy Death.* New York: T. Mason and G. Lane.

1839 Waterson, Robert C. *Arthur Lee and Tom Palmer; or, The Sailor Reclaimed.* Boston: James Munroe and Co.

1841 *The Temptation; or, Henry Thornton.* By a Minister. Boston: D. S. King.

1845 Torrey, Charles. *Home; or, The Pilgrims' Faith Revived.* Salem: John P. Jewett and Co.

1846 Alden, Joseph. *Elizabeth Benton; or, Religion in Connection with Fashionable Life.* New York: Harper and Brothers.
Allen, Elizabeth. "The Effects of Indulgence." In *Sketches of Green Mountain Life.* Lowell: Nathaniel L. Dayton.

Brace, John P. *Tales of the Devils.* Hartford: S. Andrus and Son.

Hall, Bayard Rush. *Something for Everybody: Gleaned in the Old Purchase, from Fields often Reaped.* New York: D. Appleton and Co.

1847   Alden, J. *Alice Gordon; or, the Uses of Orphanage.* New York: Harper and Brothers.

———— *The Lawyer's Daughter.* New York: Harper and Brothers.

———— *The Old Revolutioner.* New York: Harper and Brothers.

1849   Stone, David M. *Frank Forrest; or, The Life of an Orphan Boy.* New York: Dodd and Mead.

1850   Gallaher, James. *The Western Sketch-Book.* Boston: Crocker and Brewster.

Liberal and Anti-Calvinist Fiction

1812   *The Soldier's Orphan.* New York: C. S. Van Winkle.

1814   Savage, Sarah. *The Factory Girl.* Boston: Munroe, Francis, and Parker.

1820   Savage, S. *Filial Affection; or, The Clergyman's Granddaughter.* Boston: Cummings and Hilliard.

1821   Savage, S. *James Talbot.* Boston: Hilliard and Metcalf.

1822   Sedgwick, Catherine Maria. *A New England Tale; or, Sketches of New England Characters and Manners.* New York: E. Bliss and E. White.

1824   Cheney, Harriet V. *A Peep at the Pilgrims in Sixteen Hundred Thirty-Six.* Boston: Wells and Lilly.

Child, Lydia Maria. *Hobomok, A Tale of the Early Times.* Boston: Cummings, Hilliard, and Co.

Sedgwick, C. M. *Redwood. A Tale.* New York: E. Bliss and E. White.

Ware, Henry, Jr. *The Recollections of Jotham Anderson.* In *The Works of Henry Ware, Jr.* Vol. I. Boston: James Munroe and Co., 1846.

1825   Child, L. M. *The Rebels; or, Boston Before the Revolution.* Boston: Cummings, Hilliard and Co.

The Parent's Counsellor; or, The Dangers of Moroseness: A Narrative of the Newton Family. Philadelphia: E. Bacon.

Ware, H., Jr. "Robert Fowle." In *Works,* Vol. I.

1827   Hale, Sarah Josepha. *Northwood: A Tale of New England.* Boston: Bowles and Dearborn.

Sedgwick, C. M. *Hope Leslie; or, Early Times in . . . Massachusetts.* New York: White, Gallaher and White.

William Cooper and His Family; or, Christian Principle Exemplified. Boston: Wait, Greene, and Co.

1829   Flint, Timothy. *George Mason, the Young Backwoodsman.* Boston: Hilliard, Gray, Little, and Wilkins.

Postl, Karl [Charles Sealsfield]. *Tokeah; or, The White Rose.* Philadelphia: Carey, Lea, and Carey.

1830   Flint, Timothy. *Shoshonee Valley.* Cincinnati: E. A. Flint.

Hale, S. J. *Sketches of American Character.* Boston: Putnam and Hunt.

Larned, Mrs. L. *The Sanfords; or, Home Scenes.* New York: Elam Bliss.

Lee, Hannah Farnhum. *Grace Seymour.* New York: Elam Bliss.

Sedgwick, C. M. *Clarence; or, A Tale of Our Own Times.* Philadelphia: Carey and Lea.

Sedgwick, Susan Anne L. *The Young Emigrants. A Tale Designed for Young Persons.* Boston: Carter and Hendee.

1833   Sargent, Lucius Manlius. *I Am Afraid There is a God!* Boston: Ford and Damrell.

———— *My Mother's Gold Ring.* Boston: Ford and Damrell.

———— *Wild Dick and Good Little Robin.* Boston: Ford and Damrell.

1834   Sedgwick, S. A. L. *Allen Prescott; or, The Fortunes of a New-England Boy.* New York: Harper and Brothers.

1835   Follen, Eliza Cabot. *The Skeptic.* Boston: James Munroe and Company.

Hale, S. J. *Traits of American Life.* Philadelphia: E. L. Carey and A. Hart.

Lee, H. F. *The Backslider.* Boston: James Munroe and Co.

Savage, S. *Trial and Self-Discipline.* Boston: James Munroe and Co.

Sedgwick, C. M. *Home.* Boston: James Munroe and Co.

———— *The Linwoods; or "Sixty Years Since" in America.* New York: Harper and Brothers.

1836   Child, L. M. *Philothea: A Romance.* Boston: Otis, Broaders and Co.

Hall, Louisa Jane. *Alfred.* Boston: James Munroe and Co.

Mayo, Sarah E. "Annette Lee." In *Selections from the Writings of Mrs. Sarah C. Edgarton Mayo.* Boston: Abel Tompkins, 1849.

Sargent, L. M. *An Irish Heart.* Boston: William S. Damrell.

Sedgwick, C. M. *The Poor Rich Man and the Rich Poor Man.* New York: Harper and Brothers.

1837   Downer, Sarah. *The Contrast; or, Which is the Christian?* Hudson, N.Y.: Ashbel Stoddard.

———— *The Triumph of Truth.* A Tale. Hudson: Ashbel Stoddard.

Lee, H. F. *The Contrast; or, Modes of Education.* Boston: Whipple and Damrell.

———— *Three Experiments of Living.* Boston: William S. Damrell.

Mayo, S. E. "Eleonora, the Shakeress" and "The Martyr." In *Selections.*

Sargent, L. M. *Kitty Grafton.* Boston: Whipple and Damrell.

1838   Lee, Eliza Buckminster. *Sketches of a New England Village, in the Last Century.* Boston: James Munroe and Co.

Mandell, D. J. *The Adventures of Search for Life, A Bunyanic Narrative.* Portland: S. H. Colesworthy.

Mathews, Cornelius. "Parson Huckins's First Appearance" and "The Witch and the Deacon." In *The Motley Book* (1838), in *The Various Writings of Cornelius Mathews.* New York: Harper and Brothers, 1843.

Mayo, S. E. *The Palfreys.* A Tale. Boston: Abel Tompkins.

Ware, H., Jr. "David Ellington's Subscription." In *David Ellington, With Other Extracts from his Writings.* Boston: Crosby and Nichols.

1839   Hale, S. J. *The Lecturess; or, Woman's Sphere.* Boston: Whipple and Damrell.

Ware, H., Jr. "How to Spend a Day" and "The Village Funeral." In *Works,* Vol. I.

1840   Brownson, Orestes A. *Charles Elwood; or, The Infidel Converted.* In *The Works of Orestes A. Brownson,* ed. Henry F. Brownson. Vol. IV. Detroit: Thorndike Nourse, 1885.

Lee, E. B. *Delusion; or, The Witch of New England.* Boston: Hilliard, Gray and Co.

Rogers, George. "Alice Sherwood, or The Pennsylvania Valley." In *The Pro and Con of Universalism*. Utica, New York: A. B. Grosch and Co.

1841   Mayo, S. E. "The Rustic Wife." In *Selections*.

1842   Mayo, S. E. "The Gossiping of Idle Hours." In *Selections*.

1843   Child, L. M. *Letters from New-York*. New York: Charles Francis and Co.

1844   Herbert, Henry William. *Ruth Whalley; or, The Fair Puritan*. Boston: Henry L. Williams.

Sedgwick, S. A. L. *Alida; or, Town and Country*. New York: Henry J. Langley.

1845   Child, L. M. *Letters from New-York. Second Series*. New York: Charles Francis and Co.

Judd, Sylvester. *Margaret: A Tale of the Real and Ideal, Blight and Bloom*. Boston: Jordan and Wiley.

1846   Child, L. M. *Fact and Fiction: A Collection of Stories*. New York: Charles Francis and Co.

Rogers G. *Adventures of Triptolemus Tub; Comprising Important and Startling Disclosures Concerning Hell; Its Magnitude, Morals, Employments, Climate, etc.* Boston: Abel Tompkins.

1848   Lee, E. B. *Naomi; or, Boston Two Hundred Years Ago*. Boston: Crosby and Nichols.

Sedgwick, C. M. *The Boy of Mt. Rhigi*. Boston: Charles H. Peirce.

1849   Motley, John Lothrop. *Merry-mount: A Romance of the Massachusetts Colony*. Boston: James Munroe and Co.

1850   Graniss, Mrs. M. C. *Emma Clermont; or, Life's Changes*. Hartford: J. Gaylord Wells.

Judd. S. *Philo: An Evangeliad*. Boston: Phillips, Sampson, and Co.

———— *Richard Edney and the Governor's Family: A Rus-Urban Tale*. Boston: Phillips, Sampson, and Co.

Biblical: Christian Martyr and New Testament Narratives

1830   Gray, Thomas. *The Vestal; or, A Tale of Pompeii*. Boston: Gray and Bowen.

1832   Hewson, John. *Christ Rejected; or The Trial of the Eleven Disciples of Christ, In a Court of Law and Equity, as Charged with Stealing the Crucified Body of Christ out of the Sepulchre*. Philadelphia: Joseph Rakestraw.

1837   *Zerah, the Believing Jew*. New York: New York Protestant Episcopal Press.

1838   Ware, William. *Probus; or, Rome in the Third Century*. New York: Charles S. Francis and Co.

1839   Maturin, Edward. "The Christians. A Passage from the Reign of Nero." In *Sejanus, and Other Roman Tales*. New York: F. Saunders.

1841   Ware, W. *Julian; or, Scenes in Judea*. New York: Charles S. Francis and Co.

1843   Brown, John Walker. *Julia of Baiae; or, The Days of Nero*. New York: Saxton and Miles.

The Roman Exile; or, The Times of Aurelius. Boston: John G. Jones.

1847   Lippard, George. *The Legends of the American Revolution. "1776." Or, Washington and His Generals*. Philadelphia: Leary, Stuart, and Co., 1876. Pp. 403–422. First published as *Washington and His Generals; or, Legends of the Revolution*. Philadelphia: G. B. Zieber.

1849 Beecher, Charles. *The Incarnation; or, Pictures of the Virgin and Her Son.* New York: Harper and Brothers.

1850 Gallaher, James. "The Eagle and the Gnat" and "The Living and the Dead Prophets." In *The Western Sketch-Book.*

Roman Catholic Fiction

1829 Pise, Charles Constantine. *Father Rowland: A North American Tale.* Baltimore: Fielding Lucas, Jr.

1830 Pise, C. C. *The Indian Cottage: A Unitarian Story.* Baltimore: Fielding Lucas, Jr.

1836 Hughs, Mary. *The Two Schools: A Moral Tale.* Philadelphia: T. T. Ash.

1837 Damon, Norwood. *The Chronicles of Mt. Benedict: A Tale of the Ursuline Convent.* Boston: Printed for the Publisher.

1842 Cannon, Charles James. *Harry Layden: A Tale.* New York: John A. Boyle.

1843 *Father Oswald: A Genuine Catholic Story.* New York: Casserly and Sons.

1844 Cannon, C. J. *Mora Carmody; or, Woman's Influence.* New York: Edward Dunigan.

1845 Cannon, C. J. *Father Felix: A Tale.* New York: Edward Dunigan.
Pise, C. C. *Zenosius; or, The Pilgrim Convert.* New York: Edward Dunigan.

1846 Dorsey, Anna Hanson (McKenney). *The Sister of Charity.* New York: Edward Dunigan.
———— *The Student of Blenheim Forest; or, The Trials of a Convert.* Baltimore: John Murphy.
———— *Tears on the Diadem.* New York: Edward Dunigan.

1847 Brownson, O. A. *The Two Brothers; or, Why Are You a Protestant?* In *Works,* Vol. VI.
Bryant, John D. *Pauline Seward; A Tale of Real Life.* Baltimore: John Murphy.
Cannon, C. J. *Scenes and Characters from the Comedy of Life.* New York: Edward Dunigan.
McSherry, James. *Pere Jean; or, The Jesuit Missionary. A Tale of the North American Indians.* Baltimore: John Murphy.
Miles, George Henry. *The Truce of God, A Tale of the Eleventh Century.* Baltimore, J. Murphy and Co., 1871, f.p. in *United States Catholic Magazine* (Baltimore, 1847).

1848 Boyce, John [Paul Peppergrass]. *Shandy McGuire; or, Tricks Upon Travellers.* New York: Edward Dunigan.
Brisbane, Abbott Hall. *Ralphton: The Young Carolinian of 1776, A Romance on the Philosophy of Politics.* Charleston, S.C.: Burgess and James.
Dorsey, A. H. *The Oriental Pearl; or, The Catholic Immigrants.* Baltimore: J. Murphy and Co.

1850 Sadlier, Mrs. James (Mary Anne Madden). *The Red Hand of Ulster; or, The Fortunes of Hugh O'Neill.* New York: D. and J. Sadlier.
———— *Willy Burke; or, The Irish Orphan in Boston.* Boston: Patrick Donahoe.

COMBATIVE OR SATIRICAL FICTION

Miscellaneous Satire on Religion through 1850

1793   Rowson, Susanna. *The Inquisitor; or, Invisible Rambler*. Philadelphia: William Gibbons.

1797   Tyler, Royall. *The Bay Boy*. In *The Prose of Royall Tyler*, ed. Marius Peladeau. Rutland, Vt.: Charles E. Tuttle.

1799   Freneau, Philip [Robert Slender]. *Letters on Various Subjects*. Philadelphia: William L. Clements.

1817   Knapp, Samuel L. *Extracts from the Journal of Marshal Soult, Addressed to a Friend: How Obtained, and By Whom Translated Is Not a Subject of Enquiry*. Newburyport: William B. Allen and Co.
        The Yankee Traveller; or, The Adventures of Hector Wigler. Concord, Mass.: George Hough.

1818   *The Life and Adventures of Obadiah Benjamin Franklin Bloomfield, M. D. . . . Interspersed with Episodes and Remarks Religious, Moral, Public Spirited and Humorous*. Philadelphia: Published for the Proprietor.

1828   *Morganiana; or, The Wonderful Life and Terrible Death of Morgan . . . Translated from the Original Arabic Ms*. Boston: Published by the Proprietors.

1830   Owen, Robert Dale. "Darby and Susan" and "Prossimo's Experience." In *Popular Tracts*. New York: Office of the Free Inquirer.

1831   *The Confessions of a Magdalene; or, Some Passages in the Life of Experience Borgia*. New York: Printed for the Publisher.

1833   Williams, Catherine Read. *Fall River. An Authentic Narrative*. Boston: Lilly, Wait and Co.

1839   *Retroprogression. Being an Account of a Short Residence in the Celebrated Town of Jumbleborough*. Boston: James Burns.

1844   Aesop [pseud.]. *The Hypocrite; or, Sketches of American Society from a Residence of Forty Years*. New York: Thomas Fox and Co.
        Lippard, George. *The Ladye Annabel; or, The Doom of the Poisoner*. Philadelphia: R. G. Berford.
        ———— *The Quaker City; or, The Monks of Monk Hall*. Philadelphia: G. B. Zieber and Co.

1845   Bang, Theodore. *The Mysteries of Papermill Village*. Papermill Village, N.H.: Walter Tufts, Jr.

1846   Lippard, G. *Blanche of Brandywine; or, September the Eleventh, 1777*. Philadelphia: G. B. Zieber and Co.
        ———— *The Nazarene; or, The Last of the Washingtons. A Revelation of Philadelphia, New York and Washington in the Year 1844*. Philadelphia: G. Lippard and Co.

1847   Lippard, G. *Washington and His Generals; or, Legends of the Revolution*. G. B. Zieber and Co.

1848   Lippard, G. *Paul Ardenheim; The Monk of Wissahikon*. Philadelphia: T. B. Peterson.

1849   Lippard, G. *The Memoirs of a Preacher: A Revelation of the Church and the Home*. Philadelphia: Joseph Severns.

1850   Lippard, G. *The Empire City; or, New York by Night and Day*. New York:

Stringer and Townsend. First published serially in 1849 in Lippard's weekly newspaper *The Quaker City.*

Anti-Catholic Fiction through 1850

1832 Bullard, Anne Tuttle. *The Reformation: A True Tale of the Sixteenth Century.* Boston: Massachusetts Sabbath School Society.

1833 Brownlee, William Craig. *The Whigs of Scotland; or, The Last of the Stuarts. An Historical Romance.* New York: J. and H. Harper.
Bourne, George. *Lorette. The History of Louise, Daughter of a Canadian Nun: Exhibiting the Interior of Female Convents.* New York: William A. Mercein.

1834 Mr. DePotter (pseud.). *Female Convents. Secrets of Nunneries Disclosed.* New York: D. Appleton and Co.

1835 Hale, Sarah Josepha. "The Catholic Convert." In *Traits of American Life.* Philadelphia: E. L. Carey and A. Hart.
Reed, Rebecca Theresa. *Six Months in a Convent.* Boston: Russell, Odiorne, and Metcalfe.
Sherwood, S. *Edwin and Alicia; or, the Infant Martyrs.* New York: Moore and Payne.

1836 Culbertson, Rosamond. *Rosamond; or, a Narrative of the Captivity and Sufferings of an American Female under the Popish Priests in the Island of Cuba . . . written by herself.* Boston: Crocker and Brewster.
Larned, L. *The American Nun; or, The Effects of Romance.* Boston: Otis, Broaders, and Co.
Monk, Maria. *Awful Disclosures of Maria Monk, As Exhibited in a Narrative of Her Sufferings, During a Residence of Five Years as a Novice, and Two Years as a Black Nun, In the Hotel Dieu Nunnery at Montreal.* New York: Howe and Bates.

1837 *The Conversion and Edifying Death of Andrew Dunn.* Philadelphia: E. Cummiskey.
Sinclair, Catherine. *Modern Society: The March of the Intellect.* New York: R. Carter.

1845 Barker, Benjamin. *Cecilia; or, The White Nun of the Wilderness.* Boston: F. Gleason.
Jones, Justin. *The Nun of St. Ursula; or, the Burning of a Convent; a Romance of Mt. Benedict.* Boston: F. Gleason.
MacCrindell, Rachel. *The School Girl in France; or, The Snares of Popery: A Warning to Protestants against Education in Catholic Seminaries.* New York: J. K. Wellman.

1847 MacCrindell, R. *The Convent.* New York: R. Carter.

SAMPLING OF RELIGIOUS FICTION AFTER 1850

1851 Hentz, Caroline Lee Whiting. *Rena; or, The Snow Bird.* Philadelphia: A. Hart.
Huntington, Jedediah Vincent. *Alban: A Tale of the New World.* New York: G. P. Putnam.

Miles, George Henry. *The Governess; or, The Effects of Good Example*. Baltimore: Hedian and O'Brien.

Mitchell, Donald Grant [Ik Marvel]. *Dream Life: A Fable of the Seasons*. New York: Charles Scribner.

Phelps, Elizabeth Stuart. *The Sunny Side; or, The Country Minister's Wife*. Boston: John P. Jewett and Co.

Warner, Susan [Elizabeth Wetherell]. *The Wide, Wide World*. New York: G. P. Putnam.

1852 Chesebro', Caroline. *Isa, a Pilgrimage*. New York: Redfield.

Huntington, J. V. *The Forest*. New York: Redfield.

Stowe, Harriet Beecher. *Uncle Tom's Cabin; or, Life Among the Lowly*. Boston: John P. Jewett and Co.

Warner, Susan B. *Queechy*. New York: George P. Putnam.

1853 Boyce, John. *The Spaewife; or, The Queen's Secret*. Baltimore: John Murphy.

Parton, Sara Payson (Willis) [Fanny Fern]. *Fern Leaves from Fanny's Port Folio*. Auburn: Derby and Miller.

Quigley, Hugh. *The Cross and the Shamrock; or, How to Defend the Faith*. Boston: Patrick Donahoe.

Southworth, Emma Dorothy Eliza Nevitte. *The Curse of Clifton*. Philadelphia: A. Hart.

1854 Brownson, Orestes A. *The Spirit-Rapper: An Autobiography*. Boston: Little, Brown and Co.

Cummins, Maria Susanna. *The Lamplighter*. Boston: John P. Jewett and Co.

Holmes, Mary Jane. *Tempest and Sunshine*. New York: Appleton and Co.

Hornblower, Jane Elizabeth. *Vera; or, The Child of Adoption*. New York: Robert Carter and Bros.

Smith, Elizabeth Oakes. *Bertha and Lily; or, The Parsonage of Beech Glen*. New York: J. C. Derby.

———— *The Newsboy*. New York: J. C. Derby.

Terhune, Mrs. Mary Virginia (Hawes) [Marion Harland]. *Alone*. Richmond: A. Morris.

1855 Baker, Harriette N. *Cora and the Doctor*. Boston: J. P. Jewett and Co.

Ingraham, Joseph Holt. *The Prince of the House of David; or, Three Years in the Holy City*. New York: Pudney and Russell.

Richards, Maria T. *Life in Judea*. Philadelphia: American Baptist Publication Society.

Sadlier, Mrs. James (Mary Anne Madden). *The Blakes and the Flanagans*. New York: D. and J. Sadlier.

Terhune, M. V. *Husbands and Homes*. Boston: Gould and Lincoln.

Wilson, Augusta Jane Evans. *Inez: A Tale of the Alamo*. New York: Harper and Brothers.

1856 Baker, H. N. *The First and Second Marriages*. Boston: Shepard, Clark and Co.

Chesebro', C. *Victoria; or, The World Overcome*. New York: Derby and Jackson.

Dorr, Julia C. Ripley. *Lanmere*. New York: Mason Brothers.

Hentz, C. L. W. *Ernest Linwood*. Boston: John P. Jewett and Co.

Holmes, M. J. *Lena Rivers*. New York: Miller, Orton and Mulligan.

Tuthill, Louisa Caroline Higgins. *Reality; or, The Millionaire's Daughter.* New York: C. Scribner.

Warner, Susan. *The Hills of Shatemuc.* New York: D. Appleton and Co.

1857 Baker, H. N. *The Household Angel in Disguise.* Boston: Shepard, Clark and Co.

Cummins, M. S. *Mabel Vaughan.* Boston: J. P. Jewett and Co.

Holland, Josiah Gilbert. *The Bay-Path: A Tale of Colonial Life.* New York: G. P. Putnam and Co.

Richards, M. T. *Life in Israel; or, Portraitures of Hebrew Character.* Philadelphia: American Baptist Publication Society.

1858 Lee, Eliza B. *Parthenia; or, The Last Days of Paganism.* Boston: Ticknor and Fields.

Townsend, Virginia Frances. *While It Was Morning.* New York: Derby and Jackson.

Wood, George. *Future Life; or, Scenes in Another World.* New York: Derby and Jackson.

1859 Denison, Mary Andrews. *Opposite the Jail.* Boston: H. Hoyt.

Fletcher, Miriam. *The Methodist.* New York: Derby and Jackson.

Ingraham, J. H. *The Pillar of Fire; or, Israel in Bondage.* New York: Pudney and Russell.

Stowe, H. B. *The Minister's Wooing.* New York: Derby and Jackson.

Wilson, A. J. E. *Beulah.* New York: Derby and Jackson.

1860 Boyce, J. *Mary Lee; or, The Yankee in Ireland.* Baltimore: Kelly, Hedian, and Piet.

Cummins, M. S. *El Fureidis.* Boston: Ticknor and Fields.

Huntington, J. V. *Rosemary; or, Life and Death.* New York: D. and J. Sadlier.

Ingraham, J. H. *The Throne of David, From the Consecration of the Shepherd of Bethlehem to the Rebellion of Prince Absalom.* New York: Pudney and Russell.

Warner, Susan and Anna. *Say and Seal.* Philadelphia: J. B. Lippincott and Co.

1862 Sadlier, Mrs. J. *Old and New; or, Taste versus Fashion.* D. and J. Sadlier.

Stowe, H. B. *Agnes of Sorrento.* Boston: Ticknor and Fields.

———— *The Pearl of Orr's Island.* Boston: Ticknor and Fields

1863 Chesebro', C. *Peter Carradine; or, The Martindale Pastoral.* New York: Sheldon and Co.

1864 Hoffman, Mary Jane. *Agnes; or, Practical Views of Catholicity.* New York: P. O'Shea.

Sadlier, Mrs. J. *Confessions of an Apostate; or, Leaves from a Troubled Life.* New York: Sadlier.

1865 Denison, M. A. *The Mill Agent.* Boston: Graves and Young.

1866 Mitchell, D. G. *Doctor Johns: Being a Narrative of Certain Events in the Life of an Orthodox Minister.* New York: Charles Scribner and Co.

Terhune, M. V. *Sunnybank.* New York: Sheldon and Co.

1867 Wilson, A. J. E. *St. Elmo.* New York: Carleton.

1868 Beecher, Henry Ward. *Norwood: or, Village Life in New England.* New York: Charles Scribner and Co.

1869 Baker, H. N. *Juliette; or, Now and Forever.* Boston: Lee and Shepard.

Horn, Henry J. *Strange Visitors: A Series of Original Papers . . . By . . . Spirits Now Dwelling in the Spirit World.* New York: Carleton.

Stowe, H. B. *Oldtown Folks.* Boston: Houghton Mifflin.

Ward, Elizabeth Stuart Phelps. *The Gates Ajar.* Boston: Fields, Osgood and Co.

1870   Baker, William. *The New Timothy.* New York: Harper and Brothers.

Holcombe, William H. *In Both Worlds.* Philadelphia: J. B. Lippincott and Co.

1871   Eggleston, Edward. *The Hoosier Schoolmaster.* New York: J. B. Ford and Co.

Miles, G. H. *The Truce of God, A Tale of the Eleventh Century.* Baltimore: John Murphy.

Stowe, H. B. *My Wife and I.* New York: J. B. Ford and Co.

Ward, E. S. P. *The Silent Partner.* Boston: James R. Osgood and Co.

1872   Quigley, H. *Profit and Loss: A Story of the Life of the Genteel Irish-American.* New York: T. O'Kane.

Roe, Edward Payson. *Barriers Burned Away.* New York: Dodd and Mead.

1873   Holland, J. G. *Arthur Bonnicastle.* New York: Scribner, Armstrong and Co.

Eggleston, E. *The Circuit Rider: A Tale of the Heroic Age.* New York: J. B. Ford and Co.

1874   Roe, E. P. *Opening a Chestnut Burr.* New York: Dodd and Mead.

1875   Hoffman, M. J. *The Orphan Sisters; or, The Problem Solved.* D. and J. Sadlier.

1876   Southworth, E. D. E. N. *Self-Raised; or, From the Depths.* Philadelphia: T. B. Peterson and Brothers.

1878   Stowe, H. B. *Poganuc People.* New York: Fords, Howard, and Hulbert.

1880   Baker, W. *His Majesty, Myself.* Boston: Roberts Brothers.

Wallace, Lewis. *Ben-Hur. A Tale of the Christ.* New York: Harper.

1883   Ward, E. S. P., *Beyond the Gates.* Boston: Houghton Mifflin.

1885   Moore, B. P. *Endura; or, Three Generations.* San Francisco: Golden Era Co.

1887   Dorsey, Anna H. *Palms.* Baltimore: John Murphy.

Howells, William Dean. *The Minister's Charge.* Boston: Ticknor and Co.

Ward, E. S. P. *The Gates Between.* Boston: Houghton Mifflin.

1888   Deland, Margaret. *John Ward, Preacher.* Boston: Houghton Mifflin.

1889   Howells, W. D. *Annie Kilburn.* New York: Harper and Brothers.

Tourgee, Albion. *Murvale Eastman, Christian Socialist.* New York: Fords, Howard, and Hulbert.

Von Himmel, Ernst. *The Discovered Country.* Boston: For the Author.

Woods, Katherine Pearson. *Metzerott, Shoemaker.* New York: Thomas Y. Crowell.

1891   Slosson, Annie Trumbull. *Seven Dreamers.* New York: Harper and Brothers.

Ward, E. S. P. and Herbert D. *Come Forth!* Boston: Houghton Mifflin.

Daniel, Charles S. *Ai; A Social Vision.* Boston: Miller.

1892   Slosson, A. T. *The Heresy of Mehetabel Clark.* New York: Harper and Brothers.

1894   Hepworth, George H. *They Met in Heaven.* New York: E. P. Dutton and Co.

Howells, W. D. *A Traveller from Altruria.* New York: Harper and Brothers.

Pendleton, Louis H. *The Wedding Garment: A Tale of the Life to Come.* Boston: Roberts Brothers.

1895   Hale, Edward Everett. *If Jesus Came to Boston.* Boston: Lamson, Wolffe and Co.

Kingsley, Florence Morse. *Titus, a Comrade of the Cross.* Chicago: David C. Cook.

Sherwood, Margaret. *An Experiment in Altruism.* New York: Macmillan.

Van Dyke, Henry. *The Story of the Other Wise Man.* New York: Harper.
Ward, E. S. P. *A Singular Life.* Boston: Houghton Mifflin.
1896 Frederic, Harold. *The Damnation of Theron Ware.* Chicago: Stone and Kimball.
Kingsley, F. M. *Stephen, a Soldier of the Cross.* Philadelphia: Henry Altemus.
Ward, E. S. P. *The Supply at St. Agatha's.* Boston: Houghton Mifflin.
Woods, K. P. *John: A Tale of King Messiah.* New York: Dodd, Mead and Co.
1897 Allen, James Lane. *The Choir Invisible.* New York: Macmillan.
Sheldon, Charles. *In His Steps: "What Would Jesus Do?"* Chicago: Advance.
Woolley, Cecilia. *Love and Theology.* Boston: Ticknor.
1899 Churchill, Winston. *Richard Carvel.* New York: Macmillan.
Gordon, Charles W. [Ralph Connor]. *The Sky Pilot. A Tale of the Foothills.* New York: Fleming H. Revell.
Springer, Rebecca. *Intra Muros.* Chicago: David C. Cook.
1900 Allen, J. L. *The Reign of Law.* New York: Macmillan.
1901 Ward, E. S. P. *Within the Gates.* Boston: Houghton Mifflin.
1902 Van Dyke, H. *The Blue Flower.* New York: Scribner.
1903 Fox, John J. *The Little Shepherd of Kingdom Come.* New York: Scribner.
1904 Churchill, W. *The Crossing.* New York: Macmillan.
1906 Churchill, W. *Coniston.* New York: Macmillan.
1907 Wright, Harold Bell. *The Shepherd of the Hills.* Chicago: A. L. Burt.
1908 Gordon, C. W. *Black Rock.* New York: Fleming H. Revell.
1909 Wright, H. B. *The Calling of Dan Matthews.* Chicago: Book Supply.
1913 Churchill, W. *The Inside of the Cup.* New York: Macmillan.
1917 Churchill, W. *The Dwelling Place of Light.* New York: Macmillan.
1919 Wright, H. B. *The Re-Creation of Brian Kent.* Chicago: Book Supply.
1921 Marquis, Don. *Chapters for the Orthodox.* New York: Doubleday, Doran and Co.
1922 Keable, Robert. *Simon Called Peter.* New York: Dutton.
1924 Barton, Bruce. *The Man Nobody Knows.* Indianapolis: Bobbs-Merrill.
Sinclair, Upton B. *They Call Me Carpenter.* New York: Boni and Liveright.
1927 Cather, Willa. *Death Comes for the Archbishop.* New York: Knopf.
Lewis, Sinclair. *Elmer Gantry.* New York: Harcourt, Brace.
1929 Freeman, H. W. *Joseph and His Brethren.* New York: Holt.
1931 Cather, W. *Shadows on the Rock.* New York: Knopf.
1932 Douglas, Lloyd Cassel. *Magnificent Obsession.* Chicago: Willett, Clark.
1933 Douglas, L. C. *Forgive Us Our Trespasses.* Boston: Houghton Mifflin.
1935 Douglas, L. C. *Green Light.* Boston: Houghton Mifflin.
1936 Douglas, L. C. *White Banners.* Boston: Houghton Mifflin.
1939 Asch, Sholem. *The Nazarene.* New York: Putnam.
1942 Douglas, L. C. *The Robe.* Boston: Houghton Mifflin.
1943 Asch, S. *The Apostle.* New York: Putnam.
Janney, Russell. *The Miracle of the Bells.* New York: Prentice-Hall.
1948 Douglas, L. C. *The Big Fisherman.* Boston: Houghton Mifflin.
Turnbull, Agnes S. *The Bishop's Mantle.* New York: Macmillan.
1949 Asch, S. *Mary.* New York: Putnam.
1950 Buechner, Frederick. *A Long Day's Dying.* New York: Knopf.
———— *The Season's Difference.* New York: Knopf.

Robinson, Henry Morton. *The Cardinal.* New York: Simon and Schuster.

1951   Marshall, Catherine. *A Man Called Peter.* New York: McGraw-Hill.

1952   Costain, Thomas. *The Silver Chalice.* New York: Doubleday.

1956   Caldwell, Taylor. *The Tender Victory.* New York: McGraw-Hill.

1958   DeVries, Peter. *The Mackerel Plaza.* Boston: Little, Brown.

Uris, Leon. *Exodus.* New York: Doubleday.

1960   DeVries, P. *The Blood of the Lamb.* Boston: Little, Brown.

1961   O'Connor, Edwin. *The Edge of Sadness.* Boston: Little, Brown.

1968   Langguth, A. J. *Jesus Christs.* New York: Harper and Row.

1970   Caldwell, T. *Great Lion of God.* Garden City, N.Y.: Doubleday.

1971   Blatty, William Peter. *The Exorcist.* New York: Bantam.

Buechner, F. *Lion Country.* New York: Atheneum.

1972   Buechner, F. *Open Heart.* New York: Atheneum.

1973   Forrest, Leon. *There Is a Tree More Ancient Than Eden.* New York: Random House.

1974   Buechner, F. *Love Feast.* New York: Atheneum.

1975   McLean, Gordon. *Devil at the Wheel.* St. Louis: Bethany.

Updike, John. *A Month of Sundays.* New York: Knopf.

1977   Berrigan, Daniel. *A Book of Parables.* New York: Seabury.

Forrest, L. *The Bloodworth Orphans.* New York: Random House.

1978   Allnut, Frank. *The Peacemaker.* Van Nuys, Cal.: Bible Voice.

Cahill, Susan. *Earth Angels.* New York: Fawcett.

Henderson, Lois T. *Hagar.* Chappaqua: Christian Herald.

1979   Christman, Elizabeth. *Flesh and Spirit.* New York: Morrow.

Hamilton, Dorothy. *Ken's Hideout.* Scottdale, Pa.: Herald Press.

Kemelman, Harry. *Thursday the Rabbi Walked Out.* New York: Fawcett.

Nixon, Joan Lowery. *The Butterfly Tree.* Huntington, Ind.: Our Sunday Visitor.

Oates, Joyce Carol. *Son of the Morning.* New York: Fawcett.

1980   Davies, Bettilu D. *The Secret of the Hidden Cave.* Grand Rapids: Zondervan.

Kauffmann, Joel. *The Weight.* Scottdale, Pa.: Herald Press.

Levine, Faye. *Solomon and Sheba.* New York: Putnam.

Mandino, Og. *The Christ Commission.* New York: Lippincott and Crowell.

Notes

Introduction

1. *The Gamesters; or, Ruins of Innocence* (Boston: David Carlisle, 1805), pp. iv–v. The early texts are full of archaic and peculiar usage, as well as errors in English and extensive use of italics. No attempt has been made to change or correct the spelling, punctuation, or grammar in quotations from the novels and other primary sources; nor have I included "sic" after each error. See the Appendix for chronological listings by type of this and other sources.

2. *Contributions to 'The Galaxy,' 1868–1871, by Mark Twain,* ed. Bruce R. McElderry, Jr. (Gainesville, Fla.: Scholars' Facsimiles and Reprints, 1961), p. 128.

3. *Life and Letters of Catherine Maria Sedgwick,* ed. Mary E. Dewey (New York: Harper, 1872), pp. 59, 63.

4. *Travels; in New-England and New-York* (New Haven: T. Dwight, 1821), I, 518.

5. *The American Mind* (New Haven: Yale Universitiy Press, 1950), p. 165.

6. Quoted in Kenneth Murdock, *Literature and Theology in Colonial New England* (Cambridge, Mass.: Harvard University Press, 1949), p. 42 (primary source unidentified). However, as Robert Daly has pointed out, this ban against literary embellishment was in fact disregarded by several colonial poets. See Daly's *God's Altar: The World and the Flesh in Puritan Poetry* (Berkeley: University of California Press, 1978).

7. "Of Poetry, and of Style," from *Manductio ad Ministerium,* in *American Thought and Writing,* ed. Russel B. Nye and Norman S. Grabo (Boston: Houghton Mifflin, 1965), I, 344.

8. *The Duty of Searching the Scriptures* (London: James Hutton, 1739), p. 16.

9. *A Divine and Supernatural Light* (1734), in *Jonathan Edwards, Representative Selections,* ed. Clarence H. Faust and Thomas H. Johnson (New York: Hill and Wang, 1962), p. 105.

10. *A Treatise Concerning the Religious Affections* (1746), in Nye and Grabo, *American Thought and Writing,* I, 406, 417.

11. *Lectures on Rhetoric and Belles Lettres* (1783; rpt., Philadelphia: S. C. Hayes 1860), p. 417.

12. Royall Tyler, *The Algerine Captive; or, The Life and Adventures of Doctor Updike Underhill, Six Years a Prisoner among the Algerines* (Walpole, N.H.: David Carlisle, Jr. 1797), p. vi.

13. *The Power of Sympathy; or, The Triumph of Nature* (Boston: Isaiah Thomas and Co., 1789), II, 4–5.

14. *Lectures on American Literature* (1829), ed. Richard B. Davis and Ben H. McClary (Gainesville, Fla.: Scholars' Facsimiles and Reprints, 1961), pp. 82, 33, 117.

15. Throughout this study I use "orthodox" loosely to mean "Calvinist." Between 1800 and 1850 there were two main kinds of Calvinism: evangelical Calvinism, which was fervent, revivalistic, and increasingly simple, was dominant on the frontier, particularly in the South; northern seminarian Calvinism, which shared the evangelical belief in the central doctrines of orthodoxy, was nevertheless more intellectual and less mass-oriented. In general, both the more conservative evangelicals and the strictest seminarians decried fiction, while the moderate Calvinists of the mainstream came to be tolerant of it in time.

1. The Oriental Connection

1. "Education," in *The Complete Writings of Ralph Waldo Emerson,* II (New York: W. H. Wise, 1929), 984.

2. *Letters Writ by a Turkish Spy,* V (London: Strahan and Ballard, 1734), 131.

3. Quoted by Arthur Christy, *The Asian Legacy and American Life* (New York: Columbia University Press, 1968), p. 26.

4. Ely Bates, *A Chinese Fragment. Containing an Enquiry into the Present State of Religion in England* (London: J. Davis, 1786), pp. 162–163.

5. The only detailed study of early Eastern fiction in America is Mukhtar Ali Isani, "The Oriental Tale in America through 1865: A Study in American Fiction" (Diss. Princeton University, 1962). Isani connects the genre with an interest in the Orient prompted by foreign trade. Although my emphasis is quite different from Isani's, I am indebted to his identification of some three hundred Oriental tales written by Americans, as opposed to British or Continental authors, between the Revolution and the Civil War.

6. *The Literary Magazine and American Register,* 3 (June 1805), 404.

7. *A Sermon Preached at the Stone Chapel in Boston, Sept. 12, 1790* (Boston 1790), p. 15.

8. Quoted by Algernon Tassin, *The Magazine in America* (New York: Dodd, Mead and Co., 1916), p. 11.

9. *Massachusetts Magazine* 1 (February 1789), 76–77.

10. *The Algerine Captive*, II, 146, 145. For the reader's convenience, future references to this book and to other works quoted at length will be cited parenthetically in the text.

11. *Monthly Anthology*, 9 (November 1810), 346.

12. Quoted in *The Prose of Royall Tyler*, ed. Marius B. Peladeau (Portland, Vt.: Charles E. Tuttle, 1972), p. 46. Tyler was an Episcopalian judge who had almost entered the ministry. His *Bay Boy* contained much anti-Calvinist commentary, including the statement that "the Episcopal clergy are generally *Arminian* while Congregational divines are Calvinistic. We cannot be too careful to maintain this line of distinction between us" (*Prose of Royall Tyler*, p. 69).

13. *Prose of Royall Tyler*, p. 250.

14. *New York Magazine*, 2 (September 1791), 507.

15. *Humanity in Algiers; or, The Story of Azem* (Troy, N.Y.: R. Moffitt, 1801), p. 4.

16. *The Algerine Spy in Pennsylvania* (Philadelphia: Prichard and Hall, 1787), pp. 19–20.

17. *Extracts from a Journal of Travels in North America . . . By Ali Bey* (Boston: Thomas Badger, Jr., 1818), p. 111.

18. Tyler, *Algerine Captive*, II, 141.

19. *Gentleman and Lady's Magazine*, 1 (July 1784), 98–99.

20. *Letters of Shahcoolen* (1802; rpt., Gainesville, Fla.: Scholars' Facsimiles and Reprints, 1962), p. 89. In his introduction to the 1962 edition, Ben H. McClary persuasively argues that Silliman wrote this work, which has been long attributed to Samuel L. Knapp.

21. *The Wandering Philanthropist; or, Lettres from a Chinese* (Philadelphia: Bartholomew Graves, 1810), p. 102.

22. From *A Treatise Concerning Religious Affections* (1746), in Nye and Grabo, *American Thought and Writing*, I, 413, 414.

23. *A Divine and Supernatural Light*, in Faust and Johnson, *Jonathan Edwards, Representative Selections*, pp. 104, 105.

24. *The Minister's Wooing* (New York: Derby and Jackson, 1859), p. 88.

25. *A Disquisition Concerning Angelical Apparitions* (Boston, 1696), p. 24. However, the fact that Increase's son, Cotton Mather, did see an angel suggests that the Puritan mistrust of angelic visions was not universal among strict Calvinists.

26. *Heaven the Best Country* (Boston: B. Green [?], 1712), p. 29.

27. *Angels Ministering to the People of God* (Newport: J. Franklin, 1755), p. 6.

28. *The Importance and Necessity of Christians Considering Jesus Christ in the Extent of his high and glorious Character* (Boston: Kneeland and Adams, 1768), pp. 16, 15.

29. *Massachusetts Magazine*, 6 (March 1794), 154.

30. *American Magazine and Historical Chronicle*, 3 (December 1746), 546.

31. *The Autobiography and Other Writings* (New York: New American Library, 1961), p. 31.

32. *The Works of Benjamin Franklin*, ed. Jared Sparks, II (Boston: Hilliard, Gray, and Co., 1840), 2.

33. *The Complete Works of Benjamin Franklin*, ed. John Bigelow, VI (New York: Putnam, 1888), 261–262.

34. *Columbian Magazine*, 2 (May 1788), 249, 251.

35. *Massachusetts Magazine*, 1 (January 1789), 48.

36. *Massachusetts Magazine,* 2 (November 1790), 646.
37. *Massachusetts Magazine,* 5 (January 1793), 45.
38. *Massachusetts Magazine,* 7 (December 1795), 546.
39. *Columbian Magazine,* 3 (January 1789), 20.
40. *Gentleman and Lady's Magazine,* 1 (December 1784), 324.
41. *Columbian Magazine,* 1 (November 1786), 131.
42. *Massachusetts Magazine,* 5 (May 1793), 277.
43. *South Carolina Weekly Museum,* 1 (February 1797), 273.
44. *American Museum,* 11 (Marach 1792), 70.
45. *Massachusetts Magazine,* 8 (February 1796), 82–86.
46. *Gentleman and Lady's Magazine,* 1 (June 1784), 47.
47. "Talisman" in *Massachusetts Magazine,* 7 (August 1795; f.p. 1791), 259–261: "Hamet" in *Port Folio,* 3rd ser., 8 (August 1812), 184–189.
48. *American Museum,* 8 (September 1790), 110.
49. *Massachusetts Magazine,* 5 (May 1793), 275.
50. John Bunyan, *The Pilgrim's Progress* (1684; rpt., Boston: Houghton Mifflin, 1969), pp. 204, 205.
51. *Poems and Compositions in Prose on Several Occasions* (Richmond, Va.: Samuel Pleasants, Jr., 1798), p. 25.
52. Henry Sherburne, *The Oriental Philanthropist; or, True Republican* (Portsmouth, N.H.: William Treadwell, 1800), pp. 3–4.
53. *Popular Tracts* (New York: Office of the Free Inquirer, 1830), Tract 2, p. 1.
54. "An Address [Delivered before the Senior Class of the Harvard Divinity School on . . . July 15, 1838]," in *The American Tradition in Literature,* 3rd ed., ed. Sculley Bradley, Richmond C. Beatty, and E. Hudson Long, I (New York: W. W. Norton and Co., 1967), 1119.
55. *The Algerine Captive,* II, 79.
56. *Humanity in Algiers,* p. 23.
57. *Gentleman and Lady's Magazine,* 1 (October 1784), 281, 284.
58. *The American Bee; A Collection of Entertaining Histories, Selected from Different Authors* (Leominster, Mass.: Charles Prentiss, 1797), pp. 133, 135, 136.
59. *Mentoria; or, The Young Lady's Friend* (Philadelphia: Robert Campbell, 1794), II, 84, 91.
60. *Port Folio,* 8 (August 1812), 188.
61. *The Literary Magazine and American Register,* 6 (August 1806), 81.
62. Henry St. Clair, *Tales of Terror; or, The Mysteries of Magic* (Boston: Charles Gaylord, 1833), II, 52–53.
63. *New York Mirror,* 14 (May 1833), 372.
64. *Pilgrim's Progress,* p. 200.
65. "Novel-Writing and Novel-Reading" (1848), in *The Works of Orestes Brownson,* ed. Henry F. Brownson, XIX (Detroit: Thorndike Nourse, 1885), 224–225.
66. *The Wandering Philanthropist,* p. 264.
67. *Port Folio,* 5 (June 1815), 567.
68. "The Scottish Philosophy and American Theology," *Church History,* 24 (September 1955), 268.
69. *Graham's Magazine,* 30 (January 1847), 29.
70. *The Templar* (Hackensack, N.J.: J. Spencer and E. Murden, 1822), p. 33.

71. Samuel Spring, *Giafar al Barmeki: A Tale of the Court of Haroun al Raschid* (New York: Harper, 1836), I, 80, 18.

72. *Zenobia; or, the Fall of Palmyra* (1838; rpt., New York: C. S. Francis, 1854), II, 239.

73. *Autobiography and Letters of Orville Dewey, D.D.,* ed. Mary E. Dewey (Boston: Roberts Brothers, 1883), p. 87.

74. "Oriental Tale," pp. 176–179.

2. Earth Above, Heaven Below

1. "Celadon," *The Golden Age* (n.p., 1785), p. 6.

2. *The Miscellaneous Essays and Occasional Writings* (Philadelphia: T. Dobson, 1792), I, 5–6, 10.

3. *Memoirs of the Bloomsgrove Family* (Boston: Thomas and Andrews, 1790), I, 72.

4. See especially the following tales in the *Massachusetts Magazine:* "An Eclipse of the Moon," 5 (June 1793), 339–342; "Benefits of Adversity," 5 (July 1793), 411–414; "A Vision," 5 (November 1793), 694–695; and the "Memorialist" column (untitled tale), 6 (May 1794), 289–290.

5. William Hill Brown, *Ira and Isabella; or, The Natural Children* (Boston: Belcher and Armstrong, 1807), pp. iii, iv.

6. Charles Brockden Brown, *The Rhapsodist and Other Uncollected Writings,* ed. Harry R. Warfel (New York: Scholars' Facsimiles and Reprints, 1943), p. 7.

7. Quoted in David Lee Clark, *Charles Brockden Brown: Pioneer Voice of America* (Durham: Duke University Press, 1952), p. 38.

8. Quoted in William Dunlap, *The Life of Charles Brockden Brown* (Philadelphia: James P. Parke, 1815), I, 23.

9. Clark, *Charles Brockden Brown,* pp. 104, 156.

10. Clark, *Charles Brockden Brown,* p. 105.

11. Dunlap, *The Life of Charles Brockden Brown,* II, 49.

12. Dunlap, *The Life of Charles Brockden Brown,* I, 285–286; II, 61.

13. *The Literary Magazine and American Register,* 1 (November 1803), 98.

14. Clark, *Charles Brockden Brown,* p. 293.

15. *Jane Talbot* (Philadelphia: John Conrad, 1801), p. 61.

16. *The Asylum; or, Alonzo and Melissa* (1811), reprinted as Daniel Jackson, *Alonzo and Melissa; or, The Unfeeling Heart* (Hartford: S. Andrus, 1851), p. 189.

17. *Charlotte: A Tale of Truth,* in *Three Early American Novels,* ed. William S. Kable (Columbus: Charles E. Merrill, 1970), pp. 85, 121, 82.

18. *The Inquisitor; or, Invisible Rambler* (Philadelphia: William Gibbons, 1793), I, 9–10.

19. *Charlotte's Daughter; or, The Three Orphans* (Boston: Richardson and Lord, 1828), p. 156.

20. *A Flight to the Moon; or, The Vision of Randalthus* (Baltimore: A. Miltenberger, 1813), pp. 96–97.

21. Dewey, *Life and Letters of . . . Sedgwick,* p. 90.

22. *A New England Tale* (1822; rpt., New York: George P. Putnam, 1852), p. 89.

23. Quoted in Edward Halsey Foster, *Catherine Maria Sedgwick* (New York: Twayne, 1974), p. 53.

24. *Redwood. A Tale* (1824; rpt., New York: George P. Putnam, 1850), p. 402.

25. Quoted in Foster, *Sedgwick,* p. 86.

26. *Hope Leslie* (1827; rpt., New York: Harper, 1855), I, 93–94.

27. *Tales and Sketches* (Philadelphia: Carey, Lea, and Blanchard, 1835), 67.

28. *Clarence; or, A Tale of Our Own Times* (Philadelphia: Carey and Lea, 1830), I, 15.

29. *The Linwoods; or, "Sixty Years Since" in America* (1835; rpt., New York: Harper, 1861), II, 112.

30. Quoted in Foster, *Sedgwick,* p. 117.

31. *Home* (Boston: Munroe, 1835), p. 28.

32. *The Poor Rich Man and the Rich Poor Man* (New York: Harper, 1836), p. 68.

33. In *The Token and Atlantic Souvenir, a Christmas and New Year's Present,* ed. S. G. Goodrich (Boston: Otis, Broaders, and Co., 1840), p. 201.

34. *The Boy of Mt. Rhigi* (1848; rpt., Boston: Crosby and Nichols, 1862), p. 25.

35. *Married or Single?* (New York: Harper, 1857), I, 8.

36. *Letters of Lydia Maria Child with a Biographical Introduction by John Greenleaf Whittier* (Boston: Houghton Mifflin and Co., 1883), p. 7.

37. *Letters of . . . Child,* p. 169.

38. *The Rebels; or, Boston Before the Revolution* (1825; rpt., Boston: Phillips, Sampson, and Co., 1850), p. 254.

39. *Philothea: A Romance* (1836; rpt., New York: C. S. Francis and Co., 1845), p. 46.

40. *Letters of . . . Child,* p. 70.

41. *Letters of . . . Child,* p. 76.

42. *Letters from New-York* (New York: C. S. Francis and Co, 1843), pp. 12, 276.

43. *Letters from New-York. Second Series* (New York: C. S. Francis and Co., 1845), pp. 205–206.

44. *Letters of . . . Child,* p. 75.

45. *A Romance of the Republic* (Boston: Ticknor and Fields, 1867), p. 174.

46. Arethusa Hall, *Life and Character of the Rev. Sylvester Judd* (Boston: Crosby, Nichols, and Co., 1854), p. 239.

47. *Margaret: A Tale of the Real and Ideal, Blight and Bloom* (1845; rpt., Boston: Phillips, Sampson, and Co., 1857), I, 154.

48. *North American Review,* 62 (January 1846), 122.

49. *Richard Edney and the Governor's Family* (Boston: Phillips, Sampson, and Co., 1850), p. 12.

50. *The Vestal; or, A Tale of Pompeii* (Boston: Gray and Bowen, 1830), pp. 3, 86.

51. *Confessions of an Early Martyr* (Boston: Wells and Lilly, 1846), pp. 29–30.

52. *The Various Writings of Cornelius Mathews* (New York: Harper, 1843), p. 83.

53. *Adventures of Elder Triptolemus Tub* (Boston: Abel Tompkins, 1846), p. 99.

54. *The Quaker City; or, The Monks of Monk Hall* (1844–1845; rpt., Philadelphia: Leary, Stuart, and Co., 1876), p. 328.

55. *Legends of New England* (1831; rpt., Gainesville, Fla.: Scholars' Facsimiles and Reprints, 1965), p. 63.

56. *Tales of Glauber-Spa* (Boston: Harper, 1832), pp. 258–259.

57. *The Wide, Wide World* (1851; rpt., London: S. W. Partridge, n.d.), p. 449.

58. *Adonai: The Pilgrim of Eternity,* in George Lippard, *The White Banner* (Philadelphia: George Lippard, 1851), I, 70.

59. *Selections from the Writings of Mrs. Sarah C. Edgarton Mayo* (Boston: Abel Tompkins, 1849), p. 25.

60. *Seven Dreamers* (New York: Harper, 1891), p. 2.

3. Calvinist Fiction

1. *Alice Gordon; or, The Uses of Orphanage* (New York: Harper, 1847), p. 57.

2. *The Art of Courting, Displayed in Eight Different Scenes* (Newburyport: William Barrett, 1795), p. 13.

3. *The Life and Reflections of Charles Observator, in which are Displayed The Real Characters of Human Life* (Boston: Rowe and Hooper, 1816), p. 12.

4. *The Spiritual Voyage Performed in the Ship Convert* (1814; rpt., Philadelphia: Anderson and Meehan, 1819), pp. 11, 15.

5. *The Life and Adventures of Dr. Caleb* (Boston: Lincoln and Edmands, 1822), p. 53.

6. [Susan De Witt?], *Justina; or, The Will* (New York: Charles Wiley, 1823), I, 32.

7. *The Reformation: A True Tale of the Sixteenth Century* (Boston: Massachusetts Sabbath School Society, 1832), p. 7.

8. *Resignation* (Boston: John B. Russell, 1825), I, 5, 6.

9. *Triumph of Religion* (Savannah: S. C. and J. Schenk, 1825), pp. iii–iv.

10. *Lucretia and Her Father* (Hartford: D. F. Robinson, 1828), p. 5.

11. *The Reformation,* p. 39.

12. *The Wife for a Missionary* (1834; rpt., Cincinnati: Truman, Smith and Co., 1834), pp. 64, 142.

13. *Memorabilia of George B. Cheever, D.D.* (New York: John Wiley and Sons, 1890), p. ix.

14. *Memorabilia,* p. xi.

15. *Deacon Giles' Distillery, and Other Miscellanies* (New York: John Wiley, 1853), p. 345.

16. *Deacon Giles' Distillery,* p. 13.

17. *The Fatal Feud; or, Passion and Piety* (New York: T. Mason and G. Lane, 1838), pp. 100–101.

18. Phoebe H. Brown, *The Tree and Its Fruits; or, Narratives from Real Life* (New York: Ezra Collier, 1836), p. 1.

19. *A Blossom in the Desert: A Tale of the West* (New York: Scofield and Voorhies, 1838), p. 19.

20. George Raybold, *Paul Perryman; or, The Unhappy Death* (New York: T. Mason and G. Lane, 1838), p. 21.

21. Robert C. Waterson, *Arthur Lee and Tom Palmer; or, The Sailor Reclaimed* (Boston: James Munroe, 1839), p. 73.

22. *Something for Everybody: Gleaned in the Old Purchase, from Fields Often Reaped* (New York: D. Appleton and Co., 1846), p. 47.

23. See *Oldtown Folks* (Boston: Houghton Mifflin, 1869), p. 224.

24. *Something for Everybody,* pp. 61, 213.

25. Charles T. Torrey, *Home; or, The Pilgrims' Faith Revived* (Salem: John P. Jewett and Co., 1845), p. 191.

26. *Oldtown Folks,* p. iv.

27. John P. Brace, *Tales of the Devils* (Hartford: S. Andrus and Son, 1846), p. 166.

28. "The Scribbling Women and the Cosmic Success Story," *Critical Inquiry,* 1 (September 1974), 51.

29. *The Wide, Wide World,* p. 457.

30. *Elizabeth Benton; or, Religion in Connection with Fashionable Life* (New York: Harper, 1846), p. 144.

31. *The Wide, Wide World,* p. 440.

32. *The Minister's Wooing,* p. 87.

33. *Uncle Tom's Cabin; or, Life Among the Lowly* (1852; rpt., New York: Collier, 1967), p. 51.

34. *Oldtown Folks,* p. 179.

35. *Norwood; or, Village Life in New England* (New York: Scribner, 1868), p. 115.

36. *The Works of Orestes Brownson,* XIX, 299, 541.

4. Anti-Calvinist and Liberal Fiction

1. *The Parent's Counsellor; or, The Dangers of Moroseness: A Narrative of the Newton Family* (Philadelphia: E. Bacon, 1825), p. 6.

2. *Boston Unitarianism, 1820–1850. A Study of the Life and Work of Nathaniel Langdon Frothingham.* (New York: G. P. Putnam's Sons, 1890), p. 262.

3. *Review of American Unitarianism* (Boston: Armstrong, 1815), p. 21.

4. [De Witt?], *Justina,* I, 160.

5. *Something for Everybody,* p. 111.

6. Quoted in *Memoirs of . . . Rev. Joseph Stevens Buckminster* (Boston: Crosby and Nichols, 1858), p. 328.

7. Elizabeth P. Peabody, *Reminiscences of Reverend William Ellery Channing, D.D.* (Boston: Roberts Brothers, 1880), p. 20.

8. W. E. Channing, *Letter to the Reverend Samuel C. Thacher* (Boston, 1815), p. 15.

9. *Works of Charles Follen* (Boston: Hilliard, Gray, and Co., 1841), I, 193.

10. *The Soldier's Orphan* (New York: C. S. Van Winkle, 1812), p. 64.

11. Sarah J. Hale, *Northwood; or, Life North and South* (1827; rpt., New York: H. Long, 1852), p. 93.

12. Dewey, *Life and Letters of . . . Sedgwick,* p. 162.

13. *The Way to Do Good* (Boston: William Peirce, 1836), p. 191.

14. *Writings . . . of Sarah Mayo,* pp. 87–88.

15. John Ware, *Memoir of the Life of Henry Ware, Jr.* (Boston: American Unitarian Association, 1845), II, 178.

16. *On the Formation of the Christian Character, addressed to those who are seeking to lead a religious life* (1829; rpt., Boston: American Unitarian Association, 1867), pp. 152, 154.

17. *Theology Explained and Defended, in a Series of Sermons* (1818–1819; rpt., New York: Harper, 1850), I, 502.

18. *Boston Unitarianism*, pp. 241, 242.

19. *On the Formation of the Christian Character*, p. 91.

20. "Hints on Extemporaneous Preaching" (1824), in *Sacred Rhetoric; or, Composition and Delivery of Sermons*, ed. Henry J. Ripley (1849; rpt., Boston: Gould and Lincoln, 1859), p. 192.

21. *Memoirs of the Bloomsgrove Family*, II, 231.

22. *The Bay Boy*, in *Prose of Royall Tyler*, pp. 106–107, 134.

23. *Boston Unitarianism*, pp. 76, 92.

24. *The Soldier's Orphan*, p. 34.

25. *The Factory Girl* (Boston: Munroe, Francis, and Parker, 1814), p. 10.

26. *Filial Affection; or, The Clergyman's Granddaughter* (Boston: Cummings and Hilliard, 1820), p. 21.

27. *James Talbot* (Boston: Hilliard and Metcalf, 1821), p. 13.

28. *American Unitarian Biography* (Boston: Munroe, 1851), I, 336.

29. *Naomi; or, Boston Two Hundred Years Ago* (Boston: Crosby and Nichols, 1848), p. 407.

30. *The Backslider* (Boston: Munroe, 1835), p. 24.

31. *Three Experiments of Living* (Boston: William S. Damrell, 1837), p. 121.

32. *The Young Emigrants* (Boston: Carter and Hendee, 1830), p. 75.

33. Lucius Manlius Sargent, *A Sectarian Thing* (Boston: Ford and Damrell, 1834), p. 33.

34. I further discuss Arminian heroism, as well as the recent scholarly debate about "feminized" religion and nineteenth-century fiction, in "The Feminization Controversy: Sexual Stereotypes and the Paradoxes of Piety in Nineteenth-Century America," *The New England Quarterly*, 53 (March 1980), 96–106.

35. Ann Douglas, *The Feminization of American Culture* (New York: Knopf, 1977), pp. 1, 117.

36. Peabody, *Reminiscences of . . . Channing*, p. 30.

37. See Ware, *American Unitarian Biography*, I, 37, 174, 215, 227, and II, 225; and Frothingham, *Boston Unitarianism*, pp. 9, 185–186.

38. *The Factory Girl*, p. 52.

39. *Filial Affection*, p. 74.

40. *A New England Tale*, p. 24.

41. *A Peep at the Pilgrims in Sixteen Hundred Thirty-Six* (Boston: Wells and Lilly, 1824), I, 216.

42. *Alfred* (Boston: Munroe, 1836), p. 13.

43. *Delusion; or, The Witch of New England* (Boston: Hilliard, Gray and Co., 1840), pp. iii, iv.

44. *Naomi*, p. 233.

45. *The Fair Puritan. An Historical Romance of the Days of Witchcraft* (Philadelphia: Lippincott, 1875), p. 30. First published as *Ruth Whalley; or, The Fair Puritan* (1844).

46. *The Sanfords; or, Home Scenes* (Boston: Elam Bliss, 1830), I, 122.

47. *The Lamplighter* (Leipzig: B. Tauchnitz, 1854), p. 97, 181, 161.

48. *Memoirs of the Bloomsgrove Family*, II, 227–228.

49. *The Farmer's Friend; or, The History of Mr. Charles Worthy* (Boston: I. Thomas and E. T. Andrews, 1793), pp. 154–155.

50. *The Factory Girl,* p. 25.

51. *Extracts from the Journal of Marshal Soult, Addressed to a Friend* (Newburyport: W. B. Allen, 1817), pp. 40, 41.

52. *A New England Tale,* p. 167.

53. *Redwood,* p. 130.

54. *Parent's Counsellor,* p. 7.

55. *Sketch of Connecticut, Forty Years Since* (Hartford: Oliver D. Cooke, 1824), p. 25.

56. *The Mayflower; or, Sketches of Scenes and Characters Among the Descendants of the Pilgrims* (New York: Harper, 1843), p. vi.

57. J. Ware, *Memoir of . . . Henry Ware, Jr.,* I, 47.

58. "Review of *A New England Tale,*" *Christian Disciple,* 4 (1823), 205.

59. *The Recollections of Jotham Anderson,* in *The Works of Henry Ware, Jr., D.D.* ed. Chandler Robbins (Boston: Munroe, 1846), I, 56.

60. J. Ware, *Memoir of . . . Henry Ware, Jr.,* I, 185.

61. *Works of Henry Ware, Jr.,* I, 159–160.

62. H. Ware, Jr., *David Ellington, With Other Extracts from his Writings* (Boston: Crosby and Nichols, 1846), p. 69.

63. Dewey, *Life and Letters of . . . Sedgwick,* p. 239.

64. Advertisement to Sarah Savage's *Trial and Self-Discipline* (Boston: Munroe, 1835).

65. *On the Formation of the Christian Character,* p. 28.

66. *Trial and Self-Discipline,* p. 6.

67. *The Backslider,* pp. 17–18.

68. *Alfred,* pp. 13, 39.

69. Eliza Cabot Follen, *The Skeptic* (Boston: Munroe, 1835), p. 31.

70. *Nature,* in Bradley, Beatty, and Long, *The American Tradition in Literature,* I, 1067.

71. "An Address," in Bradley, Beatty, and Long, *The American Tradition in Literature,* I, 1119.

72. *Dial,* 2 (April 1841), 418.

73. *Dial,* 3 (July 1842), 112.

5. Biblical Fiction

1. *Boston Unitarianism,* p. 73.

2. Nye and Grabo, *American Thought and Writing,* I, 243, 244.

3. *The Duty of Searching the Scriptures,* pp. 7, 17.

4. "A Dessertation, & c.," in *The Major Poems of Timothy Dwight (1752–1817),* ed. William J. McTaggart and William K. Bottorff (Gainesville, Fla.: Scholars' Facsimiles and Reprints, 1969), p. 545.

5. *A Miscellaneous Collection of Original Pieces: Political, Moral, and Entertaining* (Springfield: John Russell, 1786), p. 18.

6. Quoted in Sidney Mead, *The Lively Experiment* (New York: Harper and Row, 1963), p. 41.

7. *Memoirs of the Bloomsgrove Family,* II, 94.

8. *The Farmer's Friend,* p. 230.

9. *Christian Disciple,* 4 (1817), 3–4.

10. *The American Monthly Magazine and Critical Review,* 4 (January 1819), 177.

11. *Wandering Reflections of a Somewhat Busy Life* (Boston: Roberts Brothers, 1869), p. 90.

12. *Seventy-Six; or, Love and Battle* (1822; rpt., London: J. Cunningham, 1840), p. 137.

13. *American Quarterly,* 1 (1827), 493.

14. *American Quarterly,* 6 (1829), 240.

15. *Lectures on American Literature,* pp. 22, 41.

16. *The Young Christian. A Familiar Illustration of the Principles of Christianity* (New York: American Tract Society, 1832), p. 4.

17. In Hall, *Life and Character of . . . Judd,* pp. 432–433.

18. Charles Beecher, *The Incarnation; or, Pictures of the Virgin and Her Son* (New York: Harper, 1849), p. iii.

19. *Biblical Dialogues* (Boston: Richardson and Lord, 1822), I, iii.

20. *The Vestal,* pp. 70, 72.

21. *The Roman Exile; or, The Times of Aurelius* (Boston: John G. Jones, 1843), p. 13.

22. Eliza B. Lee, *Parthenia; or, The Last Days of Paganism* (Boston: Ticknor and Fields, 1858), pp. v–vi.

23. John Hewson, *Christ Rejected* (Philadelphia: Joseph Rakestraw, 1832), p. 372.

24. *Zerah, The Believing Jew* (New York: New York Protestant Episcopal Press, 1837), p. 43.

25. *The Mayflower,* p. 318.

26. Beecher, *The Incarnation,* p. vii.

27. *Washington and His Generals* (1847), reprinted as *The Legends of the American Revolution. "1776." Or, Washington and His Generals* (Philadelphia: Leary, Stuart and Co., 1876), p. 404.

28. Maria T. Richards, *Life in Judea; or, Glimpses of the First Christian Age* (Philadelphia: American Baptist Publication Society, 1855), p. 6.

29. Joseph Holt Ingraham, *The Pillar of Fire; or, Israel in Bondage* (New York: Pudney and Russell, 1859), p. 600.

30. In M. Dewey, *Autobiography . . . of Orville Dewey,* p. 87.

31. In J. Ware, *Memoir of . . . Henry Ware, Jr.,* II, 137.

32. *Antiquity and Revival* (Boston: American Unitarian Association, 1832), p. 28.

33. M. Dewey, *Autobiography . . . of Orville Dewey,* p. 183.

34. *Julian; or, Scenes in Judea* (1841; rpt., New York: C. S. Francis, 1856), I, 48.

35. *Aurelian; or, Rome in the Third Century* (*Probus*) (1838; rpt., London: Frederick Warne, n.d.), p. 266.

36. *Probus,* p. 270.

37. *Julian,* II, 255.

38. *North American Review,* 47 (October 1838), 466–467.

39. *Probus,* pp. 190, 268.

40. *Julian,* I, 53, 157.

41. *Probus,* 17.

42. *Sketches of European Capitals* (Boston: Phillips, Sampson, and Co., 1851), p. 58.

6. Roman Catholic Fiction

1. *Redwood,* p. xv.

2. For a summary of the biographies of these writers, as well as descriptions of representative plots and typical critical reviews, see Willard Thorp, "Catholic Novelists in Defense of their Faith, 1829–1865," *Proceedings of the American Antiquarian Society,* 78 (April 1968), 25–117.

3. *Works of . . . Brownson,* XIX, 149.

4. *Father Rowland: A North American Tale* (Baltimore: Fielding Lucas, Jr., 1829), pp. 64, 65.

5. *The Indian Cottage: A Unitarian Story* (Baltimore: Fielding Lucas, Jr.), p. 125.

6. *Zenosius; or, The Pilgrim Convert* (New York: Dunigan, 1845), p. 80.

7. *Father Oswald: A Genuine Catholic Story* (New York: Casserly and Sons, 1843), pp. vii, viii. *Father Clement* (1823), an anti-Catholic novel by the Scottish Grace Kennedy, had gained wide circulation in America in the 1820s and 1830s.

8. *Harry Layden: A Tale* (New York: Boyle, 1842), pp. iii–iv.

9. *The Cross and the Shamrock; or, How to Defend the Faith* (Boston: Patrick Donahoe, 1853), p. 6.

10. *Father Oswald,* pp. 23–24.

11. Cannon, *Harry Layden,* p. 46.

12. *Mora Carmody; or, Woman's Influence* (New York: Dunigan, 1844), p. 23.

13. *Father Felix* (New York: Dunigan, 1845), p. 50.

14. Anna Dorsey, *The Sister of Charity* (New York: Dungian, 1846), p. 6.

15. Quoted in James J. Walsh, "The Oxford Movement in America," *Records of the American Catholic Historical Society of Philadelphia,* XVI (Philadelphia, 1805), 436.

16. *North American Review,* 70 (January 1850), 233.

17. *Rosemary; or, Life and Death* (New York: Sadlier, 1860), p. 162.

18. *The Forest* (New York: Redfield, 1852), p. 169.

19. *Loretto; or, The Choice* (Baltimore: Hedian and O'Brien, 1851), p. iii.

20. *The Governess; or, The Effects of Good Example* (Baltimore: Hedian and O'Brien, 1851), p. 251.

21. *Cross and Shamrock,* p. 149.

22. *Brownson's Quarterly Review,* 2nd Series, III (January 1849), 58.

23. *Brownson's Quarterly Review,* 3rd Series, I (April 1853), 279.

24. *Mary Lee; or, The Yankee in Ireland* (Baltimore: Kelly, Hedian, and Piet, 1860), p. 165.

25. *Brownson's Quarterly Review,* New York Series, No. 2 (April 1856), 272.

26. From *Charles Elwood; or, The Infidel Converted* (1840) in *Works of . . . Brownson,* IV, 178.

27. *Christian Examiner and General Review,* 28 (May 1840), 180.

28. "Charles Elwood Reviewed," *Boston Quarterly Review* (March 1842), in *Works of . . . Brownson,* VI, 318.

29. *The Two Brothers; or, Why Are You a Protestant?* (1847), in *Works of . . . Brownson,* VI, 285.

30. *The Spirit-Rapper: An Autobiography* (1854; rpt., Detroit: T. Nourse, 1884), p. 1.

31. *Brownson's Quarterly Review,* 3rd Series, II (January 1854), 23.

32. *Works of . . . Brownson,* XIX, 566.

7. Combative or Satirical Fiction

1. *Charles Observator,* p. 4.

2. *The Yankee Traveller; or, The Adventures of Hector Wigler* (Concord, Mass.: George Hough, 1817), p. 18.

3. *The Life and Adventures of Obadiah Benjamin Franklin Bloomfield, M.D.* (Philadelphia, 1818), p. 31.

4. *Morganiana; or, The Wonderful Life and Terrible Death of Morgan* (Boston, 1828), p. 34.

5. *The Confessions of a Magdalene* (New York, 1831), p. 11.

6. *Fall River. An Authentic Narrative* (Boston: Lilly, Wait and Co., 1833), pp. 64, 144.

7. *Retroprogression. Being an Account of a Short Residence in the Celebrated Town of Jumbleborough* (Boston: James Burns, 1839), p. v.

8. *The Hypocrite; or, Sketches of American Society from a Residence of Forty Years* (New York: Thomas Fox and Co., 1844), p. 7.

9. *The Mysteries of Papermill Village* (Papermill Village, N.H.: Walter Tufts, Jr., 1845), pp. 13–14.

10. *The Reformation,* pp. 18, 16.

11. *Lorette. The History of Louise, Daughter of a Canadian Nun* (New York: William A. Mercein, 1833), p. 128.

12. *Female Convents. Secrets of Nunneries Disclosed* (New York: Appleton, 1834), p. ix.

13. *The Protestant Crusade, 1800–1860* (New York: Macmillan, 1938), p. 108.

14. *Western Monthly Magazine,* 3 (June 1835), 379.

15. Quoted in Billington, *Protestant Crusade,* p. 100. For a full account of the Monk affair see Billington's book (pp. 95–108) and his article "Maria Monk and Her Influence," *Catholic Historical Review,* 22 (October 1936), 283–296.

16. *The Chronicles of Mt. Benedict: A Tale of the Ursuline Convent* (Boston, 1837), p. 111.

17. *Freeman's Journal* (September 18, 1852), p. 23.

18. *The American Nun; or, The Effects of Romance* (Boston: Otis, Broaders and Co., 1836), p. iv.

19. [John Bell Bouton], *The Life and Choice Writings of George Lippard* (New York: H. H. Randall, 1855), p. 90.

20. James B. Elliot, "Biographical Sketch of George Lippard," Introduction to Lippard's *Thomas Paine: Author-Soldier of the Revolution* (Philadelphia, 1894), p. 15.

21. *The Quaker City,* p. 2.

22. [Bouton], *The Life and Choice Writings of George Lippard,* p. 45.

23. *The Quaker City,* p. 371.

24. *The Empire City; or, New York By Night and Day* (1850; rpt., Philadelphia: Peterson, 1864), p. 89.

25. *Blanche of Brandywine; or, September the Eighth to Eleventh, 1777* (1846; rpt., Philadelphia: Peterson, 1876), p. 276.

26. *The Nazarene; or, The Last of the Washingtons* (Philadelphia: Lippard, 1846), p. 59.

27. *The Memoirs of a Preacher; or, The Mysteries of the Pulpit* (1849; rpt., Philadelphia: Peterson, 1864), p. 12.

28. *The Quaker City,* p. 379.

29. *Paul Ardenheim; The Monk of Wissahikon. A Romance of the American Revolution, 1776* (1848; rpt., Philadelphia: Peterson, 1876), pp. 324, 326.

30. *The Legends of the American Revolution,* p. 406.

31. *Blanche of Brandywine,* p. 172.

32. *Memoirs of a Preacher,* p. 59.

33. *The Legends of the American Revolution,* p. 403.

8. Into the Mainstream

1. *North American Review,* 62 (January 1846), 103.

2. "Beware of Bad Books," Tract 493, *Tracts of the American Tract Society,* XII (New York, c. 1840), 16.

3. "Novel-Reading," Tract 515, *Tracts of the American Tract Society,* XII (New York, c. 1840), 33.

4. *Authorship: A Tale* (Boston: Gray and Bowen, 1830), p. 133.

5. K. Arvine, ed., *Cyclopedia of Moral and Religious Anecdotes* (New York: Leavitt, Trow and Co., 1848), p. 578.

6. *Port Folio,* 14 (September 1822), 295.

7. *North American Review,* 65 (October 1847), 348.

8. *The Gamesters,* p. iv.

9. *Redwood,* p. x.

10. *True Womanhood: A Tale* (Boston: Ticknor and Fields, 1859), p. iv.

11. *The Circuit Rider: A Tale of the Heroic Age* (1874; rpt., New York: Scribner's, 1911), p. vii.

12. *Margaret Percival in America: A Tale* (Boston: Phillips, Sampson, and Co., 1850), p. v.

13. "Scribbling Women and Cosmic Success Story," p. 51.

14. "Religion in the American Novel: 1870–1900," Diss. Kansas, 1960, p. 293.

15. *Future Life; or, Scenes in Another World* (New York: Derby and Jackson, 1858), p. vii.

16. *Strange Visitors: A Series of Original Papers . . . By . . . Spirits Now Dwelling in the Spirit World* (New York: Carleton, 1869), p. 24.

17. *The Wedding Garment* (New York: Roberts Brothers, 1894), pp. 20, 55.

18. *They Met in Heaven* (New York: E. P. Dutton, 1894), p. 130.

19. Quoted by Suderman, "Religion in the American Novel," p. 129.

20. Publisher's Announcement, *Titus, A Comrade of the Cross* (Chicago: David C. Cook, 1894), p. 1.

21. *Come Forth!* (Boston: Houghton Mifflin, 1891), p. iii.

22. *Ai, A Social Vision* (1892; rpt., Boston: Arena, 1893), p. 198.

23. *His Majesty, Myself* (New York: Roberts Brothers, 1880), p. 220.

24. Quoted in Paul Carter, *Spiritual Crisis of the Gilded Age* (DeKalb: Northern Illinois Press, 1971), p. 66.

25. John Dart, "Producers Find 'Jesus Sells Almost As Well As Sex,' " San Francisco *Chronicle,* August 1, 1976, p. 19.

26. Quoted in John T. Frederick, *The Darkened Sky: Nineteenth-Century American Novelists and Religion* (Notre Dame: Indiana University Press, 1969), p. 188.

27. Ambrose Bierce [Dod Grile], *The Fiend's Delight* (New York: A. L. Luyster, 1873), p. 69.

28. *Chapters from a Life* (Boston: Houghton Mifflin, 1900), p. 269.

29. *Christian Disciple,* 4 (1817), 3.

30. *The Mayflower,* pp. vi–vii.

31. *My Wife and I* (1871; rpt., New York: Riverside, 1967), p. viii.

32. *North American Review,* 82 (April 1856), 373.

33. Ibid., 76 (January 1853), 110.

34. *The Criterion; or, The Test of Talk about Familiar Things* (New York: Hurd and Houghton, 1866), p. 317.

35. *Oratory* (1892; rpt., Philadelphia: Penn, 1901), p. 44.

36. *The Masque Torn Off* (St. Louis: N. D. Thompson, 1879), p. 518.

37. Quoted in *T. DeWitt Talmage: His Life and Work,* ed. Louis A. Banks (Philadelphia: John C. Winston, 1902), p. 67.

38. William R. Moody, *Dwight L. Moody* (New York: Fleming H. Revell, 1900), p. 432.

39. *Sam Jones' Own Book: A Series of Sermons* (Cincinnati: Cranston and Stowe, 1886), p. 50.

40. "Didactic Literature in America, 1825–1850," Diss. Indiana, 1954, pp. 104, 106.

41. *Yale Lectures on Preaching* (1872; rpt. New York: Fords, Howard, and Hulbert, 1881), I, 208–209. For further discussion of this topic, see my article "From Doctrine to Narrative: The Rise of Pulpit Storytelling in America," *American Quarterly* (forthcoming).

42. James K. Folsom, *Timothy Flint* (New York: Twayne, 1965), pp. 43, 27.

43. Dewey, *Life and Letters of . . . Sedgwick,* p. 153.

44. *Letters of . . . Child,* p. 139.

45. *Wandering Reflections,* p. 99.

46. Quoted in Hall, *Life and Character of . . . Judd,* p. 57.

47. *Letters of . . . Child,* pp. 193, 196.

48. *Young Christian,* p. 120.

49. *Wandering Reflections,* p. 99.

50. Herman Melville, *Clarel. A Poem and Pilgrimage in the Holy Land* (1876), ed. Walter E. Bezanson (New York: Hendricks House, 1960), p. 176.

51. *Letters of . . . Child,* pp. 56, 57.

52. Dewey, *Life and Letters of . . . Sedgwick,* p. 316.

53. Dewey, *Life and Letters of . . . Sedgwick,* pp. 328–329.

54. *The Christian Examiner,* 21 (1836), 34.

55. *Beulah* (New York: Derby and Jackson, 1859), p. 378.

Index